Ethnic Ident[i]

The Transformation of

White

America

D0404149

Ethnic Identity:

The Transformation of

White

America

Richard D. Alba

Yale University Press   New Haven and London

Tables 1.1 and 1.2 are taken from Richard D. Alba, "Cohorts and the dynamics of ethnic change," in *Social Structures and Human Lives*, ed. Matilda White Riley, pp. 211–28, copyright 1988. Reprinted by permission of Sage Publications, Inc.

Designed by James J. Johnson.

Set in Aster Roman type by The Composing Room of Michigan.

Printed in the United States of America by Vail-Ballou Press, Binghamton, New York.

Library of Congress Cataloging-in-Publication Data

Alba, Richard D.

  Ethnic identity : the transformation of white America / Richard
D. Alba.

      p.   cm.

  Includes bibliographical references.

  ISBN 0-300-04737-1 (cloth)
        0-300-05221-9 (pbk.)

  1. Minorities—United States.   2. Ethnicity—United States.
3. Whites—United States.   I. Title.
E184.A1A45   1990
305.8'034073—dc20   89-21483
                                                                      CIP

The paper in this book meets the guidelines for permanence and durability of the Committee on Production Guidelines for Book Longevity of the Council on Library Resources.

10   9   8   7   6   5   4   3   2

For Michael and Sarah

Contents

Tables

Preface

This book examines ongoing and profound ethnic changes among
white Americans through the special lens of ethnic identity, or ethnic
consciousness. Reduced to its essentials, the book addresses a paradoxical divergence to be found among Americans descended from
European immigrants: between the long-run and seemingly irreversible decline of objective ethnic differences—in education and
work, family and community—and the continuing subjective importance of ethnic origins. Through an analysis of a unique survey about
the manifestations of ethnicity in ordinary life, it attempts to answer
the crucial questions about the significance of the persisting subjective attachment to ethnicity: is ethnic identity a new basis for ethnic
solidarity and ethnic division among whites, as it is portrayed by the
many scholars who see it as heralding a revival of ethnicity in the
United States? Or should ethnic identity be viewed instead as "symbolic ethnicity," a vestigial attachment to a few ethnic symbols imposing little cost on everyday life? In its final interpretation, the book
strongly favors the symbolic ethnicity view, but it elaborates further
the theoretical conception of symbolic ethnicity, arguing that the
ethnic identities of many whites are a symptom of the emergence on
the American scene of a new ethnic group, which is the outcome of

assimilation in a society that remains fundamentally multiethnic and multiracial. As social distinctions based on European ancestry have receded into the background, a new ethnic group based on ancestry from anywhere on the European continent has formed. The emergence of this new group, which I call "European Americans," with its own myths about its place in American history and its relationship to the American identity, is an important development, with repercussions for racial minorities and new immigrant groups from Asia, Latin America, and the Caribbean.

On a more personal level, the book was conceived out of my reflections on criticisms of the research tradition of which I have been a part. That tradition, emphasizing the foundation of ethnicity in more or less objective differences among groups as registered in such familiar variables as education, income, occupation, and even intermarriage, has dominated the sociological study of ethnicity for some time. And much has been learned from its research findings, but they have not ended the debate over the evolution and future of ethnicity in the United States even if they have changed its terms. Instead, the conception of ethnicity has undergone a shift in some quarters, as scholars and laypersons alike have pointed to an ethnicity that depends far more on voluntary commitments to ethnic identities than on moorings in ethnic inequalities. One cannot fail to be struck by how often research on objective differentiation has been criticized for neglecting such factors as the tenacity of ethnic identities and ethnic pride. It is precisely to address such criticisms that the following work was conceived.

From conception to completion has taken six *long* years. Many people helped along the way. Heading the list is Herbert Gans, without whom this work would never have seen the light of day. As will be apparent to even the most cursory glance, the book owes a considerable intellectual debt to Gans's conception of "symbolic ethnicity." Moreover, he gave generously of himself early in the project, collaborating with me on the design of the complex questionnaire, and then graciously bowed out to allow me to take full control of survey materials for which he deserves considerable credit.

The project could also not have been carried out without financial support. The Ethnic Identity Survey was made possible by a grant from the National Science Foundation (grant no. SES–

8308685). The period of initial analysis and writing was supported by a sabbatical leave from the State University of New York at Albany (1986–87) and by a simultaneous Fulbright lectureship award, enabling me to spend a full year away from normal academic responsibilities. Special mention must be made here of the generosity of Professor Max Kaase at Mannheim University, my host during my Fulbright year, who understood that not too much should be asked of me in this precious year of freedom.

Collection of the data was an arduous job to which many hands contributed. Claudia Hartmark served as the first supervisor: she organized the field work and managed a cadre of nearly twenty interviewers; the quality of the data owes much to her efforts. Midway through the data collection, Beth Roberts took over from Claudia and competently saw the field work through to the end. She also did yeoman work on the coding of the data, as did Brian Fisher and Genevieve Joseph. Genevieve also did a considerable portion of the computer analysis of the data set.

As the manuscript evolved through several drafts, generating a dizzying blur of details, a number of readers helped me to see its features more clearly and to find ways to strengthen them. Paul DiMaggio, Herbert Gans, and Bill Yancey read the whole manuscript and gave me expert guidance, as did one anonymous reviewer. Judith Blau, Richard Felson, and John Logan read and commented on portions of the manuscript. Parts of the manuscript were also presented at the meetings of the Eastern Sociological Society and the American Sociological Association, as well as in talks at New York University and Washington State University. Comments of those in attendance, especially by Stanford Lyman at the Eastern Sociological Society meetings, also contributed to the manuscript's development. I was helped not only by readers—while I was writing, my thinking was stimulated by substantive discussions with various colleagues. During the year abroad, my intellectual fires were stoked by discussions with Duane Alwin, Hartmut Esser, Donata Elschenbroich, Ceri Peach, and John Stone. At home, I have benefited from talks with Victor Nee and Mary Waters, among others. Frank Femminella, John McEneny, and Gordana Rabrenovic shared with me their knowledge of ethnic neighborhoods and institutions in the Capital Region, enabling me to present a more nuanced portrait. At Yale University Press, Gladys Topkis gave me the enthusiastic support that all authors crave, and Carl Rosen took on the challenging task of editing my unruly prose into shape.

A special tribute must be paid to Kathy Vaccariello, my secretary at the Center for Social and Demographic Analysis. Throughout the entire six years of the project, she kept the project materials and the manuscript in good order. She effortlessly and uncomplainingly satisfied my frequently frantic needs for this or that thing and served as my lifeline to the survey materials while I was in Europe. She also typed all the tables, many of them going through several drafts.

I have saved the best for last. My family—Gwen, Michael, and Sarah—have seen me through a project that proved more demanding than I anticipated at the outset. Without their love and support, I might never have made it to the end.

1

The Transformation of Ethnicity among Americans of European Ancestries

✴Ethnicity is a central theme of the American experience. Today, perhaps more than ever, Americans envision their nation as formed by the melding of many other nations, a process that continues, expanding now to include new immigrant groups from Asia, Latin America, and the Caribbean. This perception is given objective form in the Statue of Liberty, whose symbolic meaning has undergone an about-face. Once, the statue stood for the political and religious freedoms available in the United States, in contrast to many of the countries from which immigrants came, and thus it represented the New World's decisive break with the Old. Today, it stands for the origins of the American nation in the immigrant experience and hence Americans' link with their immigrant and Old World roots.

A self-consciousness about diverse ethnic origins finds expression in many areas of contemporary American life. It is almost hard to remember the time—only a few decades ago, in the aftermath of World War II—when the expectation was widespread that ethnic Americans would assimilate, largely along the lines of an

1

Anglo-American prototype, and hence that consciousness of ethnicity would gradually disappear. This was a time when the melting pot was the prevailing image of American society, and it is difficult to identify the forces that overturned this image. Some point to the civil rights movement, which demonstrated that some ethnic inequalities—notably racial ones—are quite resilient and that ethnic assertiveness is a legitimate way of achieving important goals. Others point to the maturing of a third generation of ethnic Americans, who no longer needed to be defensive about their place in America and could afford to assert pride in their ethnic roots.[1]

⚹ Whatever the cause, the celebration of ethnicity and the perception of the stubbornness of ethnic difference have come to occupy a place of honor. Ethnic festivals and parades are familiar in most communities; ethnic cooking has achieved a lofty niche in American cuisine, far removed from its humble immigrant origins; and evidence of ethnicity in the form of names, accents, and behavioral styles is pervasive in the media. Accompanying these surface changes is a belief, among scholars and the lay public, that ethnic differences form a possibly permanent substructure, if not the ultimate bedrock, of American society. During the 1960s and 1970s, this belief took on particularly strong forms. Some spoke of an "ethnic revival," an increasingly assertive and prideful stance on the part of ethnics who had once been quiet out of deference to the melting pot ideal. Others spoke of "cultural pluralism," alluding to a cultural and social mosaic whose pattern derives from the persistence, even the continuous reforming, of ethnic groups.[2]

This shift in view has deeply influenced the scholarly study of American ethnic groups. An older view, dating back to the origins of sociology in the United States, tended to see assimilation as the long-run outcome of contact between different groups,[3] but during the 1960s and 1970s many scholars adopted a skeptical stance toward assimilation, questioning its validity as a concept and its desirability as an ideal. This change was heralded in *Beyond the Melting Pot*, by Nathan Glazer and Daniel Patrick Moynihan, published in 1963. Their reassessment was followed by many others—notably, the work of Andrew Greeley on Catholic ethnic groups. These reassessments, it should be acknowledged, had precursors in a longstanding research tradition emphasizing the durability of racial cleavages, particularly between whites and blacks. By the late

1970s, most scholars in this area accepted ethnicity's staying power as a matter of fact worthy of investigation, if they did not (as many did) commit themselves to theoretical positions emphasizing its permanence. Many also expressed the belief that ethnic Americans have the right to hold on to their particular traditions and differences, that these represent a valid form of self-expression under threat of obliteration by the cultural hegemony implicit in the melting pot. The reassessment of ethnicity, then, produced not simply a rediscovery of significant existing aspects of American society, but a different image of what American society *should* be.[4]

The simplistic dualism between melting pot and cultural pluralism no longer dominates debate about ethnicity, but the questions about ethnicity's role and future in the United States have not disappeared. The legacy of the reassessment of recent decades has left scholars wary of interpreting ethnic developments in terms of assimilation, and they remain attentive to the existence of ethnic differentiation. This legacy, I believe, has obscured for many the enormity of the changes taking place among some ethnic groups, specifically those derived from European ancestries. These changes and their implications for the contemporary role of ethnicity are the subject of this book.

In brief, I argue that ethnicity among whites (more precisely, non-Hispanic whites[5]) in the United States is in the midst of a fundamental transformation, whose basic outlines are not always perceived clearly, even by knowledgeable observers, and whose long-run consequences call for investigation. This transformation does not imply that ethnicity is less embedded in the structure of American society but rather that the ethnic distinctions that matter are undergoing a radical shift. Ethnic distinctions based on European ancestry, once quite prominent in the social landscape, are fading into the background; other ethnic distinctions appear more highlighted as a result. In a sense, a new ethnic group is forming— one based on ancestry from *anywhere* on the European continent.

The book is an attempt to examine the current state of this transformation and to project some of its long-range consequences through the special lens of ethnic identity, the degree to which individuals think of themselves and interpret their experience in terms of ethnic points of origin. I believe that this lens is especially revealing because research utilizing numerous "objective" indicators of ethnicity—for example, educational and occupational attainment, language use, intermarriage—makes it clear that older, structural bases for ethnic differentiation, such as labor-market niches and informal segregation, are weakening dramatically, although perhaps not disappearing. Consequently, *if* ethnic distinctions among whites are to remain associated with meaningful social differences, it must be because these distinctions are embedded in the way people identify themselves and in the actions they take as a result. In an era when ethnicity is increasingly voluntary among whites, it can continue to play an important social role only insofar as people choose to act in ethnic ways. Such choices hinge on personally meaningful identities.

These notions obviously need to be explicated more fully, but before doing so, I must document my claim that major social changes are taking place in the white population—changes that require us to reconceptualize the possible role of ethnicity.

Ethnic Changes among White Americans

That ethnicity has been an important principle of social organization in the United States is demonstrated by even a superficial glance at history. What stands out most in the social landscape are the mountainous barriers between the major groups distinguished by skin color, most notably between whites and blacks. But even among whites, the staggered arrival of immigrant groups from Europe—in a distinctive order sweeping gradually from the continent's western edges to its outer eastern and southern reaches—and their varied economic backgrounds and initial success led to a clearly perceptible ethnic hierarchy: occupying the top were the Protestant groups from the British Isles; in the middle were other groups from northern and western Europe; and at the bottom were the newest European arrivals, from eastern and southern Europe.

Admittedly, this hierarchy is only approximate. Not every group fits neatly in its compartments: where, for example, should eastern European Jews be placed? In some respects, such as the intensity of discrimination they have faced, they seem to be the companions of other southern and eastern European groups, such as the Italians and Poles; but in terms of their great socioeconomic success, they seem to be the peers of the most highly placed groups.

Even more important is the hierarchy's uncertain application to individuals. In general, European ancestry has not posed an insuperable barrier to achievement: assimilation has been possible to a greater degree than for blacks and other racially distinct groups.

Nevertheless, the outlines of this ethnic hierarchy have been evident until very recently, even though the period of mass immigration from Europe has been over for more than a half century. Writing in the early 1960s (and again in 1970), Nathan Glazer and Daniel Patrick Moynihan saw a version of this hierarchy, complicated by the addition of blacks and Puerto Ricans, as structuring ethnic patterns in New York City; they viewed these patterns as the social fundament of the city itself.

Recent research has uncovered enormous changes in this ethnic structure, which are leveling once-important social distinctions deriving from European origins. These changes represent an ongoing process, not one that has already reached its culmination, and therefore one can still find important differences among aggregate ethnic categories in the white population. But the trajectory of change is evident when one decomposes ancestry groups in two ways—by generational group and birth cohort.

Generation, of course, refers to distance in descent from the point of immigration into the United States. (By convention, generations are numbered starting with the immigrants as the "first," so that their children are the "second," their grandchildren are the "third," etc.) Generally speaking, ethnic differences appear to be strongest among the generations closest to the immigrant experience and grow fainter among those further away. This generational progression among individuals and families, insofar as it exists, is predictive of ethnic *group* change because the generational composition of ethnic groups changes over time. This has been especially true for the ethnic groups arising out of mass immigration from Europe, since they have received little inflow of new immigrants since the 1920s; accordingly, their generational composition has changed rapidly, as reflected in the fact that their young adults are now drawn overwhelmingly from the third and fourth generations.

Socioeconomic life chances, a key part of the historical picture of ethnic differentiation among whites, reveal how differences have been eroding across generations. Lisa Neidert and Reynolds Farley

(1985; also see Lieberson and Waters, 1988) show convincingly that, at least for men of European ancestry,[6] there is a broad process of convergence across the generations, even if ethnic differences are not extinguished in the third and later generations. Among men of the first and second generations, there are clear-cut ethnic differences in educational achievement and occupational positioning. In general, the attainments of men from southern and eastern European backgrounds (with the exception of Russians, a category that is mainly Jewish) lag behind those of men of English ancestry; so do those of men of Irish, French, and German ancestries. The differences, moreover, are frequently large. For instance, while 56 percent of second-generation men of English ancestry have attended college, the proportion is only about half as large for men of French, Italian, and Polish backgrounds (27, 30, and 30 percent, respectively [Neidert and Farley, 1985: 845]).

But these disadvantages have largely faded for the men in the third and later generations. Men of southern and eastern European backgrounds have caught up with their English counterparts educationally and nearly so occupationally. Some European-ancestry groups still trail the English, but these are typically ones from northern and western Europe, such as the French and the Germans, and the margins of difference are not as large; although Neidert and Farley do not pursue their origins, the differences may well result from variations in the geographical placement of groups.

The most important ethnic differences among whites of the third and later generations represent not disadvantages but the exceptional achievements of relatively small groups, such as eastern European Jews. Thus, the general picture conveyed by the research is of a broad convergence across generations of socioeconomic life chances around those for an "average" white American, as represented by men of English background, with some departures from this standard in the form of exceptional achievement for a few groups.

Even more striking in some respects is the evidence of convergence across birth cohorts of Americans of European ancestries. *Cohorts*, defined as groups born during the same period, can be seen as indexing historical changes in life chances, particularly those arising external to the group, in such processes as the structural mobility generated by shifts in the occupational distribution (see

Alba, 1985a). The result of changing opportunities is that each new cohort of an ethnic group reaches maturity under somewhat different conditions than its predecessors; and insofar as the changes are favorable to the group, the younger cohort experiences higher average levels of educational attainment and occupational positioning. Therefore, historical shifts in the opportunities open to members of an ethnic group can be read in the differences among its age strata at a given moment, much as the archaeologist can interpret the succession of civilizations through the shards found at different layers of earth.

The magnitude and pace of the cohort changes can be seen in my study of changes among individuals with south-central-eastern European ancestry (Alba, 1988). These groups are the acid test of ethnic change because of the recency of their immigration, which makes them in general the most ethnically distinctive of European-ancestry groups.

The patterns of college attainment reproduced in table 1.1 indicate the rapidity and depth of change in opportunity for these groups. Rates of college attendance and graduation among men and women are shown by birth cohort for their American-born mem-

Table 1.1   Changes in educational attainment among cohorts of U.S.-born South-Central-East European ethnics

	% Attended College		% Completed 4+ yrs. College	
	Ethnics	3d Generation British	Ethnics	3d Generation British
Women				
Before 1916	10.9	26.5	5.4	12.3
1916–1930	17.3	35.8	8.8	18.2
1931–1945	32.6	38.9	16.1	20.0
1946–1960[a]	48.8	50.0	21.4	22.5
Men				
Before 1916	20.6	30.0	12.2	17.3
1916–1930	27.7	40.6	16.0	23.9
1931–1945	49.3	52.6	31.9	34.9
1946–1960[a]	55.7	55.1	25.2	25.5

Source: Tabulations from the November 1979 Current Population Survey.
[a]The educational attainment of the cohort born after 1960 is too incomplete (as of 1979) to report.

bers and compared to those for third-generation Americans of British background.[7] The latter category has been included as an index of the typical opportunities available to the ethnic core of Americans, those most privileged as a result of ethnic background, and thus provides a way of testing directly for ethnic convergence.

Convergence is unequivocally in evidence among men. The table shows that, among older cohorts of men, Americans of British background had an edge over those of south-central-east European ancestry in terms of attending and completing college. In both older cohorts, the rates of British achievement were roughly 50 percent higher than those for the ethnic men. But a convergence begins to emerge for the men born during the 1930s and early 1940s who completed their educations in the post-World War II period. Not only has the college going and completion of the ethnic men risen sharply, but just a small difference remains between them and their British-American age peers. By the post-World War II cohort, even this small difference has disappeared. Parity has been attained.[8]

The convergence among women is even more remarkable, for the older women of south-central-eastern European ancestry were greatly disadvantaged in comparison with their age peers of British ancestry and also with men of their own backgrounds. In the cohort of women born before 1916, for example, the British women are almost two and a half times more likely to have attended and completed college. It is not hard to see why this might be the case. In general, the immigrants from south-central-east Europe came from peasant backgrounds. Jews form the main exception but represent just a small minority overall among these groups. These immigrants brought cultures that stressed the family and the distinctive role of women in the family setting—the southern Italian immigrants provide the epitome of this cultural configuration (Yans-McLaughlin, 1977; Alba, 1985a). Insofar as these groups placed much less weight on the occupational accomplishments of their daughters than on those of their sons, they were undoubtedly less likely to encourage and support women's educational careers.[9]

But the disadvantages borne by the ethnic women appear to have been reduced rather dramatically within a short period. The ethnic inequalities are about as large for the 1916–30 cohort as for the preceding one, but for the women born between 1931 and 1945, they have narrowed considerably. And they have essentially disap-

peared for the post-World War II cohort. Given t
size, the tiny differences that remain may be sta
ingful but are not substantively significant. Notew
the youngest women of south-central-eastern
ground have educational achievements that are
with those of their male counterparts. This is also
to the pattern in the oldest cohorts.

Such convergences across generations and birth cohorts are
instructive about the long-term trajectory of change and about contemporary ethnic differences. Most important, they imply that the
present is a time of transition between an older ethnic pattern
where rather strong differences prevailed and a newer one where
white ethnic groups have roughly equal life chances to attain many
highly valued statuses. Even so, these convergences are consistent
with significant difference among contemporary ethnic categories
in the white population. Any such category—Poles, say—mixes the
patterns found for early and later generations and for older and
younger cohorts. Therefore, in comparing the average attainments
of aggregated categories, one still finds evidence of ethnic differentiation. But the final implication is that ethnic differences are
declining among Americans of European backgrounds. Contemporary ethnic differences are concentrated in the first and second generations and in older cohorts; they appear more muted, if they
appear at all, among the third and later generations and younger
birth groups. Accordingly, the differences are dwindling because the
generations and cohorts where they are concentrated account for
smaller and smaller proportions of whites.

This erosion of ethnic differentiation is much further advanced
for the population of European-ancestry whites than for other racial and ethnic groups in American society (Lieberson, 1980;
Hirschman, 1983). This need not imply a permanent chasm separating Americans of European ancestries from all others. Some non-
white and Hispanic groups may be beginning to undergo processes
similar to those that have undercut ethnic differences among European whites—one thinks in this connection of Cubans, most Asian
American groups, and the many Americans of American Indian ancestry who are integrated in the white population (Nee and Sanders, 1985; Hirschman and Wong, 1986; Snipp, 1986; Bean and
Tienda, 1987; Model, 1988). Such ambiguities, however, do not

aracterize the situations of blacks and the largest Hispanic groups. For instance, Neidert and Farley show that, even in the third and later generations, there are large educational, occupational, and income differences separating African Americans, Mexican Americans, and others of Hispanic background from whites, no matter what part of Europe their ancestors came from (see also Farley, 1984; Bean and Tienda, 1987). The well-established state of ethnic convergence among European-ancestry whites highlights the value of investigating the long-run outcomes of ethnic change in this population, as I do in this book.

The changes among whites do not end with the gradual equalization of educational and labor-market opportunities. The evidence reveals a broad social integration among persons from different European ethnic backgrounds. One aspect is the decline of behaviors capable of serving as socially salient ethnic markers. Language is a crucial case in point. Ethnic languages, or mother tongues, can serve as social divides, separating the communities of those who understand or speak them from those who can do neither (Stevens, 1985). One could make the case that knowledge approaching fluency is not even necessary for ethnic languages to have this function. Characteristic accents or the use of non-English words and phrases in English speech can signal ethnic origins to others. Moreover, language represents a major repository of ethnic cultural knowledge. Culture is embedded in language, thus knowledge of large portions of an ethnic culture is lost to those who do not know the mother tongue. This, too, contributes to the decline of a basis for ethnic social differentiation.

Over the past half century, there has been a massive erosion in the use of and even exposure to European languages in the United States. (Spanish could be argued to be an exception, but its widespread use in the United States is associated with immigration from Latin America; the numbers of Greek and Portuguese speakers also appear to have increased as a consequence of immigration during the 1960s and 1970s [Veltman, 1983: 9].) On the basis of a comprehensive study of intergenerational language shift, Veltman (1983) formulates a process of anglicization over two intergenerational transitions. The first generation continues to speak an ethnic language, although its members typically also speak English; the next generation is frequently bilingual, but English dominates the ethnic language; by the third generation, knowledge of an ethnic language beyond a few words and phrases is often lost.

The erosion of European languages is revealed in strong shifts across birth cohorts. Knowledge of mother tongues is concentrated in older cohorts and is declining inevitably as a result of cohort succession. Table 1.2 shows these patterns for the south-central-eastern European groups in terms of two indicators: currently speaking a language other than English at home, and exposure to an ethnic language in one's childhood home. Only a minority of any cohort currently speaks any ethnic language at home, but the group of speakers constitutes a larger proportion of older cohorts than of younger ones. Only tiny percentages of the post-1930 cohorts, hovering around 5 percent, speak anything besides English at home. More spectacular as a shift is the plummeting level of childhood exposure to ethnic mother tongues. About three-quarters of the two older cohorts had such exposure in their childhood homes, compared to just 10 percent among persons born after 1960. This massive shift implies a rapid fall-off in knowledge of these languages during the remainder of this century as the older cohorts are depleted by death.[10]

By far the most impressive evidence of the diminishing power of ethnicity among whites is the rising tide of interethnic marriage. Marriage is a sensitive barometer of social integration because it involves great social intimacy, which typically enwraps not only the

Table 1.2   Changes in language use and exposure among cohorts of U.S.-born South-Central-East European ethnics

	% Report Non-English Language in Childhood Home	% Currently Speak Non-English Language in Home
Before 1916	76.8	18.2
1916–1930	70.2	14.9
1931–1945	45.5	6.2
1946–1960	24.9	4.3
After 1960[a]	9.8	5.8

Source: Tabulations from the November 1979 Current Population Survey.
[a]The cohort born after 1960 contains only persons aged fourteen and older for the measure of language in childhood home and persons aged three and older for the measure of current home language.

marital partners but also members of their families, who are likely to be drawn into regular contact with each other. Since the perception of disparities rooted in ethnic and other aspects of social background can create a barrier to marriage, or even to the kinds of relationship that culminate in marriage, changes in marriage patterns carry broader implications about otherwise hard-to-measure changes in the hidden depths of social structures.

Among whites, a long-term trend of increasing intermarriage, which dates at least to the immediate post-World War II period and probably earlier, has made marriage across ethnic lines now the rule rather than the exception.[11] Indeed, ethnic origins seem so weakly related to marriages among whites that the term *intermarriage* may be increasingly a misnomer (as Robert Merton foresaw in 1941)—the existence of differences in ethnic origins may not be perceived by the marriage partners themselves.

These marriage patterns are demonstrated in my own research, using census and other survey data, and in the research of Lieberson and Waters (1985, 1988). For instance, analyzing the ancestry data in the 1980 census, I found that three of every four marriages of whites involve some degree of ethnic boundary crossing (Alba, 1985b). About half of all marriages among whites occur between individuals whose ancestries have nothing in common. Another quarter are between individuals whose ancestries differ in part but also share some common element—for example, when a woman of English-French background marries a man of English-Irish ancestry, or a woman of Irish-Italian background takes a husband of Italian ancestry. (Necessarily, one or both partners in such marriages have ethnically mixed ancestry. Typically, the overlapping ancestry involves one of the three largest ancestry categories—English, German, or Irish. Not only are these categories very large, but one or more of them is present in the great majority of ancestry mixtures.) Finally, in only a quarter of marriages do the partners have the same ethnic backgrounds.

The frequency of marriage across ethnic lines among whites presents a strong contrast to the infrequency of marriage across lines of race and Hispanic ancestry. Virtually all marriages of whites not of Hispanic background (99 percent) are with other non-Hispanic whites, according to the census data. Especially rare are marriages between non-Hispanic whites and blacks, by far the

largest group outside of the white population. In 1980, onl̶
percent of non-Hispanic whites had married blacks. Indeed,
whites, blacks tend to marry within their own racial group: am̶
blacks who are not of Hispanic background, only 2 percent ̶.̶a̶u̶
married non-blacks. Intermarriage is more common than this for
U.S.-born Hispanics and Asians and for American Indians, but still
falls short of its order of magnitude in the white population. (Nevertheless, the intermarriage rates of these groups appear to be increasing.)

✗ Interethnic marriage among whites has increased in recent
decades, especially for the groups from south-central-eastern Europe. The principal evidence of increase comes from comparisons
across cohorts (owing to the absence of comparable data on marriage patterns from two or more time points). Such comparisons, it
must be noted, can be confounded by differential rates of separation, divorce, and remarriage. But in the cases of the south-central-
eastern European groups, the cohort differences are so strong that
the inference of a historical rise in intermarriage seems sound.

Consider the intermarriage rates of persons of Polish or Italian
ancestry, shown in table 1.3. These two are the largest of the ancestry
groups originating in south-central-eastern Europe, with Poles ranking seventh and Italians fifth overall among all European-ancestry

Table 1.3 Marriage patterns of U.S.-born members of major
European ancestry groups

Major ancestry groups (in order of size):	Spouse's ancestry					
	Cohort born in 1920 or before			Cohort born after 1950		
	Entirely from group	Partly from group	Not from group	Entirely from group	Partly from group	Not from group
English	40.7%	21.7%	37.6%	36.9%	18.9%	44.1%
German	28.3	20.7	50.9	21.5	28.8	49.7
Irish	18.7	27.6	53.7	10.9	29.1	60.0
French	10.4	10.7	78.9	8.2	14.3	77.4
Italian	58.1	1.2	40.7	14.8	10.2	75.0
Scots	2.6	23.2	74.2	1.1	13.7	85.2
Polish	46.7	5.5	47.8	7.2	10.5	82.3

Source: Tabulations from the .1% B Public Use Microdata Sample of the 1980 Census.

groups in the U.S. population. In 1980, more than half those persons of Polish ancestry who were 60 years of age or older had spouses who were also of Polish background (mixed with other ancestries in 6 percent of the cases). Among their compatriots under the age of thirty, the equivalent rate was less than 20 percent. Among the Italians about 60 percent of the older group had spouses of Italian background, but in the younger group the comparable figure was only 25 percent. The cohort differences are not nearly as large for the old-stock groups, but in general their intermarriage rates were already high in the older cohort. Only the two largest ancestry groups—the English and Germans—do not have majorities in the youngest cohort who marry outside the group. Their relatively high rates of marriage to fellow group members are partly explained by group size (large groups provide more potential partners) and regional concentration (Tomaskovic-Devey and Tomaskovic-Devey, 1988). In addition, these groups have large mixed-ancestry contingents, and marriages involving spouses whose ancestry is only partially from the group figure prominently in their overall patterns.[12] As already noted, such marriages can frequently be viewed as intermarriages, especially since English and German are common in complex ancestry mixtures.

The rising tide of intermarriage is also sweeping across religious lines. In other words, there has been a general decline in the influence of ethnoreligious origins on marriages between whites. (Thus, the well-known triple-melting-pot thesis [Herberg, 1955; Kennedy, 1944; cf. Peach, 1980]—which predicted a regrouping of ethnicity along religious lines because of the containment of interethnic marriage within major religious divisions—does not seem to be holding up.) The increase in interreligious marriage is perhaps best illustrated by the marriage patterns of Jews, although their ultimate significance for the Jewish group remains in dispute because of unresolved questions about how intermarried couples and their children identify themselves and what such identifications mean (see Silberman, 1985: chap. 7). Before the 1960s, only a tiny proportion of Jews married non-Jews, and such marriages were frequently regarded with opprobrium by the Jewish community. In recent years, however, the rate of intermarriage has risen to the point that a quarter to a third of Jews intermarry (the exact numbers are uncertain; see Cohen, 1987). As the rate of intermarriage has risen, so has acceptance of such marriages, by both Jews and non-Jews.

Interreligious marriage by Catholics, mostly with Protestants, has reached even greater heights.[13] National survey data show that about half of young Catholics—that is, those who have married in recent years—have married non-Catholics (Alba, 1981). No doubt, in many of these marriages, as in Jewish-Gentile pairings, religious harmony is eventually brought about by the formal conversion of one spouse to the other's religion, or by informal agreements over religious identification. Such agreements, however, do not diminish the import of the fact that religious origins play a lesser role in the choice of a spouse than they once did.

The increase in ethnic intermarriage is responsible for what may be the most profound ethnic change among whites: the wide dispersion of ethnically mixed ancestry. Mixed ancestry cuts to the very quick of ethnicity as a social phenomenon, for ancestry is inextricably bound up with perceptions of ethnic group membership. Individuals with mixed ancestry have the potential to belong to two or more groups, and this fact may undercut the strength of affiliation they feel for any one of them. In addition, such individuals are, for obvious reasons, more likely to be brought up within an ethnically mixed milieu and therefore less likely to be socialized within an ethnic culture—for example, they are less likely than persons from ethnically undivided backgrounds to be exposed to ethnic languages during childhood (Stevens, 1985; Alba, 1988). Consequently, the spread of mixed ancestry strongly threatens the traditional bases for ethnic groups.

In all probability, a majority of U.S.-born non-Hispanic whites now have ethnically mixed ancestry. According to the 1980 census, 47 percent had ethnically mixed ancestry, and there are good reasons to view this figure as an underestimate.[14] In addition, there is a strong association between birth cohort and mixed ancestry, reflecting the historical rise in intermarriage, and this implies continuing change in the overall level of mixed ancestry as a result of cohort succession. In the census data, fewer than a third of the whites born in 1920 or earlier had ethnically mixed ancestry as compared to 60 percent of those born after 1960. Among those born during the 1970s, the proportion with mixed ancestry had climbed to two-thirds (Alba, 1985b).

An Older Model of Ethnicity

It is not clear that any role is left for ethnicity in light of the trends reviewed above. But such a facile dismissal, based on the decline of prominent ethnic inequalities, risks overlooking the subtle ways in which ethnicity conditions how people live. It is plainly contradicted by the claims of many social scientists and other observers (Greeley [1971] and Novak [1971] among them) that an ethnic revival has been under way since the 1960s. There is evidence to support their claims: an increase in ethnic phenomena of some kinds, such as radio and television broadcasts in ethnic mother tongues and ethnic studies courses at colleges and universities (see Fishman et al., 1985: 489), and a growing societal sensitivity to matters of ethnicity, in marked contrast to the optimism about assimilation in the aftermath of World War II. And then there is the obvious recognition many white Americans still accord their ethnic backgrounds. Many surveys show that only 10–15 percent of whites (Lieberson, 1985: 173) fail to answer questions about ethnic background. Clearly, most Americans remember something of their ethnic background, even after their families have been in the United States for many generations. Why would they do so unless ethnicity still holds some importance for them?

To resolve these apparent conflicts, it is necessary first to take stock of fundamental theoretical conceptions of ethnicity. The definition by Max Weber provides a good starting point: an ethnic group is one whose members "entertain a subjective belief in their common descent because of similarities of physical type or of customs or both, or because of memories of colonization and migration" (Weber, [1922] 1968: 389). Weber adds, "it does not matter whether or not an objective blood relationship exists." Weber's definition has the virtues of emphasizing that ethnic groups are social groups, and thus ones whose members tend to interact with one another[15] and to share a consciousness of kind; that real or presumed ancestry is the criterion by which an individual's group membership is decided; and that central to an ethnic group's self-definition is a sense of a common history that sets it apart from others. The central role of the past—of family ancestry and group history—demonstrates that ethnic groups are different from many other types of social groups, which are defined in terms of the current characteristics of their members.

Broadly conceived, two interdependent sources for ethnicity's potential importance in social life stand out: Ethnicity may serve as a principle of *social allocation;* and it may represent a form of *social solidarity* (for supporting reviews, see Yinger, 1986; See and Wilson, 1988). To say that ethnicity is a principle of social allocation means that individuals are channeled into locations in the social structure based on their ethnic characteristics, through means that may vary from one setting to another and may involve complex combinations of voluntary and institutional factors. In American society until recently, white ethnic groups have been distinguished from one another by educational level, occupation, and residence; and much research devoted to ethnicity has attempted to measure and develop explanations for this kind of ethnic differentiation. But as the trends reviewed above strongly imply, this aspect of ethnicity is weakening steadily.

The notion of solidarity represents an extension of the group character of ethnicity. *Solidary* ethnic groups can be regarded as self-conscious communities whose members interact with each other to achieve common purposes (cf. Olzak, 1983; Nielsen, 1985; Hechter, 1987; Esser, 1988). Ethnic solidarity is made manifest when group members mobilize themselves to influence the outcome of a political issue, or when they offer each other assistance— in the form of jobs, say—that they would deny to outsiders. The solidarity notion implies not simply the recognition of some distinction between people inside and outside of the group ("we" and "they") but a consciousness of "something" that is shared by members and requires their mutual cooperation. It could be that they are conscious of being bound together by a common fate, of suffering discrimination in common (see Gordon, 1964: 53); that they are aware of shared interests, such as furthering the advancement of the group and thereby of its individual members (see Glazer and Moynihan, 1970); or that they value a heritage, however diffusely defined, that they wish to perpetuate. Evident is that solidarity should be viewed as a variable quantity, not as a fixed criterion. Groups, then, can be more or less solidary (Yancey et al., 1976).

The trends among American whites not only dent the once po-

tent role of ethnicity for social allocation, but also render problematic its importance as a form of social solidarity. The latter
implication emerges into clear focus when one considers an older
model of ethnic solidarity, made increasingly irrelevant by ethnic
trends. Ultimately, then, the trends force us to consider the possibility of an alternative model for solidarity; and this brings us to
ethnic identity as the pivotal notion.

The older model envisions ethnic solidarity as rooted, on the
one hand, in certain commonalities of culture, experience, and interests that are widely shared by the members of an ethnic group
and, on the other, in numerous informal social structures that are
more or less ethnically homogeneous. In both regards, social allocation contributes to ethnicity as a form of solidarity.

Insofar as they are culturally rooted, the commonalities are not
static traditions, brought by immigrants and handed down, with
unavoidable losses in the process, from one generation to the next.
The proponents of what I call the older model—for example, Glazer
and Moynihan (1970) and Greeley (1977)—insist on the transforming quality of the early experience of a group in the United States.
Much of the culture that immigrants bring with them is not suitable
for their circumstances in the new society (this is particularly the
case for the many groups of peasant background that settled in
American cities). Large parts of the Old World culture, then, are
jettisoned by the immigrants or by their children and grandchildren, and the surviving portions are often fundamentally altered by the cultural reshuffling brought on by the settlement and
assimilation processes.

But the complex contingencies peculiar to each ethnic group,
the product of its characteristics at entry (cultural traits, occupational experiences, intentions to return, etc.) and the opportunities
available to its members at the time and in the places of their settlement, lead to a distinctive experience and social positioning that
continue beyond the immigrant generation. Glazer and Moynihan
(1970: xxxiii) put the matter nicely in speaking of culture:

> In *Beyond the Melting Pot*, we suggested that ethnic groups,
> owing to their distinctive historical experiences, their cultures
> and skills, the times of their arrival and the economic situation
> they met, developed distinctive economic, political, and cultur-

al patterns. As the old culture fell away—and it did rapidly enough—a new one, shaped by the distinctive experiences of life in America, was formed and a new identity was created. Italian-Americans might share precious little with Italians in Italy, but in America they were a distinctive group that maintained itself, was identifiable, and gave something to those who were identified with it, just as it also gave burdens that those in the group had to bear.

This new culture, to be sure, does not arise *de novo* but is built in large part from the cultural materials brought by the immigrants; hence it is not surprising that the new ethnic culture often bears a strong resemblance to the group's Old World culture (Greeley and McCready, 1975).

An important part of these commonalities results from the channeling of a group's members into a distinctive set of occupations, itself a primary example of how complex contingencies—that is, interactions between American opportunities and Old World characteristics of immigrants—generate a common experience for a group. An ethnic group is thus economically specialized to an important degree, exploiting specific economic niches that further define its essential experience. In Glazer and Moynihan's (1970: lvii) words, "to name an occupational group or class is very much the same thing as naming an ethnic group" (see also Yancey et al., 1976; Hechter, 1978; Portes and Bach, 1985; Morawska, 1985). A similar set of contingencies helped to produce the residential concentrations of ethnic groups in American cities, which stand as vivid reminders of the social power of ethnicity.

On the basis of such commonalities as these, Glazer and Moynihan, along with other authors (for example, Bell, 1975), argue for one more, namely, common political interests. Because members of an ethnic group are relatively homogeneous with respect to occupation and residence, they are affected in the same way by government actions. Ethnic groups therefore become *interest groups,* and this fact breathes new and presumably permanent life into what might seem to be an Old World social form. Ethnicity is seen as particularly well suited for a political role in American society as the absence of sharp class divisions highlights the correspondences between ethnicity and social positioning (Olzak, 1983; Nielsen, 1985).

Ethnic social structures, the second factor in the older model, are presumed to arise in part because people prefer to associate with others ethnically like themselves, and in part because of social inertia, operating independently of such preferences. It is assumed that neighborhoods, friendship circles, and families are often ethnically homogeneous, so that even those persons who do not self-consciously identify in ethnic terms find themselves embedded in the social matrix of ethnic communal life (see Glazer and Moynihan, 1970; Greeley, 1971).

But these two presumed pillars of ethnic solidarity are overwhelmed by the accumulated weight of findings concerning the attenuation of ethnic differences among whites. Thus, research demonstrating increasing convergence in economic chances implies that economic specialization may still exist, but it has weakened considerably (see Lieberson and Waters, 1988: chap. 5). And research documenting the growing extent of ethnic intermarriage shows unequivocally that ethnic integration occurs in the most socially intimate of spheres, the family, and makes it hard to imagine how ethnic groups could remain separated in other informal social structures.

Viewed in its totality, the transformation of ethnicity implies a new primacy for ethnic identity, the subjective orientation toward ethnic origins (see also Gans, 1979). It can no longer be assumed that ethnic solidarities within the white population are sustained by salient correspondences between ethnicity and labor-market situation or by extensive patterns of informal association. Insofar as ethnicity has a role, then, it is increasingly voluntary, dependent on deliberate actions of individuals to maintain activities and relationships that have an ethnic character.

The primacy of ethnic identity can be seen, for instance, in the argument that ethnic solidarity no longer depends on the residential segregation of groups (Yancey et al., 1976). In this formulation, social relationships are becoming less confined by geography as a result of modern means of transportation and communication, and ethnic relationships can be maintained at long distances. But precisely because it envisions that the chance, everyday encounters engendered by propinquity have lost some of their significance, this argument attaches greater weight to the intentions of individuals to maintain easily lost social patterns that have some ethnic significance.

There is also a methodological importance to the questions surrounding ethnic identity. Ethnicity research has consistently relied on the assumption, often without recognizing its role, that ancestry categories can be presumed to represent social groups and can be compared to one another on that basis (McKay and Lewins, 1978). Ancestry information is thus assumed to indicate the subjective orientations of the persons involved—that persons with, say, German ancestry regard themselves, and are regarded by others, in socially meaningful ways as German. But at a time when the proportion of whites with mixed ancestry is high and continuing to increase, this assumption is questionable, to say the least (see Alba and Chamlin, 1983; Lieberson and Waters, 1986).

To recognize the new primacy of ethnic identity is not, of course, to delineate a model. But the point is that ethnic identity must come in for close scrutiny, which it has up until now not received, in order to understand contemporary ethnicity among whites. The remainder of this book is devoted to an investigation of ethnic identity as a means of pursuing the ultimate implications of current ethnic trends; thereby, it also assays the viability of a new model of solidarity grounded on ethnic identity. But next we must consider the nature of ethnic identity and the critical research issues concerning it.

Ethnic Identity

In an era when ethnicity is increasingly voluntary for whites, questions about ethnic identity go to the heart of ethnicity's possible role. But what precisely is ethnic identity? Two alternative conceptions deserve to be considered.[16]

One conception, framed in psychological terms, locates ethnic identity in deep structures of the psyche. Paradigmatic here are the theories of Erik Erikson. One of Erikson's greatest contributions to psychoanalytic theory is his concept of identity as representing an individual's personal identification in terms of the prototypes available given his or her location in time (history) and space (Erikson, 1980). This identity is formed through internalization of the models of self—"prototypes of good and evil," Erikson calls them—that exist within the family and the larger social environment. Erikson's advance beyond Freud, who hardly ever used the term *identity* (Erikson, 1980: 109), was to recognize that the crucial developments of personality are not confined to a brief period in childhood and the nuclear-family setting but that each stage of the life-cycle has its particular "crises" and developmental resolutions, and that models of self incorporated in the identity are assimilated in a number of social settings.

The relevance of the Eriksonian concept of identity for ethnicity should be obvious (for work inspired by Erikson's framework, see Femminella, 1983; McGoldrick, 1982).[17] In ethnically differentiated societies, there exist varieties of models of self linked to ethnic background. From early in life, each individual is exposed to a limited set of models, constituting a framework of acceptable alternatives based on his or her background, and elaborates a personal variant, a unique identity, within this context. The resolution of each stage of the life-cycle, then, is likely to occur in terms of an ethnically contingent set of alternatives, not only because of the individual's family origins, but also because his or her development to that point represents an accumulation of ethnically influenced past resolutions.

The appeal of the concept lies in its suggestion that the individual's personality and identity are informed by ethnicity not just on the conscious surface but also at deeper levels. Accordingly, individuals may be ethnic in their "identities" even if they consciously reject their ethnic backgrounds. That is, a person who is raised within, say, an Italian-American family and social setting will have self-conceptions impregnated with this influence—in the domain of family relationships, for example—even if he or she no longer consciously identifies as Italian or Italian American.

An alternative conception of ethnic identity lies in contemporary social psychology's theory of the self-concept. The concerns here are less with deep psychological dynamics and more with the direct articulation between social structure and the image an individual holds of him- or herself. The starting point is the notion that the social world is composed of social categories and membership groups, in terms of which the individual must define him- or herself and be defined by others (Rosenberg, 1978; Tajfel, 1981; see also

Gecas, 1982, and Ferdman, 1989). Thus, an individual can be simul-
taneously a male, a Polish American, a father, and a plumber—these
and other socially recognized names of categories and groups make
up his social identity. Generally speaking, such names are associated with other elements—evaluative and emotional loadings,
which determine the self-esteem derived from a specific identity,
and normative expectations (or roles), characteristic ways in which
a member of a group or category is expected to behave (Stryker,
1968).

Identity theory in social psychology also speaks about structuring or hierarchy in a social identity, thereby addressing an issue of
considerable importance for the study of ethnic identity. Since not
all identities are of equal importance, for society or for the individual, it is necessary to distinguish among them in these terms.
Sheldon Stryker (1968) identifies *commitment* and *salience* as critical dimensions of identities. Commitment is the degree of invest-
ment in relationships to others that is premised on a specific identity, and thus the social cost of renouncing it, and salience is the
"probability, for a given person, of a given identity being invoked in
a variety of situations" (Stryker, 1968: 560). Salience may be more
interesting for the study of ethnic identity, as it corresponds with
one possible outcome of a long-run process of ethnic change, namely, that ethnic identities continue to exist but decline in significance. To pose this endpoint in the extreme, an individual may
identify as, say, an Irish American, or an American of Irish ancestry,
but this may be perceived as simply a matter of where one's ancestors came from, without relevance for ordinary social life.

Each of these alternative conceptions of identity has something
to offer to the study of ethnicity, but neither seems entirely satisfac-
tory for addressing the implications of the transformation of ethnicity among whites. One difficulty with the Eriksonian conception
lies in what may seem its greatest strength: the notion that the
incorporation of ethnic models of the self may be below the surface
of consciousness. This may well be the case (although its application
to whites at a time when ethnic intermarriage is so widespread,
when family and intimate social milieus contain great ethnic diversity, seems questionable). But it is insufficient to address the key
issue concerning the contemporary role of ethnicity: Since social
differences among white ethnic categories are declining, if not dis-

solving, and contact between persons of different ethnic origins is pervasive, ethnic solidarity in whatever form can be maintained only if there are critical masses of individuals who *consciously* identify themselves in ethnic terms, are so identified by others, and who act, at least some of the time, in terms of these identities.

This issue might seem to be more directly addressed, then, by the social psychological conception of identity, but this too has a pitfall: It overformalizes the concept of identity, implying a strong degree of consensus about the ethnic names or labels with which people identify themselves and the expectations about behavior associated with ethnic identities. Given the contemporary fluidity of ethnicity among whites, the degree of consensus about ethnic labels and behaviors must be taken as problematic, a subject for investigation rather than a definitional matter.

The difficulties that must be faced by an appropriate conception of identity can be illustrated in the following ways. Consider the ambiguities of ethnic labels in relation to identities based on mixed, and perhaps quite complex, ethnic ancestry. An example is someone who identifies as a German-Irish-Italian (some 227,000 in the 1980 census). Should this identity be regarded as three separate ethnic memberships or as an identification with a new kind of group, based on a particular combination of mixed ancestry (the German-Irish-Italian Americans)? Or perhaps the appropriate reference group is made up of all persons of ethnically mixed ancestry, whatever the European components? Moreover, a complex identity of this sort may be situationally specific (Lyman and Douglas, 1973)—with its Irish component emphasized under some circumstances (on St. Patrick's Day), its Italian under others (when with one side of the family), and its German under still others (when choosing a language to study in school).[18]

Equally problematic is any assumption about behavioral expectations (or actual behavior). Given the voluntary nature of ethnicity among whites, individuals are freer than ever before to pick and choose among the behaviors associated with an ethnic identity, if not indeed to create new ones (Gans, 1979). The individual who consciously identifies as Italian American can interpret this identity in terms of a fondness for opera, a love of Italian cuisine (which now can be carried over to a high-status northern Italian cuisine quite unfamiliar to his or her ancestors and probably served to non-Italian guests), or a desire to combat stereotypes of Italian Americans as Mafia-linked. There is, in short, no prescription about the significance of an ethnic identity for a person's life.

A study of the contemporary role of ethnicity therefore requires a conception of identity that acknowledges the possible fluidity of ethnicity (Lyman and Douglas, 1973). Such a conception must derive from a recognition that ethnic identity may be a subtle matter for many whites, sometimes present but often not, and possibly quite variable in its form. For these reasons, I begin from a loose conception of ethnic identity, namely, a person's subjective orientation toward his or her ethnic origins. This definition, intended to be closer in spirit to the social-psychological than to the Eriksonian conception, accepts a variety of names as indicators of ethnic identities, such as, in the case of a person of Italian ancestry: "I am Sicilian," "I am Italian," "I am an American of Italian ancestry," or "my grandparents came from Italy." Although the variations are significant, each constitutes a potentially meaningful acknowledgment of an ethnic background. So, in the case of someone of mixed Irish and Italian ancestry, do such formulations as: "I am Irish and Italian," "I like to think of myself as Irish, but my father's side is Italian," or "my grandparents came from Ireland and Italy." All such formulations, and still others, can be found among contemporary Americans of European ancestry.[19]

This conception of ethnic identity leads to a number of issues that require empirical investigation. The first is the personal meaningfulness or felt intensity of identity, closely related to Stryker's (1968) concept of salience. It should be obvious that, even though individuals may on occasion label themselves in ethnic ways, these labels may be marginal to their self-conceptions. If this is the case, it is unlikely that they will see this identity as relevant to many social situations or frequently act in accordance with it. Precisely because of trends that reduce the structural connections among persons of the same ethnic background, ethnic identity is most likely to serve as a basis for solidarity when its salience for the individual is great. This stands in contrast to the situation that prevailed only a few decades ago, when ethnic social structures made ethnicity less self-conscious.

A second issue concerns the extent and manner in which identity is manifested to others. Because of the decline in grossly observable ethnic differences among whites—formerly manifested in language and mannerisms, occupation and residence—the communication of ethnic identity is now problematic in a new way. Even names, insofar as their ethnic character can be deduced, are no longer a reliable guide—intermarried women find their ethnic identities hidden behind their husbands' names, and many persons of mixed ancestry lose aspects of their identities in names that reflect paternal ancestry only. But because of the erosion of the structural foundations of ethnicity and the porousness of ethnic boundaries, solidarity is possible only if ethnic identities are socially recognized. How is this done? What are the forms of "ethnic signalling" (Plotnikov and Silverman, 1978)?

A third issue is the practical significance, the content, of ethnic identity. If ethnic identity is to have a social, as opposed to a merely personal, significance, it must be linked to activities and relationships that have an ethnic character, the behavioral correlates of identity: how is it typically expressed in terms of such culturally linked behaviors as food habits and holiday rituals? Is it rooted in social structures—relationships to others that are forged on the basis of common ethnicity? Unless ethnic identity is linked to behavior, it cannot contribute to ethnicity as a social form.

Finally, a study of ethnic identity must concern itself with an aggregation issue: are there meaningful collective ethnic identities? It is ultimately not enough to find masses of individuals who identify themselves ethnically in meaningful ways—that is, in ways that they hold to be relevant for their lives. It is necessary also to ask whether the ethnic identities of individuals aggregate in ways that sustain ethnic solidarity. Essential in this respect is that ethnicity as a collective phenomenon cannot be carried on as a largely private affair. Even if many individuals identify themselves in terms of ethnic origins, the existence of such identities need not demonstrate that ethnicity remains an important basis for social life (as Herbert Gans's [1979] thesis of "symbolic ethnicity" underscores). How, then, the identities of different individuals from the same group articulate with each other is an important question for evaluating the contemporary role of ethnicity.

Theories about Ethnic Identity

The issues surrounding ethnic identity have an obvious bearing for any assessment of the current state of ethnicity among Americans whose ancestors came from Europe. In order to provide some initial expectations about the kinds of findings that might emerge from a study of ethnic identity, it is useful to review several well-known interpretations of ethnicity that revolve quite specifically around issues of identity. This review can also provide clues about critical tests that may help to distinguish one interpretation from another.

1. Ethnicity as a working- and lower-class style. Perhaps the most popular view of ethnicity, this has a long history in the study of American ethnic groups and draws support from the classic studies of ethnic communities, such as Herbert Gans's *The Urban Villagers* (1982). It is broadly consistent with the notion, often found in assimilationist interpretations, that ethnicity is strongest among socially disadvantaged groups and is eroded by social and geographical mobility (Esser, 1988). Moreover, in a society like the United States where class ideologies are muted, ethnicity can provide an idiom by which the disadvantaged can identify and understand the nature of their disadvantage.

   An underlying premise of this view is that chiefly in the working and lower classes there is a correspondence of work, residence, and ethnicity that causes ethnicity to be subjectively perceived as a principal determinant of life chances and lifestyles (Yancey et al., 1976). This correspondence is reflected in the family- and neighborhood-based networks that define the character of working- and lower-class life (Kornblum, 1974; Stack, 1974). These draw together people of common ethnic background whose lives intersect in numerous ways (for example, having grown up in the same neighborhood, working at the same job). Ethnic sentiments should resonate easily in such insular social worlds.

   The view of ethnicity as a class-linked phenomenon has broad import—it implies, for instance, that ethnic cultural markers should be most prominent among members of the working and lower classes. But it carries implications for ethnic identity as well. Ethnic identities should be more common and more salient in lower socioeconomic groups than in higher ones, whose members have presumably more or less suppressed their ethnic identities in the interest of mixing freely with people of widely differing ethnic backgrounds. Given the popularity of the class-linked view, it is important to test this simple proposition.

But the view has another relevant implication. It suggests that there should be a close connection among class position, ethnically based networks, and identity, and in particular, that individuals whose social networks are family-based and contain many ethnic peers should have stronger ethnic identities. This proposition, too, can be put to the test.

2. The politicization of ethnicity. This interpretation, initially formulated by Glazer and Moynihan (1970, 1975), emphasizes that, even though the immigrant culture fades quickly under the impact of the settlement process, ethnicity coincides with differences in American circumstances, such as residential and occupational concentrations (see also Yancey et al., 1976). This superimposition of American experiences on ethnic outlines stimulates a sense of ethnic identity. In particular, ethnicity becomes important in the political sphere, as ethnic groups become interest groups, representing and reflecting the interests of many similarly situated individuals. Daniel Bell (1975) has added to the argument with his claim that politics is increasingly replacing the market as the chief instrument of distribution and that politics recognizes only group claims, thus enhancing ethnicity's role. Others, who see the politicization of ethnicity as an intrinsic feature of advanced industrial societies (Olzak, 1983; Nielsen, 1985), argue that ethnicity offers a wider basis for mobilization than does social class.

According to these views, ethnic identity should be strongly linked to political attitudes, participation, and behavior. Those who identify should have a sense of the ethnic group as having interests that can be advanced and attacked. It is likely that they will be involved with ethnic causes, whether these concern the minority status of Catholics in Northern Ireland, the embattled situation of Israel, or, closer to home, the persistence of degrading ethnic stereotypes and discrimination against members of the group.

3. The revival of ethnicity. Many scholars who saw an ethnic revival among whites during the 1960s and 1970s relied on a social-psychological logic that originated in Marcus Hansen's (1938) famous thesis of a third-generation return to ethnicity. Hansen argued that the second generation is often preoccupied with the problems of adapting to American society and hence self-consciously rejects its ethnic heritage, but the third generation, surer of its place in the new society, seeks to retrieve it. Hansen's memorable formulation ran, "What the son wishes to forget, the grandson wishes to remember" (quoted in Herberg, 1960: 30).

But the notion of a "return" can be stripped from a specific generation. That is, it can be argued that during an ethnic group's early period in the United States, its members are too diffident about their place in the new society to assert their identity with any vigor. But at a later point, after they have moved upward, they seek to reassert their identity (Greeley, 1971: 53–59). Thus, the notion of a revival postulates that this may have happened on a mass scale to the descendants of the nineteenth- and twentieth-century immigrants from Europe.

The notion of an ethnic revival is particularly bound up with a return to ethnic cultures, and many commentators have pointed to what they perceive as renewed interest in ethnic languages, literatures, and rituals, as well as growth in the number of ethnic festivals and other celebrations of ethnicity as evidence of the surge in ethnic identity (Fishman et al., 1985). Whether there is more here than nostalgic fascination is open to question (Gans, 1979), but this interpretation suggests a strong association between ethnic identity and involvement in ethnic cultural activities.

The return thesis also suggests that indicators of success and integration in American society may be correlated with ethnic identity. The indicators are broader than the original distinction between the second and third generations, although clearly one would expect that expressions of ethnic identity are weaker among earlier American-born generations than among later ones. But the thesis also implies that socioeconomic position may be positively related to ethnic identity—that the more highly educated, for example, may be more likely to identify ethnically than those with less education. This implication runs directly counter to the conventional assumptions about social mobility's role as an agent of assimilation and hence to the view of ethnicity as a working- and lower-class style.

4. The emergence of "symbolic ethnicity." The notion of "symbolic ethnicity" has been advanced by Herbert Gans (1979; see also Steinberg, 1981) to rebut claims of an ethnic revival among whites. Gans sees symbolic ethnicity, which he describes as an "ethnicity of last resort," in terms of a gradual, albeit inevitable, withering of ethnic differences among Americans of European ancestries. Because of widespread social mobility and intermarriage, ethnicity has become increasingly peripheral to the lives of many Americans of recent ethnic origins. But they do not relinquish ethnic identity entirely; rather, they adapt it to their current circumstances, selecting from an ethnic heritage a few symbolic elements that do not interfere with the need to intermix socially, turning ethnicity thereby into an occasionally practiced avocation. (Gans characterizes contemporary ethnicity as a matter of "feeling ethnic" as opposed to being so.) This symbolic identification with the ethnic group allows individuals to construct personal identities that contain some eth-

nic "spice." But at the same time, it represents a personalization of ethnicity and frequently amounts to little more than a token acknowledgment of ethnic background.

If symbolic ethnicity is indeed the appropriate concept to apply to contemporary ethnicity among whites, one would expect to find that ethnic identity corresponds with a limited commitment to ethnic cultural activities, or to other ethnic activities that might lead to conflict with nongroup members. The ethnic activities of the symbolic identifier are likely to have an occasional character and to be acceptable in a multiethnic setting, as is true for many holiday rituals (for example, the serving of appropriate ethnic foods on Christmas, Easter, and Passover).

Symbolic ethnicity also carries implications about the linkage between ethnic identity and ethnic social structures. Symbolic ethnicity is characteristic of persons in integrated settings, and therefore one would expect to see a detachment of ethnic identity from ethnic networks, organizations, and neighborhoods. In this respect, it directly opposes what I have called the older model of solidarity as well as the view of ethnicity as a class-linked style, both of which would lead one to expect that ethnic identity is rooted in ethnic social structures.

The Capital Region Study

The remainder of the book investigates the role of ethnic identity among contemporary whites of the second and later generations through the analysis of a survey. The data represent a random sample of residents in the core counties of the Albany-Schenectady-Troy metropolitan area (hereafter, the "Capital Region") of New York State. In 1984 and 1985, 524 randomly chosen residents were interviewed concerning their ethnic ancestries, their identification with their ethnic origins, their ethnically related experiences, and social relationships and activities that might have an ethnic character. The survey instrument was designed with the assistance of Herbert Gans, and, in addition to its specifically ethnic content, contained a range of standard survey items, including education, occupation, parental birthplaces, and many of the attitudinal items found in the General Social Survey of the National Opinion Research Center. The respondents represent a wide variety of ethnic backgrounds, principally those found in the white population, and they come from very different socioeconomic and residential settings—for example, from large and small cities, suburbs and rural areas.

Technical details of the survey are presented in an appendix, and others unfold in subsequent chapters. But some remarks about the appropriateness of the research setting seem in order at this point. To begin with, there is value in studying ethnic identity in a specific setting because ethnicity is, in important aspects, a localized phenomenon, dependent on context; this property is lost in national studies. Moreover, the study site can be taken as representative of many aging industrial areas of the northeastern and midwestern United States, where the ethnicities derived from European immigration remain prominent features of the social landscape. Its relatively small overall population size (less than one million) and small non-white populations in particular distinguish it from such ethnic conglomerations as New York City, Boston, and Philadelphia. But this perhaps means it is more typical, not less.

In terms of a broad-brush socioeconomic profile, the area seems reasonably typical of metropolitan areas in general. For instance, the 1980 census shows that a third of its adult population has attended college, approximately the same proportion as is found for the average metropolitan area in the nation.[20] The occupational distribution of the region is also broadly similar to that of the average metropolitan area. A quarter of its labor force, for example, is in managerial and professional specialty occupations, and a third is in technical, sales, and clerical jobs—fractions on a par with those for metropolitan areas in general. One difference, however, is that the regional labor force contains a slightly smaller proportion of blue-collar workers—25 percent versus 29 percent in the nation. The proportion employed in manufacturing is also smaller (18 versus 22 percent).

Yet the area is not typical in all respects. First, it contains the state capital, and a larger than average portion of the region's work force—27 percent versus 17 percent for all metropolitan areas—is employed in government. Ethnic concerns, which play a role in the politics of the state, are probably more familiar to many inhabitants than would be the case for a similar region elsewhere. Second, the region is less intensely urban than most metropolitan areas. Its largest cities are not really very large—in 1980 Albany had a population barely above 100,000 and the populations of Schenectady and Troy were smaller. Hence, a smaller part of the region's population resides in central cities than is true for the average metropolitan area (28 versus 39 percent in 1980). This adds to the area's appeal as a setting for studying ethnicity because the study of ethnic phenomena in suburban and rural areas has suffered neglect in comparison with those in large cities.

The continuing prominence of ethnicity in the region can be exemplified through the region's politics: the Albany Democratic Party, whose influence extends well beyond the boundaries of the city, remains the last stronghold in the nation of a once prevalent political form, the Irish Catholic machine. (At the time this is written, the entire political leadership in the county, including the mayor of Albany, the county executive, the state senator, and the representative in Congress, is Irish Catholic.) Further, the surface of the area's social life is crisscrossed by numerous ethnic organizations and events. For example, the city of Albany holds a Pinksterfest each spring to celebrate its Dutch origins (and a picture of young women in Dutch costume sweeping State Street invariably appears in the local newspaper); the annual Scottish Games draws participants from all over the Northeast; and the Italian tradition of religious festivals (*feste*) is still maintained by some parishes, which dedicate festivals to St. Anthony and Our Lady of Mount Carmel, among others.

Happily, moreover, for a study of this kind, there is an unusual degree of ethnic diversity in the Capital Region's white population, which includes both old-stock and newer groups (social-psychological studies suggest the importance of ethnic differences for activating ethnic identities [McGuire et al., 1978]). The earliest European settlers, arriving in the seventeenth century, were the English and Dutch, ancestries that are still represented in significant numbers in the population. Early industrialization and the region's significance as a river port brought large numbers of Irish and Germans in the nineteenth century, and Italians and eastern Europeans around the turn of the century. Proximity to Canada led to extensive settlement by French Canadians. Non-European groups, however, are represented in very small numbers, aside from the American Indian ancestry found in many old-stock mixtures.

A comparison of the ethnic composition of the Capital Region with that of the nation shows some similarities and some differences (see table 1.4). In broad terms, the ranking of groups by size is approximately the same in the region and the nation. Among

Table 1.4 Selected characteristics of major ancestry groups among U.S.-born whites in the Capital Region

| | % of U.S.-born whites in Capital Region[a] | % of U.S.-born whites in national population[a] | Selected characteristics of Capital Region ethnic groups | | | |
			Ancestry type: % with unmixed ancestry	Generation: % in third and later generations	Religion: % Catholic	Education: % who have attended college
Irish	34.8	22.0	18.1	92.4	70.6	42.5
English	34.1	26.7	5.1	92.3	42.7	47.1
German	31.3	26.5	12.5	88.3	41.7	42.7
French/French Canadian	24.1	7.3	14.4	83.3	64.9	34.2
Italian	15.2	6.5	54.3	69.6	80.0	41.4
Scots	13.7	5.3	9.5	83.6	23.8	47.6
Dutch	11.7	3.4	3.7	95.9	35.2	29.6
Polish	9.6	4.2	36.4	54.5	70.5	25.0
American Indian	5.9	2.8	3.7	95.0	29.6	33.3
All U.S.-born whites in Capital Region	—	—	33.3	78.5	54.3	38.1

[a]Because individuals with mixed ancestry can be tabulated in more than one category, the percentages in these columns total more than 100 percent. The data for the ethnic composition of the Capital Region come from the ethnic identity survey, the data for the nation from the .1% B Public Use Microdata Sample of the 1980 Census. It should also be noted that some ancestry categories, particularly old-stock ones, may be undercounted in the census data because of ancestry truncation in census data-collection and coding procedures.

native-born whites, the three largest groups—the English, Germans, and Irish—stand apart from all others. They are followed by a series of smaller groups—French and French Canadian, Italian, Scots, Dutch, Polish, and American Indian (this is the order in the region; that in the nation is only slightly different). But in terms of European groups, the region is more ethnically heterogeneous than the nation. This is somewhat disguised in the table because of the generally lower proportion each group claims in the national population. (This difference is partly a methodological artifact, resulting from the higher proportion of unreported ancestry in census data for the nation.) But the greater heterogeneity of the region is apparent in the numerical importance of groups following the "big three" in size. For example, Italians represent approximately 15 percent of the Capital Region's population—nearly three times their proportionate size in the nation. Similar characterizations apply to many of the other groups following the top three. Thus, the smaller groups appear to make up a bigger portion of the region's population than of the national one.

There are also differences in generational and religious terms. By comparison with the nation, a greater part of the Capital Region's population is within living memory of the immigrant experience. About 8 percent of whites are immigrants themselves, and even among the American-born, the children and grandchildren of immigrants predominate. The third generation is the modal one, containing roughly 40 percent of the white population; fewer than a third of whites do not have at least one immigrant grandparent. Moreover, in distinct contrast to the Protestant predominance in the national population, Catholics form a majority (54 percent) among the region's native-born whites, while Protestants constitute barely a third. Jews are represented at about the same level as in the nation as a whole (2.6 percent). The prevalence of Catholics is partly attributable to the numerical importance of some heavily Catholic groups, such as the French, Irish, and Italians. But even normally Protestant groups, such as the English, contain strong Catholic representations, presumably as a result of intermarriage over the generations.

To bring these comparisons to bear on the issues prompting the research, one might say that ethnic identities are more likely to retain some importance in the Capital Region than in other metropolitan areas of comparable size; and in this sense, the region provides a valuable setting for studying such identities and the social contexts that support them. In comparison with that of many similar-sized metropolitan areas in the southern and western United States, the Capital Region's native-born white population is more ethnically heterogeneous, closer to the immigration experience, and probably more settled in ethnic communities. In comparison with that of many large urban areas in the Northeast, such as New York City, the Capital Region's population affords an interesting balance between ethnicities associated with very long settlement in the United States and those of fairly recent vintage. As Archdeacon (1985) and others have noted, the ethnicities deriving from old-stock origins have been neglected in the study of American ethnic groups. This neglect can be addressed here.

Plan of the Book

Chapter 2 delves into the nature of the ethnic identities of U.S.-born whites in the Capital Region and the crucial relationship between identity and ethnic ancestry. It considers not just how many identify and how salient their identities are but also what kinds of whites are most likely to identify with their ethnic backgrounds—how, for instance, does the probability of identification vary with generational position and educational attainment?

Chapter 3 is the first of two chapters to consider the content of ethnic identities: how, if at all, do they correspond with experiences? This chapter searches for the cultural content in identities—for systematic differences based on identities in such areas as foods and ethnic customs. In doing so, of course, it also provides a characterization of the strength of ethnic cultural features among whites. Chapter 4 pushes the investigation of ethnically related experiences into other domains, such as discussing one's background with others, suffering prejudice and discrimination, and identifying with ethnic political issues.

Chapter 5 initiates a three-part examination of ethnic social structures and their relationship to ethnic identity. This chapter looks at the crucial topic of ethnicity in families, addressing among other issues the intergenerational transmission of ethnicity in intermarried families. Chapter 6 examines ethnicity in friendship and organizational memberships, and chapter 7 looks for ethnicity in the neighborhoods of the Capital Region.

Finally, chapter 8 provides an overview and interpretation of the results. It attempts to resolve a puzzle: why do so many whites continue to identify with their ethnic origins when "objective" differences among ethnic categories in the white population are dwindling? The resolution is given in the form of the gradual, and still incomplete, emergence of a new ethnic group on the American scene, the European Americans. The chapter attempts to account for some of the characteristics of this new group in terms of the continuing importance of ethnic and racial differences in the United States and the nature of ethnicity itself.

Fundamentals of Ancestry and Identity

Treating ethnic identity strictly as a group
phenomenon in which recruitment of membership is ascriptive forecloses study of the
process whereby individuals make use of ethnicity as a maneuver or stratagem in working
out their own life chances in an ethnically
pluralistic social setting.
—STANFORD M. LYMAN AND WILLIAM A. DOUGLAS
(1973: 350)

I'm Polish. I mean, I'm American. My family
has been here for four generations; that's a lot.
My great-grandfather came over here, from
near Cracow. I've never been to Poland. I'll
never go there. Why should I? It's in your
blood. It's in your background. But I live *here*.
My wife is the same, Polish.
—POLISH AMERICAN RESPONDENT
QUOTED BY COLES (1971: 43)

✗ Ethnicity is inherently a matter of *ancestry*, of beliefs about the origins of one's
forebears. As Max Weber ([1922] 1968:
389) put it: ethnic-group members "entertain a subjective belief in their common descent.✗ Unlike many other group
memberships, ethnicity is oriented toward the past, toward the history and origin of family, group, and nation.

But ethnic identity need not be coterminous with ancestry (or,
more precisely, with what is believed about ancestry). There are
reasons to think that ancestry and identity may be increasingly
divergent in the United States, as a result of the growing complexity
of the ancestries of the large portion of the population having mixed

37

ethnic background. In contrast to ancestry, identity involves beliefs directly about oneself. Identity is not just a matter of saying, "my great-grandparents came from Poland," but of saying in some form, "*I am* Polish" (although under some circumstances, saying one's ancestors came from Poland may be understood as equivalent to declaring oneself to be Polish).

There are a number of reasons why identity and ancestry may be discrepant (even though they are treated as equivalent in most sociological writing about ethnicity). Although an individual may know his ancestry in considerable detail, he may not perceive its ethnic aspect as relevant to himself, believing in effect, "That was long ago, not today." Or the person with multiple ethnic strands in her ancestry—and, in the contemporary United States, ancestries are increasingly complicated—may not be able to extract from them an ethnic identity. She may think in essence, "I am a mixture," removing herself thereby from the ethnic character of her ancestry. Or someone may have little or uncertain knowledge of his ancestry; more certain knowledge may have been lost because of the distance in time from immigrant ancestors or because a prior generation did not care enough about ethnic backgrounds to pass on knowledge about them. Such a person may not be able to say anything other than that his ancestors have been American for as many generations as he knows about (Lieberson, 1985).

The ability to describe oneself in ethnic terms is obviously at the core of ethnic identity, but it should not be treated as that concept's entirety. An ethnic identification, that is, an ethnic label attached to the self, may have little emotional power associated with it or be a very occasional thing, springing to life only in narrowly defined settings (for example, while carrying out a particular holiday ritual) and otherwise out of mind as far as ordinary life is concerned (McKay and Lewins, 1978). Thus, the concept of identity must be extended to include the *salience* of identity, its felt intensity and the associated likelihood that it will be perceived as relevant in different social settings (Stryker, 1968).

A fundamental erosion of the structural basis of ethnicity is underway among Americans with European ancestries. This transformation renders ethnicity as a social phenomenon more problematic and more dependent on the strength of ethnic identities than has been true at any time since the onset of mass immigration.

Yet the same transformation also threatens ethnic identities, especially because of the growing complexity of ancestries engendered by high rates of intermarriage among whites. The current chapter opens up an empirical survey of the state of ethnic ancestry and identity among the American-born descendants of European immigrants.[1] It begins to address the issues surrounding the viability and significance of ethnic identities in an era when the social structures supportive of ethnicity are breaking down and an increasing number of white Americans—perhaps even a majority— have ancestry from two, three, or even four different European nations.

Measuring Ancestry and Identity

Because of the potential for discrepancy between ethnic ancestry and identity, it is essential that they be measured in different ways. The failure to perceive the necessity for this separation is one of the most critical errors in past research on ethnicity in the United States. Indeed, many of the important bodies of data available to social scientists inextricably confound the two concepts, with significant consequences for the results. The 1980 census, for example, asked in its long-form version about every member of a household, "What is this person's ancestry?"—an apparently straightforward question. But the questionnaire refers the person who feels uncertain how to complete the question to the instruction guide. There, he or she is told to write in "the ancestry group with which [the person in question] *identifies*" (U.S. Bureau of the Census, 1982: 34; emphasis in original). What began as an ancestry question now probes for an ethnic identity. Although most people completing the form probably did not refer to the instruction booklet to answer the question, the confounding of ancestry and identity may be one reason why the proportion of the population claiming ethnically mixed ancestry is lower in the census than in some other surveys, such as the National Opinion Research Center's General Social Survey.[2]

But not only questions may confound ancestry and identity— respondents may interpret questions about ancestry as if they were questions about identity and respond accordingly. Insofar as ethnic background remains a frequently remarked personal trait, many people become used to answering questions about their background and develop stylized ways of reducing complex ancestral backgrounds to readily digested answers (Waters, 1990). As one indicator, Stanley Lieberson and Mary Waters (1986) have noted the frequency of apparent "errors" in census reports about ancestry—for example, truncations or simplifications of ancestry that become apparent when one compares the reports of different members of the same household (in particular, children with their parents).

One reason that ancestry and identity may be so difficult to separate is because we possess so little independent knowledge of identity.[3] It is rare for surveys to ask about ethnic identity (especially if they also inquire about ethnic ancestry); when they do, they frequently go astray because of conceptual limitations. The General Social Survey, for example, asks respondents of mixed ancestry which part of their background they feel closest to. The intent of the question is obviously to place as many respondents as possible in single ethnic categories, accounting for the question's narrow focus. Accordingly, the question collects identity data only for those persons of mixed background who identify with a single group; it fails completely to distinguish between persons who identify with more than one group and those who do not identify at all in ethnic terms. Moreover, it neglects the issue of identity for persons whose ethnic ancestry is undivided, assuming by default that they must identify with their ethnic backgrounds.

The questions about ancestry and identity for our survey[4] of the Capital Region were designed with such considerations in mind. The opening question about ancestry is from the General Social Survey: "From what countries or parts of the world did your ancestors come?" To guard against truncation, this question was followed by, "Was that on both your mother's and father's sides?" In the event that parental ancestries differed, the respondent was then asked separately about each side. A number of respondents gave initially truncated answers to the first question, but then modified them to give greater detail as they answered the questions about their maternal and paternal sides.

The approach to asking about ethnic identity was, of necessity, less straightforward. Our fear was that many people, when asked a question of the sort, "What are you?" or "How do you think of yourself?" would shy away from directly applying ethnic labels to themselves in front of a stranger. Indeed, our fears were borne out in the interviews because many respondents were at pains to assure the interviewers that they are Americans far more than Irish Americans or German-Irish-Italian Americans.[5] Nor did we want to provide respondents with a ready-made identifying label, as we would have done had we constructed an identity question out of the ancestries they named to us. Precisely because so little is known about ethnic identity, we wanted to obtain identities as respondents describe them. For both these reasons, our question was indirect: "When people ask you what your ethnic background is, what—in your own words—do you answer?"

There is a danger in such indirectness—the resulting answers may overstate the existence, or at least the meaningfulness, of ethnic identities. Therefore, the basic identity question was followed immediately by, "Is this the way you in fact think of yourself?" Respondents were next asked, "How important is your ethnic background to you? Would you say it is very important, somewhat important, or not important?" Both questions allow for an evaluation of the subjective meaningfulness and salience of the ethnic self-identifiers respondents provided. There is also the danger of missing some experiences of ethnic identity. Perhaps most, if not all, Americans have occasional moments when they are reminded of their ethnic background and feel themselves to be ethnic—when they are in the presence of certain family members, for example. These occasional experiences may occur to people who are not willing to give an ethnic answer to our basic identity question. Our questionnaire did, in fact, solicit information about such experiences (to be discussed later in this chapter), but I have chosen not to regard them as sufficient to constitute an ethnic identity, at least for the purposes of my analysis. Precisely because ethnicity is undergoing a transformation among whites, ethnic characteristics are increasingly voluntary and are frequently not evident from behavioral and other cues. Hence, the presentation of self as ethnic in a range of social situations is crucial for ethnicity as a social form; it is generally a necessary condition for involvement in ethnically related activities and relationships (at least, for those outside of the family). It is this willingness to acknowledge one's ethnic background that is tested in our first question.[6] But mere acknowledgment is still a passive form of identification. More active engagement requires that ethnicity be felt as personally meaningful and varies with its perceived importance. These are tested in the questions that immediately follow the initial one on identity.

Knowledge of Ancestry

A prerequisite issue for the study of ethnic identity is what people know about their ethnic ancestry. Ethnic identities apart from a diffuse sense of being American cannot continue on a mass scale without widespread knowledge of ancestries. Such knowledge alone does not guarantee that people will identify themselves in ethnic ways, but it is a necessary condition. Stanley Lieberson and Mary Waters (1986) have pointed to drift in the knowledge of ancestry, an increasing gap between knowledge and "true" ethnic origins, as one of the mechanisms leading to a weakening of ethnic social distinctions in the United States.

But precisely construed, knowledge of true ethnic origins is not crucial. As Lieberson and Waters recognize, true origins are in some sense unknowable for most people, if only because they are too far back in time (one knows perhaps that an ancestor came from a particular country but not whether preceding ancestors had moved there from somewhere else).[7] Rather, what matters is the degree of belief about one's ancestry, and the phenomenon of drift becomes important as people lose confidence in their ancestry knowledge. A large number of factors may contribute to drift of this sort: death or separation of a parent, and thus lack of detailed knowledge about one part of the family tree; one generation's lack of interest in family history, with the result that this knowledge is lost to subsequent generations; or, simply, distance in time and the resultant weakening of family memory.

It is important, then, to distinguish between lack of knowledge about ancestry and diminished confidence in the knowledge one has. Indeed, very few whites in the Capital Region are without some knowledge of their ethnic ancestry. In this respect, they are rather different from American whites as a whole, perhaps because they are on average generationally closer to their immigrant ancestors and reside in a more ethnically conscious region. Just 3 percent of the native-born whites in our survey were unable to identify at least some of their ethnic ancestry (virtually all of this group described their ancestry as "American" only). By comparison, the General

Social Survey and the census find that some 10–15 percent of American whites cannot name the countries or parts of the world from which their ancestors came (Alba and Chamlin, 1983; Lieberson, 1985).

Considerably more respondents, however, displayed some uncertainty about their origins. Although we didn't ask respondents directly about their confidence in their knowledge of their ancestry, a significant number exhibited some uncertainty as they answered our questions. For some, the uncertainty was global, clouding the entire picture they possess of their ancestry—such respondents might say something like, "I don't know for sure. German, I guess. My family's name is originally German, I think." For others, the uncertainty extends only to a limited and perhaps minor part of their background. For a third group, the uncertainty emerges in relation to their parents' backgrounds. There are, for example, people who have a sense of their ethnic background based on knowledge about one side of the family only, and know little or nothing about the other side.

These various forms of uncertainty extend the relevance of ethnic drift for native-born whites in the Capital Region. Approximately 4 percent display some global uncertainty about ethnic ancestry (not counted here are those, already mentioned, who do not know their ancestry), and another 2 percent display some selective uncertainty. In addition, 5 percent appear uncertain about the ancestry of a parent. With the group who lack any knowledge included, about 15 percent of native-born whites have some degree of uncertainty about their background. Thus, for every person who is unable to answer a question about ethnic origins, there are three or four who are unsure of their answer. If anything like this same ratio applies to whites in the nation as a whole, then clearly ethnic drift in the form of uncertainty must be widespread.

Lack of knowledge of ethnic origins and uncertain knowledge can be related to several other factors—in particular, generational status, education, and age.[8] Uncertainty grows with increasing distance from the point of immigration, and it is less among persons with high levels of educational attainment. More interesting, young adults appear more likely than adults of other ages to be confident in their knowledge of their ancestry. The reason for this relationship is not immediately clear, but it could reflect somewhat greater interest in ethnic origins among the young, or the fact that many of these young people still live in parental households and thus have greater immediate exposure to their parents' backgrounds. Other factors, such as sex and where a respondent grew up (in a rural versus urban area), do not have statistically significant relationships to ancestry knowledge.

The Increasing Complexity of Ethnic Ancestries

A second major aspect of ethnic ancestry among whites lies in its increasing complexity. Ethnic ancestry is no longer a simple matter: nearly two-thirds of native-born whites in the Capital Region have ethnically mixed ancestry, while one-third report a single ancestry only (the small remainder consists of the persons whose background is unknown; see table 2.1). Moreover, the ethnic mixtures are frequently complicated. Our results in this respect stand in contrast to the ancestry patterns found in the census and other standard sources, because our questions elicited more complete ancestry reports. Of those with ethnically mixed ancestry, slightly more than half have two ethnic components in their backgrounds— nearly half have three or more. Consequently, persons with three or more ethnicities in their backgrounds amount to more than a quarter of all native-born whites in the Capital Region. Among these complicated backgrounds, ancestries with three ethnic components predominate, but persons with four or more ethnic components—we found as many as seven among the members of our sample—accounted for approximately a tenth of all native-born whites.

Both the occurrence of mixed ancestry and its complexity are related to generational status and birth cohort in predictable ways. Because these relationships are well known (see chapter 1), I will only suggest something of their magnitude in the example of generational status. Among members of the fourth and later generations, 80 percent have mixed ethnic ancestry, nearly half of whom have complex ancestries, including three or more ethnic components. In the second generation, only one-third report mixed ancestry, and mixtures with two components are most common. Consequently, persons with complex mixed ancestries account for nearly 40 percent of the later generations, but only 11 percent of the second.[9]

Another issue relates to the presence of ancestry mixtures

Table 2.1   Ethnic ancestry: Complexity and uncertainty among native-born whites in the Capital Region

Number of ethnic components in ancestry	% of native-born whites	Five most common ethnic backgrounds (%)[a]		% uncertain about background[b]
0	3.3	"American"	(93.3)	100.0
1	33.3	Italian	(24.8)	16.3
		Irish	(19.0)	
		German	(11.8)	
		French	(10.5)	
		Polish	(10.5)	
2	35.9	German	(39.4)	6.1
		Irish	(37.0)	
		English	(33.3)	
		French	(27.3)	
		Polish	(10.9)	
		Scots	(10.9)	
3	16.5	English	(69.7)	13.2
		Irish	(51.3)	
		German	(47.4)	
		French	(27.6)	
		Dutch	(25.0)	
4 or more	11.1	English	(80.4)	11.8
		Irish	(60.8)	
		French	(56.9)	
		German	(49.0)	
		Scots	(45.1)	

Note: N for table is 460, the number of native-born whites in the sample.
[a]Percentages are based on numbers in ancestry categories defined in the left column and add to more than 100 percent in categories of mixed ancestry.
[b]Respondents who displayed any degree of uncertainty are counted as uncertain.

among the parents of respondents. One reason that mixed ancestry is thought to play a critical role in ethnic change is that persons from mixed backgrounds are presumably less likely to be fully exposed in childhood to ethnic cultures, sentiments, and social life (for mother tongues, this is clearly established by Stevens [1985]). Persons of mixed ancestry may have some exposure to ethnic influences, but this would seem more likely when one or both parents are themselves from unmixed backgrounds, and less likely when both have mixed ancestry.

Overall, the great majority of persons coming from mixed backgrounds have unmixed ancestry on at least one side. Nearly half say that their ancestry is unmixed on both sides, and another third have unmixed ancestry on one side. Only about 20 percent come from mixed backgrounds on both sides. But these proportions seem likely to change in conjunction with the increasing complexity of ancestries. Such change is implied by the concentration of ethnic mixtures among whites born after 1940, the parents of children now growing up in the Capital Region. Approximately three-quarters of these adults have ethnically mixed ancestry. If one assumes, therefore, as a rough approximation that native-born whites choose marital partners without much regard for ethnic background (see Alba and Golden, 1986) and that there are not sizable fertility variations among different marriage types, then half or more of the children in white families today would have mixed ethnic ancestry on both sides.

People who have mixed ancestry on both sides may still have some ancestry common to these sides, and in some cases this may counteract the diluting effect of being raised by ethnically mixed parents. In the Capital Region's mixed ancestry population, the proportion with an ethnic ingredient common to both sides is still just a quarter, but it seems certain to rise as ancestries become increasingly complex, raising the probability that there is some match between parental backgrounds. Nevertheless, it is questionable whether this common ancestry, perhaps only one ethnic ingredient in a complex stew, is enough to offset the effect of mixed ancestry itself. One reason is that the ethnic ingredient most frequently shared is one (or more) of the three largest old-stock ancestries— English, German, and Irish. This is understandable on purely numerical grounds. Not only are the ancestry groups large, but they are frequent ingredients in ancestry mixtures, as table 2.1 indicates. Close to 90 percent of ancestry mixtures in the Capital Region include one or more of these ancestries. But with the partial exception of the Irish, these ancestries rank among the most assimilated, thus limiting the potential for shared ancestry to counteract ethnic dilution.

The division of particular ethnic backgrounds between single and mixed ancestry is another important aspect of ancestry mixture. Largely because of generational concentrations, some ancestries are found chiefly in mixtures, while others are represented frequently by persons of undivided ethnic heritage. To the extent that ethnic characteristics are most likely to be found among persons of unmixed background, this division helps to shape the typical ethnic accents found in a region. It is quite visible in the ancestry patterns in table 2.1.

At one extreme are the English and Dutch, groups of long residence in the Capital Region: 95 percent of persons with these ancestries come from mixed backgrounds, and frequently from very intermixed ones. Sixty percent of persons of English ancestry have two or more other ancestries as well, as do three-quarters of those of Dutch heritage. Other ancestries that are found in great part only in ethnic mixtures include: Scots (90 percent); German (88 percent); French (86 percent); Irish (82 percent); and the small group with American Indian ancestry, virtually all of whom claim other ancestry as well.[10] At the other extreme are the groups of southern and eastern European origin, which contain relatively high proportions of persons of unmixed ancestry. The most extreme case is that of the Italians, 54 percent of whose native-born members are of ethnically unmixed ancestry; among the Poles, 36 percent are. Even in these groups, of course, the proportions with mixed ancestry are substantial, and they are increasing as a result of intermarriage. Among persons of Italian ancestry born after 1940, for example, two-thirds come from ethnically mixed backgrounds. Equally sharp changes by cohort are found among the Poles.

Not only are there clear patterns of division between single and mixed ancestry, but there are also frequently occurring combinations that occur in ancestry mixtures. In general, these configurations are quite understandable in terms of the sizes of groups, the recency of their immigration, and to a lesser extent their religious affiliations.[11] Predominant among these ethnic configurations are those involving the big three ancestries. Most persons of English background are descended from immigrants of the seventeenth and eighteenth centuries, while the high-water marks of Irish and German immigrations occurred in the mid-nineteenth century. As a consequence, nearly half of the native-born whites of mixed ancestry in the Albany region have at least two of these three major ancestry groups in their heritage. The most common combination is English-Irish. It is included in nearly a quarter of all ancestry mixtures, usually not alone but in combination with other ethnic ingredients, most frequently with French, German, or Scots. The pairing English-German is almost as common, appearing in 20 percent of ancestry mixtures. Again, it is typically combined with some other ancestry, most often with Irish or French.

But pointing to the frequent occurrence of combinations involving the three major ancestry groups risks understating the diversity and complexity of ethnic mixture. More than half of ancestry mixtures *do not* involve a combination of these groups, although most of these other mixtures combine one of these ancestries with smaller ancestry groups. In addition, most of the mixtures that involve combinations of the three largest groups also include other ancestries. The combination English-French-Irish, for example, alone or mixed with other ancestries, accounts for about 7 percent of all ancestry mixtures; the combination English-Irish-Scots is equally common.

Beyond the three largest ancestry groups, one finds that most ancestry mixtures in the Capital Region draw primarily on a limited number of "old-stock" groups, which have their origins in northern and western Europe and have resided in the United States for a century or more. In addition to the three major ancestries, these ethnic origins include American Indian,[12] Dutch, French (or French Canadian), and Scots. Virtually all ancestry mixtures in the region (95 percent) include one or more of these origins, and almost two-thirds are made up exclusively from them.

Groups from southern and eastern Europe, such as the Italians and Poles, are also a noticeable presence in the mixed-ancestry population but are not yet as widely dispersed as old-stock origins. Two reasons account for this difference: First, the southern and eastern European groups are smaller in size than the most important old-stock ones; second, they are still relatively more concentrated among persons of undivided ethnic ancestry, largely because of their more recent arrival. Nevertheless, certain ancestry constellations figure prominently among persons whose mixed ancestry includes some southern or eastern European components, and these constellations frequently include old-stock ancestry as well as that of newer origin. The southern and eastern European groups are clearly mixing with the more established groups. In the Capital Region, Italian ancestry is most frequently mixed with Dutch, English, French, and Irish ancestry; the last two, of course, are to be expected on the basis of common Catholicism, but the first two exhibit the joining of a relatively new ancestry with those at the heart of the old-stock core. Polish ancestry most frequently appears in combination with German, a linking perhaps unsurprising given the shared roots of these two groups in central Europe. But also noteworthy is the appearance of Polish ancestry in combination with Irish and French. More than Italian ancestry, though, Polish ancestry is combined with other central and eastern European ancestries, such as Austrian, Russian, and Ukrainian.

In the Capital Region as in the nation, the ancestral origins of native-born whites are changing rapidly. An increasing percentage of this population belongs to the third, fourth, and even later generations, and intermarriage is spreading across ethnic boundaries. Not only do a majority of whites come from mixed ancestral backgrounds, but their ancestries are increasingly complex, often including three or more ethnic components, and more frequently inherited from parents who are themselves of mixed background. The growth of mixed ancestry prompts the question: What does ethnicity mean to whites in the United States?

Ethnic Identities: Some Basics

The difference between self-image (identity) and knowledge of an objective family past (ancestry) is critical to understanding contemporary ethnicity in the United States. Knowing where one's ancestors originated is one matter; regarding oneself as ethnic may be quite another. The two are surely connected: it is difficult to have an ethnic identity other than the purely American one if one lacks knowledge of one's ancestry, but such knowledge is no guarantee that ethnicity is a meaningful self-identification.

Our approach to asking about ethnic identity was indirect—it cast the net widely on the assumption that ethnic identity may be a subtle matter for many whites. The same approach was used in sifting the answers to the identity question. For many respondents the answer was straightforward—"I'm Irish" or "half German and half French" illustrate such replies. But for others answers contained elements of uncertainty, if not of contradiction—"I guess I would say French Canadian" or "I usually say Irish but actually I'm

just American" suggest the hesitancy of some respondents. But in
the spirit of casting the net widely, these responses, too, were treated as defining ethnic identities.[13]

Following this approach, I find that about two-thirds of native-
born whites describe their ethnic backgrounds in ways consistent
with an ethnic identity (see table 2.2). The vast majority of these
ethnic identifiers describe their ethnic background with nationality
labels. (This characterization includes a small number who describe themselves as WASPS, and other occasional respondents who
combine nationality with religious labels.) Also counted among
them is a small number of respondents who describe themselves as
"Jews." This is consistent with standard views of ethnicity, since in
contrast with other major religious groups in the United States
Jews can view themselves as a "people" and thus satisfy ethnicity's
sine qua non. Other religious labels by themselves were not treated
as ethnic identities.

Of those who did not identify themselves in ethnic ways, persons who describe themselves simply as "American" form the
largest group (approximately 20 percent of all native-born whites).
The remainder are heterogeneous. About 2 percent view themselves
as very mixed in background ("mutt" was a not uncommon self-
description from this group); just under 2 percent describe themselves racially, as "whites." Four percent give some sort of religious
identification (other than Jewish); this small group is about evenly
divided between Catholics and Protestants. Finally, about 6 percent
say they cannot answer a question about ethnic identity.

A substantial minority, about a quarter, of those who identify
themselves ethnically qualify their self-description in some significant way. About 10 percent qualify it as they state it, in ways described above, either by appearing unsure of how to identify themselves or distancing themselves from their ethnic response. In
addition, about 20 percent disavowed their ethnic self-identification
when asked whether this was in fact the way they thought of themselves. (There is some overlap between the two groups. Together they
add up to less than 30 percent.) Most of these disavowers explained
that ethnicity is not important to them, generally indicating that
they really think of themselves as Americans only.

It would no doubt be incorrect to regard a qualification or
disavowal as negating altogether an ethnic self-description. Never-

theless, many respondents appeared hesitant to express too strong an ethnic identity, lest it be seen as contradicting their American identity. Such hesitancy may be in part a function of the interview setting, of what people are willing to say to a stranger. But this explanation still leaves it as a significant limitation, since many social situations where ethnicity is potentially relevant would require expression of an identity to strangers. Thus, a substantial minority of persons who are initially willing to define themselves in terms of an ethnic identity are not willing to make a strong commitment to one, at least to strangers.

Taking qualifications and disavowals into account divides the native-born whites of the Capital Region into two roughly equal groups with respect to ethnic identity. The members of one group identify themselves in ethnic terms and think of themselves in this way (at least on some occasions); the members of the other group either do not state an ethnic identification or qualify (or disavow) a stated one.

Let us accept for the moment the ethnic identities of native-born whites at face value, for they have a number of interesting properties. To begin with, the probability of identifying in ethnic terms is influenced by a number of major demographic and socioeconomic factors, which can in turn be related to what I described in chapter 1 as the transformation of ethnicity. These influences emerge from a logistic regression analysis (see table 2.3).[14] Since the factors involved will be used repeatedly in analyses throughout the book, the discussion that follows can also serve as an introduction to them.

In the main, the demographic and socioeconomic forces associated with the transformation of ethnicity also correspond with a diminished probability of identifying ethnically. Type of ancestry (single or mixed) is a case in point: Persons of single ancestry are more likely to identify ethnically than those of mixed ancestry. Net of other factors, the difference associated with ancestry type is about 15 percentage points. But aside from the distinction between single and mixed ancestry, the complications of ancestry appear to have little impact on the probability of identifying. That is, no difference exists between persons whose mixed ancestry consists of just two elements and those with three or four—it is the fact of having mixed ancestry in the first place that is relevant.

Table 2.2 Ethnic identities of native-born whites

Type of ancestry	Type of identity	% of native-born whites	Five most common ethnic backgrounds (%)	Five most common ethnic identities %	% qualifying or disavowing identity
unmixed	unmixed	26.3	Italian (28.1) Irish (19.0) Polish (12.4) French (9.9) German (9.9)	same as backgrounds	19.0
mixed	unmixed	19.1	English (53.4) German (46.6) Irish (42.0) French (22.7) Scots (19.3)	Irish (31.8) German (20.5) English, WASP (14.8) Jewish (10.2) French (5.7) Italian (5.7)	31.8
mixed	mixed	22.0	Irish (48.5) English (45.5)	Irish (45.5) English (38.6)	33.7

		%					
unmixed	none	7.0	German (42.6) French (33.7) Scots (20.8)	German (18.8) Irish (18.8) French (12.5) Italian (12.5) Scots (12.5)	German (38.6) French (31.7) Scots (18.8)	American (62.5) "Don't know" (12.5) Catholic (12.5) Protestant (6.3) Several others (1 case each)	—
mixed	none	22.4	English (54.4) Irish (43.7) German (40.8) French (39.8) Dutch (19.4)			American (54.4) "Don't know" (20.4) "Mixed" (9.7) White (5.8) Protestant (5.8)	—
unknown	none	3.3	American (93.3) "Don't know" (6.7)			American (80.0) "Don't know" (13.3) Catholic (6.7)	—

Table 2.3   Logit analysis of ethnic self-identification

	Change to log odds of identifying	Statistical significance	% diff. at sample mean[a]
Number of ethnic components in ancestry:		p < .05	
one	+.585		+11.4
two	−.292		−6.7
three	−.088		−2.0
four or more	−.205		−4.7
Generational status:		p < .10	
second	+.546		+10.7
third	−.216		−4.9
fourth or later	−.416		−9.7
unknown	+.086		+1.9
Confidence about ancestry knowledge:		p < .10	
confident	+.340		+7.0
uncertain	−.340		−7.9
Education[b]	+.251	p < .05	+5.3
Sex:		N.S.	
male			
female			
Age:		N.S.	
under 30			
30–44			
45–59			
60 and older			
Place grew up:		p < .05	
rural	−.290		−6.7
nonrural	+.290		+6.0
Proximity to relatives:		p < .10	
yes	+.266		+5.6
no	−.266		−6.1
A likelihood-ratio $\chi^{2,c}$	41.21 (14 d.f.)	p < .001	

Note: Respondents whose ancestry is unknown are not included in the analysis.

[a]The percentage-difference column indicates the approximate order of magnitude of the differences associated with an independent variable. These percentage differences are calculated by assuming that each logit coefficient represents a change from the mean ethnic identity for the sample (% = 67.4, logit = .726). For the mechanics of such a calculation, see Alba (1987).

[b]Education is a scale coded in five categories: 1 = elementary school; 2 = some high school; 3 = high school diploma; 4 = some college; 5 = college graduate.

[c]The χ^2 statistic here provides a joint test of statistical significance for all coefficients except the intercept (see footnote 14).

Generational status is a second major influence on the probability of identifying ethnically.[15] This probability is greater among
those who are closer to the immigrant experience. Ethnic identities
are most common among the second generation, the children of
immigrants, and least so among the fourth and later generations;
the third generation, composed of the grandchildren of immigrants,
stands in between.[16] With other variables controlled, including ancestry type, the difference between the second and fourth generations is about 20 percentage points. Age (or birth cohort), another
important correlate of the transformation, however, has no significant relationship to ethnic identity in the logistic equation.

The process of ethnic drift described by Stanley Lieberson and
Mary Waters (1986), which affects knowledge of ancestry, is also
consequential for ethnic identities. Ethnic drift is measured in the
equation by the degree of confidence in knowledge of ancestry, and
the analysis demonstrates that uncertainty in this knowledge reduces the probability of identifying by approximately 15 percentage points.

Not all the influences suggest the diminishing of ethnic identity
over time. Most important in this respect is education. Although
rising educational attainment among some white ethnic groups is
part of the transformation of ethnicity, education has been included
in the equation principally as a measure of socioeconomic standing.[17] Ethnicity is frequently seen as an ingredient of a working-
class style, leading to the expectation that ethnic identities would
be more common among those with a high school education or less.
The notion that education should have a negative impact on ethnic
identity is also bolstered by the common view of education as an
agent of assimilation. But, on both counts, the analysis disappoints:
the higher the level of education, the more likely is the expression of
an ethnic identity. The effect is not as large as some others—for
example, the expected difference between high school and college
graduates, a big step in educational terms, is about 10 percentage
points. Nevertheless, this counters widely accepted expectations
and the general direction of assimilatory changes among whites.

Two other notable influences represent social contexts that can
enhance or constrain ethnicity. Given the connection between ethnicity and family origins, family ties can be presumed to strengthen
ethnic identities. This hypothesis is represented in the equation by

proximity to relatives[18] and is supported by the fact that persons who live near their relatives are more likely to identify ethnically than are those who do not. Ethnicity thus may be a function in part of closeness to the family. A final influence is where one grew up, reflecting childhood exposure to ethnic diversity. Rural areas, more ethnically homogeneous, are less likely to contain salient ethnic differences, and persons who grew up in them are less likely to identify ethnically.

Qualifications and disavowals of ethnic identities strengthen this general picture (see table 2.4).[19] Analysis of these distancing methods underscores the identity-weakening impacts of ancestry complexity and uncertainty; but also repeated is the positive influence of closeness to family. In this case, differences even emerge among persons with mixed ancestry. In general, the more complex the ancestry, the greater the probability of distancing oneself from a stated identity: for example, persons with four or more ethnic components in their backgrounds are about 20 percent more likely to distance themselves than are those whose mixed ancestry includes just two ethnic components. Uncertainty about background, which is associated with the growing complexity of ancestry, also plays a role: Persons unsure of their ethnic ancestry are 20 percentage points more likely to distance themselves from an ethnic identity than are those confident in their knowledge.

But proximity to relatives strengthens the unqualified sense of an ethnic identity. The comparative sturdiness of ethnic identity among those who live near other relatives implies again a close linkage between ethnicity and family and suggests that embeddedness in a family network breathes life into what might otherwise become an abstract commitment to an ethnic label.

In sum, ethnic identities, at least in the minimal sense of a willingness to apply ethnic labels to oneself in front of a stranger, are widespread among native-born whites, despite the transformation of ethnicity evidenced by more objective measures of ethnic difference. Nevertheless, this transformation is having its effects: The influences of mixed ancestry, diminished confidence in ancestry knowledge, and membership in the fourth and later generations suggest that ethnic identities may become less important among American whites in the future. These characteristics are increasing inexorably in the white population, and this shift should decrease

Table 2.4   Logit analysis of qualification and disavowal of identity

	Change to log odds of qualifying or disavowing	Statistical significance	% diff. at sample mean[a]
Number of ethnic components in ancestry:		$p < .05$	
one	−.578		−9.9
two	−.231		−4.4
three	+.113		+2.3
four or more	+.696		+15.7
Generational status:		N.S.	
second			
third			
fourth or later			
unknown			
Confidence about ancestry knowledge:		$p < .05$	
confident	−.506		−8.9
uncertain	+.506		+11.1
Education		N.S.	
Sex:		N.S.	
male			
female			
Age:		N.S.	
under 30			
30–44			
45–59			
60 and older			
Place grew up:		N.S.	
rural			
nonrural			
Proximity to relatives:		$p < .05$	
yes	−.391		−7.1
no	+.391		+8.4
A likelihood-ratio χ^2	34.13 (14 d.f.)	$p < .01$	

Note: Only respondents who identify in ethnic terms (N = 302, after deletions due to missing data) are included in the analysis.

[a]The percentage differences are calculated in the manner described in the notes for table 2.3. The percentage assumed as a reference point is 27.4%, the overall percentage who disavow or qualify a stated ethnic identity.

the probability that whites identify in terms of European origins. Moreover, increasing ancestry complexity and uncertainty about ancestry are related to increased distance from ethnic identity, and hence to a reduction in its salience.

But the effects are not all one way. Education, in particular, increases the probability of identifying ethnically, despite its reflection of the transformation and the reasons grounded in assimilation theory to expect the opposite effect. Far from being part of a working-class style, ethnic identity appears to be associated with the cosmopolitanism that goes along with higher levels of education.[20] Given the consistently negative effects of advanced generation and mixed ancestry on identity, it seems unlikely that the positive effect of education reflects a "return" to ethnicity of the kind anticipated by some interpreters (see chapter 1). Rather, ethnicity may be part of the "cultural capital" imparted by advanced education—the repertoire of cultural codes that highly educated persons acquire in order to be able to establish prompt and effective communication in diversified social worlds not strongly bounded by kinship and locality (DiMaggio and Mohr, 1985). As Paul DiMaggio (1987) points out for artistic taste, cultural codes play an increasingly basic role in establishing the social identities of the members of highly mobile social strata, who, because of the physical and social distances they cross, cannot always rely on kinship or physical property to establish who they are. (DiMaggio notes, for instance, the use of such codes in preliminary conversational signaling to establish whether the basis for a trustful relationship exists.) If the increasing role of cultural capital enhances the worth of interest in the arts, it may also do so for ethnicity, which provides yet another system of cultural symbols and references. This line of speculation hardly pins down the precise value of ethnic identity for the highly educated, but it does suggest why ethnic identities may be maintained even in the face of the decline in objective ethnic differentiation. Accordingly, the relationship between education and ethnicity bears watching.

The Ethnic Composition of Identities

The influences on ethnic identity are important not only for what they presage about changes in its extent, but also for how they shape the composition of the pool of identities. This pool, in turn, determines the recognizable social contours of ethnicity; it mirrors the ways people are likely to identify themselves in ordinary social interaction (see table 2.2).

In contrast to the situation among ethnic ancestries, single ethnic identities are considerably more frequent than mixed ones. Persons who identify themselves in terms of a single group outnumber those who identify themselves in a mixed fashion by a margin of two to one. This happens because persons of single ancestry are disproportionately represented among those who identify ethnically and because a fair number of people from mixed backgrounds identify themselves in terms of a single group. Indeed, people with mixed ancestry are about as likely to identify with a single group as with multiple ones. Consequently, in ordinary social interaction, the strength of identifications with single groups emerges, not the frequency of mixed and complex ancestries. Equally striking, the proportions of different ethnicities in the pool of identities differ considerably from the overall ethnic profile of ancestries. In particular, the major old-stock ethnicities are less prominent among ethnic identities than they are among ancestries. The most common ancestries in the Capital Region, Irish, English, and German, are each claimed by about a third of native-born whites. Irish occurs almost as frequently among ethnic identities as it does among ancestries (31 percent versus 35 percent), but English and German are less common—each appears only in about 20 percent of identities. Also reduced among identities is French or French Canadian, the fourth largest ancestry group in the region's population.

By contrast, the ethnicities from southern and eastern Europe are enhanced in *relative* prominence among identities. Notably, Italian ancestry is claimed by about 16 percent of persons who identify ethnically, the same as its proportion as an ancestry. But as an identity, it is as important as French and not far behind English and German, even though as an ancestry it trails all of these by considerable margins. A similar phenomenon on a smaller scale occurs with Polish. Both phenomena are further enhanced, incidentally, when qualifications and disavowals are taken into account, for these are more likely to occur for identities based on old-stock ancestries.

The reduction in the prominence of old-stock ethnic identities results in part from demographic influences. Contributing to this pattern, for instance, are the lower probabilities of ethnic identification among persons who have mixed ancestry or belong to the fourth and later generations: the old-stock ancestries are heavily represented in these groups. There may also be some influence here of what can be called the "supply side" of ethnicity[21]—collective ethnic phenomena, such as ethnic neighborhoods, organizations, and cultural trappings (restaurants and festivals, for instance). These are in general more frequent among the newer European groups and thus may lend their ethnicities a greater appearance of vitality, making them more attractive and meaningful as loci of identification.

Further insight can be gained by examining how identity varies by the ethnic specifics of ancestry. Some ethnic ancestries appear in identities only in combination with others or are frequently passed over in favor of others, while other ancestries are almost always present, and frequently alone, when persons possessing them identify in ethnic terms. Dutch and Scots ancestries illustrate one extreme. Of persons with Dutch ancestry who identify ethnically, only 6 percent identify themselves as "Dutch only" and approximately 40 percent drop Dutch identification altogether; the story is virtually identical among those with Scots ancestry. The picture among persons with English ancestry who identify ethnically is slightly different, perhaps because of the association of English background with prototypical American origins. Almost 20 percent of persons of English background who identify ethnically describe themselves solely as "English" (this includes persons who label themselves as "wasps"), although 40 percent drop their English identification altogether.

At the other extreme are the Irish, Poles, and Italians. Among persons of Irish or Polish ancestries who identify ethnically, about half describe themselves solely as members of these groups; among the Italians, the figure reaches almost 75 percent. And among the Irish and Italians, only 10 percent neglect these ancestries if they state an identity. Such loyalty diminishes somewhat among the Poles, but two-thirds of those who identify themselves ethnically include "Polish" as part of their identity.

These patterns are not only tied up with the frequency of ethnic mixtures, but also with the manner in which persons with mixed ancestry identify. One influence on self-identification, which must be acknowledged even though it does not contribute to an explanation of these differential ethnic patterns, is paternal ancestry. Persons of mixed ancestry tend to identify along the lines of their fathers' backgrounds. Among those who chose to identify with a single group, identities based on paternal ancestry were preferred by approximately two to one. This ratio is the same for men and women, suggesting that identification is not so much based on closeness to a particular parent as on self-image in the world outside the family, where surnames play an important role (see Waters, 1990).

Loyalties to different ethnic origins also color the identities of persons with mixed ancestry. Persons of mixed Irish ancestry, for example, are more likely than others of mixed background to identify ethnically, and when they do, their Irish ethnicity plays a prominent role. This is shown rather clearly by those who choose a single ethnic identity from the multiple possibilities in their ancestries, for those identifying themselves as Irish only outnumber those choosing some other part of their background by a margin of three to one. Among those of mixed English ancestry, by comparison, the ratio is reversed.

These ethnic variations shed some light on the possibility of ethnic mobility operating through the identification process. Among whites in the contemporary United States, identification with an ethnic group is a choice, not something externally imposed. For this reason, one might expect to see patterns of identification that favor old-stock, more prestigious origins (see Lieberson, 1985), but this is not the case, with perhaps the exception of the Irish. Dutch and English origins, the most prestigious (or, at least, the oldest) in the ethnic spectrum of the Capital Region, are frequently passed over and rarely singled out in stating identities. Rather, the process of identification appears to favor groups whose ethnicities seem most conspicuous. This characterization applies not only to the strength of Italian and Polish identities but also to that of the Irish, the one old-stock group that retains a hold on persons with ancestry from it. Irish ethnicity remains prominent, particularly in the region's politics and cultural life. The patterns of ethnic choice among persons of mixed ancestry thus suggest that ethnic collective phenomena in the form of neighborhoods and institutions may be central, functioning like ethnic beacons and even drawing the attention of assimilated group members.

The Ethnic Inclinations of Nonidentifiers

People who are unwilling to identify in ethnic terms may still at times feel close to one or more parts of their backgrounds. These ethnic inclinations can vary in strength. For some people, they may be an established preference, perhaps reflecting the influence of a parent or grandparent during childhood. For others, they may be almost whimsical predilections, a sense that it is nicer to be an X, rather than a Y. In either event, they could be a latent form of identity, which could spring to life under the proper set of circumstances.

The survey gathered considerable data on persons whose identities and ancestries are not in agreement, including their feelings about their background and the reasons why their self-identifications differ from their ancestries. We asked these respondents whether they ever felt close to any part of their background and under what circumstances, and if their ancestry is mixed, whether they would be willing to choose between the parts of their background, what choice they would make, and why.

The data suggest that most nonidentifiers do incline toward some part of their ethnic background, but that these inclinations are typically mild or even inconsistent. The issue of inconsistency arises for the majority of nonidentifiers, who are of mixed ancestry and who, in answering our questions, could "vote" for some part of their background in two ways: by feeling close to it and by expressing a preference for it. Nearly half of nonidentifiers of mixed background were inconsistent, either feeling close to an ethnicity they do not prefer or preferring one they do not feel close to; another third displayed no apparent inclinations. Just 20 percent gave consistent replies.

Among persons of either single or mixed ancestry, the reasons for ethnic inclinations seem diverse, but two broad themes stand out. Some respondents explained their propensity in terms of family influences and particularly those of a specific family member, usually a parent or grandparent, although aunts and uncles were also mentioned. Others saw it in terms of properties of the group they favored, typically expressing admiration or liking for some presumed traits. At times, the traits seemed stereotypical, suggesting that the inclinations have little to do with actual involvement in ethnic activities or relationships and reflect instead some distance from ethnicity. Examples are liking the French part of one's background because of admiration for French wines and fashions, or the Irish part because the Irish are "fun-loving."

Undercutting the inclinations are the reasons respondents give for their failure to identify with their backgrounds. These are fairly consistent, and three are prominent: the respondents identify only with the United States; they do not think about their ethnic backgrounds; or their ethnic origins are too far back in time. About two-thirds mentioned one or more of these reasons. (Less frequently given reasons usually ran along similar lines—for example, that backgrounds are very mixed or that the respondents do not know what "ethnic background" means.) In sum, these explanations uphold the meaningfulness of the distinction between those who are willing to describe themselves ethnically in answering our basic question about ethnic identity and those who are not. Although the vast majority of native-born whites, regardless of the number of generations their families have been in the United States and the degree of complexity in their ancestries, retain some sense of their ethnic backgrounds, those who do not identify ethnically by our criterion appear to have a meaningful reason for their refusal, one that would curtail expression of ethnic identity in a variety of social settings.

The Perception of Ethnicity's Importance

That people can identify themselves to others in ethnic terms and perhaps even think of themselves in this way does not demonstrate that ethnicity is salient or important to them. From the comments of some of our respondents, it seems clear that their self-identifications are descriptions they have fashioned to answer still-common questions about ethnic background, not identities that have everyday meaning in their lives. For others, ethnicity seems clearly anchored in recurrent experiences. To investigate the importance attached to ethnic backgrounds, we asked our respondents directly about this, offering them the categories "very," "somewhat," or "not" important (see table 2.5). The assessments must be seen in the context of the respondents' self-identifications, since these are implicit in the question.

Table 2.5 The perceived importance of ethnic backgrounds

		"very important"			"somewhat important"			"not important"		
Type of ancestry	Type of identity	% of native-born whites	three most common: ethnic backgrounds	identities	% of native-born whites	three most common: ethnic backgrounds	identities	% of native-born whites	three most common: ethnic backgrounds	identities
unmixed	unmixed	9.3	Italian Irish Polish	same	11.2	Italian Irish French[a] German[a]	same	7.2	French Polish[a] English[a]	same
mixed	unmixed	3.5	English Irish German	Irish[b]	10.0	English Irish German	Irish Jewish German	7.0	German English French[a] Irish[a]	German Irish English
mixed	mixed	4.0	Irish French[a] German[a]	Irish French German	9.8	English German Irish	English German[a] Irish[a]	9.5	Irish English German	Irish German English
single	none	2.8	Italian[b]	American Catholic	1.9	Scots[b]	American[b]	1.6	Irish[b]	American[b]
mixed	none	4.7	German English[a] French[a]	American[b]	7.0	English Irish French	American Protestant[a] White[a]	7.7	English German Irish	American "Mixed"[a] "Don't know"[a]
unknown	none	1.2	—	American[b]	0.7	—	American	1.2	—	American[b]

[a] Indicates a tie in rank.
[b] Indicates the presence in a cell of additional small ethnic categories (containing two or fewer cases each).

64

Overall, whites tend to attribute a middling importance to ethnic background, avoiding the extremes of elevating it to a central place or denying it any value. But it is not obvious at first sight just how important this middle ground is. The pattern is most apparent among the approximately two-thirds who identify ethnically, for their assessment has an unambiguous ethnic referent. Only a quarter of this group feel that their ethnic background is very important to them; but just a third ascribe no importance to it at all. The largest part of the group, but still not a majority (about 40 percent), evaluate ethnicity as somewhat important.

Some whites who do not identify ethnically still attribute importance to ethnic background. Estimating the size of this group is difficult because many nonidentifiers described their ethnic background as "American" and also evaluated it on this basis as very important. But an estimate can be made by sifting the explanations respondents gave us for their evaluations, looking for indications that respondents are evaluating only the importance of their ethnic backgrounds. On this basis, it appears that 5 to 10 percent of nonidentifiers feel that their ethnic background is very important, despite the fact that they do not readily identify themselves in these terms. About 25 percent feel that ethnic background is somewhat important. Still, two-thirds either denied the importance of ethnic background or attributed importance to something other than ethnicity.

The tendency to describe ethnicity as "somewhat" important prompts closer scrutiny of respondents' explanations. Underscoring the significance of these explanations is the generally clear-cut nature of those given by respondents with more extreme evaluations—positive or negative—of ethnicity's importance. Among those who felt that ethnicity was of great personal importance, three explanations stood out. One explanation stressed that ethnicity is an intrinsic part of the self, influencing, for instance, values and beliefs (one typical comment was that ethnicity "shaped a lot of my viewpoints and who I am today"). Closely related was an explanation emphasizing the way in which respondents were brought up. Finally, there was an explanation that reiterated ethnicity's importance, declaring pride in ethnic background. While this hardly explicates ethnicity's meaning, it does indicate the depth of feeling certain respondents possess.

Very different explanations were given by respondents who evaluate ethnicity as unimportant. They frequently explained that they feel themselves to be simply Americans; many also voiced patriotic themes, saying for example that "America is the land of opportunity" and "this is the best country." Such explanations may leave room for ethnic feelings that are not expressed in the interview, perhaps because they are overshadowed by the respondents' desire to present themselves as fully American. Indeed, there were a few second-generation respondents who appeared to fit well the first part of Hansen's dictum, "What the son wishes to forget, the grandson wishes to remember." But this aspect should not be exaggerated. Many who gave this explanation came from old-stock backgrounds and had roots deep in American history.

The explanations of many other respondents in this category leave no doubt that ethnic background carries little weight in their lives. The most frequently given ran along the lines that "ethnic background makes no difference in my daily life"; closely related was a second explanation, "I almost never think about it." (Others said that they lacked knowledge about their ethnic roots, or that these were just too far back in time to care about.) A further interesting twist was a normative explanation: People should not be viewed in terms of ethnic background. Some put this in more or less factual terms: "I'm not prejudiced. I don't take notice of people's ethnic backgrounds." Others were more explicitly normative: "We should all be equal." But no matter which way they put it, some respondents appeared to be concerned that an emphasis on ethnic background could give rise to prejudice.

In comparison to both of these extremes, the explanations of those attributing a middling importance to ethnicity were more mixed. This reveals the heterogeneous nature of this middle category, which was used by those for whom ethnicity holds some genuine importance as well as by those for whom it is of marginal significance. Some respondents gave explanations similar to the most positive views of ethnicity's importance, although these reasons do not come up as frequently. But others gave reasons appearing to downplay ethnicity's significance (for example, "I don't really think much about ethnic background"), although—once again—such reasons are by no means as frequent in this group as among those for whom ethnicity is unimportant.

Two distinctive notes were sounded by many in the middle category. One grounds ethnicity's importance in a sense of family—indeed, for many of these respondents, ethnicity seems to be confused with family. A frequent explanation suggesting this view was that "it's nice to know where you came from." Many respondents apparently meant that it is good to know about your ancestral roots—some even talked about their interest in family genealogy. This explanation was cited by approximately a quarter of those who hold ethnicity to be somewhat important, making it the most popular for this group. It implies that, for some, ethnicity as a contemporary influence is not as important as the sense of family history.

The second note is one of self-consciousness about ethnicity, a sense that ethnicity needs to be cultivated because of its larger meaning in society or because it can easily slip away. This sense emerged most clearly in an explanation, given by 10 percent of the middle category, that it is important to have a heritage or roots to hold on to. Those perceiving this need generally connected it with a sense that ethnic backgrounds still play a role in American society, and therefore it can be valuable to have one: it helps to place a person relative to others, forming a kind of social shorthand. (As one respondent astutely remarked, "Rarely do you hear Americans say [just], 'I am an American.'" He went on to conclude, "it's important that I have an identity.") Still, by comparison with the explanations given by the strongly identifying, self-consciousness here implies a sense that ethnicity is weakening, that it can no longer be taken for granted.

An analysis of influences on the perception of ethnicity's importance suggests that this self-consciousness may be well founded: ethnicity appears to be declining in salience along with the broad changes occurring in the white population. Of the factors considered earlier, type of ancestry and generational status stand alone here. Both are associated with a fall-off in ethnicity's importance; and in this case, there is no countervailing influence of education. (Since the two factors emerge from a regression analysis as virtually the only statistically significant influences, they can be discussed in terms of a percentaged table [table 2.6],[22] without fear that confounding factors are present. The analysis is restricted to respondents who identify ethnically, since only for them is the ethnic reference being evaluated unambiguous.)

Table 2.6   Subjective importance of ethnic background
by ancestry type and generation

	Ancestry type					
	Single			Mixed		
	background is			background is		
	very important	somewhat important	not important	very important	somewhat important	not important
Generation:						
second	39.1%	39.1%	21.7%	25.0%	41.7%	33.3%
third	34.0	42.6	23.4	20.5	50.0	29.5
fourth	22.2	38.9	38.9	9.1	45.5	45.5
unknown	25.0	37.5	37.5	23.5	17.6	58.8
Total	33.6	40.3	26.1	17.0	45.2	37.8

Significance levels: Ancestry type X import, $p < .05$
                                        Generation X import, $p < .01$

Note: Only respondents who identify ethnically are included in the analysis.

Indicative of future decline in the salience of ethnicity is the lower importance attached to ethnic background by persons with mixed ancestry, since this group represents an increasing proportion of whites. Summarized across generational groups, just 17 percent of persons of mixed ancestry feel their ethnic backgrounds to be very important; the comparable figure among persons of undivided ancestry is twice as large. The ethnically mixed are also more likely to rate ethnic background as having no importance.

The evaluations of persons of mixed ancestry do not seem to be affected by whether they identify with a single ancestry or more than one; in either case, more persons say that ethnicity is unimportant than greatly important. But the degree of intermixture does make a difference: Individuals with four or more ethnic strands in their backgrounds are quite unlikely to attach great importance to ethnic background—just 3 percent do (this is not shown in the table). This group presents a contrast even to other persons of mixed ancestry.

The impact of generational status also suggests the diminution of ethnicity's potency over time, for the core of those with the strongest feelings about ethnic background is concentrated in the second and third generations. This pattern emerges most clearly when one compares across the same categories of identity status. Among persons of single ancestry who identify ethnically, for instance, about 40 percent in the second generation say that their ethnic background is very important to them; in the third generation, 34 percent, and in the fourth, only 22 percent. There is a comparable rise across the generations in the proportion denying any importance to ethnic background. A similar shift, but with a lower average salience of ethnicity, appears among ethnic identifiers having mixed ancestry.

As an indicator of possible change in the salience of ethnicity, a corollary of these two major influences is the receding in the importance of ethnicity across age groups. Age does not have an independent influence on ethnicity's importance, but changes across age groups emerge as reflections of the historical rise in the proportions of whites who have mixed ancestry or belong to the fourth and later generations. Accordingly, young people tend to attribute less importance to ethnic background than their elders do. Only 15 percent of persons under the age of forty-five rate their ethnic background as very important to them. Among those forty-five and older, the proportion is double this. There is, however, no difference between the age groups in the proportion declaring ethnicity to be unimportant. The shift, then, lies in rating ethnicity as "somewhat" rather than "very" important, and it may reveal the reception young people find for any strong expressions of ethnic identity. Although ethnicity is not generally dismissed as unimportant by their peers, the shift probably implies additional limits in the toleration of intense ethnic identities and commitments.

Gender is the only other influence on ethnicity's importance to emerge from the multivariate analysis. Women view their ethnic backgrounds as more important than men do by a considerable margin. Among ethnic identifiers with single ancestry, women were twice as likely as men to rate their ethnic backgrounds as very important (43 percent versus 20 percent). Men, however, are twice as likely to view ethnicity as unimportant. The gender difference is not so pronounced among persons of mixed ancestral background, but it conforms to the same pattern. One possible explanation lies in the close linkage between ethnicity and family in the minds of many respondents. Since women typically are charged with greater responsibility for maintaining family relationships and traditions (di

Leonardo, 1987), they tend to see ethnicity, at least in the specific sense of family origins, as quite important. And since women are less likely to be in the labor force, they have fewer alternative identities to draw on, thus enhancing ethnicity's importance (De Vaus and McAllister, 1987).

The evaluations of ethnicity's importance further alter the portrait of prominent ethnic identities, in particular sharpening the distinction between the region's ancestry profile and the pool of salient ethnic identities. Greater importance is attached to the identities associated with more recently arrived groups, namely, the Italians and Poles. Few with such old-stock identities as Dutch, English, French, and German, however, attribute much importance to ethnic background; only the Irish are a partial exception.

These patterns seem comprehensible on the basis of the influences on ethnicity's perceived importance—generation and ancestry type. In general, the old-stock identities are disproportionately found among the fourth and later generations and in complex ancestry mixtures, where ethnic background tends to be seen as not very important. But there may again be some independent contribution of ethnic loyalties derived from ethnic collective phenomena. Individuals may attach greater importance to ethnicities that are *visible* in the larger environment, feeling that there is more value in being perceived as members of these groups than in being seen as members of less visible, more assimilated groups. (And more value there may in fact be, for groups with distinct neighborhoods, organizations, and informal networks may have more to offer.)

Whatever the source, the differences between old-stock and newer ethnic identities are sharply defined. Of persons with old-stock identities, whether single or mixed in with other ethnicities, typically between 10 and 20 percent feel their ethnic background to be very important. Between 40 and 50 percent say that their background holds no importance at all for them. The picture is different for the Italians and Poles. Among persons identifying with these groups, roughly 40 percent ascribe great importance to ethnic background, and comparatively few rate it as unimportant. Among the Italians, in fact, just 8 percent is willing to say that ethnic background is altogether unimportant.

The Irish seem to stand midway between the other old-stock groups and the Italians and Poles. Persons with an Irish identity are not more likely than their old-stock counterparts to view their ethnic background as very important, but they are less likely to deny it any role. Moreover, when their ancestry is solely Irish, then the Irish resemble the southern and eastern European groups in their estimation of ethnicity.

These ethnic variations in the perceived importance of background would seem to have an undeniable impact on the ethnic landscape, because they determine the ethnicities most likely to emerge in ordinary social interaction as strongly defined. If one accepts that identities felt to be important are more likely to make themselves manifest, then the distance between the pool of identities and that of ancestries grows. In the pool of identities to which great importance is attached, for example, many major old-stock ethnicities have practically vanished. To be specific, English and Dutch are each represented by only 4 percent of persons with such strongly felt identities. The two most important ethnicities in the pool are Irish and Italian, each claimed by about a quarter. Polish has now risen to the same level as German and French, with each of these three identities claimed by about 15 percent.

Old-stock identities are not so underrepresented among persons who evaluate their ethnic backgrounds as somewhat important. In this group also, Irish is the most frequent ethnic identity (a third of the entire group), while Italian has slipped. But even so, the latter is even with English and German in a virtual tie for second place, a ranking quite different from its frequency among ancestries.

Summary

The findings of this chapter provide ample reason to view ethnic identity as a critical issue for the future of ethnicity among Americans of European ancestries. Three broad conclusions have emerged.

First, many white Americans, perhaps a majority, continue to identify themselves in ethnic terms. There is a paradox here: The decline of objective differences among ethnic categories in the white population is not matched by an equivalent receding of ethnic identities. In the Capital Region, where, admittedly, ethnicity is still a prominent feature of the social landscape, about two-thirds of native-born whites are willing to describe themselves to an interviewer in terms of ethnic labels and presumably do so in a range of social situations; approximately half acknowledge thinking about themselves in such terms. Not all of the individuals who describe themselves in ethnic ways concede any importance to ethnic background; perhaps some use ethnic labels more out of deference to the questioner than out of genuine conviction about who they are. But a majority of the ethnically identifying view their ethnic backgrounds as at least somewhat important, and a significant minority view them as very important. The social ramifications of presenting oneself in terms of ethnic labels are underscored by the reactions of respondents when asked how others could know their ethnic backgrounds.[23] Nearly half said, one way or another, "They can't know—unless I tell them," thus pointing up the pivotal role of ethnic identity.

The second major conclusion draws attention to the complex interplay between personal ethnic identities and collective or aggregate ethnicity. On the one hand, ethnic identities help to shape the visibility of different ethnicities, that is, their relative salience in everyday interactions. On the other, the supply side of ethnicity—such collective features as ethnic neighborhoods and institutions, as well as the number of identifiers—makes some ethnicities more attractive than others or instills deeper loyalty to them, thus encouraging ethnic identity. This individual-collective interaction is reflected in the large aggregate discrepancies between the ethnic identities and ancestries of whites in the Capital Region. The discrepancies arise in part because of compositional differences among ethnic groups: that is, personal ethnic identities and their salience vary in patterned ways according to the complexity of ancestry, generational status, and the degree of confidence in knowledge of ancestry, to name just some of the influences. These characteristics vary in turn by ethnic group. But there is also an influence of collective group properties, which can be seen in the loyalty some ethnicities (for example, Irish) call forth. Groups that are conspicuous because of neighborhoods, organizations, cultural distinctiveness, *and* many adherents appear to offer more reasons for affiliation and thus are likely magnets for ethnic identities. Such patterns of identification favor visible groups, which typically are recently arrived in historical terms, over prestigious or more established ones.

The net product of these forces is the characteristic ethnic topography of the region, the bulges and depressions that define the ethnic surface to an observer. Prominent in this topography are newer ethnicities, such as Italian and Polish, even though they are not the largest ancestry groups. They are favored by patterns of identification and are especially numerous among strongly held identities. By contrast, most old-stock ethnicities, such as English and German, are relatively faint, particularly because of their underrepresentation among identities felt to be important to their possessors. Also contributing to this pattern may be the connection of these origins, specifically those from the British Isles, with an American ethnic identity. Persons of old-stock background may therefore have difficulty in discerning any ethnic distinctiveness in their background. Of these ethnicities, only Irish is as prevalent among identities as among ancestries (and, accordingly, its relative importance among identities is increased). It exemplifies the supply-side principle because of its prominent role in the region's politics and culture.

The third major conclusion is that some of the erosive forces reflecting the transformation of ethnicity also have effects on ethnic identity. The weight of the evidence appears to suggest a long-term decline in the role of ethnic identities among whites. In terms of the analysis presented above, the impact of some large-scale and seemingly irreversible demographic changes in the white population seems quite plain: mixed, and especially complex, ancestry; membership in the fourth and later generations; and uncertainty about one's ethnic background. All reduce the probability of identifying in ethnic terms and the personal meaningfulness of ethnic identity. These characteristics are increasing in the white population as a result of such forces as advancing generational status and high rates of interethnic marriage, making it likely that ethnic identities will, in the future, decline in frequency and in felt importance.

But the evidence does not run all in one direction. Higher levels of education, in particular, are associated with a moderately greater probability of expressing an ethnic identity. The widely held assumption that social mobility promotes assimilation does not hold up when it comes to ethnic identity, which seems instead to receive a boost from the increasing cosmopolitanism and contact across ethnic lines that are generally associated with education beyond high school. Given its isolation, this effect hardly seems to betoken a return to ethnicity. A better interpretation may be that the value of cultural goods in general is greater for those in more highly placed social strata; those with more diversified symbolic repertoires have a wider range of social contacts, and this encourages the use of ethnic identity. Moreover, increasing education among formerly disadvantaged white ethnic groups is one outcome of the transformation of ethnicity among whites. In this respect, then, the impact of the transformation establishes a countercurrent tending to increase the expression of ethnic identity, although, admittedly, education's combined effects on identity and its salience are not as large as those associated with ancestry and generation. But the countervailing influence of increasing education indicates the possible presence of forces in American society that tend to sustain ethnic identity even as the objective basis of ethnicity is crumbling.

What must next be established is the *content* of ethnic identities: do they resonate with the experiences of whites, or are they rather symbolic assertions of little practical consequence?

The Cultural Expressions
of Ethnic Identity

And it is probably in tastes in *food* that one
would find the strongest and most indelible
mark of infant learning, the lessons which
longest withstand the distancing or collapse of
the native world and most durably maintain
nostalgia for it.
—PIERRE BOURDIEU
(1984: 79; italics in original)

To have value in comprehending the contemporary role of ethnicity in the United
States, ethnic identity must not be reduced to a matter of psychology, that is,
translated purely into terms of self-concept and inner orientation, or left at the
level of how one presents oneself to others. As important, if not more
so, are the behavioral and experiential expressions of identity, its
crystallization into concrete patterns of action and relationship.
These manifestations, as much as identity itself, are capable of nour-
ishing social structures supportive of ethnicity. Such mundane actions as eating ethnic foods, enacting holiday rituals, peppering
English speech with mother-tongue words and phrases, and participating in ethnic social clubs give meaning to an otherwise abstract assertion of ethnic identity and breathe life into ethnicity as a
social form. Conversely, no matter how strongly an individual identifies with an ethnic background, if this identity is not reflected in
action and experience, it makes little contribution to sustaining
ethnicity. If an ethnic identity has no *content*, no commitments in
terms of action, then it represents a pure form of what Herbert Gans

75

(1979) has called "symbolic ethnicity," a self-conscious attempt to "feel ethnic," to the exclusion of "being ethnic."

No manifestations of ethnic identity are probably more critical for defining a content than those falling under the rubric of culture. The term *culture* is used here in a broader sense than the arts, or the trappings of high-brow culture, and with a meaning closely approximating that found in anthropology. Ethnic culture embraces the patterned, commonplace actions that distinguish members of one ethnic group from another, including food, language, and holiday ceremony. Although social theorists recently have avoided the inclusion of specific cultural dimensions in the definition of ethnicity, on the grounds that these vary too much in prominence from one group to another to be construed as defining traits,[1] it is nevertheless clear that ethnic groups generally define their uniqueness in regard to other ethnic groups largely through the medium of culture. It is, in truth, difficult to imagine that an ethnic group could successfully maintain a distinctive sense of identity among its members without the presence of some cultural elements seen as a positive heritage worth holding onto. But ethnic culture need not represent an unchanging set of traditions. For European-ancestry groups, the ethnic trends imply major declines in cultural distinctiveness, taking place within a brief historical span.[2] Even in the face of such changes, however, the possibility of cultural elements serving as important foci for ethnic identity remains.

Do Americans of European ancestries maintain ethnic cultural patterns? And if so, which ones? The most relevant answers come in terms of patterns that are regarded as ethnic by those who practice them. American cooking, language, music, and so forth have been so infused over the centuries with the contributions of different groups that all Americans could be described as maintaining ethnic patterns in their daily activities.[3] But these sorts of contributions are not at issue here, for in general they have come to be regarded as American, and their ethnic origin is often known only to scholars of American popular culture. Unless a cultural pattern is viewed as ethnic, it cannot serve as a rallying point for an ethnic group.

One must also grapple with the questions, difficult though they may be, of the quality and depth of ethnic cultural patterns. It is not enough to observe that such patterns exist, even if they are found among individuals many generations removed from immigration.

The thesis of "symbolic ethnicity" is a reminder that ethnic cultural commitments may be shallow, confined to a few ethnic symbols that do not intrude on a life that is otherwise nonethnic. It suggests skepticism about some of the evidence put forward on behalf of a renewal of ethnicity—such as greater interest in ancestral languages or folk music and dancing (Fishman et al., 1985). These activities by themselves need not revitalize ethnicity, for they may remain confined to a sphere of personal curiosity instead of feeding into the ongoing life of ethnic networks and institutions. This communal dimension is vital. The study of an ancestral language, for instance, no matter how earnestly it is pursued, is a purely academic affair if there is no one to speak the language with. Hence, one must address such questions as: How regular in occurrence are ethnic cultural patterns? And what are their social contexts—who are the significant others who participate?

Although the mere description of ethnic cultural patterns in the general population is of great interest because they have been so little studied outside of the limited confines of a few ethnic groups, my focus is mostly on their connection to ethnic identity. This connection is crucial in light of the transformation of ethnicity—the erosion of the structural foundations of ethnicity among whites, throwing far greater weight on the role of ethnic identity than ever before. An implication is that ethnic cultural activity in the absence of an ethnic identity—for example, the unself-conscious consumption of ethnic foods—is likely to remain on a purely personal or familial plane, without contributing to the fragile tissue of connections necessary for ethnic social structures to survive. Thus, the relationship between identity and cultural activities can be seen as synergistic—each necessary for the other to contribute positively to ethnicity as a social form; that is, ethnic identity without any cultural content represents a pure form of symbolic ethnicity, and an adherence to ethnic culture in the absence of ethnic identity represents a private form of ethnicity that does not feed into the ongoing life of an ethnic community.

Central to this book are tabular analyses displaying how cultural patterns and other ethnically relevant experiences are related to whether or not individuals identify ethnically and to the salience, that is, subjective importance, of their ethnic background. Such analyses can tell us whether or not ethnic traits congeal around ethnic identities in such a way as to give these identities substance in terms of everyday experience. They cannot inform us, however, about causality—whether identity leads to cultural patterns (and other experiences), or vice versa. The causal relationship between these two seems almost certain to be reciprocal. Thinking of oneself in ethnic terms is likely to increase the probability of maintaining some ethnic cultural patterns. Likewise, the presence of such patterns undoubtedly boosts the probability of identifying ethnically, since cultural patterns serve as regular reminders of the distinctiveness and value of ethnic origins. Given the cross-sectional nature of the Capital Region survey, it is not possible to disentangle these mutual causal relationships from one another in the data. But their reciprocity must be kept in mind in reading the results that follow.

Another reason for proceeding cautiously with respect to causality is that ethnic identity and its salience vary systematically with a number of other factors reflecting the transformation of ethnicity, such as generational status and confidence in knowledge of ancestry. Presumably, some of these factors also influence ethnic cultural patterns, and therefore the culture-identity relationship may prove ultimately to be a reflection of these underlying forces. This possibility should not diminish our interest in the relationship, which still describes whether ethnic identity is expressed in concrete actions. But it does affect any evaluation of the staying power of cultural patterns and other expressions of identity. Therefore, descriptive analyses of the relationships between ethnic identity and specific cultural traits are followed by more systematic scrutiny through models incorporating demographic, socioeconomic, and other variables—as well as ethnic identity—to take into account the larger processes of ongoing change among white ethnics.

Data about Ethnic Experiences

The basic data about cultural and other ethnically relevant experiences come from a checklist of sixteen experiences that was presented to respondents (see table 3.1). The experiences ranged in character from the cultural ("practicing customs or traditions of your ethnic background"), to the political ("feeling strongly about an issue because of your ethnic background"), to the social ("feeling a special sense of relationship to someone else because that person

Table 3.1   Ethnic experiences (during preceding five years)

	% of native-born whites indicating
Eating special foods or dishes of your ethnic background	47.0
Practicing customs or traditions of your ethnic background	21.3
Teaching your children about your ethnic background	15.0
Attending or participating in ethnic festivals or celebrations	27.2
Visiting an ancestral homeland	9.8
Using words or phrases from an ancestral language	29.8
Feeling strongly about an issue because of your ethnic background	15.0
Being discriminated against because of your ethnic background	4.3
Seeing or hearing about discrimination against others who have your ethnic background	15.4
Coming into contact with stereotypes or fixed ideas about people with your ethnic background	21.7
Feeling curious about the ethnic background of someone else	31.7
Being asked by someone else about your ethnic background	16.1
Feeling a special sense of relationship to someone else because that person has your ethnic background	21.3
Discussing your ethnic background with someone else	32.8
Feeling special interest in the career of a public figure or celebrity because that person has your ethnic background	12.2
Getting special help in your business or profession from someone with your ethnic background	2.2

Note: The table shows the experiences in the order in which they appeared on a list presented to the respondent.

has your ethnic background"). Respondents were asked to indicate which of the experiences they had had during the preceding five years and were then asked a series of follow-up questions about each experience they checked in order to gain greater depth of knowledge about its quality and frequency. The data collected in this way provide the basic source about the cultural experiences to be discussed here. But before pursuing the theme of culture, it is useful to give a brief overview of the ethnic experiences.

In the aggregate, the ethnic experiences of native-born whites appear to fit the metaphor of the glass that defies easy characterization because it is half full and therefore half empty. For most white Americans, ethnic experiences do not appear to constitute a rich tapestry of everyday life. But most do have some experiences that they think of in ethnic terms. Just a quarter of native-born whites in our survey indicated having none of the experiences on our list (see table 3.2). At the other extreme, a quarter reported six or more of them (interestingly, no one claimed all of them). Half of native-born whites, then, had between one and five experiences, and the bulk of this group was concentrated at the lower end, indicating one, two, or three experiences.

The most common experiences were fairly mundane ones, such as eating ethnic foods or attending an ethnic festival. These are precisely the kind of quotidian experiences that can establish regular ethnic patterns in people's lives, but there were important limits to their extent, for none was reported by a majority. The most frequently reported of the experiences was, in fact, the culinary one: 47 percent of respondents indicated that they eat some special foods of their background. Several other experiences were also quite common—discussing one's ethnic background with someone else (33 percent); feeling curious about another person's ethnic background (32 percent); using words or phrases from a mother tongue (30

Table 3.2   Distribution of ethnic experiences among native-born whites, immigrant whites, and non-whites

	Native-born whites	Immigrant whites	Non-whites
No experiences	25.9%	15.0%	18.2%
1	12.8	7.5	9.1
2	13.0	5.0	0.0
3	12.2	7.5	4.5
4 or 5	12.6	17.5	18.2
6 or more	23.5	47.5	50.0
N	(460)	(40)	(22)

Overall significance level (by χ^2 test): p < .01

percent)[4]; and attending ethnic festivals (27 percent). These four, and the eating of ethnic foods, constitute the staples of contemporary ethnic experience. They account for about half of all the experiences reported by our respondents and an even greater share among those with just a few experiences.

The infrequency of some experiences on the list is noteworthy in light of theories that are often proposed to account for the role of ethnicity in the United States and other advanced industrial societies. It has been argued—in *Beyond the Melting Pot,* among other places—that ethnicity has, over time, taken on a political role (Glazer and Moynihan, 1970, 1975; Nielsen, 1985). But we found that only 15 percent of native-born whites said they have felt strongly in recent years about an issue because of their ethnic background. An economic role for ethnicity has also been described: ethnic groups have been viewed as occupying specific economic niches and therefore able to provide their members with special opportunities for advancement through ethnic businesses or with the assistance of informal networks.[5] But only 2 percent of native-born whites in our survey claimed to have gotten special help in their business or professional life from a fellow ethnic. Even if one allows for considerable underreporting because of respondents who have not been economically active in recent years or because not all ethnically based transactions are perceived as ethnic in character by their participants, the figure remains remarkably small.

Other surprisingly uncommon experiences included hearing about discrimination practiced against the members of one's ethnic group, indicated by 15 percent of respondents. Only 4 percent of respondents reported suffering discrimination themselves. Teaching one's children about their ethnic background was indicated also by just 15 percent (although this figure is deflated by the inclusion of respondents without children). And only 10 percent visited an ethnic homeland within the five years preceding the survey.

A comparison to immigrants and non-whites demonstrates that ethnic experiences loom larger for these groups than for native-born whites. Only a quarter of American-born whites reported more than five ethnic experiences; by comparison, this many were claimed by about half of foreign-born whites and about the same proportion of non-whites (see table 3.2). Comparatively few in the foreign-born and non-white groups reported a minimal level of experience—a quarter mentioned two or fewer ethnic experiences, compared to half of native-born whites.

Nevertheless, the ethnic experiences of native-born whites are linked to ethnic identity, as must be true if identity is to be pivotal for ethnicity: these experiences are more numerous among those who identify themselves ethnically. Table 3.3 presents the relevant data, and employs a set of distinctions that are invoked under the label of "ethnic identity status" throughout the book. This variable combines ancestry and identity information, forming all six logically possible categories of ancestry type (unknown, single, mixed)

Table 3.3   Level of ethnic experience by ethnic identity status and importance of background (% with six or more experiences)

Ethnic identity status (ancestry type/identity type)	All native-born whites	Importance of background		
		very	somewhat	none
Ethnically identifying:				
single/single	31.4	45.0	39.6	0.0
	(121)	(40)	(48)	(31)
multiple/single	27.3	46.7	30.2	13.3
	(88)	(15)	(43)	(30)
multiple/multiple	24.8	52.9	33.3	4.9
	(101)	(17)	(42)	(41)
Nonidentifying:				
single/none	12.5			
	(32)			
multiple/none	16.5	24.3	14.6	8.9
	(103)	(37)	(41)	(45)
unknown/none	0.0			
	(15)			
Significance levels:	$p < .05$	identity status × experiences, $p < .05$ importance × experiences, $p < .001$		

Note: Ns (bases) for percentages appear in parentheses, and remain virtually the same throughout this and the next chapter. For this reason, they are not repeated in subsequent tables. For purposes of classification by importance of background, the nonidentifying respondents are combined into one category because of small numbers in the full table. This will be done in other tables as well.

and identity status (none, single, mixed). The three categories of persons who identify in ethnic terms—those of single ancestry; those of mixed ancestry who identify with a single origin; and those of mixed ancestry who identify also in a mixed fashion—each have approximately equal levels of ethnic experience. Between a quarter and a third of each, for example, reports six or more ethnic experiences (the small variations among the categories are not statistically significant).

The overall level of ethnic experience is manifestly weaker among persons without an ethnic identity. Fourteen percent of this group claimed to have had more than five of the ethnic experiences on our list.[6] Two-thirds indicated either none or just one or two. Also among those without an ethnic identity, the aggregate patterns of ethnic experience do not vary according to whether ancestry is mixed or unmixed. Ethnic experience is just as infrequent for those of undivided ethnic background as for those whose ethnic heritage is mixed. But one small category in our sample that does appear distinctive is that containing whites with no knowledge of their ethnic origins. Unsurprisingly, its members reported very low levels of ethnic experience.

The level of ethnic experience is also strongly associated with the salience of ethnic identity, the degree of importance an individual attributes to his or her ethnic background.[7] The strength of this relationship has the incidental value of confirming that the judgments of ethnicity's importance are not casual by-products of the interview situation, but are well grounded in experience. Thus, close to half of those who identify ethnically and also say that their ethnic background is very important have had six or more of the ethnic experiences. A third of ethnically identifying persons who acknowledge their background as somewhat important (the middle category) report an equally high level of ethnic experience. But just 6 percent of whites overall who attribute no importance to background but still identify in ethnic terms report six or more experiences.

Even among those who do not identify in ethnic terms, the level of ethnic experience corresponds to some degree with evaluations of ethnicity's importance, although the relationship does not have the same magnitude as among the ethnically identifying. This finding is consistent with the observation that some in the nonidentifying group perceive their ethnic background to be very important, despite their apparent reluctance to identify with it: about a quarter of them indicated six or more of the ethnic experiences. This proportion is only half that of persons who identify ethnically, but it is well above the average level of experiences reported by other nonidentifying respondents.

Cultural Experiences

Three experiences we asked about stand out for their potential to provide ethnicity with a cultural "substance," composed of behavior and ritual distinguishing group members from others and helping to define an ethnic uniqueness worth maintaining. These are the eating of ethnic foods, the use of words and phrases from a mother tongue, and the upholding of ethnic customs and traditions. Each was indicated by a significant minority among our respondents. To these can be added a fourth, participation in ethnic festivals, since these festivals generally celebrate ethnic cultures and thereby help to preserve a sense of their special value. This was also one of the most common experiences among native-born whites.

For these experiences, the mundane rituals and practices involved in cultural maintenance are potentially of greater significance as carriers of subtle ethnic attitudes and values, as markers of ethnic boundaries, and as ceremonies for the building of ethnic solidarity. This potential is illustrated by the use of a mother tongue. As Gillian Stevens (1985) points out, important aspects of ethnic culture are embedded in language and thus are accessible only to those who know the mother tongue. The complex of attitudes and values surrounding the Italian-American family system, for instance, often seen as this group's cultural hallmark, are communicated through the shadings of meaning attached to such words as *compare* or *godfather* (Gambino, 1974).

Language has not only a cultural significance as a conveyor of special meanings, but it also provides a way of marking out ethnic boundaries. Obviously, speech in a mother tongue cuts out anyone who does not know the language and thus provides a way of communicating things intended to be understood only by those who share an ethnic bond. But for purposes of boundary demarcation, fluency in an ethnic language may not even be necessary. The use of words and phrases from a mother tongue in an English conversation can remind others of a shared ethnic background, a form of "ethnic signalling" (Plotnikov and Silverman, 1978). Thus, even extensive acculturation may not extinguish the important role of ethnic cultural residues in sustaining ethnicity.

Yet one must avoid concluding that any cultural survival inevitably contributes to ethnic distinctiveness. The ethnic transformations of late-twentieth-century America require one to pay attention to the contexts and occasions of cultural experience. Food or language can provide the basis for celebrating and renewing the solidarity of common ethnic background, but they can also allow others, not of that background, to appreciate an ethnic heritage. They can, in other words, foster a solidarity that transcends conventional ethnic confines and is based on a mutual appreciation of ethnic heritage, a recognition of the shared experience of being the descendants of ethnics whatever their specific origins may be. One, then, must ask not simply whether culturally laden experiences occur to Americans of European ancestry, but what purposes they may serve when they do.

To start with an overall characterization, it appears that these experiences are not spread with much uniformity among the various groups in the native-born white population. They are concentrated in specific ways that suggest they approximate the trajectory of "straight-line" assimilation theory (Crispino, 1980)—most frequent and richest in substance among the groups that are closest to the immigration experience and less frequent and more superficial as one moves away. This is demonstrated first by an examination of how each experience varies in terms of ethnic identity and its salience. Subsequently, I consider how other factors, such as generation and age, affect each experience.

Culinary Loyalties

Consider the tantalizing case of ethnic cuisine. Ethnic foods have been incorporated into American cooking at all levels of refinement, but this incorporation has a double edge. On the one hand, it implies that there need be no contradiction between eating in an American style and eating ethnic foods. The popularity of certain ethnic cuisines means that their main ingredients are easy to obtain and that their dishes are served in many restaurants, often not just ethnic ones (as with pasta dishes, for example). Hence, even outside of geographical areas of ethnic concentration, ethnic food may be widely available and serve as a continual reminder of one's ethnic origins. On the other hand, the incorporation of ethnic foods into the American cuisine may come at the cost of diluting the original distinctive taste of the food. Over time, a dish may become so thoroughly American that its ethnic associations, if not altogether lost, become only faintly perceptible, like those of the frankfurter.

Although some ethnic cuisines have survived and even prospered in America, there are few homes of native-born whites in which ethnic foods are set on the table every day.[8] Only 1 percent of our respondents said that they eat ethnic foods daily, and only 15 percent indicated eating them at least once a week. About as common is eating such foods one or a few times per month, reported by 14 percent of native-born whites. A similar percentage indicated very occasional consumption of ethnic foods, perhaps one or a few times in the year. About half, as noted above, denied eating ethnic foods at all.

To judge by our respondents' reports, some cuisines have fared better than others. In the Capital Region, Italian is an example of a flourishing cuisine.[9] About 85 percent of the ancestry group, persons of mixed Italian background included, eat Italian dishes at least occasionally. Moreover, persons of Italian background generally described a large number of Italian dishes as part of their diet; this was not confined to the stereotypical spaghetti and pasta dishes. Last, Italian food is consumed with regularity: More than 60 percent of American-born respondents of Italian background indicated eating Italian food at least once a week. To put this figure into a larger perspective, these regular Italian-food eaters constitute almost two-thirds of all those who eat ethnic foods with weekly frequency.[10]

No other cuisine in the Capital Region is as popular as the Italian one, but a number of other ethnic cuisines crop up frequently and are eaten with some regularity. They, however, are not always represented by a variety of dishes. In order of mention, the most important are Irish and German, followed by French and Polish. The cuisine that comes closest to matching the Italian pattern is Polish. Half of the American-born members of the ancestry group indicate eating Polish dishes, and a variety of dishes were mentioned by these respondents, though a smaller variety than the Italian one. In terms of regularity, Polish cuisine also lags behind Italian. Only about 10 percent eat Polish food with weekly frequency. More common is the consumption of Polish food one or a few times per month.

The cuisines associated with the French, German, and Irish tend to be even more limited in variety and regularity of consumption than Polish and especially Italian. Irish food stands as an extreme case. Just a few foods, particularly corned beef and cabbage, are mentioned with any frequency. About 30 percent of the ancestry group consumes Irish dishes, but in many cases they do so only occasionally: Nearly half of those who eat Irish foods do so only a few times a year.

The cuisines of other major old-stock groups have largely disappeared or at least blended with traditional American cooking. Only a few persons mentioned distinctive English dishes, such as trifle, and virtually no one indicated eating Dutch foods, despite the annual festivals that remind the region's residents of its Dutch heritage. An example of the gradual disappearance of an old-stock cuisine is that of the Scots. Only a small part of the ancestry group (11 percent) eats Scottish dishes, despite the opportunity provided by the annual Scottish Games festival. The majority who do so eat these foods no more than a few times a year.

If one stands back from the ethnic specifics, it becomes apparent that loyalty to an ethnic cuisine is, as a general rule, strongly related to the salience of ethnic identity and also to whether ethnic ancestry is single or mixed.[11] Specifically, the consumption of ethnic foods occurs most frequently among persons who identify ethnically and come from an undivided ethnic background, especially when they feel that their background is at least somewhat important (see tables 3.4 and 3.5). Overall, almost two-thirds of ethnic identifiers of single ancestry eat ethnic foods at least occasionally, and about half do so monthly or more frequently.

In the single-ancestry group, the frequency of ethnic-food consumption is higher for those who feel that their identity is important. Three-quarters of those saying their background is at least somewhat important eat ethnic foods, and 60 percent do so with at least monthly regularity. But among those who say their back-

Table 3.4   Ethnic food customs by ethnic identity status

	% who eat ethnic food	% who eat ethnic food at least once a month	% who eat ethnic food at home	% who use special ingredients in preparing food[a]	% who eat ethnic food on special occasions
All native-born whites	47.0	29.6	38.7	23.0	28.9
Ethnic identity status (ancestry type/identity type)					
single/single	62.8	47.9	56.2	29.4	47.9
multiple/single	50.0	22.7	36.4	15.6	27.3
multiple/multiple	41.6	23.8	35.6	22.2	22.8
single/none	34.4	18.8	25.0	—[b]	15.6
multiple/none	40.8	26.2	32.0	21.2	21.4
unknown/none	6.7	6.7	6.7	—[b]	6.7
Significance levels:	p < .001	p < .001	p < .001	N.S.	p < .001

[a]Based only on those who eat ethnic food at home.
[b]Percentage not reported because of small base (N < 10).

Table 3.5   Frequency of eating ethnic food by ethnic identity status and importance of ethnic background (% eating ethnic food at least once a month)

Ethnic identity status (ancestry type/ identity type)	Importance of background		
	very	somewhat	not
single/single	57.5	62.5	12.9
multiple/single	33.3	23.3	16.7
multiple/multiple	29.4	35.7	7.3
non-identifying	29.7	26.8	20.0
Significance levels:	identity status × food, p < .001 importance × food, p < .001		

ground is not important, the situation is essentially the reverse: only a quarter eat ethnic foods, and just 13 percent eat them on a monthly basis. For those feeling that background is unimportant, the fact that their ethnic identity is derived from an undivided heritage apparently does not boost their loyalty to an ethnic cuisine.

Persons of mixed ancestry consume ethnic foods less frequently than those of unmixed background, even though they have greater opportunity, having two or more ancestral cuisines to draw on. Overall, 54 percent of ethnically identifying persons of mixed ancestry do not eat ethnic foods at all, and only 23 percent eat such foods monthly or more frequently. In terms of loyalty to a cuisine, it makes little difference whether respondents of mixed ancestry identify ultimately with a single group or with more than one, as the frequency of ethnic-food consumption is about the same in both cases. The strength of feelings attached to an identity, however, does make a difference. Those of mixed ancestry who attribute at least some importance to their ethnic background are more likely to eat ethnic foods and to do so with regularity, but they still do not approach the frequencies found among identifiers of single ancestry.

Finally, ethnic foods are consumed least frequently by persons who do not identify ethnically. Overall, 64 percent said that they do not eat ethnic foods (however, this figure is partly attributable to the presence of the group of unknown background, whose members are very unlikely to eat ethnic foods). Curiously, the likelihood of eating foods with monthly regularity is about the same as among ethnically identifying persons of mixed background. In the nonidentifying group, the importance attached to ethnic background appears to make little difference for food patterns.

The ethnic-food consumption differences across categories of identity are not just a matter of whether people eat such foods. Even among those who eat ethnically, differences in frequency emerge. Among ethnic identifiers of single ancestry, for example, those who eat ethnic foods with monthly regularity outnumber more occasional consumers by three to one; in fact, those who eat such foods at least once a week are almost half of the food-consuming group. The food-consumption patterns of ethnic identifiers of mixed ancestry present a marked contrast. In this group, persons who eat ethnic foods just occasionally are equal in number to those who eat them at least once a month, and weekly consumers of ethnic foods represent just a small minority.

In other ways as well, it appears that loyalty to ethnic-food traditions is strongest among ethnically identifying persons of single ancestry, particularly for those who attribute some importance to their backgrounds. The great majority of ethnic-food consumers eat these foods in their homes, especially those who eat them frequently. But nearly 20 percent eat ethnically only outside of the home, presumably with family or friends or in restaurants. This percentage is lowest (11 percent) among the ethnically identifying of single ancestry; by comparison, it is 21 percent among their counterparts of mixed ancestry. The percentage who eat ethnic foods at home monthly or more frequently is also correspondingly higher in the single-ancestry group. When combined with the differences in the probability of eating ethnic foods in the first place, these variations lead to a marked concentration of ethnic food consumption in the homes of ethnic identifiers from unmixed ancestral backgrounds, as table 3.4 shows.

A valuable indicator of the role of food in maintaining a sense of ethnic tradition is its use in celebrations, which raises it out of the realm of the mundane and may be particularly likely to call forth pristine culinary traditions, enhancing the ritual and boundary-demarcating significance of food (see Goode et al., 1984, on wedding menus among Italian Americans). Sixty-two percent of native-born whites who eat ethnic foods report using them in celebrating special occasions. For most people the ceremonial use of ethnic foods is confined largely to a few holidays a year. Christmas was mentioned by about half of the respondents reporting a ceremonial use of food, and Easter by more than a third. These holidays, together with St. Patrick's Day and Thanksgiving, account for three-quarters of all the special occasions reported. Surprisingly, only a small number of respondents mentioned such family events as weddings and gatherings as the occasions for celebration with ethnic dishes.

This use, too, varies by identity type, even among those who eat ethnic foods, and is most likely to be found among ethnically identifying persons of single ancestral background and among those who feel their backgrounds are important. About 75 percent of ethnic-food consumers who identify ethnically and come from undivided backgrounds say that ethnic foods are served on special occasions.

Among ethnically identifying persons of mixed ancestry the figure is down to 55 percent. In fact, the concentration of the ceremonial use of ethnic foods in the single-ancestry group is even stronger than these figures suggest, because of its members' greater probability of eating ethnic foods in the first place (see table 3.4).

The Transmission of Ethnic Cuisines, or Who Does the Cooking?

Given the growing proportion of the population that is intermarried or comes from a mixed ancestral background, a significant issue is how ethnic cuisines are maintained from one generation to the next. No sooner is the issue posed but a seeming paradox emerges. If ethnic homogeneity can no longer be taken for granted within most families, one would expect that women, more likely to be the cooks, would have a greater chance than men to keep their culinary heritage alive. But this is not the case, at least in the Capital Region, where men are as likely as women to report eating foods of their ethnic background.

It appears that intermarriage does not do much to hinder the preservation of ethnic cuisines. The complexities of ancestry make classifying marriages a less simple endeavor than it may seem in the abstract. But the impact of intermarriage on cuisine can be assessed by looking at two groups of married respondents: those whose spouses' ancestries are the same as their own, and thus are married endogamously[12]; and persons whose spouses have ethnic ancestries that do not overlap with their own. The latter respondents are plainly intermarried.

There is not a great difference between these two marital groups. About half of the endogamously married respondents reported eating ethnic dishes at home, compared to 42 percent of those who are intermarried. But the figure was somewhat lower (36 percent) for intermarried men, who, one might imagine, are especially disadvantaged in satisfying any taste they may have for their own ethnic foods. Among the intermarried men, nevertheless, about 25 percent said that they eat dishes of their ethnic background at home at least once a month. The comparable figure was barely higher among endogamously married men

Who prepares ethnic dishes in intermarried households? Women typically prepare the dishes of their own ethnic background—

about 90 percent indicated doing so, although in a few cases they receive help from their husbands or another member of the household. Intermarried men, however, rely on their wives to a great extent for their own ethnic foods. About half indicated that their wives prepared these dishes, and another quarter said that the dishes were prepared by both. Only a quarter of the men cooked ethnic foods without any help from their wives. Clearly, then, in many intermarriages, women learn to make the ethnic dishes of their husbands' backgrounds. Cooking appears to be transmitted not only from mother to daughter, but also from mother-in-law to daughter-in-law.

But one area of culinary tradition that still appears to depend on the preceding generation is that of cooking ethnic dishes for special occasions, such as holidays and family gatherings. Although few consumers of ethnic foods (other than young adults) depend on their mothers and other older relatives for regular ethnic meals, about 40 percent do so for special occasions. Moreover, it appears from an examination of the menus respondents described that the holiday dishes they and their spouses prepare may be less elaborate than the dishes made by their mothers, and also confined to fewer occasions in the year. Thus, the question is open as to which holiday food traditions will be maintained once the older generation is gone.

Although the mothers of the previous generation appear to have been able to pass on food traditions from either side of the family, some cuisines may not have retained their full authenticity. The survey yielded evidence of the weakening of ethnic food traditions, even in those families where they continue: the evidence is in the form of respondents' evaluations of the quality of the ethnic dishes they eat. Overall, 36 percent reported that the ethnic foods prepared in their own homes compare unfavorably to those they ate in their parents' home, while 15 percent claimed that ethnic foods had improved.[13] (About half said they were of the same quality.)

It is tempting to write off this depreciation of ethnic cooking as just a nostalgic veneration of parental homes—many respondents, in fact, made comments to the effect that one's own cooking couldn't compare to mother's. But speaking against such a simple explanation is that the sense of deterioration was sharpest in the very group where ethnic culinary traditions are strongest, namely, the ethnically identifying of single ancestry. Almost half of the ethnic-food consumers in this group said that these foods had gotten worse since their parents' days. Perhaps the sense of deterioration is so strong because its members are the most familiar with the original traditions. But this implies that the others who continue to eat ethnic foods haven't been as exposed to the culinary traditions of their background. The ethnic foods they eat are more likely to have been diluted and Americanized in taste.

Mother-Tongue Survivals

In the case of ethnic foods, the statistical patterns appear to indicate a drift away from ethnic cultural traditions, for example, in the concentration of food loyalties among persons of single ancestry, a group that is declining as a proportion of the native-born white population. Nevertheless, these patterns are leavened with many indicators of the continuing vitality of ethnic cuisines. The general picture of drift is sharper when it comes to mother tongues. Our findings, and those of others, indicate that language as a basis of ethnicity is rapidly eroding among those of European ancestry. Even though 30 percent in our survey indicated the use of words and phrases from a mother tongue as an ethnic experience, the knowledge and, even more so, the use of a mother tongue appears limited to a small minority among the American born.

The data collected from our Capital Region respondents allow a far more searching examination than census data do. We asked the respondents with this experience for considerable detail about their knowledge and use of a mother tongue. Our questions included whether they were exposed to a mother tongue (other than English) in their childhood home; whether they currently could speak a mother tongue or, at a minimum, knew words and phrases from one; and whether they used such a language in their daily life or interspersed words from one in English conversation. To my surprise, 13 percent of the respondents who initially claimed this experience subsequently told us that they had no knowledge of a mother tongue, including knowledge of words and phrases from one.[14] Nearly half of the respondents indicated no use of a mother tongue, even in the restricted sense of occasional words and phrases in conversation. Perhaps our more detailed questions failed to include some sporadic and very restricted use that respondents had in mind when they originally checked this experience, but even so, relatively few respondents reported specific experiences consistent with the use of language as a medium for maintaining ethnicity. Only 16 percent of native-born whites said that they actively use a mother tongue, either as a language for conversation or as an ethnic garnish when speaking English.

This figure is the proportion of all native-born whites who use a non-English mother tongue, and it is the proper index of the extent to which language can serve as a locus for ethnic differences in the population with European ancestry. But from the standpoint of measuring the *survival* of mother-tongue use, it is not the best index, since it includes, for example, people of solely English ancestry, who have no mother tongue other than English, and others, such as those of Irish ancestry, who are unlikely to have a non-English mother tongue.[15] Nevertheless, even with a generous rule of exclusion, the magnitude of survival is only slightly affected. Limiting the proportion to persons having some ancestry from outside the British Isles, one finds that just 20 percent indicate some use of a non-English mother tongue.[16]

It is not just a question of limited use. Even the knowledge of mother tongues is now uncommon among native-born whites. In this respect, our findings are consistent with, but also go well beyond, recent research on mother-tongue loyalty. In *Language Shift in the United States*, Calvin Veltman has documented how English has dominated the other languages brought by immigrants. Veltman focuses more on regular use of a mother tongue than on knowledge of one, and he does not address the issue of whether snatches from mother tongues are mixed with English in ways that can highlight ethnic differences among predominantly English speakers. But he demonstrates that each new generation appears to experience a strong shift away from mother tongues and toward English. Thus, the children of parents who maintain a minority language household are typically bilingual, with the minority language often relegated to a secondary role; and the children of bilingual parents are frequently monolingual in English. Within a few generations, then, most mother tongues as living languages are confined to small parts of their original ancestry groups, even though such "language islands" (Fishman, 1966) may persist over long periods.

Our findings are consistent with such a shift toward English. About 17 percent of native-born whites reported that a non-English language was spoken in their childhood home. (This is a measure of exposure, not of knowledge. It could be the case that a parent spoke a mother tongue with a grandparent and used only English with children, with the result that the children had no fluency in the mother tongue.) But only 11 percent claim to speak a mother tongue now. Of those exposed to a mother tongue during childhood, just half can currently speak the language. Also, a small group of persons say that they can speak a mother tongue but were not exposed to it during childhood. But this small inflow to the pool of mother-tongue speakers is far outweighed by the magnitude of the outflow.

In addition to those who can speak a mother tongue, 15 percent of native-born whites have some knowledge of words and phrases from one, though this knowledge appears to be quite limited on average. Only 10 percent of this group said that they knew "many" words and phrases, and 14 percent characterized their knowledge as limited to just "one or two" words. More than 60 percent of the group estimated their knowledge at fewer than ten words.

Even this limited knowledge of a mother tongue hinges on childhood exposure, implying that it too is fading. Virtually all of the respondents exposed to a mother tongue in childhood claimed knowledge of words and phrases from one. About half of the respondents who know more than ten words or phrases come from this small group. But few respondents who were not exposed in childhood knew even words or phrases, and when they did, they tended not to know many. Only 12 percent of those lacking childhood exposure knew anything of a mother tongue, and most estimated their knowledge at less than ten words or phrases.

Like ethnic food traditions, knowledge of a mother tongue is related to type of ancestry and identity, and speaking knowledge in particular is concentrated among the ethnically identifying of single ancestry (see table 3.6). Ancestry type is pertinent because exposure is most likely when parents are from the same ethnic background and continue to speak a mother tongue with each other and with their children (see Stevens, 1985). For persons of mixed ancestry, exposure to a mother tongue, if it happens at all, is most likely to result from a parent speaking with another relative. Accordingly, the child's knowledge is more likely to be limited to words and

Table 3.6 Mother-tongue knowledge and use by ethnic identity status

		Knowledge (in %)			
	Speaking ability	Ten or more words and phrases	A few words (less than 10)	No knowledge	Total
All native-born whites	10.9	5.7	9.3	74.1	100.0%
Ethnic identity status (ancestry type/identity type)					
single/single	24.0	7.4	6.6	62.0	100.0
multiple/single	6.8	6.8	10.2	76.1	99.9
multiple/multiple	4.0	6.9	14.9	74.3	100.0
single/none	15.6	0.0	6.3	78.1	100.0
multiple/none	5.8	3.9	8.7	81.6	100.0
unknown/none	0.0	0.0	0.0	100.0	100.0

Overall significance level: identity status × knowledge, p < .001

	Use (%)			
	Speech[a]	Only words and phrases[a]	No use	Total
All native-born whites	4.6	11.3	84.1	100.0%
Ethnic identity status (ancestry type/identity type)				
single/single	9.1	20.7	70.2	100.0
multiple/single	3.4	9.1	87.5	100.0
multiple/multiple	4.0	11.9	84.2	100.0
single/none	6.3	0.0	93.8	100.0
multiple/none	1.0	6.8	92.2	100.0
unknown/none	0.0	0.0	100.0	100.0
Overall significance level:	identity status × use, $p < .001$			

[a]Most mother-tongue speakers also use words and phrases when speaking English. Therefore, overall use of words and phrases is closely approximated by the sum of these two columns.

phrases. Altogether, nearly 40 percent of the ethnically identifying of single ancestry can claim some knowledge of a mother tongue. About a quarter report being able to speak one. An additional 14 percent say that they have some words and phrases, and half of this group estimate their knowledge at more than ten words or phrases. Knowledge is less common, and shallower, among ethnic identifiers of mixed ancestry. Among them, just 5 percent overall claim to speak a mother tongue. Twenty percent do know some words and phrases, but two-thirds estimate that they know fewer than ten words or phrases. Knowledge of an ethnic language is even less among persons who do not identify in ethnic terms.

Mother-tongue knowledge corresponds also with the importance attached to ethnic background. Among the ethnically identifying of single ancestry who view their ethnic backgrounds as very important, 55 percent claim some mother-tongue knowledge (see table 3.7), and 43 percent have a speaking knowledge. At the other extreme, just 10 percent of persons who view their backgrounds as unimportant claim any mother-tongue knowledge.[17]

What about the use of mother tongues? Knowledge is certainly important—use cannot occur without it—but it is use that implies active participation in those aspects of an ethnic culture that depend on language and in the forging of ethnic social boundaries through language. Nevertheless, few native-born whites speak a mother tongue on a regular basis: only 5 percent said that they use a mother tongue in their daily lives.[18] This small group does not represent even half of those with speaking knowledge.

Further, the contexts in which mother tongues are spoken indicate that this use is typically confined to a limited set of situations and that the erosion in knowledge of ethnic languages is continuing. We asked our respondents with whom they spoke a mother tongue. The group of speakers is quite small, thus any results must be taken as suggestive. About half of the speakers cited only one context in which the language was used ("with neighbors" or "with parents"). Also, about half named only relatives, indicating that mother-tongue speech is often confined to family settings. A fair number of respondents said that they speak a mother tongue only with their parents or with their parents and family members of their own generation. Few, just a quarter, indicated speaking a mother tongue

Table 3.7   Knowledge and use of a mother tongue
by ethnic identity status and importance of background

Ethnic identity status (ancestry type/identity type)	Background is		
	Very important	Somewhat important	Not important
% reporting any knowledge of an ethnic mother tongue			
single/single	55.0	41.7	9.7
multiple/single	46.7	20.9	16.7
multiple/multiple	29.4	38.1	12.2
non-identifying	21.6	26.8	11.1
% reporting any use of an ethnic mother tongue			
single/single	50.0	27.1	6.5
multiple/single	13.3	16.3	6.7
multiple/multiple	23.5	19.0	9.8
non-identifying	13.5	7.3	2.2

Significance levels: identity status × knowledge, $p < .05$
importance × knowledge, $p < .001$
identity status × use, $p < .001$
importance × use, $p < .001$

with their children. On this basis, it would appear that few children of our respondents will possess any fluency in a mother tongue.

The mixture of words and phrases from a mother tongue into English conversation is considerably more common than full-blown speech. But even this use is limited to about 15 percent of native-born whites.[19] The use of words and phrases seems to be a function of knowledge of a minority language: those who know more are more likely to use a mother tongue in this way. Two-thirds of those who claim to speak a mother tongue reported this kind of use. It is about equally common among persons who cannot speak a language but know ten or more words or phrases from one. But among those with knowledge of less than ten words or phrases, only about 40 percent intersperse English-language conversation with snatches from a mother tongue.

The number of people who use mother-tongue words and phrases represents only a small proportion of the population, but this use may be a significant indicator of ethnicity's salience for some. One reason for thinking so is that mother-tongue words and phrases are not generally confined to the family setting, unlike full-blown speech. The great majority of respondents citing this use named more than one type of person whom they address with ethnic words and phrases, and just a small minority named only family members. Outside of the family, friends and coworkers were the most commonly named. A second reason is its frequency of occurrence. For about half the group, this use occurs one or more times in the week (and for a fifth, it is a daily occurrence). The most frequent use, however, is disproportionately found among the diminishing group of persons who continue to speak a mother tongue on a regular basis.

Further speaking for the decline of language as a foundation for ethnic identity is that mother-tongue use of any sort is strongly related to ancestry and identity type. It is concentrated among the ethnically identifying persons of single ancestry (see table 3.6). Almost 10 percent of this group speaks a mother tongue at least occasionally, and another 20 percent or so use ethnic words and phrases when speaking English. Among the ethnically identifying of mixed ancestry, just 4 percent speak a mother tongue, and 11 percent more employ ethnic words and phrases in English speech. Use is even less common among those who do not identify in ethnic terms.

The use of a mother tongue is also strongly linked to the felt importance of ethnic background. This relationship is particularly prominent among ethnically identifying persons of single ancestry (see table 3.7). Among the members of this group who feel their ethnic backgrounds to be very important, half use a mother tongue in some way. At the other extreme, there is virtually no use of a mother tongue among the ethnically identifying of single ancestry who attach no importance to ethnic background—none of our respondents in this category reported speaking a mother tongue, and less than 10 percent said that they use words and phrases.

These relationships seem full of portent for the survival of European mother tongues, for languages cannot be sustained as purely private affairs. A minority language can be kept alive only when there is a critical mass of speakers to provide occasions for regular use and to socialize each new generation. For the languages brought by European immigrants, such conditions appear to be dissolving. Language knowledge and language use are largely concentrated among persons of single ancestry. As the proportion with mixed ancestral backgrounds increases, because of the high rates of intermarriage of the past few decades, knowledge of mother tongues will dwindle. So, too, will the opportunity to use a mother tongue, even for those who have the knowledge.

The decline of mother tongues may also have a powerful impact on the importance native-born whites attach to their ethnic origins. At least this is suggested by the strong relationship of mother-tongue use to perceived importance, since the use of a mother tongue, which has its origins extending back to childhood, almost certainly precedes and conditions a person's evaluation of the importance of ethnicity. Accordingly, as the number of mother-tongue users declines, so may the proportion for whom ethnicity is a salient concern.

Ethnic Customs

The maintenance of ethnic customs and traditions still appears to be part of the experience of a significant minority of native-born whites. But it is no doubt symptomatic of the ethnic flux among whites that many respondents who initially claimed to maintain customs and traditions seemed unsure which practices constitute them.[20] The experience of keeping customs and traditions was indicated by 21 percent of our respondents. But some of this group, when asked directly to describe the ethnic practices that they keep, were unable to identify any or even disclaimed keeping any. Others answered in terms of fidelity to religious, not ethnic, practices. This was especially true for religiously faithful Catholics, who described as ethnic customs their weekly Mass attendance, regular confession, and other observances.[21] Yet other respondents described what appear to be family traditions without ethnic overtones, such as gathering together on certain holidays. After the elimination of questionable responses, the proportion who keep some ethnic customs is 13 percent.

Moreover, the great majority who keep customs or traditions do so not as part of their everyday lives but only on a few major holidays during the year. Many respondents described their ethnic customs as limited to traditions on the most important religious holidays of the year, such as eating fish on Christmas Eve (an Italian custom), using traditional decorations, handed down within the family, on the Christmas tree, or maintaining a special Passover ritual. Other respondents mentioned customs associated with ethnic holidays, the majority of which are nominally religious holidays. One of the most important observances was St. Patrick's Day, mentioned by a quarter of all who keep some customs. This could be viewed as a religious holiday, but it is probably more often observed as an ethnic one, an occasion for the "wearing o' the green"; some, in fact, identified wearing green on St. Patrick's Day as their only cultural practice. Other ethnic holidays cited include Fasching (the German equivalent of Mardi Gras), Norwegian Liberation Day (seventeenth of May), and saints' feast days (observed by some Italians).

Few respondents identified customs not confined to holidays. Among those of Italian ancestry, there was an occasional mention of practices to ward off the *malocchio* ("evil eye"). A few respondents of Scots ancestry indicated wearing kilts at times. Finally, 13 percent of those who keep some customs (but only 2 percent of all native-born whites) referred to ethnic music or dancing.

Our respondents, then, did not describe a rich fabric of custom and ritual but a few symbolic practices that preserve some sense of ethnic identity. Few seem to want to maintain more. Two-thirds of those keeping customs told us that they did not want to keep more. Most said that they did enough or that additional customs would not be compatible with their lives.

The customs maintained are typically ones that were practiced by parents. Indeed, respondents gave this as the major reason that they maintain customs, although some respondents also cited their own enjoyment as important in determining their practices. Nevertheless, there is a definite sense of loss across the generations. Nearly 40 percent of the respondents who keep some customs said that they keep fewer than their parents did. Undoubtedly, had we put the question of parental practices to all respondents, and not just those who maintain some customs, the magnitude of intergenerational loss would appear even larger. Virtually no one claimed that their ethnic practices exceed those of their parents.

Perhaps because the notion of ethnic customs is unclear to many native-born whites, there is not a well-defined relationship between keeping customs and the status of a person's ethnic identity (see table 3.8). In fact, though the broad pattern of the relationship resembles those for ethnic food and languages, that is, ethnically identifying persons of single ancestry are more likely than others to keep some customs, the differences involved are so small that the relationship is not statistically significant.

Table 3.8   Ethnic customs and traditions by ethnic identity status
and subjective importance of background (% keeping any customs
or traditions)

Ethnic identity status (ancestry type/identity type)	All native-born whites	Importance of background		
		Very	Somewhat	None
single/single	16.5 ⎫			
multiple/single	13.6 ⎬	23.6	15.9	5.9
multiple/multiple	12.9 ⎭			
single/none	9.4 ⎫			
multiple/none	12.6 ⎬	13.5	14.6	8.9
unknown/none	0.0 ⎭			
Significance levels:	N.S.	identity status × customs, N.S. importance × customs, p < .01		

The relationship to the subjective importance of background is
more meaningful: the more salient ethnicity is to individuals, the
more likely they are to keep some customs. Twenty-four percent of
ethnic identifiers who feel their background to be very important
maintain some customs compared to just 6 percent of those who feel
it to be unimportant. Those who feel their background to be important are also more likely to want to keep additional customs. As with
food and language, there is a correspondence between cultural
practice and the salience of ethnic identity. The causal connection
between the two has not been proved, but almost certainly they are
mutually reinforcing. This might seem to suggest optimism for the
survival of ethnic cultural residues, but it also implies that any
further cultural decline is likely to impact negatively on the salience of ethnicity for many Americans of European ancestry.

Ethnic Festivals

> The German-American Club of Albany will ob-
> serve St. Patrick's Day with a dinner-dance on
> March 19.
> —ANNOUNCEMENT IN THE ALBANY TIMES-UNION
> (1988)

Attendance at ethnic festivals, the final culturally relevant experience on our list, is a reminder of group culture and an occasion for

its celebration. Over the course of a year, numerous ethnic celebrations occur in the Capital Region—some on a large scale, drawing participants from a broad area, and others on a much smaller one, perhaps not larger than a single neighborhood. The festivals represent the spectrum of ancestries in the region's population. Some of the better known ones celebrate groups whose roots in the region go back to the early period of its settlement by Europeans—the Pinksterfest, for example, recognizes Albany's Dutch origins. Other festivals, such as Oktoberfest, St. Anthony's Bazaar, and the Polka Festival, are connected with groups of more recent origin.[22]

There are also festivals, usually centered on foods, with an explicitly multiethnic character. In a sense, all ethnic festivals have become multiethnic. They draw typically on an audience that extends well beyond the boundaries of the group and frequently on ethnic elements unrelated to the explicit identities of the festivals themselves. It is not surprising, for example, to find Italian food stands at the German Oktoberfest or to see Tulip Queens whose family names are far removed from any Dutch traces. Increasingly, ethnic festivals have become celebrations of ethnicity itself rather than of a particular ethnic heritage, and in this way they can be enjoyed by everyone, regardless of ethnic background.

Accordingly, attending ethnic festivals is a relatively common experience among native-born whites in the Capital Region. Twenty-seven percent of our respondents indicated attending at least one such festival within the preceding five years, and 17 percent said that they do so at least once a year.

Curiously, the relationship between festival attendance and ethnic identity status is very tenuous. Given that such attendance, unlike the practice of ethnic customs, is a clearly identifiable, discrete event, this tenuousness suggests that mere attendance frequently lacks an ethnic character and can be quite casual, rooted in sociability and the limited alternatives available on an evening or weekend afternoon out. Among the ethnically identifying of single ancestry, 30 percent acknowledge some festival attendance (see table 3.9), and 21 percent assert that they attend festivals at least once a year. The figures are very similar among the ethnically identifying of mixed ancestry but fall off only modestly among the nonidentifying, 19 percent of whom have attended one or more festivals and 11 percent of whom do so at least once a year. Once again,

Table 3.9 Festival attendance by ethnic identity status
and subjective importance of background (% attending any festival)

Ethnic identity status (ancestry type/identity type)	All native-born whites	Importance of background		
		Very	Somewhat	None
single/single	29.8 ⎫			
multiple/single	35.2 ⎬	36.1	39.1	16.7
multiple/multiple	28.7 ⎭			
single/none	18.8 ⎫			
multiple/none	22.3 ⎬	35.1	17.1	13.3
unknown/none	0.0 ⎭			
Significance levels:	p < .05	identity status × festivals, p < .05 importance × festivals, p < .001		

though, the relationship to ethnicity's salience is stronger. Among
ethnic identifiers who attach at least some importance to their
background, more than a third reported attending an ethnic festival, compared to just 17 percent among those who view their
backgrounds as unimportant.

Practicing ethnic customs and attending ethnic festivals appear to have a very different character from eating ethnic foods and
using a mother tongue. The differences are at least partly due to
regularity: food and language are part of ordinary experience, and
even if their ethnic dimension is not present on an everyday basis, it
generally is on a regular one. This regularity may help to account for
the strong and consistent relationships these experiences display
with ethnic identity status and salience. Practicing ethnic customs
and attending ethnic festivals seem to be part of a thinner and much
more occasional stratum of ethnic experience. These experiences
therefore do not have relationships to identity that are as clearly
delineated as those associated with ethnic foods and language.

Other Influences

By and large, the same influences that play important roles in determining the level of ethnic identity, such as generational status and
educational attainment, affect the cultural experiences. Because of

their correlation with each other, their effects are best seen in the form of a logistic regression analysis,[23] which also includes two indicators of ethnic identity, identity status and the salience or importance attached to ethnic background, as well as occasional other variables as needed. (The discussion that follows is based on far too many regression equations to show them all, but several of the most important ones, exemplifying patterns discussed in the text, are presented in table 3.10.) The analyses clarify that differences in cultural loyalty among identity types are not much explained by other factors, for in every equation one or both of the identity indicators plays a significant role.

Aside from ethnic identity, the dominant forces for cultural experience are largely demographic in character, and the most theoretically significant is generational status. Its presence in the equations addresses issues surrounding the relationship between ethnic cultural experience and generational distance from the point of immigration into the United States. This relationship represents a major question mark for the future of cultural diversity among the descendants of the European immigrants. On the one hand, contemporary ethnic cultural experience can be seen as a matter of cultural "survivals," residues of the immigrant culture suitably modified to fit American patterns. This view lends itself to the expectation that cultural experience is inevitably eroded across the generations: indeed, the so-called straight-line theory of ethnicity (Sandberg, 1974; Gans, 1979; Crispino, 1980) predicts a weakening of ethnic forms with each generation. If such a linear relationship holds, then the contemporary existence of ethnic cultural diversity among whites of European background results from the still large size of the second and third generations and will fade as these groups dwindle in size. On the other hand, it has been argued that ethnic cultures are as much a product of American experiences as they are of Old World importations (Glazer and Moynihan, 1970; Yancey et al., 1976; Greeley, 1977). This argument implies that there is no inevitable attrition of an ethnic culture across generations, as long as members of an ethnic group share a more or less similar set of American conditions and experiences.

The patterns of generational variation in the data are broadly consistent with the straight-line theory, although the fit is not perfect, and the strength of generational differences varies across the cultural experiences of food, language, and festival attendance. (Generation does not have a statistically significant relationship to the maintenance of ethnic customs; perhaps the lack of clarity in the notion of such customs for many respondents interferes with the ability to detect a generational pattern.)

The strongest generational relationship exists with respect to language (this is clearer in the logit coefficients than in their translation into percentages). With other influences controlled, there is a steep drop-off in knowledge and use of a mother tongue between the second and later generations. According to the logit equation in table 3.10, for example, members of the third generation are 28 percentage points less likely than members of the second to know at least ten mother-tongue words and phrases.[24] This is an extremely large difference given that only 17 percent of all native-born whites has this level of knowledge to begin with. The drop-off continues into the fourth and later generations, and generational differences are close to the same order of magnitude when it comes to using a mother tongue.

Differences across the generations are almost as strong with respect to the eating of ethnic foods. There is a steady decline in the consumption of ethnic foods between the second and fourth generations, with members of the fourth generation 25 percentage points less likely than members of the second to report eating any ethnic foods. The generational difference is nearly as large for eating ethnic foods monthly or more frequently. Thus, the most important implication of straight-line theory, an attrition of cultural survivals with increasing generational distance from immigrant origins, does seem to hold.

Age is a second demographic factor influencing cultural experience. Its influence is especially critical to the extent that age differences can be interpreted as indexing historical variations in the experiences of different cohorts, thus pointing to future changes arising from cohort succession. But the interpretation of age differences is not inevitably straightforward. Cultural experience may not only differ among age groups because of their different exposures to and deeply engrained degrees of loyalty to ethnic cultures—the cohort factor rooted in systemic, historical change—but also because of variations over the life course. That there must be some variation due to aging seems obvious: the elderly in particular

Table 3.10   Selected logit analyses of ethnic cultural indicators

| | Eating ethnic foods | | | |
| | at all | | at least monthly | |
	logit coefficients	% change at mean	logit coefficients	% change at mean
Generation:	p < .01		p < .01	
second	+.784	+19.0	+.712	+16.5
third	+.258	+6.4	+.609	+14.0
fourth	−.243	−6.0	−.142	−2.9
unknown	−.799	−18.5	−1.179	−18.1
Age:	p < .01		p < .05	
under 30	+.686	+16.8	+.575	+13.2
30–44	+.085	+2.1	+.201	+4.3
45–59	−.126	−3.1	−.192	−3.8
60+	−.645	−15.2	−.584	−10.6
Sex	N.S.		N.S.	
Education	N.S.		N.S.	

	Column 1			Column 2		
		$p < .01$			$p < .05$	
Confidence about ancestry knowledge:						
confident	+.521		+12.9	+.556		+12.7
uncertain	−.521		−12.5	−.556		−10.2
Living with parents:		not included			not included	
yes						
no						
Other relatives near:		not included			$p < .10$	
yes				+.306		+6.7
no				−.306		−6.0
Ethnic identity status:		$p < .05$			$p < .001$	
single/single	+.681		+16.7	+.943		+22.3
multiple/single	+.067		+1.7	−.330		−6.4
multiple/multiple	−.187		−4.6	−.268		−5.3
single/none	−.435		−10.5	−.623		−11.2
multiple/none	−.126		−3.1	+.278		+6.1
Importance of background	+.262	$p < .10$	+6.5	+.640	$p < .001$	+14.8
Identity status-importance interaction	+.421	$p < .01$	+10.5		not included	
χ^2	84.78 with 15 degrees of freedom ($p < .001$)			84.52 with 15 degrees of freedom ($p < .001$)		

(continued)

109

Table 3.10 (Continued)

| | Mother-tongue indicators | | | | |
| | Knowing 10+ words and phrases | | Using mother tongue at all | | |
	logit coefficients	% change at mean	logit coefficients	% change at mean
Generation:	p < .001		p < .01	
second	+1.260	+24.6	+1.040	+18.9
third	−.239	−3.0	−.238	−2.9
fourth	−.618	−6.9	−.731	−7.5
unknown	−.403	−4.8	−.071	−0.9
Age:	N.S.		N.S.	
under 30				
30–44				
45–59				
60+				
Sex	N.S.		N.S.	
Education	+.328	+5.0	+.262	+3.8
	p < .05		p < .10	
Confidence about ancestry	N.S.		N.S.	
knowledge				
Living with parents:	p < .05		p < .01	
yes	+.569	+9.4	+.895	+15.7
no	−.569	−6.4	−.895	−8.7

	Model 1		Model 2	
Other relatives near	not included		not included	
British ancestry only:	p < .001		p < .01	
yes	−1.362	−11.7	−1.652	−12.4
no	+1.362	+27.1	+1.652	+33.7
Ethnic identity status:	p < .05		p < .01	
single/single	+.830	+14.7	+1.133	+21.1
multiple/single	−.057	−0.8	−.086	−1.1
multiple/multiple	−.337	−4.1	+.340	+5.1
single/none	−.130	−1.7	−.921	−8.9
multiple/none	−.306	−3.8	−.466	−5.3
Importance of background	+.465	+7.4	+.872	+15.2
	p < .05		p < .001	
Identity status-importance interaction	not included		not included	
χ^2	106.24 with 16 degrees of freedom (p < .001)		110.90 with 16 degrees of freedom (p < .001)	

Notes: Persons of unknown ancestry ($N = 15$) are excluded because of their small number and low rate of participation in these experiences.

    N.S. indicates that a variable was included in an equation but was not statistically significant. Some ancillary variables are not included in equations where they are not significant.

    Coding of noncategorical variables: Importance of background ranges from $+1$ (very important) to -1 (not important). Education ranges from 5 (college graduate) to 1 (grammar school education only).

    Means of dependent variables: eating ethnic foods (47.0%); eating ethnic foods at least once a month (29.6%); knowing ten or more words and phrases (16.5%); using a mother tongue (15.9%).

are likely to have less opportunity for some of these experiences, such as attendance at ethnic festivals.

Because of this interpretive ambiguity, the age differences in cultural experience seem less clear-cut in their meaning than do the generational ones. For one important type of experience—namely, language—there is no relationship to age, net of the other influences taken into account in the analysis. But for the other experiences, substantial relationships to age exist, although their meaning remains ambiguous. In general, the young are more likely to report food, custom, and festival experiences, and there are relatively sharp breaks between young adults, that is, persons under the age of thirty, and their elders and also between persons aged sixty and older and everybody else; for instance, according to the coefficients in table 3.10, young adults are about 15 percentage points more likely to eat some ethnic foods than are persons between the ages of thirty and forty-four, and they are roughly 30 points more likely to do so in comparison to those sixty and older. In terms of festival attendance, young adults are about 10 percentage points more likely to go to at least one festival a year than are members of the next oldest age group, and nearly 20 points more likely than members of the oldest group.

Several sorts of forces seem to be at work here. One is certainly the decline of some experiences due to aging—a decline that is especially prominent among elderly persons. Indeed, the overall level of ethnic experience in general is markedly lower among the elderly. Undoubtedly, advanced age is associated with diminished opportunity for some kinds of experience as well as with settled patterns of routine that tend to preclude taking advantage of experiences that occur only occasionally. In the preparation of ethnic foods, for instance, the elderly may confront difficulties in shopping for necessary ingredients, particularly unusual ones sold only in specialty shops, and also in carrying out any complicated recipes demanding lengthy preparation times. Restricted travel, especially at night, limits their involvement in ethnic festivals.

A simple life-cycle factor may also be at work at the other end of the age spectrum. Young adults are still close to their parents' home and culture—in fact, a significant number of our young-adult respondents were still living with their parents at the time they were interviewed. Such proximity suggests that the level of ethnic experience may decline as young adults establish their own households and as their contact with the older generation is reduced.

But closeness to parents does not seem sufficient to explain the relatively high levels of some of these experiences among young adults (controlling for living with parents does little to reduce age differences in the consumption of ethnic foods, for example). Thus, there must be something else involved. One possibility is that young adults have a greater sensitivity to ethnic dimensions of experience, if not also a greater involvement in ethnic experience, than other age groups. This sensitivity to ethnicity could be a result of the greater attention Americans have paid to the diversity of their ethnic origins since the mid-1960s. This, in other words, could be a genuine cohort effect, a reflection of the affirmations of ethnic diversity to which young adults have been exposed throughout their lives, in contrast to the emphasis on assimilation and the melting pot dominant when their parents were growing up.[25] But another possibility is that the lives of young adults are still unsettled—they are more available for certain kinds of experience, such as festival attendance and eating ethnic foods in restaurants, both of which are compatible with youthful gregariousness. Moreover, many young adults have not yet reached the point when considerations of career and family overshadow other identities; there is, then, less competition with ethnic identities and activities. But both of these alternatives seem inconsistent with the absence of any age effect on ethnic identity and its salience (see chapter 2). In the final analysis, the relationship between age and experience remains ambiguous. Whether and how much it is due to cohort versus life-cycle variations cannot be determined.

Besides generation and age, other influences are less powerful. A principal case in point, given its prominence in the analysis of ethnic identity, is education. It is unrelated to the maintenance of customs, attendance at festivals, or the consumption of ethnic foods (with the exception of a positive relationship to using food to celebrate special occasions, which is not shown in table 3.10). The one area where education has substantial impact is language. Although it is not related, net of other factors, to having a speaking knowledge of a mother tongue, education does positively influence the knowledge of words and phrases. The full range of its effect is revealed by a comparison of its extreme categories (not shown explicitly in the table): college graduates are about 25 percentage points more likely than persons with only a grade school education to know at least ten mother-tongue words and phrases. No doubt, the greater knowledge of the more highly educated reflects formal study of a mother tongue by some respondents as well as a more general exposure to cosmopolitan forms of culture. Education also has a positive impact on use of a mother tongue. Though the influence of education on ethnic language demonstrates anew that expressions of ethnicity are not just a working-class style, evidence of a generalized interest in ethnic cultural codes among the highly educated is missing.

The analyses also reveal a linkage between familism and ethnic culture: embeddedness in family networks helps to sustain cultural patterns connected with food and language. This is implied by two variables, although each is included, based on statistical criteria, in only a few equations. One is living with parents or grandparents, which has a sizable effect on virtually all the language indicators; for example, living in the parental home increases by 16 percentage points the probability of knowing ten or more words and phrases of a mother tongue, and it lifts the probability of using a mother tongue by almost 25 points. It follows that departure from the parental home decreases substantially the probability of significant knowledge of a mother tongue and, more so, the probability of its use, even in a limited sense. The influence of this variable underscores, then, the erosion of the fragile base of mother tongues among the European-ancestry groups. These languages are concentrated among the early generations in the United States and are weakened as contact with these generations declines.

Living in the vicinity of relatives has modest effects on some of the food indicators. This makes good sense in terms of the role food plays within kinship networks, even when kin are not living under the same roof. It suggests further that patterns of socializing with relatives help to keep ethnic food traditions alive. Living near relatives raises the probability of eating ethnic foods at least once a month by 13 percentage points, and it also increases the probability of preparing ethnic foods at home (not shown in table 3.10).

Other factors that appeared consequential in the analysis of ethnic identity—notably, confidence in the knowledge of one's ancestry and gender—are less important here. Confidence in ancestry knowledge is primarily related to food experiences; for instance, persons who are unsure of their ancestry are 25 percentage points less likely than others to eat ethnic foods at all. Gender's effects are the most modest, and it is statistically significant in just a few equations. One example is the use of ethnic foods to celebrate special occasions, which is more likely to be reported by women—but by just a 10-point margin, net of other factors.

Finally, we come to the role of ethnic identity in the equations. It bears repeating that ambiguity surrounds this role, since ethnic identity is not only capable of influencing these cultural behaviors, but also of being influenced by them. This sort of reciprocal influence is not modeled in the equations (and, indeed, it would be very difficult to do so). Its absence means that the coefficients of the identity variables should not be construed as direct influences on the cultural indicators, but as relationships between identity and its cultural expressions, net of the other factors controlled in the equations.

With this interpretation in mind, one sees that the relationships of ethnic identity status to the various cultural indicators remain much as described earlier, where other factors were not controlled. Ethnic identity status has statistically significant relationships to food and language indicators, but not to the maintenance of ethnic customs or attendance at ethnic festivals. For both food and language, the principal contrast lies between the ethnically identifying of single ancestry and other identity categories, and the differences involved are sizable; for example, the differences in monthly consumption of ethnic foods generally range between 15 and 30 percentage points, and those for use of a mother tongue are of the same magnitude.

Even larger differences tend to be associated with the subjective importance of ethnic background, the salience factor, which plays a significant and generally powerful role in all the equations. Because the variable is scaled from -1 (not important) to $+1$ (very important),[26] the full range of its relationship is revealed by doubling the logit coefficients presented in table 3.10; for example, in the case of eating ethnic foods monthly or more frequently, the difference between those holding their ethnic background to be very important and those giving it no importance is about 30 percentage points, net of other variables. A similar difference occurs for use of a mother tongue.

The differences associated with subjective importance also vary somewhat between identifiers and nonidentifiers, as one ought to expect, since the meaning of ethnic background is presumably not the same in the two groups. This distinction is tested by a statistical interaction between ethnic identity status and subjective importance, and the interaction is significant in two equations—for eating ethnic foods in general and for eating them at home (only the first is shown in table 3.10). In both cases, the interaction can be interpreted as indicating that subjective importance corresponds with large cultural differences among the ethnically identifying but not among nonidentifiers.[27] Since such an interpretation is plausible for other cultural experiences as well, the question can be raised as to why the interaction is not statistically significant elsewhere. The answer may lie in the fact that the interaction is significant for the two cultural indicators that occur the most frequently (and hence have the greatest variance[28]). Thus, the relatively small size of the survey and the limited frequency of occurrence of other cultural experiences probably hinders detection of the interaction in other equations.

Ethnic Groups

The cultural expressions of identity vary considerably among ethnic groups, and these variations are of great consequence for what appears on the ethnic surface of American life. In particular, the critical nature of the interaction between the individual's propensity to identify in ethnic terms and the collective properties of the group stands out; and especially intriguing is the interaction's supply side—the cultural resources the group provides for identity. For the more vital cultural expressions among some groups imply that their members, even those of later generations or with mixed ancestry, are more likely than their counterparts from other groups to be exposed to some remnants of their cultural backgrounds and to encounter frequent reminders of their ethnic origins, with further consequences for the construction of their identities. In general, cultural expressions are most prominent among the more recently arrived European groups, that is, those with southern and eastern European origins, although the pattern is complicated by factors such as group size and the prestige and acceptability of an ethnic culture. Moreover, for some ancestries—for example, Dutch and Scots—even ethnically interested persons would have difficulty locating the cultural materials needed to give substance to their inner orientations.

The ethnic variations in cultural survivals are illustrated by cuisine. Loyalty to an ethnic cuisine is strongest for the most recently arrived European ethnic groups—their culinary traditions are still quite powerful. By contrast, high percentages of old-stock ancestry groups say that they do not eat ethnic foods, and few acknowledge eating them with any regularity. Undoubtedly greater percentages of these groups do in fact eat ethnic foods, particularly those that have found their way into American cooking, such as frankfurters or corned beef and cabbage. But for most of their members, these foods are no longer ethnic and thus no longer serve an ethnicity-preserving function.

But even among the groups whose culinary traditions retain some vitality, there is a sense of decline in the quality of ethnic foods—perhaps this sense exists *because* of the vitality of culinary traditions and the memories of the food prepared by preceding generations. About 40 percent of the Italians and Poles who eat ethnic foods said that these foods have deteriorated from their parents' days. The perception of a decline is more prevalent in these groups than it is in others, no doubt because the Italians and Poles have been more exposed to culinary traditions in their original form.

The details are somewhat different but the overall pattern of a concentration of cultural resources in a recently arrived group is repeated for the maintenance of ethnic customs and traditions. Persons of Italian ancestry are about twice as likely as those of most other backgrounds to report keeping some ethnic customs—about 20 percent, compared to 10 to 12 percent, or even less, in most other ancestry groups. The Irish are the second most likely to keep some traditions, owing to the continued popularity of St. Patrick's Day observance. For both the Irish and the Italians, maintenance of customs appears to be especially concentrated among the ethnically identifying of undivided background—among the Italians, for instance, a third of the members of this category describe some customs they maintain. But, as with the quality of ethnic foods, the sense of a decline in comparison with the parental generation is quite prevalent among the Italians (although not so much among the Irish, whose parents presumably also limited their customs to the observance of St. Patrick's Day). About half of the Italians who keep some customs say that they keep fewer than their parents did.

Somewhat different from both cuisine and customs are the ethnic patterns in language maintenance. The recency of a group's arrival is important here too; but since the retention of language hinges on opportunities to use it and thus on the number of others who speak it, the sizes of groups affect mother-tongue survival, as undoubtedly do other factors, such as the prestige associated with a language and its culture.

Of the European immigrant languages surviving among the Capital Region's residents, the most prominent in numbers are French, German, and Italian. In terms of current speaking knowledge, Italian is the most frequently cited: 23 percent of the ancestry group can still speak the mother tongue, although just 10 percent acknowledge speaking it in their daily lives. Moreover, speaking knowledge is heavily concentrated among persons of unmixed Italian ancestry and appears to represent a substantial decline from the previous generation, since nearly 40 percent of the ancestry group say that Italian was a language spoken in their childhood home. The current level of knowledge thus appears to be only about half of what it was in the preceding generation.

Nevertheless, this level of childhood exposure, greater than that for any other European ethnic group, may be significant as an indicator of a broader exposure to ethnic culture and experience and hence part of the explanation for the relatively greater strength of ethnic feelings and identity apparent among persons of Italian ancestry. This exposure is reflected in a knowledge of mother-tongue words and phrases among those who can no longer speak the language, for this is markedly greater among the Italians than among other groups. Overall, 34 percent of the ancestry group claims knowledge of some words and phrases; added to the portion of the group that retains a speaking knowledge, the figure indicates that almost 60 percent of the entire ancestry group has some familiarity with the mother tongue.[29] But even among the Italians, the knowledge of words and phrases is often quite fragmentary, and the majority of those who claim it say they know fewer than ten words.

Language loyalty is much lower among those of French and German ancestry than among the Italians, but these languages also show lower intergenerational losses than Italian does. About 10 percent of the French ancestry group claims a current speaking knowledge of French, and 8 percent of persons of German background can still speak their mother tongue. (The percentages of these groups who do speak in their mother tongues on a regular basis are of course much lower—between 2 and 3 percent.) But while the ability to speak a mother tongue is infrequent among the French and Germans, small proportions of these two ancestry groups were exposed to one in the first place (only 13 percent of the French and 10 percent of the Germans). Accordingly, the rate of intergenerational shift toward English is lower for these groups than for the Italians.

The contrast between Italian, on the one hand, and French and German, on the other, appears to correspond to a phenomenon noted by Calvin Veltman (1983) in his study of language shift. An immigrant language typically loses adherents very rapidly during the early generations in the United States—this is the situation of Italian—but then the rate of loss often subsides and the population speaking the language becomes more stable in size. The mother tongue is carried on by "language islands," which generally represent just a small proportion of the overall ethnic group and also continue to suffer losses, albeit at a reduced rate. Given the large number of French and German speakers who were once present in the United States, the phenomenon of language islands may best correspond with the experiences of very large groups, who, even after the initial heavy erosion of the mother tongue, retain sufficient numbers of speakers to support the institutional structure—schools, newspapers, and so forth—needed to socialize fully a new generation of speakers.

But outside of the language islands, familiarity with French and German appears to be less widespread than is familiarity with Italian. Only 13 percent of the overall French ancestry group and 17 percent of the German indicate a knowledge of words and phrases, as distinct from a full speaking knowledge. In other words, about three-quarters of the members of these two ancestry groups indicate no knowledge of any mother tongue. And as is generally the case, those who know words and phrases typically know just a few: about two-thirds estimate their knowledge at fewer than ten words or phrases.

The comparison between Italians and these older groups suggests a general direction of future cultural change. For the current prominence of cultural expressions among such groups as the Italians is not likely, in light of demographic trends, to be enduring. These groups still have large numbers of second- and third-generation members with undivided ethnic heritage, but this is changing rapidly as a result of such forces as generational succession and the high intermarriage rates in the post-World War II era. Cultural expressions seem certain to pale as the groups come to resemble older ethnic groups in demographic terms. But whether they will fade as completely as they have for some old-stock groups such as the Dutch and Scots is certainly open to question. There is an in-between possibility, represented by the language islands of the French and Germans. Thus, "cultural islands," in the form of neighborhoods and networks representing just small portions of the ancestry groups, may continue to generate cultural "supplies" for other group members. These can serve as a stimulus for ethnic identity, but the gradual erosion of cultural stock is likely to diminish, overall, the possibilities for ethnic identification on the part of people with ancestry from the newer groups. They may be less and less likely to find cultural echoes of any interest they may feel in their ethnic origins. As chapter 2 shows, after all, French and German usually are not the foci for intense identities.

Summary

Probably no aspect of ethnic experience is more critical to the survival of ethnicity in the United States than culture, when taken in the broadest sense to include the mundane, everyday behaviors and rituals that help to distinguish members of one social group from those of another. Culture's cardinal importance stems in part from its contribution to features that signal group membership in social interaction. Equally important, culture can define a heritage viewed as the essence of a group and thereby create a rationale for preserving an ethnic connection. Ethnicity is then justified as a way of preserving traditions handed down by forebears.

My investigation of cultural expressions of ethnic identity is premised on the transformation of ethnicity. The reduction in group inequalities and the massive intermingling across ethnic lines (in the native-born white population) highlight the role of *visible* cultural features that are *socially recognized* as ethnic, for these can serve as badges of ethnic membership and commitment in the many social situations where ethnic background and its meaning cannot be taken for granted by participants. In focusing on such cultural forms as food, language, and customs, I am not denying that ethnic cultural heritages can also have less overt manifestations, in impacts on personality and values (Greeley and McCready, 1975; Schooler, 1976; McGoldrick, 1982). But I suspect that these subtler effects are not likely to form a basis for ethnic bonding—in general, they lack the quality of visibility. (Ethnic differences in families and in anything touching on the family may be a significant exception.)

The analysis affirms the critical role of culture, for it reveals a frequently close linkage between ethnic identity and cultural expression, particularly in the areas of food and language. Adherence to ethnic culture is most frequently found among ethnic identifiers, especially those of undivided ethnic background, and varies strikingly with the subjective importance of ethnicity. It seems almost certain that some mutual influence is involved: persons who identify in ethnic terms are more likely to seek out cultural expressions for their feelings; at the same time, those exposed to, or involved in, cultural activities, have more occasion to perceive themselves in ethnic terms and identify accordingly. This mutual influence underscores the repeated theme of the interaction between the identities of individuals and the collective features of groups. Groups that have a greater supply of cultural resources provide their members with more material to stimulate a sense of identity. Conversely, these groups also depend on that sense of identity; without it, the critical mass necessary to maintain the ethnic cultural supply would dissipate.

Yet it is hard to be sanguine about ethnic culture as a long-term basis for ethnic identity. Even in their contemporary extent, let alone their future one, it is difficult to see the cultural expressions of identity as more than a fragile and thin layer alloyed to a larger body of common American culture, with its complex class and place variants. Two cultural domains stand out for their potential to provide an everyday basis in experience for ethnic identities—namely, cuisine and language. In the case of language, it is apparent that knowledge and use of a mother tongue are concentrated in diminishing parts of the white population—such as persons of ethnically undivided background, members of the second generation, and their children who still live at home. The explanatory power of living with parents (in table 3.10) suggests how greatly language behavior depends on frequent contact with the generation that still uses mother tongues to any degree. My examination of language goes well beyond prior studies because it takes account of limited knowledge and use of a mother tongue—of words and phrases that can appear as an ethnic garnish in English speech—that are still capable of signaling ethnic membership and contributing to feelings of solidarity based on ethnicity. The analysis reveals that even this limited capability is waning.

By contrast, some ethnic cuisines appear quite vital; and the consumption of ethnic foods is, by a good margin, the most widespread of all the ethnic experiences we inquired about. The significance of food for ethnic continuance is enhanced by the incorporation of many ethnic foods and their tastes into American cooking, which increasingly celebrates its ethnic diversity. But even granting that ethnic cuisine is here to stay, there is evidence of cultural weakening in this domain, too. Ethnic food consumption generally and the ceremonial use of food specifically, to celebrate holidays and other special occasions, are most common among a group representing a declining part of the population—namely, the ethnically identifying of single ancestry. Further, they decline across the generations. Given this weakening of ethnic food traditions and the incorporation, as well as dilution, of ethnic foods into American cooking, one has to wonder if the occasional eating of ethnic foods is sufficient to preserve a sense of ethnic identity, unless there are also other salient domains of experience in which ethnicity is prominent.

Neither of the other two experiences analyzed seems capable of filling the gap. Attendance at ethnic festivals is a sporadic event—only one of every six native-born whites attends festivals at least once a year. Moreover, many of these festivals are no longer strongly tied to the presence of an ethnic community (which, in many cases, is long since dispersed), and their ethnic character has weakened over time so that they include a variety of contradictory ethnic elements (Italian foods at the Oktoberfest) and draw an audience well beyond the boundaries of the ethnic group. Perhaps the best that can be said is that festivals are frequently occasions for celebrating ethnicity per se. But stating their role in this way does much to illuminate the direction of ethnic change among whites.

Equally illuminating are the vague notions many native-born whites have about ethnic customs. A substantial number of our respondents who initially indicated keeping some ethnic customs described practices that do not appear ethnic but are family traditions and religious observances. And most of the customs that are kept are fully compatible with what Herbert Gans (1979) describes as "symbolic ethnicity"—they are practices that add some ethnic flourishes to major holidays, such as special foods served at Christmas and Passover. Like ethnic food in general, the ethnic customs our respondents described form cultural patterns that are quite appropriate in ethnically integrated social settings, where the great majority of our respondents, like most Americans of European ancestry, are found.

Ethnicity's Shadow in Social Experience

The Jew thus finds himself in a paradoxical
situation: it is perfectly all right for him to gain
a reputation for honesty, just as others do and
in the same ways, but this reputation is added
to a primary reputation—that of being a Jew—
which has been imposed on him at one stroke
and from which he cannot free himself no
matter what he may do. . . . Let him multiply
acts of disinterestedness and honesty, and perhaps he will be called a *good* Jew. But Jew he is
and must remain.

—JEAN-PAUL SARTRE
(1948: 74; emphasis in original)

Culture is not the only realm where ethnicity can be manifested. When ethnic
identities are salient, they cast shadows
over much of experience; the tints of the
ordinary social world are altered by their
presence. Encounters with others, for in-
stance, can be shaped by the ethnic identities of the participants,
with a sense of commonality and even kinship quick to spring out of
common identity and one of indifference, wary distance, or even
hostility out of dissimilar ethnic backgrounds. Persons who hold
ethnicity to be important may also be prompt in perceiving ethnic
slights, in seeing the actions of others as deriving from prejudice or
involving discriminatory intent.

This chapter continues to explore areas of experience in which
ethnic identities may find expression. I begin by considering ethnicity's influence on everyday social interaction and then on encounters with prejudice and discrimination, followed by ethnicity's

reflection in the political sphere and a few miscellaneous but infrequent experiences, such as travel to ancestral homelands.

Sensitivity to Ethnicity in the Quotidian Social World

Wherever ethnicity is important, it is a salient feature of the everyday social world. Ethnicity potentially divides the universe of ordinary social interaction between those with whom one shares a common origin, or at least some similarity of origin, and those who are ethnically different. In societies where ethnicity represents a fundamental social cleavage, ethnic divisions have concrete and often powerful repercussions for ordinary social life. Trust, for example, may be largely limited to one's fellow ethnics, and interactions across ethnic boundaries may be marked by some degree of suspicion or wariness. This characterization is not only applicable to societies like Lebanon and Northern Ireland, where ethnic divisions take on a life-or-death significance: Gerald Suttles' study, *The Social Order of the Slum*, shows that trustful interaction in a lower-class Chicago neighborhood tended to be confined to people of the same ethnic background. His study, conducted during the 1960s, is brought up to date by recent news reports, which show that, in some major American cities, straying into the wrong neighborhood at night can be punished by verbal abuse, beating, and even death.[1]

On a less violent note, an orientation toward interaction with others who share one's background must be regarded as a defining property of an ethnic *group*.[2] Without some tendency to draw social distinctions based on ethnic background, it is impossible to achieve any degree of solidarity, which is properly seen as an aspect of ethnicity with broad social import, the foundation of ethnic collective action (Olzak, 1983; Nielsen, 1985). But ethnically based interaction is increasingly problematic for whites in the United States. Intermarriage rates demonstrate that ethnic divisions are hardly rigid among European ancestry groups. As a practical matter, ethnic integration has been achieved in the most intimate of social relations. By implication, it must have occurred in many other relational spheres as well; otherwise, the cross-ethnic contacts leading to marriage would never take place.

For any sort of ethnic bond, high levels of ethnic integration pose problems that are not found in societies where ethnicity is reflected in rigidly segregated social realms. In an ethnically homogeneous environment, the individual is embedded—independently of his or her own conscious intent—in ethnic networks and other social structures supportive of ethnicity. In the United States, however, everyday interaction brings an individual into contact with people of diverse backgrounds. The ethnic origins of these others may not even be apparent. Name changes through intermarriage and anglicization and the attenuation, if not disappearance, of overt behavioral indicators make ethnic origins frequently difficult to guess. This is true not only for people whose ethnic backgrounds differ from one's own but even for those from the same background. Even when origins are known, ethnic identities need not be. Given, for instance, the frequency of mixed ethnic backgrounds, how—or whether—a person identifies ethnically cannot be presumed from knowledge of his or her ethnic ancestry. Nor can the significance that ethnicity holds for him or her. In short, even the knowledge that another comes from the same, or a similar, ethnic background as oneself does not permit the presumption that the basis for a special bond exists.

In light of the ethnic flux among whites, the American setting imposes sensitivity to the ethnic backgrounds of others on the person who regards ethnicity as a matter of personal importance. A person who is oriented toward establishing relationships based on common ethnic background is forced to be alert for frequently unobtrusive indicators of ethnic background, if not to ask directly about it. But even when backgrounds turn out to be the same, some discussion of ethnicity may be necessary to establish whether common ethnic origin can contribute to a relationship.

Accordingly, examining the role of ethnicity in the quotidian social world of American whites involves not simply looking for relationships where common ethnic background may play a role but also for sensitivity to ethnicity as a dimension of ordinary social life. The list of ethnic experiences (table 3.1) is helpful in both respects. In particular, respondents were asked: whether they ever felt curious about the ethnic backgrounds of others; whether they discussed their own ethnic backgrounds with others; and whether they felt a special sense of relationship to others who shared their ethnic background. About half of native-born whites indicated at least one of these experiences, and a quarter indicated at least two of them. In fact, two of the three experiences—feeling curiosity about others' ethnic backgrounds and discussing one's own ethnic background— are among those most often mentioned by our respondents, each cited by about a third of native-born whites. Feeling a special sense of relationship based on common ethnic background was also relatively frequently indicated, checked by a fifth of respondents.

Despite the commonness of these experiences, they do not seem to reflect a preoccupation with ethnicity for most respondents who report them. Feelings of curiosity about the backgrounds of others can serve as the revealing illustration here, for such feelings are obviously a sine qua non of ethnic consciousness as a way of orienting oneself to the social world. According to those respondents who acknowledge having them, such feelings typically are not very frequent (see table 4.1). Respondents who said that they have such feelings "hardly ever" or "occasionally" outnumbered those who have them "often" or "all the time" by more than two to one.[3] (The "occasional" category accounts for the lion's share, indicated by about 60 percent.) Putting this another way, only 9 percent of all native-born whites feel frequently curious about the ethnic backgrounds of others; for the other 91 percent, such feelings either do not occur or are not more than an occasional stirring of interest.

Feelings of curiosity are also not necessarily acted on. A quarter of persons acknowledging such feelings said that they do not ask people directly about their ethnic backgrounds. Among those who do, people who ask just occasionally (or rarely) again outnumber those more frequently concerned about ethnic backgrounds by a wide margin—in this case, better than three to one.

Discussions of their own ethnic backgrounds are also not regarded by most respondents as frequent occurrences. In asking about such discussions, we offered respondents a different set of frequencies ("a lot," "sometimes," "infrequently"), not directly comparable to those for feelings of curiosity. Half of the respondents reporting the experience indicated it as infrequent, and virtually all the rest described it as occurring "sometimes." Just 8 percent of these respondents (about 3 percent of native-born whites) said that they discuss their ethnic backgrounds "a lot." As with feelings of

Table 4.1   Frequencies of experiences of sensitivity to ethnicity in the everyday social world among native-born whites

	Feel curious about the ethnic background of someone else	*Ask about ethnic background*
No experience	68.5%	76.9%
Hardly ever	3.0	3.3
Occasionally	19.3	14.6
Often	6.5	4.6
All the time	2.6	0.7

	Discuss one's ethnic background
No experience	67.2%
Infrequently	16.5
Sometimes	13.7
A lot	2.6

	Feel a special sense of relationship based on common background
No experience	78.7%
No current friends	3.7
One friend	2.0
Two to four	7.8
Five or more	7.8

Note: The percentages are based on 460 native-born whites, the total in the Capital Region sample.

curiosity, these results imply that the vast majority of native-born whites (about 85 percent) either do not discuss their ethnic backgrounds or do so only infrequently.

Two commonly mentioned topics give further insight into the potential role of such discussions.[4] The most frequently indicated amounts to family history, as reflected in such specifics as the ethnic character of one's name and the place of origin of one's family. More than half of our respondents indicated discussing aspects of their family history, and for a third, this is the only topic concerning their background they remember discussing with others. The other major topic concerns ethnic cultural patterns. Such topics as ethnic foods, holidays, and other cultural patterns were mentioned by a third of respondents who indicated having discussed their ethnic background in recent years.

The comments of many respondents make clear that these discussions do represent a general form of sensitivity to ethnicity as a feature of the social world, but not typically for the purpose of establishing narrowly ethnic bonds. Discussions of ethnicity are most often exchanges of information between people who may or may not be of the same ethnic background; they are part of the process of getting to know one another better ("comparing notes about different backgrounds," as one respondent aptly put it). Often the discussions have the function of identifying the backgrounds of the participants—a substantial number of respondents reported that the topic of ethnicity arises when someone else hears their surname and asks what kind of name it is. (One respondent's description is revealing: "I let them know I'm German; it gives them a little information.") Also often, discussions fill in the details, giving others the sense that they know one in greater depth. This characterization could be applied to the many respondents who described telling about the way they were brought up, the regions of a homeland their immigrant grandparents came from, recipes for ethnic dishes, and so forth. The tenor of many comments is summarized in one respondent's remark, "I want to know their backgrounds as quickly as possible, where they came from and all. I ask them about holidays—what they do special." Much less common than this sort of introductory discussion is one focused on more narrowly ethnic concerns, those likely to be discussed by people who already know they share the same ethnic backgrounds. By way of illustration, few respondents mentioned such topics as discrimination or other problems faced by their group as part of their discussions.

The third experience in this set, having a special sense of relationship to someone based on common ethnic background, was the least frequently cited. But for many indicating it, the experience seems to tap a significantly ethnic aspect of their social lives. This "special sense" is a form of sensitivity to the ethnicity of others rather than an objective measure of relationship to persons of common ethnic background. And the explanations respondents gave for this feeling highlighted features of their backgrounds that continue to have resonance for them.[5] Moreover, beneath the details of presumably shared experiences such as food, custom, language, and ways of growing up ran a common thread of unstrained empathy that some respondents feel when with fellow ethnics, revealed in such phrases as "rapport," "a sense of security," or "an understanding of why people act a certain way." The feelings of many respondents were summed up in one comment, "You figure they were brought up the same way, so you feel you share something."

For those who have it, the experience is generally not an isolated part of their social lives. Three-quarters said that they have this special sense of relationship with more than one current friend. A third described it true of a large number (five or more) of current friends. Still, these proportions apply to a relatively small fraction of the whole native-born white population. Measured against this larger population, just 16 percent reported feeling this sense of relationship about more than one current friend, and 8 percent about five or more current friends.

The experiences of social sensitivity are generally related to ethnic identity (see tables 4.2 and 4.3). But the relationship to identity is somewhat different from that of cultural experiences (see chapter 3), where the category of identity containing persons of undivided ancestry stands apart from all the rest. Here, the frequency of experience is approximately the same among ethnically identifying persons of single and mixed ancestry and tends to be

Table 4.2   Experiences of ethnic social sensitivity by ethnic identity status

Ethnic identity status (ancestry type/identity type)	% curious about ethnic backgrounds	% discuss own background	% feel special sense of relationship
single/single	34.7	41.3	25.6
multiple/single	35.2	38.6	26.1
multiple/multiple	35.6	40.6	23.8
single/none	12.5	12.5	25.0
multiple/none	29.1	21.4	10.7
unknown/none	13.3	0.0	6.7
Significance levels (by χ^2 test):	p < .10	p < .001	p < .05

Table 4.3   Experiences of ethnic social sensitivity by ethnic identity status and importance of background

Ethnic identity status (ancestry type/identity type)	Importance of background		
	Very	Somewhat	Not
	% curious about ethnic backgrounds		
single/single	47.5	33.3	19.4
multiple/single	46.7	34.9	30.0
multiple/multiple	52.9	31.0	34.1
non-identifying	21.6	31.7	26.7
	% discuss own background		
single/single	55.0	50.0	9.7
multiple/single	60.0	41.9	23.3
multiple/multiple	52.9	45.2	29.3
non-identifying	27.0	26.8	11.1
	% feel special sense of relationship		
single/single	42.5	27.1	0.0
multiple/single	46.7	25.6	16.7
multiple/multiple	35.3	31.0	9.8
non-identifying	21.6	14.6	6.7
Significance levels:	identity status × curious, N.S.		
	importance × curious, N.S.		
	identity status × discuss, p < .01		
	importance × discuss, p < .001		
	identity status × relationship, p < .05		
	importance × relationship, p < .001		

lower among nonidentifying categories.[6] As was also true for cultural experience, however, the relationship to identity comes into sharper focus when the subjective importance of background is brought into the picture. The experiences of social sensitivity are considerably more common among those with salient identities than among everyone else.

This pattern is especially strong for the experience of discussing one's ethnic background, which we have seen is not typically linked to an interest in forming narrowly ethnic relationships. Even without taking salience into account, about 40 percent of ethnic identifiers report such discussions, a proportion about twice that among nonidentifiers. But among those with intense ethnic identities, the proportion discussing background rises to between 50 and 60 percent, making the experience very common indeed. It is a bit less common among ethnic identifiers who view their backgrounds as of moderate importance. The experience of feeling a special sense of relationship to someone of the same ethnic background seems rather different in its nature, but it displays a similar profile in relation to ethnic identity, although with somewhat lower levels of experience overall.

Curiosity about the backgrounds of others exhibits the weakest relationship to identity, suggesting that it may not in fact be a very good indicator of sensitivity to ethnicity. Perhaps this experience is too haphazard—the product of occasional encounters that pique curiosity—to be revealing. The level of curiosity among those with the most intense identities—between 45 and 50 percent—is just modestly higher than it is among some categories of persons who do not identify at all or who view their backgrounds as unimportant.[7]

The distinctiveness of these experiences compared to those associated with culture continues when other variables are introduced into the picture through logistic regression analysis, thus demonstrating conclusively that there is no uniform pattern of change in ethnic experience. The apparatus of analysis is exactly the same as employed in chapter 3, and several of the regression equations are exhibited in table 4.4 in order to show the basic pattern of the results.[8]

The experience that approximates most closely the pattern of results in the preceding chapter is that of discussing one's ethnic background. Like such cultural experiences as eating ethnic foods and using a mother tongue, it falls off across the generations, dropping by almost 25 percentage points between the second and the fourth generations (net of other variables). And it declines by approximately the same magnitude with loss of confidence in one's ancestry knowledge. Both of these influences are indicative because of their generic relationship to the transformation of ethnicity. But they are not repeated for the other two experiences. In particular, the pattern of "straight-line assimilation," an increase of assimilation with each generational remove from immigration, is absent for the experience of feeling a special sense of relationship based on ethnicity, which we have seen has a definite ethnic significance for the minority who have it.

Also distinctive for these experiences are the consistent patterns of relationship shown by age, gender, and education. This is
not to deny the role of these factors for cultural experience, but they
did not display in the preceding chapter the consistency of effect
that they have here. The young are more likely than their elders to
report the experiences of social sensitivity to ethnicity; women are
more likely to do so than men; and the more highly educated more
likely to do so than those with less education. Only the absence of an
age effect in the analysis of experiencing a special sense of relationship keeps these patterns from perfect consistency. The effects,
moreover, are frequently sizable. To take a telling example, the
effect of education on discussing ethnic background, each step on
the educational scale (between, say, completing high school and
attending college) makes a difference of 13 percentage points.

The influence of these three variables supports the idea of ethnicity as cultural capital (see chapter 2). The effect of education, in
particular, demonstrates anew that ethnicity cannot be viewed simply as a working-class pattern. Ethnicity and its symbols presumably contribute to schemes of reference that enable people meeting
for the first time to place each other quickly and establish communication. But as the experience of one's discussing ethnic background reveals, communication opened up by ethnic topics is not
typically confined to people of the same ethnic background.

This interpretation of the role of ethnicity seems also consistent
with the relationship of age to the experiences of being curious
about the ethnicity of others and of discussing one's own background with them. Both experiences, and especially that of discussing one's background, are more common among those under the age
of forty-five and are least common among the elderly. It is highly
plausible that this is more a life-cycle effect, one that changes as
people age, than a cohort effect. As we saw in chapter 2, the young
are not more interested in their ethnic backgrounds per se (and such
interest, in the form of ethnic identity, is controlled in the analyses).
But their social lives are more unsettled; they are meeting people
and forming new relationships. Thus, they have more need to be
curious about the backgrounds of others and to discuss the facts of
ethnicity (and other aspects of background), all the more so because
the objective level of contact across ethnic lines may be greater for
younger cohorts than for older ones (in this sense a cohort effect may

Table 4.4 Logistic regression analyses of ethnic social sensitivity

	Curious about ethnic backgrounds		Discuss own ethnic background		Feel special sense of relationship	
	Logit coefficients	% change at mean	Logit coefficients	% change at mean	Logit coefficients	% change at mean
Generation:	N.S.		p < .05		N.S.	
second			+.599	+14.3		
third			+.065	+1.4		
fourth			−.505	−10.1		
unknown			−.159	−3.4		
Age:	p < .10		p < .001		N.S.	
under 30	+.291	+6.6	+.625	+14.9		
30–44	+.302	+6.8	+.419	+9.8		
45–59	−.033	−0.7	−.113	−2.4		
60+	−.560	−10.7	−.931	−16.7		
Sex:	p < .05		p < .05		p < .01	
male	−.243	−5.0	−.278	−5.8	−.425	−6.3
female	+.243	+5.5	+.278	+6.4	+.425	+8.0

	Model 1		Model 2		Model 3	
Education	+.478 p < .001	+11.1	+.549 p < .001	+13.0	+.470 p < .001	+8.9
Confidence about ancestry knowledge:	N.S.		p < .05		N.S.	
confident			+.601	+14.3		
unconfident			−.601	−11.7		
Ethnic identity status:	N.S.		p < .01		p < .10	
single/single			+.613	+14.6	+.217	+3.9
multiple/single			+.212	+4.8	+.080	+1.4
multiple/multiple			+.644	+15.4	+.244	+4.4
single/none			−1.260	−20.7	+.316	+5.8
multiple/none			−.209	−4.4	−.857	−11.0
Importance of background	+.468 p < .01	+10.8	+.898 p < .001	+21.7	+.954 p < .001	+20.0
χ^2	70.49 with 14 degrees of freedom (p < .001)		129.76 with 14 degrees of freedom (p < .001)		82.47 with 14 degrees of freedom (p < .001)	

Note: Persons of unknown ancestry (N = 15) are excluded here and in other logistic regression analyses in this chapter.

Coding of non-categorical variables: Importance of background ranges from +1 (very important) to −1 (not important). Education ranges from 5 (college graduate) to 1 (grammar school education only).

be at work). Older people may be less overtly interested in ethnic aspects of the backgrounds of others because they already know about them (or perhaps think they do), having circles of friends and acquaintances that have remained largely stable over long periods of time. In addition, young adults may be more oriented toward ethnicity as an idiom of communication because their lower involvement in careers provides them with less work-related material for this purpose.

Gender is the last variable in the trio. Like young adults, women may find ethnicity to be effective in communication because they frequently lack the dominant interest in work most men have. But there is probably something else at work in women's greater sensitivity to ethnicity, namely, the connection between ethnicity and family. The gender difference is largest for the experience of a special sense of relationship based on ethnicity. As the comments of numerous respondents indicated, this feeling is usually linked to a sense of common family experiences (quite often during childhood). Since women are undoubtedly more likely than men to seek out information about the family backgrounds of friends and acquaintances, they are more likely to strike a spark of friendship because of biographical parallels originating in ethnicity.

Controlling for these influences does not explain the relationship of ethnicity identity to the experiences of sensitivity. Ethnic identity status is statistically significant in two of the three equations: in that for discussing one's ethnic background, persons who identify ethnically are shown to be more likely than the nonidentifying to have such discussions, even when such factors as generation and education are controlled; in that for feeling a special sense of relationship, nonidentifiers of mixed ancestry remain especially unlikely to have this experience. The subjective importance of ethnicity is more consistent still.[9] Thus, those who believe their ethnic backgrounds to be important are far more likely to have these experiences. The sizes of the differences associated with subjective importance rival those associated with the most powerful of the other influences; for example, one step on the scale of importance makes a difference of more than 20 percentage points for discussing ethnic background. Thus, the multivariate analyses affirm the correspondence between the salience of identity and sensitivity to ethnicity in the social world.

Further differences between sensitivity, as an exemplar of the social experience of ethnicity, and cultural experience emerge when ethnic groups are considered. There is some variation across groups (persons with some kinds of ancestry are more likely to report the experiences of sensitivity), but it is by no means as pronounced or as consistent as is ethnic variation in cultural experience. For the sensitivity experiences in general, it is once again true that the Italians report the highest levels and thus appear to be the most "ethnic" of the major ancestry groups in the Capital Region. But in this case, the differences between the Italians and other native-born whites are smaller, and the Italians are not followed closely by the Poles, the other major European ancestry group in the Capital Region originating in early twentieth-century immigration. Instead, the ranking of other groups shifts from one experience to another. In short, ethnic variations for these experiences are not as prominent or systematic as was the case for cultural experiences.

Nevertheless, sensitivity to ethnicity does stand out among the Italians. A third of the ancestry group (including those whose ancestry is mixed) reports feeling a special rapport with others because of common ethnic background (the figure is even higher among those who identify ethnically as Italian). By comparison, this is said by approximately 20 percent of members of such old-stock ancestry groups as the English, French, and Germans. Moreover, the Italians are unusually likely to say that this feeling characterizes a large number of their current friendships. In the Italian case, sensitivity to ethnicity is combined with a considerable number of ethnic social circles—family, friendship, and neighborhood groups that are disproportionately Italian. The Italians represent, after all, a historically recent European immigration, and the social structures associated with immigrant and second-generation communities, although weakening, are still in existence.

Further, Italians are more likely than most other groups to discuss their ethnic backgrounds. About half of persons of Italian ancestry checked this as an experience, compared with 30 to 35 percent of the English, French, and Germans. By itself, this is not such a large difference, but the Italians tend to discuss their backgrounds more frequently than do their counterparts in the old-stock groups. Among them, those discussing their backgrounds "sometimes" or "a lot" outnumber those who do so "infrequently" by two to one. Among the old-stock groups, persons who reported infre-quent discussions are as numerous as those who reported more frequent ones. The Italians are also more likely than members of the major old-stock groups to indicate feelings of curiosity about the backgrounds of others, but the difference is not large (43 percent among the Italians versus about 30 percent among the old-stock groups). The Italians are no more likely than anyone else to claim this as a more than occasional experience.

Two groups that appear surprisingly ethnic in terms of some of the experiences under discussion here are American Indians and Scots. One must be cautious about leaping to conclusions from the data for these groups, however, because both are small compared to other ancestry groups and dominated by persons with mixed ethnic ancestry, raising an issue of ethnic misattribution (since, for per-sons of mixed ethnic background, it is often unclear which part of their ancestry prompts sensitivity to ethnicity). Nevertheless, per-sons of Scots ancestry are almost as curious about ethnic back-grounds as the Italians are, and American Indians are as likely as Italians to discuss their ethnic backgrounds. Reasons for this un-usual degree of sensitivity to ethnicity are not apparent (although American Indian ancestry may be sufficiently rare among whites to stimulate exchanges of information about ethnic background). Per-haps the surprising distinctiveness of these groups is simply a re-minder that sensitivity to ethnicity is potentially a universal experi-ence in the United States, not one highly concentrated among people who are ethnic in other ways as well.

This is probably the most important conclusion to be drawn from these experiences. Sensitivity to ethnicity is a common experi-ence, but it is not for most whites a frequent or intense one. About half of native-born whites indicated having at least one of these experiences but most described them as occasional or infrequent. Only the question about a special sense of relationship founded on common ethnic background seemed to identify a core of respon-dents for whom ethnicity is a prominent feature of their social world, but they still represent a small minority among whites. The broadly scattered, but superficial nature of this sensitivity, then, seems reflective of the continuing attention to ethnicity in Ameri-can society, reinforced in schools and by the media. Consequently, many white Americans, even those quite distant from the immigration experience and those who do not think of themselves in ethnic terms, feel occasional twinges of curiosity and a desire to exchange information about ethnic and family backgrounds. But given the massive contact that occurs across what were once ethnic divisions, their social worlds are not structured around ethnicity. Only for a small minority, concentrated among those who feel strongly about their ethnic backgrounds, is there evidence that sensitivity to ethnicity runs deep.

Experiences with Prejudice and Discrimination

Ethnic identity need not be entirely voluntary (or voluntary at all). Discussions of race in the United States usually point out that assimilation is not always a matter of choice. Non-whites who want to assimilate into the majority society may be barred from doing so by their visibility and by the prejudice of whites. Thus, an identity as an African American may be forced on them by the reactions of others and by discriminatory treatment. Although the far greater intensity of discrimination and prejudice directed against non-whites and Hispanics is beyond dispute, the same argument can, in its essentials, be applied to many whites. In the past, immigrants and their descendants have suffered at the hands of prejudiced, nativist Americans, and vestiges of this treatment and the beliefs that nurtured it may survive. Thus, a continuing, even if milder, level of hostility directed against white Americans of particular ancestral backgrounds (such as Italians and Jews) may help to keep ethnic identities alive (Novak, 1971).

It may not even be necessary to suffer personally the pain inflicted by prejudice and discrimination in order to feel their impact on ethnic consciousness. Milton Gordon (1964: 52–53) describes the identification that is built up from the recognition of prejudice and discrimination directed at fellow ethnics: "'I am ultimately bound up with the fate of these people' is the type of [psychological] constellation attached to the ethnic group as a whole." Gordon contrasts this type of identity with those derived from a sense of similarity or a feeling of social ease with coethnics. By comparison, the recognition of an "interdependence of fate" may be more likely to generate intense feelings of solidarity with the entire ethnic group rather than with the limited segment like oneself.

The causal ordering need not run in one direction only. Ethnic identity, particularly when it is salient, may contribute to the perception of prejudice and discrimination, making an individual sensitive to any occurrence of ethnic slights and quick to point out continuing injuries to members of his or her group. Additionally, the combination of salient ethnic identity and the negative experiences of prejudice and discrimination may be quite potent for the political manifestations of ethnicity, spurring people to involve themselves in political activities and in ethnic organizations.

But how widespread among native-born whites are experiences with prejudice and discrimination? A good deal of anecdotal and survey evidence suggests that prejudicial views of European ethnic groups have abated in the post-World War II period (for Jews, the European group with the deepest historical record of suffering from prejudice and discrimination, see Silberman [1985]). But perhaps compensating for this decline is the power of the mass media to magnify any vestiges of ethnic bias. Television, in particular, can transport into homes throughout the country expressions of these once potent forces occurring in far-away corners of the United States. Even in the face of an objective decline, prejudice and discrimination may retain a good deal of subjective importance to the extent that ethnicity among whites mimics the experiences of the African-American civil rights movement. Many scholars perceived a resurgence of ethnicity among white groups during the 1960s and 1970s, which some interpreted as a response to the apparent success of the civil rights movement and increased economic competition with African Americans. If this thesis is correct, then it would not be surprising if whites who identify in ethnic terms also see members of their group as still suffering under unfair burdens, regardless of the objective magnitude of such burdens.

Nevertheless, experiences with prejudice and discrimination were not frequently reported by our respondents. Our survey asked about these in several ways—inquiring whether the respondent had encountered stereotypes about his or her ethnic background (described as "fixed ideas about people with your ethnic background"), had suffered from ethnic discrimination, or had heard about discrimination against others of the same background. None of these experiences was mentioned by even as many as a quarter of native-born whites. The most common was coming into contact with stereotypes. This was claimed by 22 percent of native-born white respondents. It is not among the most common experiences (each of which was mentioned by at least a quarter of respondents), but it is frequent enough to be regarded as part of a second tier of important ethnic experience. Experiences with discrimination were less common. Very few native-born whites (4 percent) believed that they had been the victims of discrimination (though our questions asked only about ethnic experiences during the preceding five years). Fifteen percent said that they had heard of discrimination against others with their ethnic background.

That stereotypes provide the most common of these experiences should not come as a surprise. Stereotypes are certainly alive in the mass media, which frequently use explicit references to ethnicity as a kind of shorthand to suggest the social variety of American life. The pervasive quality of many of these stereotypes is suggested by television advertisements for spaghetti sauces, which frequently feature tastings in Italian family kitchens, celebrating, as well as drawing sustenance from, the notion that Italian families are unusually cohesive and centered around food. It is consistent with the wide dissemination of ethnic stereotypes that respondents, who typically reported more than one stereotype, provided us with rich detail about the stereotypes they encounter. Thus, stereotypes appear to embody familiar ideas for some respondents. In fact, many of the stereotypes we heard about were familiar to us also, and not all of them are negative, although even positive stereotypes frequently have a cutting edge, such as the notion that all Jews are smart and do well in school, which can imply that they are excessively competitive.[10]

There was a definite ethnic pattern in the clustering of stereotypes. The larger a group in the region's population and the more recent its arrival in the United States, the greater the number of stereotypes described by our respondents. Stereotypes appear to be a function of visibility, and therefore the more a group seems to blend into the old-stock population, the less it is stereotyped (or, at least, the less its members perceive themselves as meeting up with stereotypes). Of the major ancestry groups in the region, Italians seem to possess the greatest number of stereotypes. These run the gamut from preconceptions of physical appearance and mannerisms ("big noses" and "talk with their hands"), to family life ("family oriented" and "good with children"), to the Mafia ("they all have something to do with organized crime").

Next in order by number of distinct stereotypes come the Irish. Their stereotypes, too, cover familiar ground, including those of the politician and policeman, the heavy drinker, and the poet ("good with words"); and not to be forgotten is the notion of Irish women as "long-suffering." Another group with a substantial number of stereotypes is the Germans. Surprisingly few stereotypes were reported about Jews and about Poles, although this may simply be a reflection of the relatively small sizes of these two groups in the Albany population. There were also few stereotypes about such old-stock groups as the English, French, and Scots.

Stereotypes, although they are generally exaggerated ideas and inappropriately applied too broadly to members of a group, may often contain a grain of truth. Many of our respondents conceded that some of the stereotypes they reported are true, and a considerable number even applied them to themselves.[11] Just a third of respondents reporting on stereotypes denied that any of them were true; a slightly larger number not only said some were true but conceded they were true of themselves.

But despite these admissions about the truth of many stereotypes, respondents did not often feel that others expected them to behave according to stereotype.[12] This suggests that, even though stereotypes are still a living part of the American ethnic heritage, they are not often applied to individuals in daily life. Perhaps they survive more in the mass media and in the form of ethnic jokes than in normal day-to-day interaction. Roughly 60 percent of respondents encountering stereotypes said that they were not expected to behave like the stereotypes. Only 2 percent said that they frequently came across such expectations. Most of the remainder reported occasionally encountering them.

Likewise, the burden of discrimination does not seem to fall heavily on the vast majority of native-born whites. Just one of every twenty-five respondents believed that they themselves had been recent victims of discrimination. Somewhat more common, but hardly widespread (reported by 15 percent of native-born whites) was the experience of hearing about discrimination against the members of one's group. Even these low figures risk overstating the degree of discrimination perceived by our respondents. We asked those respondents who reported either a personal or a vicarious experience with discrimination how much discrimination they believed currently existed against people of their ethnic background, and how this present discrimination compared to the level that existed in the past.[13] About half of these respondents characterized the present level of discrimination as just "a little" or even "none." Put differently, not even 10 percent of all native-born whites were willing to say that there is a significant amount of discrimination directed against people like themselves. And the great majority of our respondents who had encountered discrimination, either personally or vicariously, said that the current level of discrimination is less than it was in the past.[14] In fact, half characterized the present level as "much" less than in the past.

The episodes of discrimination described by our respondents are also revealing. We asked only those respondents who had directly suffered discrimination to tell us what happened. Most of the occurrences they mentioned involved slurs or other negative comments (for example, a person of Polish background being called a "dumb Polack" or being told a Polish joke). Only a handful described events with tangible, damaging consequences, such as the denial of a job or a place to live. On this basis, most of the experiences that our respondents call "discrimination" cannot be separated entirely from the encounter with stereotypes. The ethnic characterizations involved in the events described may be more unambiguously negative than is often the case with the sterotypes noted earlier, but both belong to the same spectrum of phenomena: in a society where ethnic social distinctions have a long history, ethnic labels, including quite negative ones, live on after the decline of the objective social differences in which they were once rooted. But the great infrequency of reported acts that deprive someone of some tangible value on the basis of ethnic origin is indicative that discrimination is, in fact, quite weak among whites.

Unlike all the ethnically relevant experiences discussed so far, the experiences with prejudice and discrimination have little or no relationship to ethnic identity status per se. Ethnically identifying individuals are scarcely more likely than the nonidentifying to report them. Only the encounter with stereotypes differs significantly between the two groups, and this is chiefly because of an unusually high level of this experience among persons with mixed ancestry who identify with a single group (see table 4.5).[15] Perhaps the involuntary character of these experiences explains their distinctive lack of profile in relation to ethnic identity status. To present oneself to others in ethnic terms is a choice, and it is linked to ethnic experiences that are also volitional in some degree. But encountering prejudice or discrimination is an exogenous event, imposed on the individual by others, and may bear little relationship to a chosen social identity.

Yet the picture is somewhat puzzling, for these experiences exhibit a moderately strong relationship to the subjective importance of ethnic background, especially among ethnic identifiers (see table 4.6). The encounter with stereotypes, to take the strongest instance of the pattern, is most common among ethnic identifiers who view their backgrounds as at least somewhat important—nearly a third of this group reported the experience (the figure is higher still among its members with mixed ancestry), compared to just 15 percent of all other native-born whites. Likewise, the vicarious experience with discrimination attains its high-water mark among ethnic identifiers who feel strongly about their ethnic background (and, again, is even more common for persons with mixed ancestry).[16] Perhaps these experiences have the effect of enhancing the salience of ethnicity for those who identify; this effect may be especially powerful for persons, such as those with mixed ancestry, who believe they should not be judged by ethnic criteria. But this remains a speculation inasmuch as the same pattern is absent for the personal experience of discrimination.

Table 4.5   Experiences with prejudice and discrimination by ethnic identity status

Ethnic identity status (ancestry type/identity type)	% encounter stereotypes	% suffer discrimination	% hear about discrimination
single/single	21.5	3.3	14.0
multiple/single	36.4	9.1	19.3
multiple/multiple	18.8	3.0	16.8
single/none	9.4	0.0	6.3
multiple/none	18.4	4.9	15.5
unknown/none	6.7	0.0	13.3
Significance levels:	p < .01	N.S.	N.S.

Table 4.6   Experiences with prejudice and
discrimination by ethnic identity status and the
subjective importance of ethnic background

Ethnic identity status (simplified)	Importance of background		
	very	somewhat	none
% encounter stereotypes			
ethnic identifying	30.6	32.3	11.8
nonidentifying	13.5	17.1	20.0
% suffer discrimination			
ethnic identifying	6.9	6.0	2.0
nonidentifying	8.1	2.4	0.0
% hear about discrimination			
ethnic identifying	26.4	19.5	5.9
nonidentifying	18.9	14.6	13.3

Significance levels: identity status × stereotypes,
  $p < .10$
  importance × stereotypes, $p < .01$
  identity status × discrimination
  (personal), N.S.
  importance × discrimination
  (personal), $p < .05$
  identity status × discrimination
  (vicarious), N.S.
  importance × discrimination
  (vicarious), $p < .01$

Note: Because the infrequency of some of these experiences
makes the percentages in small cells unstable, detailed categories of ethnic identity status have been combined for this
presentation.

In this connection, it is interesting to examine the sort of logistic regression equations that have already been used to analyze
other experiences (see table 4.7). Of the variables in them, subjective
importance of ethnicity has the most consistently strong relationship to these experiences. Its coefficients are generally quite
large, although less so for the encounter with stereotypes than for
the experiences with discrimination (this evaluation emerges more
clearly from the logit coefficients than from the percentage dif-

Table 4.7 Logistic regression analyses of experiences with prejudice and discrimination

	Encounter with stereotypes		Personal experience of discrimination		Vicarious experience of discrimination	
	Logit coefficients	% change at mean	Logit coefficients	% change at mean	Logit coefficients	% change at mean
Generation:	$p < .10$		$p < .05$		$p < .01$	
second	+.608	+12.0	+.899	+5.7	+.430	+6.5
third	+.628	+12.5	+.180	+0.8	+.543	+8.5
fourth	+.190	+3.4	-2.024	-3.8	-.740	-7.4
unknown	-1.426	-15.5	+.945	+6.1	-.233	-2.8
Age:	$p < .01$		N.S.		$p < .05$	
under 30	+.743	+15.1			+.656	+10.6
30–44	+.377	+7.1			+.226	+3.2
45–59	-.377	-5.7			+.074	+1.0
60+	-.743	-10.1			-.956	-8.9
Sex:	$p < .10$		N.S.		N.S.	
male	-.249	-3.9				
female	+.249	+4.5				
Education	+.467 $p < .001$	+9.0	+.588 $p < .05$	+3.2	+.266 $p < .10$	+3.8
Confidence about ancestry knowledge:	N.S.		N.S.		N.S.	
confident						
unconfident						
Ethnic identity status:	N.S.		N.S.		N.S.	
single/single						
multiple/single						
multiple/multiple						
single/none						
multiple/none						
Importance of background	+.449 $p < .05$	+8.6	+.991 $p < .05$	+6.6	+.848 $p < .001$	+14.4
χ^2	83.12 with 14 degrees of freedom ($p < .001$)		33.59 with 14 degrees of freedom ($p < .01$)		62.54 with 14 degrees of freedom ($p < .001$)	

ferences, which are depressed by the infrequency of the two discrimination experiences).

Also rather consistent is the effect of generational status. Experiences with ethnic bias (or, at least, the reporting of them) decline
across the generations, but the pattern does not fit the straight-line
prototype. In general, there is little difference between the second
and third generations.[17] Experiences with discrimination drop off
sharply in the fourth generation, while the critical difference for the
experience of stereotyping lies between those who do not know their
generational status and everyone else. Perhaps this last is as much
an effect of mental distance from ethnicity, that is, a lack of interest
in the facts of family origins, as it is one of generational position.

Otherwise, two influences stand out, both of which have already proved to be important for sensitivity to ethnicity in the
social world: education and age. Personal experiences with discrimination and stereotyping are quite strongly related to education:
the more highly educated are more likely to have personally encountered ethnic bias (hearing about discrimination is also related
to education, but less strongly). In one sense, this is the opposite of
what one should expect, since the most highly educated members of
a group should be less likely than others to meet up with barriers
based on ethnic background, especially in a period when such forces
are in retreat. And the more highly educated are no more likely than
others to believe that a significant amount of discrimination exists
against people with their ethnic background. The results suggest
that they are more sensitive to ethnic slights, which they may perceive as particularly inappropriate given their educational attainment and social position. It may also be the case that, because some
of them have attained entry to social strata where there are few
others of their ethnic background, they are more likely to run into
residues of prejudice and discrimination. Socially mobile members
of minority groups are often a "beachhead" for the advance of the
group's mass and have to suffer hostility that later-arriving group
members are spared. Yet one must keep in mind that the personal
experience of discrimination is not common for any group of native-
born whites. Only 9 percent of the college educated claim to have
suffered it. (The experience of stereotyping, which is also related to
education, is far more common than this, but also more likely to be
viewed as fairly benign.)

Experiences with prejudice and discrimination are also more frequent among the young. The important exception is the direct experience of ethnic discrimination. But the young are more likely to have heard about discrimination and to have encountered stereotypes, and the differences are sizable. In the case of stereotyping, the relationship to age is almost perfectly linear, with each older category less likely to report this experience. In the case of hearing about discrimination, the principal distinction lies between the elderly and all others; differences among other age categories are smaller (although they still favor young adults).

Here, too, one might see the influence of somewhat greater sensitivity to ethnic slights, combined with somewhat more attention to social aspects of ethnicity in general. The social lives of the young are more in flux; as we have seen, they have more reason than others to discuss backgrounds, including their ethnic dimension. Thus, they have a greater chance of encountering ethnic stereotypes and stories of ethnic discrimination. As with the college educated, however, one must be careful not to exaggerate the extent and significance of the experience with bias. The most widespread of these experiences in the young-adult age group is the encounter with stereotypes, cited by 36 percent, but this is the least deleterious of the experiences. Just a quarter claim to have heard about discrimination against people of their ethnic background, and only 6 percent say that they themselves have suffered from discrimination. Further, the young give little credence to the existence of significant levels of prejudice and discrimination from which people like themselves might suffer. Just 14 percent are willing to say there is more than a "little" discrimination directed against their group. And virtually all who have heard of acts of discrimination say that the discrimination against their group is less than it was in the past.

If the pattern in relation to ethnic identity and some other variables is somewhat puzzling, the ethnic concentrations of these experiences are not, for especially subject to ethnic bias are the groups from southern and eastern Europe. Italians and Jews stand out as the groups whose members most frequently report ethnic stereotyping. Generally speaking, the proportions of old-stock groups who meet up with stereotypes about their groups resemble the proportion among native-born whites as a whole: with some minor variations, about a fifth of each old-stock ancestry group indicates having this experience. Even the Irish, with their large number of reported stereotypes, do not stick out from this mass. Among those of Italian ancestry, the experience is about twice as common, reported by approximately 40 percent. It appears to be even more frequent among those of mixed Italian background, suggesting again that the experience with stereotypes may be most salient to those who deem it inappropriate. The experience occurs most often to Jews.[18] Given the religious composition of the Capital Region, this group is very small in our sample, but the proportion of it (two-thirds) who reports this experience is so impressive that it seems unlikely to be a statistical artifact (and this is confirmed by a statistical test of significance).

These two groups, joined by Poles and American Indians, are also the most likely to indicate some experiences, direct or indirect, with discrimination. Except for Jews and Poles, direct contact with discrimination is rare. Even among persons of Italian ancestry, just 4 percent indicate having personally suffered from discrimination, which is on a par with the frequencies to be observed among old-stock groups. Among persons of Polish ancestry, however, the frequency of direct experience with discrimination is three times as high, reported by 13 percent.[19] And among Jews, it rises to nearly 40 percent, indicating that the experience is about ten times as common in this group as it is in the native-born white population as a whole. Another way of putting this remarkable concentration: even though Jews and Poles make up only about one ninth of the white population of the Capital Region, they account for fully half of all the reported direct experiences with discrimination.

Jews and Italians are the groups most likely to have heard about discrimination directed against their ethnic compatriots. In general, 10 to 15 percent of old-stock groups have heard of incidents of discrimination against people like themselves. The proportion seems moderately (though not significantly) higher among persons of American Indian or Polish ancestry. In either case, between 20 and 25 percent of the group reported this experience. But among the Italians, about a third have heard of discrimination, and 20 percent believe that there is still more than a minor amount of discrimination directed against their group. (By comparison, among native-born whites overall, only 9 percent believe there is more than "a little" discrimination against their groups.) About half of the Jewish group reported having heard of discrimination, and a quarter believe that its current level is more than minor.

But even though members of the Jewish and Italian groups are considerably more likely than the average white American to perceive a significant amount of ethnic bias, they share the general faith that discrimination directed against people like themselves is on the wane. The great majority of the members of both groups who have, personally or vicariously, encountered discrimination assert that the level of discrimination against their group has declined from what it was in the past. (This is also the case among Poles.) Among the Italians, those who see progress are about equally divided between those willing to declare that discrimination is "much" less than it was and others who say it is just "somewhat" less. Among the Jews—admittedly few in number in our sample—the magnitude of progress is not perceived to be this strong: most prefer the more subdued assessment that discrimination is now "somewhat" less than it was.

Ethnicity in the Political Domain

The frequency of experiences with prejudice and discrimination among some ethnic groups seems broadly consistent with the view that ethnicity increasingly has a political dimension in advanced industrial societies. Daniel Bell (1975) and Nathan Glazer and Daniel Patrick Moynihan (1975) perceive a new basis for ethnic solidarity in this trend (see also Olzak, 1983; Nielsen, 1985). The perception of prejudice and discrimination directed against people from one's ethnic background seems a likely spur to activity on behalf of specifically *ethnic* interests. Ethnic political organizations in the United States do typically devote a considerable portion of their efforts to combating ethnic bias and to overturning perceived barriers to the advancement of group members. For white ethnic groups, such organizations as the National Italian American Foundation and the B'nai Brith Anti-Defamation League can serve as examples. But for those who perceive ethnicity as increasingly political in character, the civil rights movement is the true prototype, demonstrating that mobilization on behalf of ethnic interests can be effective in achieving some, even if not all, goals.

But not all interest in ethnic politics need be seen as evidence of politically based, ethnic resurgence. In his essay on "symbolic ethnicity," Herbert Gans (1979) equates some ethnic political interests with this new form of ethnicity, which he characterizes as possibly "an ethnicity of last resort." He notes that ethnic concerns in political spheres are frequently with international issues, such as the plight of Catholics in Northern Ireland or the preservation of Israel. Concerns with homelands can have a very different character from ethnic involvement in domestic issues, especially in muting the potentially divisive nature of ethnic political issues: "Old countries are particularly useful as identity symbols because they are far away and cannot make arduous demands on American ethnics. . . . American ethnics can identify with their perception of the old country or homeland, transforming it into a symbol which leaves out its domestic or foreign problems that could become sources of conflict for Americans" (Gans, 1979: 10–11). Undoubtedly not everyone would agree with this characterization; for example, some American Jews see old-fashioned anti-Semitism behind domestic opposition to Jewish support of Israel. Still, it seems highly plausible that even if ethnic international issues can give rise to American conflicts, these conflicts are less intense than they would be if ethnic political concerns were focused squarely on the domestic arena.

Generally speaking, the political concerns we found among native-born whites appear to match the profile of symbolic ethnicity rather than of politics as a fundamental dimension of contemporary ethnicity. We inquired about ethnic political concerns as inclusively as possible, asking respondents if they had felt "strongly about an issue because of [their] ethnic background." Even with this broad wording, which implies no practical action on their part, only 15 percent of native-born whites claimed this as an experience.

Consistent with symbolic ethnicity, the issues of concern to our respondents lie mainly in the international sphere: it does seem as if countries across the sea offer far safer ground on which to express ethnic political interests than do issues closer to home.[20] The single most-frequently cited issue was the situation of the Catholic minority in Northern Ireland, named by about 40 percent of those indicating political concerns. A variety of other international issues, such as the plight of Soviet Jewry, the Solidarity movement in Poland, and the division of Germany, were also mentioned, but none with a frequency approaching that of Northern Ireland. The only consequential set of domestic concerns related to prejudice and discrimination. Altogether, about a third of respondents with political interests mentioned such concerns, which scattered broadly from anti-Semitism, to concern over the Mafia image of Italians, to nonspecific expressions of concern about ethnic and racial bias. As this list suggests, domestic concerns were not often focused on well-defined, recognizable political issues. Indeed, the concerns of some respondents seemed less matters of politics than of somewhat diffuse worries about American society. Such respondents talked about the "need to keep an open mind" or to give everyone the same chance, using terms far removed from the concrete language of American politics.

The issues mentioned by our respondents often do not involve even the minority concerned about them in activities and networks that might nourish ethnic solidarity. We asked our respondents what actions, if any, they took with respect to the issues they perceive in ethnic terms. We took note of even very informal actions, such as keeping informed about an issue and talking to friends about it. A surprisingly large proportion (nearly half) of the respondents who felt strongly about some issue reported taking no action whatsoever. Only a quarter indicated an action that went beyond informal steps. We counted as more than informal even such modest political actions as signing petitions and writing letters (as well as, of course, participating in demonstrations and voting). Put in terms of all native-born whites, only 8 percent were actively involved in an issue that had some ethnic resonance for them, and just 4 percent engaged in traditional forms of political activity, even at the minimal level of petition signing.

Like a number of other experiences examined so far, ethnic political concerns are concentrated among individuals with salient ethnic identities (see table 4.8) and—interestingly—reach their highest levels among such persons who come from mixed ancestral backgrounds. Altogether, persons who identify ethnically are about twice as likely as those who do not to express concerns with ethnic issues (18 versus 9 percent). The picture sharpens further when the salience of ethnic identity is introduced, for ethnic political concerns are quite strongly related to ethnicity's subjective importance. Among the ethnically identifying, persons who feel their

Table 4.8   Ethnic political concerns by ethnic identity status
and subjective importance of background (% reporting concerns)

Ethnic identity status (ancestry type/identity type)	All native-born whites	Importance of background		
		very	somewhat	none
single/single	16.5	25.0	18.8	0.0
multiple/single	21.6	46.7	23.3	6.7
multiple/multiple	16.8	52.9	7.1	12.2
single/none	3.1 ⎫			
multiple/none	11.7 ⎬	16.2	7.3	4.4
unknown/none	0.0 ⎭			
Significance levels:	p < .05	identity status X concerns, p < .05 importance X concerns, p < .001		

backgrounds to be very important are, overall, five times more like-ly to have such concerns than are those who attribute no impor-tance to background—36 percent of the former express such con-cerns, compared to just 7 percent of the latter. The level of political concerns in the group with salient ethnic identities is also much higher than it is among nonidentifiers, although even among the latter, there appears to be some effect associated with the impor-tance attached to background.

The highest levels of ethnic political concerns occur among persons with mixed ancestries, underscoring a theme running throughout the experiences in this chapter. Half of such persons with salient ethnic identities reported political concerns—a pro-portion well above the average level for all native-born whites (see table 4.8). Because the proportion of mixed-ancestry individuals who identify so strongly is small, one must be careful not to over-state the implications of this difference. Nevertheless, it shows again that ethnic social experiences—unlike cultural involve-ments—are not concentrated among persons of single ancestry, a group that is dwindling in the white population as a consequence of extensive intermarriage. Thus, political concerns and other non-cultural experiences may provide an avenue for persons of mixed ancestry to a fairly salient ethnic identity. But the general limits of all of these experiences must also be kept in mind: most are not widespread, and they tend to occur at low levels of intensity and involvement.

The connection between the salience of ethnicity and ethnic political concerns is borne out in logistic regression analysis, in which the coefficient of the subjective importance variable is very large (see the left-hand column of table 4.9). But the analysis also reveals that these concerns are eroded by demographic forces. Thus, a loss of confidence in ancestry knowledge, reflecting ethnic "drift," substantially reduces interest in ethnic political issues. Interest also falls off in the transition to the fourth generation (and drops even further among those who do not know their generational status). These diminishing influences are only modestly offset by the final significant factor, education. Rising education has a positive impact on the level of ethnic political concerns, but the effect of education is smaller here than for most of the other experiences discussed in this chapter.

Given that the predominant political concerns of white ethnics are focused on prejudice and discrimination, whether in the United States or abroad, it is of interest to see if these concerns are specifically linked to perceptions of bias against one's group. Accordingly, the right-hand column of table 4.9 reports the results of logistic regression analysis when experiences with bias are added to variables in the basic model. The two experiences with discrimination—personal and vicarious—have significant and, in concert, powerful relationships to ethnic political concerns. (As befits the more benign encounter with stereotypes, this experience is not significant in the model.) The more consequential of these two experiences is the personal one: people experiencing discrimination themselves are almost 25 percent more likely than others to have ethnic political concerns. The introduction of experiences with discrimination into the analysis also changes the remaining results. Specifically, generational status and education no longer have significant effects, implying that their influence on ethnic political concerns may occur through heightened perceptions of discrimination. Confidence in ancestry knowledge and the salience of ethnicity do retain their effects, however.

In light of the general nature of political concerns, it should come as no surprise that they are more prevalent among some eth-

Table 4.9   Logistic regression analysis of ethnic political concerns

	Equation without experiences of prejudice and discrimination		Equation with experiences of prejudice and discrimination	
	Logit coefficients	% change at mean	Logit coefficients	% change at mean
Generation:	p < .10		N.S.	
second	+.666	+10.6		
third	+.569	+8.8		
fourth	−.239	−2.8		
unknown	−.996	−8.9		
Age:	N.S.		N.S.	
under 30				
30–44				
45–59				
60+				
Sex:	N.S.		N.S.	
male				
female				
Education	+.365 p < .05	+5.3	N.S.	
Confidence about ancestry knowledge:	p < .10		p < .10	
confident	+.911	+15.5	+1.064	+18.8
unconfident	−.911	−8.4	−1.064	−9.3
Ethnic identity status:	N.S.		N.S.	
single/single				
multiple/single				
multiple/multiple				
single/none				
multiple/none				
Importance of background	+1.228 p < .001	+22.6	+1.031 p < .001	+18.1
Personal experience of discrimination:	not included		p < .01	
yes			+.892	+15.1
no			−.892	−8.3
Vicarious experience of discrimination:	not included		p < .01	
yes			+.636	+10.0
no			−.636	−6.5
Encounter with stereotypes:	not included		N.S.	
yes				
no				
χ²	77.44 with 14 degrees of freedom (p < .001)		107.72 with 17 degrees of freedom (p < .001)	

nic groups than among others. Yet despite the linkage to perceptions of discrimination, there is not an exact correspondence between the groups where the perception of discrimination is prominent and those with high levels of political concerns. One group, Jews, does stand at the top of both lists. The group most commonly experiencing discrimination (and stereotyping), it also displays the highest degree of political concerns, being evenly split (in our small sample of this group) between those who report ethnic political concerns and those who do not.[21] Jews are also unusually likely to be involved in some activity as a result. In fact, all of our Jewish respondents with political concerns reported some form of active involvement with political issues, and for all but one, this involvement rose above the merely informal.

Persons of Irish background have the second highest level of political concerns, overwhelmingly focused on Northern Ireland. Close to a quarter of persons with Irish ancestry expressed ethnic political concerns, and the proportion was even higher among those who identify ethnically as Irish. When it comes to political activity, however, the Irish resemble native-born whites in general. About half with political concerns reported taking no action, and only a small minority indicated some action that is more than informal.

Otherwise, the groups that are conspicuous for their experiences with prejudice and discrimination—the Italians and Poles—are not so when it comes to political concerns. The Italians come closer; a fifth of the ancestry group, and a slightly higher fraction of those who identify as Italian, reported some concerns, typically with the Mafia image, but their difference from old-stock groups is not large enough to be statistically significant. The lack of prominence of these groups makes the case of the Irish all the more intriguing. Why do the Irish, who are quite unexceptional when it comes to experiences with prejudice and discrimination, stand out among old-stock groups when it comes to political concerns? Perhaps the answer lies partly in the continuing influence of this group on the politics of the region, which translates into networks of Irish Catholic politicians, concentrated in the Democratic party, who are able to seize on and make visible an issue of potential ethnic importance. Added to this is the existence of an overseas, or homeland, issue, which involves ethnic division and violent strife. The Italians, by comparison, have no comparable *international* issue to serve as a political standard; this explanation, however, fails to account for the unexceptional Polish case.

Other Ethnic Experiences

Among the miscellany of other experiences about which we collected data, none was claimed by a large number of respondents. One is visiting a homeland, an experience that implies a continuing connection with a country of ancestral origin and a contact with its culture and people that possibly can rekindle a sense of ethnic identity. About 10 percent of native-born whites reported having made such a visit (implied by our question was a visit during the preceding five years, but it appears likely from the responses that some persons checked this experience based on visits occurring before this period). In terms of the lifetime number of visits, this group divides evenly between those who have made one visit and those who have made more than one.

A limited number of countries account for most of the visits. Leading the pack, undoubtedly because of proximity to the United States (and New York State in particular), is Canada, an ethnic homeland for many persons of French ancestry. Canada, by virtue of its proximity, was unusually likely to have been visited multiple times by individual respondents. The other countries most frequently visited were Britain (including Scotland), Germany, Ireland, and Italy. No countries in eastern Europe were mentioned, suggesting that persons with eastern European ancestries face considerable difficulties in maintaining links with these homelands once direct communication with family members who remained there has lapsed.

Tourism along with the desire to meet relatives and see the sites connected with one's family history seem the dominant motivations among those who make such visits. About two-thirds of this group indicated visiting with relatives abroad or going to places connected with their family origins (or doing both). The remaining third indicated tourist reasons for their trip (a European tour that included a homeland as one stop was a common pattern). Some of the respondents who visited people and places connected with their background also indicated tourism as a reason for their visit.

Visiting a homeland has a marginal relationship to ethnic identity (to conserve space, the data in this section are not reported in a tabular form). Most likely to have done so are persons who identify strongly with a single group, especially when their ancestry is also unmixed. About a quarter of such persons reported this experience. In most other categories of identity and salience, the proportion is below 10 percent.

The introduction of other factors through logistic regression analysis helps to clarify the ethnic significance of travel to a homeland. One major influence is generational status: there is a discernible fall-off in the probability of visiting a homeland between the second and third generations and again between the third and fourth ones. The role of generational status in influencing homeland visits among the American born suggests that some connections to family members who remained behind survive the transition between the immigrant and second generations, but that they fade further with each new generation on American soil. In this respect, there is a limit on family memory.

Age, too, plays a role, and a predictable one: the middle-aged are most likely to have made a visit. There is probably an affluence factor at work here, as well as the greater leisure that comes when children are grown and a work career is secure (or, even more so, coming to an end). Also involved may be a desire to see the place of one's family origins that grows stronger with advancing age (until the declining health of the elderly years hinders long-distance travel). Some scholars who stress ethnic persistence have made much of this sort of "return" to ethnicity. In this context, however, one should keep in mind that visits to a homeland are not common in any category of native-born whites.

The final influence is education: homeland visits rise with increased education. Again, there is undoubtedly some effect of affluence, which is obviously associated with education. There may also be an impact due to the greater cosmopolitanism of the highly educated, which engenders a desire to visit foreign countries and experience their cultures first-hand, thereby increasing the likelihood of visiting countries from which ancestors came.

A very different sort of experience is that of identifying with celebrities or public figures from the same ethnic background as oneself. This experience was reported by 12 percent of native-born whites, who typically named well-known and not always living figures from politics and the entertainment world as the persons whom they followed with special interest. (Curiously, almost no one mentioned a sports figure.) Frank Sinatra, New York governor Mario Cuomo, and Geraldine Ferraro (then the Democratic vice-presidential candidate) appeared on many of our respondents' lists, as did members of the Kennedy family and "Tip" O'Neill (then Speaker of the House of Representatives). Of interest to respondents of Polish ancestry was Pope John Paul II. As these examples show, the figures mentioned by our respondents typically enjoy a high level of national and international fame; only a few respondents mentioned figures of local prominence.

Although infrequent, the experience of identifying with an ethnic celebrity closely mirrors ethnic identity status and salience. It rises to its zenith among persons of single ancestry who have highly salient identities, nearly 40 percent of whom reported the experience. It is also fairly common among persons of mixed ancestry who identify strongly. But it is at very low levels in most other categories; for example, among those who do not identify ethnically or those who do but view their backgrounds as unimportant. Logistic regression analysis reveals that little aside from ethnic identity is associated with this experience. The one other variable with some impact is age: identification with ethnic celebrities is a middle-aged phenomenon, which drops off in frequency among young adults and the elderly.

The final experience is that of receiving business or professional help based on ethnic background. Despite the great scholarly attention that has been paid to the possible economic role of ethnicity and to the part played by ethnic networks in steering individuals to ethnic niches in the labor market, this experience is very uncommon among native-born whites in the Capital Region. In fact, just 2 percent checked it. (Restricting the percentage to whites who are economically active hardly changes this figure, raising it to just 3 percent.) So few are the respondents who have had the experience that statistical analysis is meaningless.

An examination of the descriptions of the help respondents have received indicates two prevalent situations in which people receive occasional help: when looking for a job and when running a small business. Several respondents told of having received various forms of help in trying to get a job, but only one claimed to have been hired on the basis of ethnic considerations. Others told of getting recommendations or other unspecified forms of assistance that increased their prospects of getting a job. The forms of ethnic assistance seemed even clearer to individuals operating small businesses. These respondents described friends who steered business their way, and one respondent said it happened all the time. The others described single incidents.

Summary

Most of the experiences considered here can, indeed, be seen as expressions of ethnic identity, or at least of salient ethnic identity. As a general rule, they attain their highest levels among persons who identify ethnically and attach some importance to their ethnic backgrounds, and they drop off considerably among nonidentifiers and persons who ascribe little or no importance to ethnicity. But whether these experiences can help to *sustain* ethnic identity, and hence ethnicity, is not so simple to answer, for they turn out to be different in character from cultural experiences. Some of the differences suggest a potentially wider role for these experiences than was found for cultural traits, while others indicate severe limits on their intensity and function and, by implication, on their ultimate import.

On the positive side of the ledger is that these experiences are not as demographically confined as such cultural experiences as eating ethnic foods and using a mother tongue. This is pointed up principally in relation to ancestry type (whether ancestry is mixed or unmixed). The noncultural experiences, such as ethnic social sensitivity, encounters with prejudice and discrimination, and ethnic political concerns, are not concentrated among persons of unmixed ancestry, who represent a declining part of the white population. Unlike the major cultural experiences, then, the experiences considered here are at least as common and in some cases more common among ethnically identifying persons from mixed ancestral backgrounds. They are also more widely dispersed among the various ethnic groups than the cultural experiences appear to be.

Other demographic forces associated with the transformation of ethnicity, such as advancing generational status and diminished confidence in ancestry knowledge, do generally weaken the non-cultural experiences. But the declines linked to them do not seem quite as pervasive or as precipitous as they do for ethnic cuisines and mother tongues; for instance, generational status has an effect on each of the experiences with ethnic bias and also on the related concern with ethnic political issues, but these experiences typically remain at a fairly constant level in the second and third generations, dropping only when the fourth generation is reached, in contrast to the more rapid generational decline of the mother-tongue experiences. And the loss of confidence in ancestry knowledge affects only political concerns and has no influence at all on experience of bias. The effects of demographic forces are even spottier when it comes to social sensitivity to ethnicity. Neither growing generational distance from immigration nor weakening ancestry knowledge hinders the experiences of feeling rapport with a fellow ethnic and of being curious about ethnic backgrounds.

Moreover, there are some countervailing forces, revealed in the typical relationships the noncultural experiences have to education, age, and gender. Virtually every one of the experiences is more common among the highly educated, and young adults and women tend to have higher levels of them. The consistency of these relationships underscores the potentially wide role of these experiences, since increased education among some ethnic groups is linked to the transformation of ethnicity, as are a broad set of changes evidenced by younger cohorts. But the relationships also suggest that these experiences have a distinctive part to play, one compatible with the notion that ethnic symbols and references are now commonly a form of cultural capital for individuals whose social worlds cut through traditional ethnic boundaries. In this conception, ethnic codes become a means of communicating and engendering feelings of solidarity with others whose social identities are not immediately apparent because of the great frequency of contact across ethnic lines and the decline of overt indicators of ethnicity. This use of ethnicity can occur just as easily in interactions between people of different ethnic origins as in those between people of the same origin (as the experience of discussing one's ethnic background demonstrates).

It bears on the value of ethnicity for cultural capital that the noncultural experiences seem quite bounded for most people who have them. Generally, they lack the intensity required to make any identity linked to them of great consequence for individuals, having for the most part an occasional, and even incidental, character. The experiences I have described as indicating a social sensitivity to ethnicity can serve as pertinent illustrations. Certainly, they must be pivotal to any maintenance of ethnic distinctions among whites, given the massive erosion of ethnic concentrations in the labor market and residential areas, as well as the great extent of marriage across ethnic lines (see chapter 1). If ethnic distinctions are to remain socially meaningful, it must be because people seek out others of like ethnic background. The relevant experiences appear to be widespread, as about half of native-born whites report having one or more of them. But for most people, the experiences are not frequent in occurrence: "occasional" is the category that stands out in the reporting of them. Few of our respondents seem to have ethnic considerations in the forefront of their minds in their daily encounters with others. The episodic nature of these experiences suggests that, while ethnicity as a social characteristic may receive occasional recognition, it pales in comparison to other features of the social world. Only for the experience of feeling rapport based on common ethnic background does there seem to be a stratum of whites, albeit constituted by a small minority, who are strongly oriented toward relationships with fellow ethnics.

Also revealing in this connection are the experiences connected with prejudice and discrimination. Although hardly widespread, they have not disappeared among native-born whites (nearly 30 percent of whom indicated one or more of them). But, fittingly, the most commonplace is that of coming into contact with ethnic stereotypes, and indeed ordinary observation indicates that ethnic stereotypes are still very familiar to Americans as a result of the historical and contemporary ethnic diversity of American society. But few respondents felt that such stereotypes are applied directly to them, and many discussed them in ways implying that stereotypes may have lost much—though surely not all—of their sting. Discrimination, however, can never lose its sting as long as it exists. But few of our respondents have personally suffered discrimination (at least in the five years preceding the survey covered by our question). Somewhat more, but still just a small minority, have heard of incidents of discrimination against members of their group. The majority of respondents having some personal or vicarious experience with discrimination seem optimistic about its decline. All in all, ethnic bias does not seem potent enough to do much for ethnic identities on a mass scale.

Ethnicity in Families

The taproot of ethnic identity nestles in families. Ethnic identity is, first and foremost, a matter of ancestry, of a self-definition that is both handed down within the family and created on the basis of family history. In the setting of the family, the child has the early experiences that can promote feelings of ethnic self-consciousness. The family is the arena where the cultural substance of the ethnic group—given mundane expression in food and language, but also communicated through family traditions—is initially acquired. The family is also likely to be the first group for the child in which the existence of ethnic differences is openly discussed, in which the putative characteristics of one's own group are praised (or bemoaned, as the case may be), and those of others are disparaged, envied, or perhaps appreciated. These matters seem so obvious that it is taken for granted among scholars that the family provides the original nurture for ethnicity.

In American society, the significance of the family for transmitting ethnicity is magnified by the comparative weakness of ethnicity in more public spheres, such as schools and workplaces. The

American experience in education, for instance, is dominated by the common-school tradition, in which an important goal has been the assimilation of students coming from diverse immigrant backgrounds. Accordingly, contemporary American school systems are not ethnically segregated, at least not in terms of ethnic divisions among whites (race is, of course, another story); and there are few schools that take the preservation and transmission of the ethnic cultures of their students to be important tasks[1]; bilingual programs constitute, arguably, an exception. Such programs are often justified as transitional necessities on the way to full integration of minority students in English-language classrooms, but they have little impact on European-ancestry groups. Insofar as schools deal with ethnic themes, it is typically to teach such values as tolerance and the appreciation of other ethnic cultures and histories.

The weakness of ethnicity outside of the family in enforced by normative consensus over the inappropriateness of ethnic considerations in many institutional spheres. In the workplace, there is almost universal belief in equality of opportunity for people of all groups (Schuman et al., 1985), to say nothing of legal prohibitions against job discrimination based on "color, religion, sex, or national origin" (in the Civil Rights Act of 1964). The consensus envisions the world of work as ethnically integrated, drawing together people from different ethnic backgrounds on a basis of equality. Obviously, this view need not deny the reality that some economic niches are ethnically exclusive, but these are generally assumed to be exceptions to the more general, normative pattern. Even affirmative-action policies, opposed by many people as an affront to this consensus, can be seen as broadly consistent with it, in the sense that such policies promote racial and ethnic integration in workplaces and represent attempts to rectify long-standing and deeply entrenched inequalities of opportunity. The absence of *normatively recognized*, systematic ethnic variations among schools and workplaces impedes the development of ethnic consciousness rooted in those differences that exist in fact. This point applies with particular force to Americans of European background, whose earlier occupational concentrations have been largely dissipated by processes of social mobility (see Lieberson and Waters, 1988: chap. 5). The situations of many non-European groups are rather different. Some recent immigrant groups, for example, are strongly concentrated in specific industrial sectors and occupational strata, forming ethnic economic enclaves, which are built on and further fortify shared ethnic identities (Portes and Bach, 1985; Waldinger, 1986).

Even with respect to European-ancestry groups, one can push the distinction between the family and public institutional spheres too far. Ethnicity is recognized as important in at least one public sphere, politics, and it is not difficult to point out significant ethnic concentrations in the economy as well (for example, Jews in New York's diamond trade and Greeks in the restaurant industry). Nevertheless, in the United States, great burdens fall on the family and some other "private" institutions (for example, social clubs and friendship networks) as the preserves of ethnicity. Although law and normative consensus may limit the ability of individuals to choose to work with coethnics, the freedom to choose to associate with others ethnically like oneself is recognized in settings like the family, the social club,[2] and friendship circles (Glazer, 1975: chap. 1). In these contexts, social structures may arise that are more or less ethnically homogeneous and supportive of ethnic cultures and consciousness.

The special role of such private spheres in preserving ethnicity has long been recognized by interpreters of ethnicity in the United States. Milton Gordon, for example, sees ethnic subsocieties as having some rough correspondence with the domain of primary relationships, while secondary relations are necessarily more ethnically integrated:

> The American social structure may be seen, then, as a national society which contains within its political boundaries a series of *subsocieties* based on ethnic identity. The network of organizations, informal social relationships, and institutional activities which makes up the ethnic subsociety tends to pre-empt most or all primary group relationships, while secondary relationships across ethnic group lines are carried out in the "larger society," principally in the spheres of economic and occupational life, civic and political activity, public and private nonparochial education, and mass entertainment. (1964: 37)

Of these private spheres, the family is paramount in importance. It is a setting in which individuals spend a great portion of their lives and which has an enduring impact on children. But what remains of its role when marriage across ethnic lines is as common as in the contemporary United States? For understandable reasons, great stress has always been placed on intermarriage as an indicator of assimilation. Intermarriage tests, and also perforates, ethnic social boundaries. It depends on the willingness of people from different ethnic backgrounds to accept each other in a long-lasting, exclusive, and largely nonhierarchical relationship. It also forges not just one relation spanning ethnic boundaries but a host of them, creating new kinship relations between the relatives of the intermarrying couple. Perhaps the greatest significance for intermarriage lies in its implications for the next generation. An intermarriage virtually guarantees that children will grow up in an ethnically mixed family setting, which may be less likely to have any ethnic character and seems certain to convey a less consistently ethnic character than an ethnically unified family.

Thus, the changes taking place among ethnic groups of European origin must be traced through families in order to understand their ultimate significance. This chapter, therefore, examines some of the ethnic characteristics of families in the Capital Region, beginning with a consideration of intermarriage—its extent and relationship to other ethnic characteristics—and then turning to the critical subject of whether and how children are raised to have ethnic identities.

Intermarriage among Whites

Intermarriage is now very widespread among whites of European background, although it occurs less commonly across the European/non-European divide, especially between blacks and whites. The 1980 census data on ethnic ancestry show that approximately three of every four marriages by American-born whites involve some crossing of ethnic boundaries. One in two are between partners whose ethnic ancestries share nothing in common; and for one in four, there is some partial overlap in ancestry, but also some difference, so that boundary spanning is once again involved (similar findings are reported by Lieberson and Waters, 1985, 1988). The contrast with marriages that span the confines of race and Hispanic ancestry is great, since only a tiny fraction of non-Hispanic whites (about 1 percent in the 1980 census) marry non-whites or Hispanics.

The intermarriage research at the national level suggests that the incidence of interethnic marriage has increased substantially over recent decades among whites, especially for the groups from southern and eastern Europe, which were largely composed of immigrants and their children until the era of World War II. Considered in historical terms, the changes among these groups have been very rapid. The principal basis for this conclusion rests on comparisons of intermarriage proportions among different birth cohorts, although it is also bolstered by the typical generational relationship to intermarriage, namely, that intermarriage is more common with greater generational distance from immigration. The cohort comparisons typically reveal that proportions married to spouses of the same background decrease from older to younger cohorts, and such differences are generally large for such southern and eastern European groups as the Italians and Poles. But for just about all the major ancestry groups, intermarriage proportions are higher among younger, more recently married cohorts. Since interreligious marriage has also increased, one can speak of a general decline in the influence of ethnoreligious factors on marriages between whites.

An intriguing feature of contemporary marriage patterns, and one that has potential implications for ethnicity, is the increasing frequency of marriage between persons whose ancestries overlap in part, but not completely. This phenomenon is connected with the spread of mixed ancestry, a consequence of rising intermarriage, since the possibility of partial overlap arises only when one or both partners come from mixed ancestral backgrounds. And, for essentially numerical reasons, the probability of such marriages increases as the proportion of the population with mixed ancestry grows and as the ethnic complexity of these ancestries increases, with the consequence that more possibilities for overlap are present. But even if the growth in the number of marriages involving partial ancestry overlap is an outcome of trends in mixed ancestry and intermarriage, it could involve consequences that counteract the apparent significance of these trends; that is, shared ethnic ancestry, even in the presence of other distinguishing ethnic ingredients, could provide the basis for some of the properties of an ethnic in-marriage. The couple could define themselves as endogamously married, thereby highlighting the ethnicity they share and pushing other aspects of their ancestries into the background, and they could emphasize this common element to their children, thus imparting a particular ethnic tone to the latter's emerging sense of ethnic identity. (Lieberson and Waters, 1986, follow this line of speculation in attempting to account for inconsistencies in the reporting of ancestry in intermarried families.)

How are these broad national trends reflected in the marriages of native-born whites in the Capital Region? To measure intermarriage, our survey asked married respondents about the ethnic ancestries and identities of their spouses in precisely the same way that it asked about this information for the respondents themselves. As is only to be expected, respondents' knowledge of their spouses' ethnic backgrounds does not appear to be as complete as their knowledge of their own, but nevertheless respondents gave us considerable detail about their spouses' ancestries. Only 5 percent claimed to have no knowledge of their spouses' backgrounds.[3] Even though the degree of complexity was not as great in respondents' reports about their spouses' backgrounds as it was in those about their own, half still reported mixed ancestral backgrounds for their spouses (compared to two-thirds for themselves); and approximately 20 percent cited three or more ethnic components in their spouses' backgrounds (compared to 28 percent for themselves). Thus, while the information about spousal backgrounds is undoubtedly not quite as complex as the reality (there being no reason to believe that the complexity of spouses' ancestries is, on average, less than that of respondents), it is complete enough to give confidence in the resulting portrait of intermarriage.

These survey data have two important advantages over census and other frequently used sources of intermarriage data. One lies in the greater completeness of the ancestry reports. As noted earlier, the ancestry data we have collected are more complete than is the case for other sources of ethnic data—they are less subject to errors of truncation or simplification. This is also true for the ancestry data for spouses, and consequently it is easier to evaluate whether there is any degree of ancestry overlap, what portion it represents of the ancestries involved, and how it is related to ancestry complexity.

The second advantage is still more critical and stems from the identity data. Especially because of the great and growing extent of mixed ancestry, the analysis of intermarriage cannot confine itself to simple measurements of ancestral overlap. Marriages involving some partial degree of common ethnicity are increasing in frequency. What is to be made of this trend? Its implications cannot be teased out of patterns of ancestry alone, for these cannot reveal the subjective meaning attached to common ancestry. Even the demonstration that marriages of this type are more frequent than would be predicted from chance (see Lieberson and Waters, 1985; Alba and Golden, 1986) does not prove the existence of felt affinities between persons who share some element of ancestry, for there can be other factors, such as geographic concentration, that account for the apparent nonrandomness.[4] Hence, the identity data, as well as other information in our survey about respondents' views of their marriages, permit me to probe more deeply into the ethnic significance of shared ancestry in marriage.

The first conclusion to be drawn from the data is that marriage across ethnic lines is exceedingly common among the residents of the Capital Region, as in the nation as a whole. A comparison of the ethnic ancestries of husbands and wives indicates that a majority of native-born whites in this region are intermarried by any plausible definition of the term (see table 5.1). In about half of marriages, the ancestries of husbands and wives have no ethnic element in common. To this group should probably be added the 5 percent of mar-

Table 5.1   Ethnic overlap in the marriages of native-born whites

	Overlap of ancestry	Overlap of identity
Complete overlap[a]	13.6%	12.5%
Partial overlap:		
Two or more components	7.0	0.0
One component	22.6	3.9
No overlap	52.1	41.6
Spouse's ancestry/identity unknown	4.7	30.0
Respondent's identity undefined	—	12.1
Number of cases	257	257

Note: Respondents whose ancestry is unknown are excluded from this and subsequent marriage tables.
[a]Overlap is determined from the point of view of the respondent. Therefore, in some cases of complete overlap, the spouse's ancestry includes elements not found in the respondent's.

ried respondents who appear not to know about their spouses' ethnic backgrounds. Although, obviously, one cannot say for certain that these are intermarriages in the strict sense of marriages that span ethnic boundaries, it is hard to view them as anything else, inasmuch as the respondents' evident lack of knowledge demonstrates that no common ethnic ancestry is recognized by these couples, even should it exist.[5]

At the other extreme, 14 percent have taken spouses whose ancestries entirely overlap their own.[6] I describe these couples as endogamously married, although it is open to doubt whether this term is appropriate for every case. First, the ethnic identities of husbands and wives are not always in agreement. Second, a quarter of these marriages involve matching mixed ethnic ancestry. Whether such marriages should be regarded as endogamous can at least be questioned, since the shared background need not imply an unambiguous ethnic affiliation.

Finally, there is an intermediate group, constituting 30 percent of the marriages of native-born whites. These are marriages in which the ethnic ancestries of husbands and wives overlap partly, containing some elements in common but also differing in some respect (by definition, therefore, all of these marriages involve mixed ancestry on one or both sides). In about three-quarters of these marriages, husband and wife share exactly one ethnic component in common. There is then a small minority, amounting to 7 percent of the marriages of all native-born whites, where this partial overlap involves more than one ethnic element; typically, the ancestries of the partners in these marriages are quite complex.

The fact that a spouse shares some ethnic ancestry with a person having mixed ethnic ancestry raises the possibility that the common ethnicity is strengthened, overshadowing other ethnic elements. In this sense, such a marriage might counteract what would seem the inherent tendency of mixed ancestry to dilute ethnic affiliations. But if this possibility is realized in some cases, it does not appear appropriate as a general characterization of marriages of this type. For one thing, these marriages are most frequent among persons with complex ancestries, since such persons have more ethnic possibilities for a partial match. Among respondents with two ethnic components in their ancestries, 35 percent have spouses whose ancestries partly overlap their own. Among those with three, the proportion rises to 45 percent, and among those with four or more, to 77 percent. It is in this last group that the majority of marriages where husband and wife share two or more ethnic elements is to be found.

Thus, the complexity of the ancestries involved would appear to lessen the possibility that marriages involving some partial ancestry overlap should be regarded as a new form of endogamy. Also speaking against it is the kind of ethnic element that is usually shared; in the great majority of cases, this is one of the three most prominent old-stock ancestries (English, German, or Irish), and in most of the others, it is also an old-stock origin such as French or Scots. This pattern is understandable on the basis of purely numerical reasons. The three most prominent old-stock ancestries are numerically largest, and the old-stock ancestries in general are the ones most likely to be involved in ancestry mixtures. Hence, the probability is rather high that when persons with mixed ancestry marry, their spouses will by chance share some English, Irish, or German ancestry with them. This is the case even for persons with some southern and eastern European background, since mixed ancestries involving these backgrounds are also likely to involve some old-stock element (see chapter 2). But, as we have already seen, the old-stock ancestries, with the partial exception of the Irish, are not typically associated with strong ethnic identities or salient forms of ethnic cultural expression. Thus, that they are so frequently the common ethnic ingredients when ancestries overlap does not generally offer the prospect of forging strong ethnic identities on this basis alone.

This brings us to the issue of ethnic identity. If, when viewed from the perspective of ancestries, marriages now commonly span ethnic boundaries, the question arises as to how they appear when viewed in terms of the ethnic identities of husbands and wives. Ancestries, after all, are only the "objective" material and may differ from the subjective definition of ethnicity. Hence, marriages that appear to be not fully endogamous when viewed from the standpoint of the ancestries involved may become so when judged by the criterion of ethnic identity.

But, in fact, the lack of congruence between the ethnicities of husbands and wives, and hence the extent of intermarriage, is even more apparent when it comes to ethnic identity. In a great number of marriages, one or both partners do not identify ethnically, or their ethnic identities are unknown to each other. In either case, shared ethnic identities cannot be considered as part of the marriages; for instance, nearly a third of respondents were unable to describe the ethnic identities of their spouses[7] (see table 5.1). Saying such things as, "she almost never talks about the subject," or "I don't know—you'll have to ask him," or "she's an American just as I am," these respondents generally indicated that ethnic background is not a topic of much concern in their families. These marriages are not typically recent in origin; included in this group are many marriages of long duration (almost three-quarters have witnessed their tenth anniversaries), where husbands and wives presumably have had many opportunities to discover common ethnic concerns, if these exist.

Among marriages where the identities of spouses exist and are known (at least to respondents), an absence of any shared ethnic element is the most common situation. Marriages of this type account for roughly 40 percent of all the marriages of native-born whites. Only in what remains after this group is subtracted, some one-sixth of marriages, is there some overlap of ethnic identities: for 4 percent, the overlap is partial, while for 13 percent, it is complete. By the measure of ethnic identity, then, endogamy is certainly no more common, and probably less so, than it is in terms of ancestry.

The rarity of any overlap in the ethnic identities of husbands and wives stands in some contrast to the pattern for ethnic ancestry, since overlapping ancestries occur for a substantial minority of marriages. The obvious explanation is that many of the marriages in this minority lose their ethnic commonality when viewed in terms of the identities of husbands and wives. Remarkably, this is true even when the overlap in ancestry is complete. In about a third of such marriages, there is no commonality in terms of ethnic identity, typically because one or both spouses do not identify themselves ethnically. (Table 5.2 presents the relationship between the ancestry and identity views of marriages.)

Even more interesting, because of their increasing frequency among native-born whites, are marriages where ancestries overlap partly. In general, these marriages display little convergence in terms of ethnic identities. In only 13 percent of these cases are the identities of both spouses the same, and in another 12 percent of

Table 5.2   Ancestry overlap by identity overlap

Ancestry overlap:	Identity overlap					
	Complete overlap	Partial overlap	No overlap	Spouse's identity unknown	Respondent's identity undefined	Tot
Complete overlap	62.9	2.9	8.6	22.9	2.9	100.2
Partial overlap	13.2	11.8	25.0	30.3	19.7	100.0
No overlap	0.0	0.0	63.4	25.4	11.2	100.0
Spouse's ancestry unknown	0.0	0.0	0.0	100.0	0.0	100.0

Overall significance level: p < .001

cases there is some shared ethnic ingredient. About 30 percent of these respondents, however, are unable to say what, if anything, the ethnic identity of their spouse is; another 20 percent lack an ethnic identity themselves; and in a quarter of the cases, the identities of husbands and wives are simply different (despite the overlap in their ancestries).

To complete the portrait of intermarriage among whites requires that some of the details of interreligious marriage be painted in, even if with broad brush strokes (justified on the grounds that this form of intermarriage will play no role in the discussion to follow). Marriage between and within religious groups is influenced by the region's religious composition, which is more heterogeneous than that of the nation. In contrast to Protestant domination in the nation as a whole, the majority of the Capital Region's population is Catholic, but this majority is not as large as the Protestant one at the national level. In the married population, 56 percent were raised as Catholic, 40 percent as Protestant, and not quite 3 percent as Jewish. This above average religious diversity makes for a fairly high occurrence of interreligious marriage, although interreligious marriage is still not as prevalent as interethnic marriage.[8] In terms of religious origin rather than current affiliation, almost 40 percent of marriages cross religious lines, with the rate of intermarriage higher among the smaller groups (Jews and Protestants) and lower among the largest (Catholics). Since there is a tendency for one partner in a religious intermarriage to convert formally or informally to the religion of the other, the degree of religious exogamy looks smaller when it is measured in terms of current religion—not quite 30 percent are intermarried by this criterion. It appears that about 40 percent of marriages between individuals of different religious origins become endogamous through conversion. While recent marriages are mixed in here and thus this figure may become higher over time, it is surprisingly low and thus may serve as a measure of the widespread acceptability of interreligious marriage.

Curiously, interreligious marriage does not have much of a relationship to interethnic marriage. In other words, marriage to someone of similar ethnic background does not offer much protection from religious difference. Only the small group of marriages where there is complete overlap of ethnic ancestry is an exception: Virtually all of these are endogamous in terms of religious origin. Otherwise the degree of ethnic overlap makes no difference for religious endogamy. About 40 percent of marriages involving partial overlap of ancestry are religiously exogamous; the same approximate percentage is found among marriages where no ethnic overlap is present.

By any standard, then, intermarriage appears to be very widespread among the Capital Region's residents of European ancestry. In this respect, the region appears to be further along than the nation as a whole. Compared to the nation, the Capital Region shows a lower frequency for marriages between spouses of identical ancestry and a higher one for marriages involving some partial ancestry overlap. These differences between the region and the nation are partly artifacts of methodology, as our survey collected more complete ancestry information than did the national census. This reduces, for example, the apparent frequency of identical ancestry, which is higher in the census because of ancestry truncation. But the difference rests on a real foundation as well. My analysis of census data for the Capital Region shows strict endogamy—husbands and wives having identical ancestries—to be less common there than in the nation. The explanation, I suspect, is that the region is so ethnically heterogeneous that few groups offer the critical mass of eligible partners necessary to sustain even moderate levels of endogamy, in the absence of either strong in-group marital preferences or institutional factors (such as segregated school systems) promoting in-group interaction. This explanation plays on the much noted role of group size in determining the frequency of in-group versus out-group interaction (Blau, 1977; Blau et al.,

1982): small groups have higher rates of interaction with outsiders. From the point of view of this book, the region's distinctiveness in intermarriage makes it more, not less, interesting and germane, since the level of interethnic marriage is climbing among whites in the nation as a whole. In this respect, the Capital Region may be indicative of the nation's future.

How are Marriages Viewed?

By the measure of either ancestry or identity, interethnic marriage appears prevalent and endogamy infrequent, although not every marriage is readily classifiable in these terms. The very commonness of intermarriage piques curiosity about how such a marriage is viewed by its participants: is it perceived as a marriage that crosses social boundaries, that is, as an intermarriage, or as a marriage between people whose backgrounds are the same in some sense? Merely because a marriage appears to an outside observer to be an intermarriage based on an objective criterion such as ancestry does not mean that it appears this way to its participants. Particularly when there is a broad convergence among different ethnic groups along lines of culture and socioeconomic position, ancestry differences may not be associated with behavioral or other social disparities that create the perception of social distance or of a social boundary.[9] To the extent that the perception of intermarriage is lost, ethnicity could be described as truly having receded into some hinterground, if not disappearing altogether.

We asked our respondents whether they viewed their spouses as coming from the same ethnic backgrounds as themselves.[10] In terms of their subjective views of their marriages, there is much less intermarriage than the data about ancestry and ethnic identity indicate. A majority of native-born white respondents (56 percent) said that they and their spouses come from the same ethnic background, while 44 percent declared the backgrounds to be different (see table 5.3). From these numbers alone, it would appear that a significant fraction of respondents perceive the ethnic aspect of their marriages in terms that have little to do with actual ancestry or with ethnic identity.

Nevertheless, there is some correspondence between the more objective ethnic characteristics of marriages and respondents'

Table 5.3   The perception of ethnic sameness in marriage
by degree of overlap

| | *% saying spouse is from* | |
	same ethnic background	*different ethnic background*
All native-born whites	56.0	44.0
Ancestry overlap:		
complete	94.3	5.7
partial	75.0	25.0
none	35.1	64.9
spouse's ancestry unknown	58.3	41.7
Identity overlap:		
complete	96.9	3.1
partial	70.0ª	30.0ª
none	31.8	68.2
spouse's identity unknown	64.9	35.1
respondent's identity undefined	71.0	29.0
Significance levels:	for ancestry overlap subtable, p < .001 for identity overlap subtable, p < .001	

ªPercentage based on very small number of cases (ten or fewer).

views of them. In particular, when there is some overlap between
the ethnic ancestries of husbands and wives, respondents are very
likely to perceive their marriages as endogamous. Virtually all of
the respondents in marriages involving a complete overlap of ancestral backgrounds perceive their marriages this way. This perception is also frequent where there is some partial overlap of ethnic
ancestries. Yet it also occurs in many marriages where no overlap of
ancestries exists. Despite the absence of common ethnic ancestry,
about a third of respondents in such marriages maintained that
they and their spouses are from the same ethnic background. The
same was also said, incidentally, by almost 60 percent of the small
group who do not know the ethnic ancestry of their spouses.

Crucial for the explanation of such anomalous perceptions is
ethnic identity status. Respondents who do not identify in ethnic
terms are nonetheless likely to assert that they and their spouses
come from the same ethnic background, regardless of the actual

facts of ancestry. This tendency suggests than when ethnicity is not salient to people, they are likely to overlook the existence of "objective" ethnic differences. Roughly 70 percent of respondents who do not identify ethnically perceive their marriages as endogamous (see table 5.3); the percentage is almost as high (nearly 60 percent) when it is limited to such respondents whose marriages involve no ancestral overlap at all (this last percentage does not appear in the table).

There is a hint in the data that the perception of being endogamously married gains strength over time in a marriage, as differences that may have seemed more prominent during its early years fade into the background (or, perhaps, marriages where these differences are pronounced are prone to disintegrate after a while). Couples that have been married for twenty years or more are more likely than others to describe themselves as endogamously married even when the facts of ancestry say otherwise. Among such couples where the ethnic ancestries of husband and wife have no common element, 44 percent still describe themselves as endogamously married, compared to 24 percent among similar couples married for less than twenty years. The effect of time seems nevertheless uncertain because it is absent for marital durations less than twenty years.

The heterogeneity behind the perception of endogamy is pointed up in the explanations respondents gave for their perceptions. Revealingly, many respondents who perceived their marriages as endogamous did not explain this by referring to the facts of ethnic ancestry—only half made reference to these. And this proportion is derived by a generous rule of counting, which includes respondents who referred not to ancestry in the same country but in similar countries (in the eyes of respondents) or the same general part of Europe (for example, northwest Europe or the British Isles). Thus, a rather broad concept of perceived shared ancestry was allowed.

The other reasons do not fall into a neat classification, precisely because they lack the common denominator of an ethnic reference. About a fifth perceive no difference in backgrounds because they view background as unimportant (or, in another variant, because they and their spouses are American). Closer to a valid ethnic reference was a second, somewhat smaller group, who answered in terms of shared religious backgrounds. A third group, also small, explained their answer in terms of their general compatibility with their spouses ("we think alike"). A variety of other reasons were cited by even smaller clusters of respondents, such as growing up in the same place or coming from the same social and economic strata.

The reasons given by respondents who perceive themselves to be intermarried were in some respects simpler. Ironically, ethnicity is more consistently salient in the group with this perception than it is in the group describing their marriages as endogamous. More than half directly referred to the differing ancestral backgrounds of themselves and their spouses. A kindred explanation, offered by a minority, was that the marital partners come from different cultural backgrounds or have different traditions. These two reasons were the only ones offered by sizable numbers of respondents. Otherwise, explanations were spread among a number of distinct reasons, no one of which attracted more than a few respondents.

The seeming lack of relevance of ethnicity for many marriages and the wide acceptability, if not invisibility, of intermarriage are on display in respondents' assessments of whether being intermarried or endogamously married, as the case may be, has made a difference to them.[11] Only a minority thought so. Approximately 70 percent of married respondents denied that the ethnic background of their spouses had any impact on their marriages, although this figure may be inflated a bit by the perception of some respondents that they had nothing to which to compare their marriages ("I've only had one husband/wife," said some). For many respondents, the sense that ethnic backgrounds have not played a large role in their marriages is undoubtedly linked to the lack of salience ethnic characteristics have for them in general; these respondents appear to be denying the relevance of ethnicity for their marital relationships. This is especially true for respondents who perceived themselves as intermarried: only 21 percent of them believed that ethnicity has made a difference in their marriages, compared to 35 percent of those respondents who perceived themselves as endogamously married.

Further revealing of the general acceptability of intermarriage are the explanations of respondents in the majority who believed their marriage type made no difference. These explanations typically emphasized the lack of importance of ethnicity in general or specifically for marriage. About half said in one way or another that ethnicity was unimportant or not relevant ("we are both Americans" was one form of this answer, but far from the only one). Others, fewer in number, stressed the personal, idiosyncratic factors in marriage ("marriage is just two people" and "we get along" were typical responses in this group). Only in the small minority of whites who perceive themselves as endogamously married *and* believe this has made a difference is there a sense that common ethnicity is to be valued in marriage. These respondents pointed to positive benefits of being married to someone from the same or a similar background, such as liking the same foods or sharing the same customs and traditions; and many felt that their marriages were stronger as a result. There were also some intermarried respondents who felt their marriage type has made a difference. They, too, stressed positive aspects of their marriage situation, usually stating that marriage to someone of a different background is more interesting, or that they had developed a new tolerance or acquired new points of view as a result of intermarriage.

Intermarriage's Bearing on Individual Ethnicity

Intermarriage has been viewed as a cardinal indicator of assimilation in the belief that intermarried couples are likely to be less "ethnic" in their characteristics than the endogamously married. Because of differences in ethnic and cultural background, it is reasoned, partners in an intermarriage may find it necessary to submerge their ethnic identities, lest these give rise to conflict. For a similar reason, they may find it difficult to maintain ethnic cultural traits—language, customs, and perhaps cuisine as well (though the data in chapter 3 dispute this point on cuisine). Adoption of mainstream American culture is made likely because it is a common denominator, a cultural *lingua franca*. Needless to say, any association between intermarriage and weak or absent ethnic traits may not be a product of the marriage itself but a prior condition which enhances the probability of intermarriage in the first place. But, either way, this reasoning would lead one to presume that there should be consistent differences in ethnic traits between intermarried and endogamous couples.

Remarkably, such differences are not to be found in our survey, at least not to any important degree. Consider, for example, the relationship between marriage type, as defined on the basis of the ancestries of husbands and wives, and whether individuals identify in ethnic terms, displayed in table 5.4. In this table, married individuals have been divided according to whether their ancestry is mixed or unmixed (since ancestry type affects the likelihood of ancestry overlap in marriage and also that of ethnic identity). For neither ancestry type is there any significant connection between marriage and ethnic identity; for instance, regardless of whether they have married spouses of the same background or not, 80 to 90 percent of respondents of single ancestry identify in ethnic terms. For persons of mixed ancestry, it is tempting to seize on the high proportion of identifiers (90 percent) in the category where there is complete overlap between the ancestries of respondents and their spouses as evidence of a link between marriage and identity. But this category is so small, since such complete overlap for persons of mixed ancestry is rare, that it is not significantly different from the others; and even if it were, the rarity of the situation would make it of little practical import.

Intermarriage also makes little or no difference for the subjective importance attached to ethnicity, a factor strongly related to most other aspects of ethnic behavior and identity. Whether one examines marriages by overlap in the ancestries or the identities of husbands and wives, the results are the same—there is no statis-

Table 5.4   Ethnic identity by ancestry overlap in marriage and ancestry type

Ancestry overlap	Single-ancestry persons	Mixed-ancestry persons
	% who identify	% who identify
Complete	88.0	90.0[b]
Partial	—[c]	61.8
None[a]	82.5	69.9
Significance levels:	N.S.	N.S.

[a] The small group of respondents who do not know their spouses' ancestry is included in this category.
[b] Percentage based on a very small number of cases (ten or fewer).
[c] By definition, partial overlap cannot occur for single-ancestry respondents.

tically meaningful relationship to ethnicity's felt importance. In sum, there is no evidence to indicate that endogamous marriage supports a strong ethnic identity or that intermarriage retards one. Nor is there evidence for the simple proposition that persons who identify strongly tend to marry within their group.

The absence of a vital link between marriage type and an individual's ethnic characteristics is shown further by the ethnically relevant experiences. The essential pattern is revealed by the index that counts all ethnic experiences reported by a respondent (first used in chapter 3). By this measure, there is no difference between the two extreme categories of marital type: first, respondents who are married to spouses of the same ancestry and, second, those whose spouses have entirely different, nonoverlapping, ancestry (see table 5.5). Turning from ancestry to identity overlap, one finds that there is some relationship between marriage and ethnic experience, but chiefly because identity overlap surreptitiously introduces the respondent's own identity status, which is known from earlier chapters to correspond with the level of ethnic experience;

Table 5.5   Selected levels of ethnic experience by degrees of ancestry and identity overlap in marriage

	% with no experiences	% with six or more
All married native-born whites	22.2	24.9
Ancestry overlap		
Complete	28.6	28.6
Partial	14.5	25.0
None	23.9	25.4
Spouse's ancestry unknown	33.3	8.3
Identity overlap		
Complete	15.6	37.5
Partial	20.0[a]	10.0[a]
None	13.1	30.8
Spouse's identity unknown	39.0	14.3
Respondent's identity unknown	19.4	22.6

Significance levels: for ancestry overlap subtable, N.S.
                       for identity overlap subtable, $p < .01$

[a]Percentage based on a very small number of cases (ten or fewer).

that is, aside from the tiny category involving partial identity over-lap, the relationship in the table arises because of low levels of ethnic experience in categories where the degree of identity overlap is undefined, and especially that for marriages where the spouse's identity is not known to the respondent (and may not exist). This last category contains a disproportionate number of respondents who do not identify themselves, and it should be obvious that if they also do not know their spouses' ethnic identities, ethnicity in gener-al is probably not salient for them. When respondents' and spouses' identities are known, however, there is no meaningful relationship between identity overlap and ethnic experience: in particular, the level of experience among respondents whose spouses' identities have nothing in common with their own is not significantly different from that among the endogamously married.

By combing through the list of experiences, one finds hints that endogamous marriage may be associated with slightly greater probabilities for some experiences. But the differences are, gener-ally speaking, not large or consistent, and the number of cases of endogamy is small, so that this conclusion cannot be backed up with statistical confidence. In the main, these differences appear for experiences that have a cultural character (as opposed, for example, to experiences with prejudice and discrimination), and this is con-sistent with expectations of intermarriage's effects. To take one of the largest differences as an example, almost 30 percent of the endog-amously married (by the criterion of ancestry overlap) report at-tending ethnic festivals at least once a year, compared to 13 percent of respondents married to spouses with nonoverlapping ancestry. This difference is statistically significant, but a number of others in the same direction are not: the endogamously married are more likely than the intermarried to eat ethnic foods at least once a month (by a margin of 44 percent to 31 percent), to use them to celebrate special occasions (by a margin of 41 to 31 percent), to practice ethnic customs and traditions (24 versus 13 percent), and to use a mother tongue (24 versus 16 percent).

There are some ethnic experiences, however, that appear to be at least as common, if not more so, among the intermarried; for example, respondents with spouses of nonoverlapping ancestry are as likely as the endogamously married: to feel strongly about an ethnic political issue, to have heard about discrimination against the members of their groups, to have come into contact with ethnic stereotypes, to feel curious about the ethnic backgrounds of others, and to discuss their backgrounds with others. But the endogamously married are significantly more likely to report some personal incident of discrimination (by a margin of 12 to 4 percent).

Despite some mild differences, the outstanding finding here is the absence of a pronounced relationship between intermarriage and ethnic experience. The differences just noted have been obtained without any controls for other relevant variables (given the small number of endogamous marriages, such controls would be inadvisable here). But surely other variables are relevant, for instance, type of ancestry (single versus mixed), since persons of single ancestry are overrepresented among those who are endogamously married and are also more likely to have some of the experiences in question.

Thus, ethnic traits are not markedly more muted among the intermarried, or more intense among those with spouses of the same ethnic background. One could perhaps take this as an indication that the generally accepted relationship between intermarriage and assimilation is a chimera, not found in reality. But far more plausible, I think, is a hypothesis that the weakness of this relationship is characteristic of a particular stage of the dissolution of ethnic boundaries. When intermarriage is as widespread as it is in the Capital Region, which may well prove a forerunner for the United States more generally, then even persons who come from quite ethnic family environments are likely to intermarry. The ethnic communities and networks that supported endogamy in the past have eroded. Even though they have not disappeared, they are not extensive enough to provide the critical mass of appropriate, ethnic partners. Thus, processes of assimilation at the level of ethnic groups and communities mean that persons with ethnic identities and experiences are found increasingly in the ranks of the intermarried. It is also inevitable that some persons with weaker ethnic traits choose by chance marital partners from similar or overlapping ethnic backgrounds. The end result of these two processes is to muddy the cultural and social distinction between the exogamously and endogamously married.

This muddying is exemplified by the Italian group, which has stood in bold relief for the vigor of its ethnicity in the Capital Region. But this prominence is not repeated when it comes to endogamy. Close to 85 percent of respondents of Italian background have spouses with no Italian ancestry at all (about 15 percent have spouses whose ancestries overlap with their own in some other respect). The proportion married to spouses with some common ancestry is, in fact, higher for some of the old-stock groups, especially the Irish, English, and Germans. Undoubtedly, this happens not because of any greater tendencies to pick spouses of the same background but for numerical reasons, because these three ancestry groups are larger and more extensively represented in the mixed ancestry population. In short, strong Italian identities are by and large not supported by endogamous marriages.

The current stage of ethnic change brings further consequences in its wake. One is that the link between identity and social structure is increasingly vitiated; that is, persons with relatively intense ethnic identities are more and more likely to find themselves in social contexts that have no resonance for their particular identities. This does not necessarily mean a diminishing of their ethnic identities or behavior, but it may change the nature of these traits as they become increasingly personal and lose a sense of obvious connection to ethnic groups and settings.

The Ethnic Socialization of Children

No issue carries greater weight for the survival of ethnic groups than the socialization of children to have a distinct consciousness of their ethnic background, an identification with their ethnic group. Should the transmission of ethnicity from one generation to the next be interrupted, then ethnic groups are obviously imperiled.

The family plays the paramount, albeit not the only, role in instilling ethnic identity in children. This is true almost by definition, given the linkage between ethnic identity and ancestry. Although systematic evidence on the early socialization of children to have an ethnic identity is lacking, many scholars of ethnicity assume that childhood experiences in the context of the family provide the first nurture for ethnic identity (for example, Isaacs, 1975).

This view, although not demonstrated in this book, is at least consistent with it. In explaining the importance they attach to ethnic backgrounds (see chapter 2), many respondents associated ethnicity with their upbringing and other aspects of their early family experiences. Without these experiences, then, there might be little ethnic identity.

That the transmission of ethnicity runs through families has been argued to be one of the strengths of ethnicity in the American context. Most interpreters have accepted an inevitable attrition of ethnicity in public spheres. But ethnicity can presumably retain its vitality if it is sheltered in private spheres, most prominently in families. In this argument, it is not even necessary for families to make self-conscious attempts to inculcate ethnicity, since ethnic groups differ from one another in family structures and in the values, living styles, and tastes associated with family life. A frequently cited example is a distinctive Italian-American family type (Gambino, 1974; Femminella and Quadagno, 1976), in which the roles of parents and other relatives have ethnically determined nuances and in which there is an unusual emphasis placed on family solidarity. Accordingly, the experience of growing up in ethnic families should be so distinctive that it breeds a sense of ethnic identity. (This is a frequent theme in the autobiographical literature of Italian Americans; see Jerre Mangione, *Mount Allegro*, and the more contemporary statement by Elizabeth Stone, 1988.)

But can so much be assumed about the connection between the family and ethnic identity for whites in the contemporary United States? As we have just seen, intermarriage is extremely common—the rule, rather than the exception, among Americans with European ancestries. Therefore, it cannot be taken for granted that families will socialize, whether intentionally or inadvertently, their children to have a sense of ethnic identity. It is unlikely that intermarried couples will recreate the ethnic family types that are portrayed in the literature on ethnicity. Moreover, marital partners often do not share a common ethnic identity, even when there is some overlap in their ancestries. Hence, one cannot assume that couples will attempt to communicate an ethnic identity to their children; nor can one assume what direction such an identity will take. The ethnic socialization of children is problematic.

Are Parents Concerned about the Ethnic Identities of Their Children?

As an initial step in addressing the issues surrounding socialization, our survey asked the parents in our sample whether they want their children to think of themselves as having a definite ethnic background.[12] Given the great extent of intermarriage, this is obviously a crucial question. Parents who do not care about their children's ethnic identity would be unlikely to expose them to the ethnic influences necessary to nourish identity. The ethnic diversity in most marriages would appear to require some deliberate effort on the part of parents to instruct their children about ethnicity. I have restricted the analysis to parents who still have at least some of their children living with them on the assumption that parents whose children have left their home are likely to feel that matters of identity are properly their children's concern.[13]

The majority of parents with children in the house do not seem to be concerned over whether their children identify themselves in ethnic terms (see table 5.6). About half of these parents said simply that they did not care about their children's ethnic identities, and another 10 percent or so said that they wanted their children to identify as Americans (also counted here are a small number of parents who said either they did not know how their children should identify or their children could identify in any way they want). Close to 40 percent of parents care that their children acquire some ethnic identity. While this is clearly a sizable minority, it is considerably smaller than the proportion of ethnic identifiers among white adults—two-thirds. Thus, if the ethnic identities of children hinge on parental intentions, the strength of identities among whites is likely to decline in the future.

Of the parents who want their children to identify ethnically, most (almost 60 percent) describe identities that are ethnically mixed. Here, too, there is a difference from the ethnic identities of contemporary adults, where unmixed identities prevail. The preference for mixed versus single identities in children stems principally from the ancestry and identity status of parents and their marital (and, in some cases, former marital) situations. Mixed identities are desired for children when parents themselves have mixed ancestry

Table 5.6   Desire for children's ethnic identity
by parent's ethnic identity status

	Desired children's identity		
	None[a]	Single	Mixed
Total for native-born white parents	60.7%	16.4%	23.0%
Ethnic identity status (ancestry/identity):			
single/single	46.8	31.9	21.3
multiple/single	63.6	18.2	18.2
multiple/multiple	46.8	8.5	44.7
single/none	80.0[b]	10.0[b]	10.0[b]
multiple/none	81.6	7.9	10.5
unknown/none	87.5[b]	12.5[b]	0.0[b]

Overall significance level: p < .001

Note: This and the next two tables are restricted to respondents with children living at home (N = 183 among native-born whites).
[a]"American" and similar identities are counted as non-ethnic.
[b]Percentage based on a very small number of cases (ten or fewer).

and especially when they identify themselves in a mixed fashion. Thus, among parents who have ethnically unmixed ancestry, single identities outnumber mixed ones in their desires for their children by a margin of three to two. In contrast, among parents of mixed background who identify with more than one group, mixed identifications are preferred for children by a margin of five to one. Parents of mixed background who identify with a single group fall in between.

In terms of honoring the ethnic diversity of their marriages, our respondents in general did not seem to be "selfish" in defining the ethnic identities they desire for their children. When their spouses' (or ex-spouses') ancestries and identities differ from their own, respondents tended to describe identities that included ethnic elements from both backgrounds. Intermarriage therefore tends to produce greater complexity in the identities parents try to transmit to their children. Intermarried parents do not typically try to resolve the ethnic difference in their families by deciding on a single ethnicity to transmit to their children.[14] Among parents whose spouses' ancestries do not overlap at all with their own, for example, mixed identities are typically desired for children (outnumbering single identities by a margin of three to one), while among parents who are endogamously married, single identities for children are the rule. Given the great extent of intermarriage, a significant number of the identities parents desire are rather complex; more than a quarter involve three or more ethnic components. Nevertheless, parents frequently do simplify when it comes to the identities they want to transmit to their children, just as they do with their own identities. The identities desired for children, while often complex, are generally not as complex as the sum total of the ancestries of both parents.

The complexity of identities desired for children can be seen as related to an ambiguity in the nature of ethnic identity which appears also in respondents' descriptions of their own identities (see chapter 2). Is ethnic identity an affiliation with a contemporary ethnic group, or merely a sense of family origins, of where ancestors came from and how they came to settle in the United States? Certainly, some parents wish to transmit what they view as a cultural heritage. But others made clear in asides to our interviewers that it is really the sense of family origins, of family memory, that they wish to transmit. Typical is the statement of one parent who wants his children to think of themselves as a complex blend of old and new European ethnic origins: "I care that my children are interested in where their family came from." Something similar seems also at work among those intermarried parents who described an identity that drew liberally from both sides of their children's ancestries. In describing the identities they wanted for their children, some of these parents did not even bother to specify the individual components but simply said, "All of their background," as if the individual elements are not so important. A few parents even made clear in their description that they want their children to identify a little with each element in their ancestry, and not to give preference to any single part of it.

Typically, parents who desire some ethnic identity for their children attach some importance to its acquisition, although few seem to rate it overall as a very important goal. When we asked these parents how important they held their children's ethnic identities to be, only 11 percent attached little importance to it. Some 60 percent said it was somewhat important, and 30 percent described it as very important. (These percentages are based on the minority of parents who desire ethnic identities for their children. The percentage of all parents who attach great importance to their children's ethnic identities is just 12 percent.)

What are the characteristics of parents who want their children to identify in ethnic terms? One factor is their type of marriage: parents who are in endogamous marriages (that is, where there is full overlap in the ancestries of spouses) are more likely than others to want their children to identify ethnically—two-thirds of them do (although the number of parents involved is small in our sample). By comparison, only about 40 percent of parents married to spouses of nonoverlapping background want their children to identify.[15] Aside from the distinctive, endogamously married group, the extent of ancestry overlap does not make any difference; that is, parents in marriages where some partial overlap is present are about as likely to want their children to identify as those where the ancestries of husbands and wives have nothing in common.

A parent's own ethnic identity plays an even more central role. Parents who identify ethnically are more likely to want their children to do so also. About half of ethnically identifying parents desire some identity for their children, compared to roughly 20 percent of nonidentifying parents (see table 5.6). Moreover, parents' desires for their children vary quite directly with the degree of importance they attach to their own ethnic backgrounds. For example, among parents with the most salient ethnic identities, three-quarters want their children to identify as well (see table 5.7). By contrast, among parents who identify ethnically but attach little or no importance to their ethnicity, less than a quarter want this. Conforming to a common pattern, the parents who attach just some importance to their backgrounds fall in between.

The close correspondence between parents' desires for their children and the condition of their own ethnic identities is reaffirmed by logistic regression analysis (see table 5.8). The analysis reveals that none of the demographic and socioeconomic background variables have much effect here. But parents' own ethnic identity status and the subjective importance they attribute to ethnicity stand out as powerful determinants of their desires for their children to identify. In terms of ethnic identity status, the principal

Table 5.7　Desire for children's ethnic identity by parent's ethnic identity status and subjective importance of ethnic background (% desiring an ethnic identity, single or mixed, for their children)

	Subjective importance of parent's background		
	Very important	Somewhat important	Not important
Parent's ethnic identity status:			
Does identify	77.3	55.7	21.4
Does not identify	25.0	25.0	16.7

Significance levels:　identity status × parental desire, p < .001
importance × parental desire, p < .001

Note: Ethnic identity status has been simplified for this table because of small numbers in some cells of the more detailed table.

difference remains between parents who identify themselves in ethnic terms and those who do not, although there is a suggestion that parents who identify in a mixed fashion may be the most likely of all to desire children to identify (perhaps out of a sense that the transmission of such complex identities cannot be taken for granted). The combined effect of the two parental identity variables, status and salience, is as large as any effects uncovered in prior analyses.[16]

The ethnic tenor of parents' lives, the manifestation of ethnic identity in concrete experiences, adds further to the explanation of parents' desires for their children's identities. This effect is indicated by the index of ethnic experiences.[17] Parents with several ethnic experiences are highly likely to want their children to identify ethnically; parents with few experiences, much less so. The difference is great even when the ethnic identities of the parents are taken into account; for instance, compared to parents who report no ethnic experiences, parents who report four or more ethnic experiences are about 60 percent more likely to want their children to identify. Parents who report a low level of experience (one, two, or three experiences) fall in between these two poles, although in terms of logit coefficients (a more accurate guide than the percentage approximations), they are closer in their desires to the parents with a high level of experience than to those with none.

Lack of proximity to relatives also increases parents' desires to

Table 5.8   Logistic regression analysis of desire
for children's ethnic identity

	Regression coefficient	% change at mean
Ethnic identity status	p < .05	
single/single	+.369	+9.1
multiple/single	+.158	+3.8
multiple/multiple	+1.252	+30.1
single/none	−.844	−17.5
multiple/none	−.935	−19.0
Subjective importance of	p < .01	
background	+.929	+22.8
Gender	N.S.	
Age	N.S.	
Generation	N.S.	
Education	N.S.	
Confidence in ancestry knowledge	N.S.	
Level of ethnic experience	p < .001	
0	−2.204	−32.7
1, 2, or 3	−.018	−0.4
4 or 5	+.944	+23.2
6 or more	+1.278	+30.6
Living near relatives	p < .01	
yes	−.888	−18.3
no	+.888	+21.8
Endogamous marriage	p < .10	
yes	+.589	+14.6
no	−.589	−12.9
χ^2	76.88 with 19 degrees of freedom, p < .001	

Note: The dependent variable contrasts parents who want their
children to identify with parents who do not want this.

transmit an identity to their children. This effect, which runs counter
to conventional expectations, may reveal a wellspring of many parents' concern with their children's identities in their desire to transmit a sense of family. Conventionally, proximity to relatives would be
interpreted as an indicator of embeddedness in family networks,
which ought to make parents more likely to desire their children to
identify. But the effect in table 5.8 is in the opposite direction. It could
perhaps be seen as compensatory: parents who live far from their

relatives may perceive the ethnic identity of their children as more problematic and therefore make a more self-conscious effort to transmit one. But why these parents would be more willing to make this effort when intermarried parents in a similar situation are not is a question that renders such an interpretation tenuous. Consequently, I favor a different way of looking at the impact of distance from relatives: namely, in the confounding of ethnicity and family by many native-born whites. Thus, what is problematic for the children of parents who live far from relatives is knowledge about their family backgrounds; such parents who want their children to identify ethnically are expressing, at least in some cases, a desire for their children to know more about their families.[18]

There is an ethnic factor, too. The Italians stand apart for the strength of their desires to impart some ethnic identity to their children. In a pattern strongly contrasting with that found for all other major ancestry groups in the Capital Region,[19] two-thirds of parents of Italian background want their children to identify ethnically, and among parents who identify themselves with the Italian group, the proportion reaches three-quarters. In every case, the identities these parents desire for their children contain an Italian component; and the parents of Italian background attach an unusual degree of importance to their children's ethnic identities. Of the parents who express concern, half feel that their children's identities are very important.

This degree of concern with children's identities is largely attributable to the relative strength of ethnic identity in the Italian group and exists despite a high level of intermarriage. The Italians display a greater than average tendency to identify in ethnic terms and to attach substantial importance to their identities. They are also unusual in the high proportion of persons with unmixed ancestry. Nevertheless, insofar as the small size in our sample of the group of parents with mixed Italian ancestry allows any conclusion, there does not appear to be much difference between parents with unmixed and mixed Italian ancestry in the desire that children identify as Italian, so long as both identify ethnically with the Italian group. But there is a difference in the type of identity desired, as parents with mixed ancestry are much more likely to desire an ethnically mixed identity for their children.

It may be useful to contrast the Italians with another important ethnic group in the Capital Region, the Irish, whose ethnic identity is quite noticeable in some respects, such as concern with ethnic political issues. But when it comes to their children's ethnic identities, parents of Irish ancestry are no different from others of other old-stock backgrounds. Just one-third are concerned that their children have some form of ethnic identity. The desired identities mostly include multiple ethnic strands, and in some cases, the Irish component is even lacking. Few parents of Irish ancestry attach great importance to their children having some ethnic identity, for just a quarter of the group indicating this as a concern say that it is very important to them. Even among the parents who identify ethnically with the Irish group, a strong contrast to Italian parents remains.

What Do Parents Do to Promote Their Children's Ethnic Identities?

Parental desires are one thing, actions to implement them something else. Since few parents are endogamously married, an ethnic atmosphere in the home that would instill in children a sense of their ethnic background without much effort by their parents cannot be taken for granted. What actions, then, do parents take in order to instruct their children about their ethnic background?

The list of ethnic experiences comes to our assistance at this point. One of the experiences listed was that of "teaching your children about your ethnic background." Only 24 percent of parents with children living at home indicated this as an experience they had had during the five years preceding the survey. This group of parents may be too loosely defined, since it includes those whose children, in the parents' eyes, are too young to be interested in ethnic backgrounds.[20] Eliminating these parents from consideration raises the proportion of parents who have tried to teach their children; but, at 27 percent, it remains a small part of the parental group.

It comes as no surprise that teaching children about their ethnic background is strongly related to parents' desires for their children's ethnic identities. Attempts to teach children are more common among parents who want their children to identify in ethnic terms and vary directly with the importance parents attach to this goal (see table 5.9). Parents who want their children to identify are

Table 5.9   Percentage teaching children
about their ethnic background, by
parent's desires for children's identity

Total for native-born white parents	27.3
Parent's desires:	
No ethnic identity desired	18.2
Identity desired:	43.6
not important	12.5[a]
somewhat important	39.3
very important	61.1
Significance level:	p < .001

Note: This and the remaining tables include only
parents with children at home who are old enough
(in the parents' eyes) to be interested in ethnicity
(N = 143).
[a]Based on a very small number of cases (ten or
fewer).

about twice as likely to report teaching their children as are parents
who do not. But only in the subgroup of parents who feel that their
children's ethnic identities are very important to them is there a
majority who teach about ethnicity. Still, teaching is not uncommon among parents who describe their children's ethnic identities
as just "somewhat" important. Parents who attach little or no importance to their children's identities, however, are no different
from parents who are simply not concerned about instilling identity.

What sorts of actions do parents take? A commonly cited one is
teaching about family history, mentioned by about a quarter of
parents who have taught their children. It might be objected here
that, surely, other parents, not conscious of having taught their
children about ethnicity, have also told them about the family history. It is therefore revealing of conceptions of ethnicity that parents
who are conscious of teaching their children see instruction in family history as a primary instance of this, providing another illustration of the conflation of family origin with ethnicity. This form of
teaching would also appear most likely in families that still retain
some memories of the immigration experience, whose adult mem-

bers have had some direct acquaintance with their immigrant ancestors and are thus familiar with some of the details of immigrant
life—which villages and towns they came from, what they did on
arrival in the United States, what were the living conditions during
their early years here, and so forth. This is strongly suggested by
some of our respondents' descriptions of the actions they have taken
to teach their children—representative is one parent who has told
her children "where their grandparents were born and what kind of
work they did in the old country."

Telling children about their family histories can easily extend
into telling them about ethnicity in a larger sense, when, for example, family stories get to the customs of the immigrants. Many of our
respondents also did this directly and self-consciously. About a
quarter of parents (in the group who have taught) indicated teaching an ethnic language, or at least something of its flavor (the qualification seems necessary in light of the limited mother-tongue
knowledge of many respondents). Other significant subgroups—
about a sixth of parents in each case—have taught about ethnic
foods and about ethnic customs and traditions. Parents mentioned a
variety of other actions, including teaching about the history of the
ethnic group or its homeland, teaching about holidays, and taking
children to ethnic festivals as a way of introducing them to their
ethnic background. Altogether, about three-quarters of the parents
who indicated having taught their children described actions of this
kind, which can be seen as instructing children quite directly about
the culture and history of their ethnic groups. The remainder either
limited their teaching to family history or described other actions,
such as setting a moral example and teaching tolerance of other
groups, that are only distantly related to socialization for ethnic
group identity.

The actions taken by the minority of parents who teach their
children about their ethnic background seem reinforced by the general ethnic character of these parents' lives. Specifically, parents
who teach children are also likely to have other ethnic experiences
that can introduce children to aspects of ethnicity. There is, in fact, a
rather tight nexus between teaching children and cultural experiences; for example, about three-quarters of parents who teach
about ethnicity also eat ethnic foods at home, and more than half do
so at least once a month. Among parents who do not report teaching

their children, on the other hand, just a third eat ethnic foods at home. In a similar vein, more than 60 percent of parents who teach report using ethnic foods to celebrate special occasions, compared to just 20 percent of parents who do not teach. This kind of consistency can be repeated with mother tongue knowledge and use, the maintenance of ethnic customs, and attendance at ethnic festivals. In each case, there is a marked difference between parents who teach and those who do not.

Behind this constellation of relationships lies the influence emanating from the parents' own ethnic identities, for the probability that parents will teach their children varies directly by their sense of their own ethnicity. As is to be expected, parents who identify in ethnic terms are more likely to teach about ethnic background than parents who do not, and they are all the more so when they feel strongly about their ethnic backgrounds. In fact, among parents who identify ethnically and attach a lot of importance to their ethnic backgrounds, a majority reported teaching their children (see table 5.10). Among the ethnically identifying who rate their backgrounds as somewhat important, the proportion who reported teaching dips under 40 percent. Among parents who identify ethnically but view their backgrounds as unimportant, this proportion plummets to just 6 percent. Thus, among parents who identify eth-

Table 5.10 Teaching children by parent's ethnic identity status and subjective importance of background (% teaching their children about ethnic background)

| | Subjective importance of parent's background | | |
	Very important	*Somewhat important*	*Not important*
Parent's ethnic identity status:			
Does identify	61.1	37.8	6.5
Does not identify	27.3	7.1	12.5
Significance levels:	identity status × teaching, p < .05		
	importance × teaching, p < .001		

Note: Ethnic identity status has been simplified for this table because of small numbers in some cells of the more detailed table.

nically, the degree of importance attached to ethnic background makes a tenfold difference in the probability of teaching about it. It appears to make some difference even among parents who do not identify ethnically, but in general teaching actions are not very common in the nonidentifying group: overall, just 15 percent of its members report them.

There also appears to be a role for endogamous marriage when it comes to teaching about ethnic background, but it is necessarily limited by the rarity of endogamy. Indeed, this same fact makes the statistical basis for a conclusion tenuous, since there are few endogamous marriages in the data for parents with children at home. But the difference by marriage type is quite consistent with the notion that endogamously married parents are more likely than others to attempt to instill a sense of their ethnic background in their children. No matter whether one measures endogamy as full overlap of ancestry or of identity, the results are the same: At least half of these parents indicate teaching their children. The partial sharing of ancestry does not increase the probability of such teaching, however.

Other factors related to teaching children about their ethnic background include parents' confidence in their knowledge of their own ancestry, a measure of ethnic "drift," and the kind of place where parents grew up (rural versus nonrural). (The effects of these variables appear in a logistic regression analysis. See table 5.11.) The influence of confidence in ancestry knowledge represents another aspect of the close link between parental ethnic identity and the self-conscious attempt to transmit an identity to children. Forces that weaken knowledge of ancestry reduce the probability of identifying in ethnic terms; they also lower the likelihood that parents attempt to teach about ethnicity. The latter effect is quite powerful: According to the equation, parents with diminished confidence in their ancestry knowledge are about 50 percent less likely to teach their children than are other parents. The magnitude of the effect rivals that of the subjective importance of ethnic background, here as elsewhere a very strong predictor of ethnicity-related behavior. The influence of where parents grew up is not as impressive. Parents who grew up in nonrural settings, where ethnic diversity is more likely to be present, are more likely to teach their children about their ethnic backgrounds.

Table 5.11 Logistic regression analysis of teaching children

	Regression coefficients		% change at mean
Ethnic identity status		N.S.	
Subjective importance of background	+1.630	p < .001	+38.4
Gender		N.S.	
Age		N.S.	
Generation		N.S.	
Education	+.394	p ≅ .10	+8.5
Confidence in ancestry knowledge		p < .05	
confident	+1.475		+34.8
not confident	-1.475		-19.4
Place where grew up		p < .10	
rural	-.693		-11.5
nonrural	+.693		+15.6
χ^2	49.2 with 14 degrees of freedom,		
	p < .001		

A possible effect of parental educational attainment should also be mentioned (although it only borders on statistical significance in table 5.11).[21] It seems plausible that educational attainment would have some influence, since teaching about ethnic background presupposes some self-conscious and organized knowledge of one's ethnicity, and this seems more likely among the more highly educated. This is the direction implied by the logistic regression coefficient, which suggests that more highly educated parents are more likely to teach their children.

In summary, the logistic regression analysis confirms the dominant part played by parental ethnic identity in determining whether children are taught about their background. The subjective importance of ethnic background has a powerful relationship to teaching even when factors such as age, generation, and education are taken into account. And, although ethnic identity status is not significant in the equation, another factor related to identity, the degree of confidence in knowledge of ancestry, is. Other influences are small in comparison to these two.[22] With parental ethnic identity controlled, parental desires for children's identity are no longer significant; apparently, they are so closely tied to parental identity that their effects cannot be distinguished in a multivariate analysis.

Also losing significance in the logistic regression equation is endogamy, although its statistical insignificance may be as much a function of the small number of endogamous marriages as of anything else.[23]

How Interested Are Children in Their Ethnic Backgrounds?

The obvious next questions are how much interest children take in their ethnic backgrounds and how they manifest their interest. We asked the parents we interviewed about these matters.[24] The resulting data make clear that at least a minimal level of interest is fairly widespread. Almost half of the parents reported that their children are interested to some extent. But the fraction of parents who reported more than minimal interest on the part of their children is, in terms of rough order of magnitude, rather similar to the proportion who care about their children's ethnic identities. About a third of parents said that their children are "very" or "somewhat" interested in their ethnic backgrounds, while a group about half as large (15 percent of parents) described their children as "just a little" interested. (The remainder of parents said their children are not interested.)

Perhaps these parental assessments should be taken with a grain or two of salt, for there is such a close correspondence between the children's level of interest as perceived by parents and the parents' own desires for them that one has to question whether the perception of interest is in many cases independent of the desires (see table 5.12). For example, among the parents who are not concerned about their children's ethnic identities (the majority of parents), two-thirds describe their children as uninterested in the parents' ethnic background and another 13 percent as interested only slightly. Not even a quarter, then, view their children as having more than just a minimal interest in their background. At the other extreme, among the parents who attach great importance to their children's ethnic identities, the proportions are practically reversed: almost 90 percent describe their children as having an interest in their backgrounds, and about 80 percent describe this interest as more than minimal.

Even if parents' perceptions of children tend to mirror their

Table 5.12   Children's interest in their background
by parent's desires for children's identity

	Children are			
	Not interested	A little interested	Somewhat interested	Very interested
Total for native-born white parents	52.1%	14.8%	20.4%	12.7%
Parent's desires:				
No ethnic identity desired	65.9	12.5	14.8	6.8
Identity desired:	29.6	18.5	29.6	22.2
not important	50.0[a]	25.0[a]	25.0[a]	0.0[a]
somewhat important	35.7	25.0	25.0	14.3
very important	11.1	5.6	38.9	44.4

Overall significance level: p < .001

[a]Based on a very small number of cases (ten or fewer).

desires for them, it is of interest to examine the ways in which parents perceive their children as showing interest in background, for these offer clues about parents' (respondents') conceptions of ethnicity as well as about the nature of emerging ethnic identities. In the reports, the tension between ethnicity as family and ethnicity as cultural heritage or an affiliation with a group larger than the family emerges anew. An interest in family history was explicitly mentioned by 15 percent of parents who perceive some interest in their children. Further, about 40 percent of parents indicated that their children manifest their interest by asking questions or by talking about their backgrounds, and my guess is that a substantial proportion of these children are in fact primarily interested in family origins rather than ethnic-group heritage in the broader sense (as one parent told the interviewer, "he is very interested; whenever we look through old photos, he asks who is this and who is that"). But other children were perceived as interested in the heritage of one or more of the groups in their backgrounds. Nearly half of parents indicated that their children were interested in such aspects of ethnic heritage as food, language, and traditions or cultural practices.

Given the close linkage between parental desires for children and the perception of children's interest in background, it is to be expected that this perception has a familiar relationship to the parents' own ethnic identities. Thus, parents who identify ethnically are more likely to perceive their children as interested than parents who do not identify. The perception of interest also varies markedly with the degree of importance parents attach to their ethnic backgrounds. Among parents who feel their backgrounds to be very important, about 80 percent perceive their children as interested in these backgrounds, and more than 60 percent believe them to be more than just slightly interested. Among parents who attach no importance to their backgrounds, however, just 30 percent perceive their children as interested, and only 15 percent believe that their interest is more than minimal.

The final question is whether parental attempts to transmit an ethnic identity are successful. The answer must be equivocal. Certainly, parents appear to believe their actions have some impact on their children's level of interest. At least, parents who have taught their children about their ethnic backgrounds are far more likely to report that they are interested. Approximately three-quarters of these parents indicate some level of interest on the part of their children, compared to less than 40 percent of parents who have not taught about ethnicity. But whether there is a direct effect of teaching on children's interest is impossible to determine from these data, and this is not just because the children's interest is seen only through the parents' eyes. When the teaching variable is included in a logistic regression equation with other variables, it is no longer statistically significant (once again, the limited number of cases implies a need for caution in drawing a firm conclusion). As before, the big effect is associated with the subjective importance parents attach to their own ethnic backgrounds.

Many parents expressed little concern over whether their children displayed any interest. This lack of concern may be a signal that parental desires to pass on ethnicity, insofar as they exist at all, do not run very deep, or that parents see their children's identities as ultimately a matter for the children to decide. We asked parents whether their children's interest or lack of interest, as the case may be, mattered to them. Most parents were not concerned—two-thirds said that they were not. Indeed, parents who perceived their children as uninterested were virtually unanimous in saying this was not of concern. Among parents who describe their children as having some degree of interest, one-third said that they didn't care.

Statistical analysis of the expressions of concern over children's interest adds little to what has gone before. But the data can still give further insight through parents' reasons for their concern or the lack of it. This insight is especially valuable for parents who are not concerned with children's identities. Up to this point, the focus has been almost entirely on the minority of parents who want their children to identify and who take steps to promote an identity; the majority of parents have remained in the background. But the reasons parents give about their lack of concern can give us some understanding of the views of this majority about the ethnic identities of the next generation. These reasons confirm what one could guess: the lack of concern of many of these parents is explicable in terms of feelings that ethnicity is not very important. About half said outright that ethnicity is not important (or, in an alternative formulation, that they and their children are "Americans first"). Others who may also feel that ethnicity is not important—at least, not important enough for them to transmit a distinct identity to their children—said that their children's interest in their ethnic backgrounds is a matter for the children to decide rather than for their parents to determine. About a sixth mentioned this reason. Among those who care about children's interest, the reasons were more varied. One group again stressed family connections, feeling that children should know their roots and where their ancestors come from. Another emphasized the preservation of ethnic cultures and traditions. Yet a third believed that children should take pride in their origins. Finally, there was a sizable group who asserted simply that it is good for children to be interested in their ethnic background.

Summary

The findings here come close to yanking ethnicity's roots out of the family. To begin with, the great majority of families of native-born whites lack any unifying ethnic element (other than the purely American one). Intermarriage has been found to be very widespread among white Americans. This finding has been repeated for the whites in the Capital Region—indeed, because of the region's diverse European-ancestry composition and perhaps also because of the finer measurement of ethnicity in our survey, intermarriage appears even more common there than in the nation as a whole. Only a small percentage of whites can be considered endogamously married, even by a generous counting rule, which includes some marriages in which both partners have identical, mixed ancestry. As in the nation, there are also numerous marriages in which the ancestries of husbands and wives are partly overlapping. But in such marriages, the shared ethnic elements in general do not seem to provide a basis for ethnic unity, as evidenced by the typically divergent ethnic identities of the spouses.

Marriage, therefore, is of little help in explaining the prevalence and intensity of ethnic identity. Previous findings indicate that ethnic identities are still alive for many white Americans, despite the dwindling of objective ethnic differences in the European-ancestry population. And most white Americans can point to ethnic experiences of some kind. But marriage type has little or no relationship to whether individuals identify in ethnic terms, to whether they attribute significant importance to these identities, or to the extent and depth of their ethnic experiences. While this finding can be seen as positive for ethnicity's survival—further intermarriage implies no necessary decline in ethnic identity and its manifestations—its more intriguing implication concerns the social contexts in which ethnic identity is found, for it removes a possible social underpinning for identity. That intermarriage per se does not diminish the salience of ethnic identity or the level of ethnic experience underscores the personal and voluntary nature of ethnicity among whites in the contemporary United States. Those who wish to emphasize their ethnic background or to maintain some sense of affiliation with it, by preserving some of its traditions, are not prevented from doing so by being married to someone of a different ethnic background. But if this is the case, then it must be because these commitments are not of a kind that can be damaged or hindered by intermarriage, or vice versa. The finding therefore highlights the symbolic nature of many contemporary ethnic commitments—they are not intrusive enough in terms of everyday life to interfere with such a marriage. Likewise, they do not depend on ethnic homogeneity in the family to be preserved. The contrast with interreligious marriage is rather striking. While there are pressures to agree on a single religious identity for a family, especially when it comes to the religious upbringing of children, there appear to be no similar pressures in interethnic marriages, as witnessed by the frequently divergent ethnic identities of spouses.

With respect to children, the analysis goes further: It challenges the notion that families can be relied on to transmit ethnic identities to their children. Only a minority of parents want their children to identify, and an even smaller minority take forthright steps to encourage them to do so. If the identities of the next generation depend on the decisions and actions of contemporary parents, then ethnic identity will undergo a decline in the future, for parents are more likely to identify themselves than to want their children to do so.

The voluntary, personal nature of ethnic identity comes through also in the findings about parental concerns with children's identities. By far the most important determinant of such concerns is the strength of parents' own ethnic identities, not the marital contexts in which they find themselves. Parents who attach some importance to their ethnic identities are likely to want their children to identify as well (although they are frequently willing to have their children identify as much with their spouses' background as with their own); and they are likely—at least more likely than others—to teach their children about ethnicity. Again, the thrust of the findings is to diminish the role of the family as a social context which can reinforce ethnicity and, in tandem, to upgrade the importance of individual identity. Ethnicity, which was once transmitted by a communal web enmeshing families, neighborhoods, and informal networks, is now dependent on the identities of individuals. The change is not merely quantitative, affecting the likelihood that the next generation will identify and retain some of an ethnic heritage, but qualitative as well, altering the character of ethnicity.

In stating the findings about marriage's lack of impact on many contemporary ethnic phenomena, there is a danger of overlooking the long-run importance of intermarriage. But even in a narrow reading of the evidence, intermarriage has not left the stage, for it is implicated in the dampening of parental concerns with their children's identities. Parents who are endogamously married are more likely to want their children to identify than those who are intermarried, implying that the lack of concern of many parents with their children's identities is a product in part of the prevalence of intermarriage. Even when intermarried parents want their children to identify, they generally do not settle on a single ethnicity to communicate but describe a mixture that draws from both sides of the family. Complexity probably does not serve well the purpose of instilling an ethnic identity that is more than superficial.

In the long run, intermarriage does diminish ethnic identity. This must be the case because of the intimate connection between ethnic identity and ethnic ancestry. Thus, ancestry mixture, a direct outcome of intermarriage in preceding generations, reduces the probability of identifying ethnically and the degree of importance attributed to ethnic background. The same effects are produced by the loss of confidence in knowledge of ancestry, which can be seen as a by-product of intermarriage and the increasing complexity of ancestry that results from intermarriages across several generations.

Perhaps most critical is how the historical rise in intermarriage seems implicated in the emerging nature of ethnic identity among whites. Intermarriage acts, ultimately, as a form of restraint on the range and depth of ethnic expression. Ethnic activities and beliefs that demand too much of everyday life or that contain too strong a potential for conflict are generally incompatible with intermarriage. Therefore, the great and rising extent of intermarriage in the white population is a force, although surely not the only one, that tends to confine the expression of ethnic identity to symbolic forms, such as customs that are enacted on a major holiday. Accordingly, the absence of strong correlations between marriage type, on the one hand, and ethnic identity and its expression, on the other, does not indicate intermarriage's lack of importance. Rather, it presumes the profound historical surge in marriage across the lines of European ancestry.

6

Ethnic Social Structures: Friends and Organized Groups

In addition to the links of interest, family and fellowfeeling bind the ethnic group. There is satisfaction in being with those who are like oneself. The ethnic group is something of an extended family or tribe.

—NATHAN GLAZER AND
DANIEL PATRICK MOYNIHAN (1970: 18)

Ethnic identity in the absence of ethnic social structures threatens to lapse into a purely private affair. Imagine an individual whose interest in his or her ethnic background is keenly felt but who lacks any close contact with fellow ethnics. Such a person would be unconstrained by social pressures in choosing the form this interest will take. Perhaps it will be reflected in a desire to know more about the family tree, culminating in a visit to the old-world villages from which ancestors came; or in the adoption of a holiday ritual, which can also help to instruct children about the traditions of their immigrant great-grandparents. Perhaps it will be reflected in study of a mother tongue (but, then, with whom would he or she speak it?); or in private (and occasionally public) railings against stereotypes and those who denigrate the group. It could take several or all of these forms. If he or she were now to meet another person with the same identity, what would they share in common aside from an ethnic label, what basis would there be for feeling that they share a special bond which is not present when two people of different ethnic backgrounds meet?

The answer could well be "not much." When the manifestations of ethnicity are determined solely by individual interest, detached from the framework provided by social structures, then there is little to guarantee that one person's choice of ethnic expression will resemble another's. This is all the more true when intermarriage and mixed ancestry are widespread and hence socialization to common ethnic forms cannot be taken for granted. On a mass scale, ethnic identity that is not harnessed in some fashion to ethnic social structures implies a diversity so great within ethnic groups that the basis for ethnic solidarity—the quality in ethnicity that "facilitates group formation of any kind," Max Weber put it ([1922] 1968: 389)— is undermined.

Thus, ethnic social structures, in such forms as families, friendship groups, and organizations, are essential if ethnicity is to be a collective phenomenon, rather than a purely personal one (McKay and Lewins, 1978; Yancey et al., 1985). If such structures exist and individuals who ethnically identify participate in them, there is some foundation for the elaboration of common expressions of ethnicity, which can distinguish members of a group from nonmembers and generate such feelings of a shared heritage as interpretations of group history, distinctive values, points of view, and rituals.[1] Although the existence of ethnic social structures does not guarantee the creation of widely shared ethnic expressions, it is a requirement for them. Hence, any evaluation of the ultimate significance of ethnic identity hinges on its relationship to social structure.

But the role of the family as a form of ethnic social structure is weakening steadily under the relentless pressure of rising intermarriage. Not only is marriage across lines of ethnic ancestry now the rule rather than the exception, but most individuals who identify ethnically are intermarried. Little relationship, therefore, exists between marriage type and ethnic identity and experience.

The search for ethnic social structures cannot stop at the family. Other social settings, such as friendships and organizations, can harbor relationships where shared ethnicity is a salient element and where, therefore, matters pertaining to ethnicity can be freely aired and discussed. Intermarried individuals may have access to relationships of this sort when they gather with friends from the "old neighborhood," or when they attend meetings of an ethnic organization such as the Ancient Order of Hibernians. To point out such possible footholds for ethnic social structures is not to suggest that structures of the sort just named are likely to be as powerful in their impact as ethnically unified families, which have an unrivaled hold on the lives of their individual members and leave an indelible imprint on the generation growing up. But, even so, ethnically based friendships and organizations offer an arena where the idiom of ethnicity—the sentiments, concerns, and outlooks that distinguish members of a group from others and contribute to the sense of a bond among them—can be developed and preserved. Thus, the search for the elements of ethnic social structures must go on.

Friendship

To what extent do whites choose close friends who are ethnically like themselves? Do ethnically based friendship circles contribute to ethnic identities and behaviors? To enable us to address such questions, our survey gathered data about the persons whom our respondents consider as "good friends, or people [they] feel close to," employing procedures that are now becoming standard in social surveys investigating informal social relations (see Marsden, 1987). To these procedures, we added some novel elements: questions about the ethnic backgrounds of friends and the presence of mutual ethnic awareness and discussion.

Specifically, we began by asking respondents to write down the first names of their close friends.[2] They could write as many names as they wanted, but we requested further information only about the first five friends.[3] For each, we asked such questions as: how the respondent first met the friend, and how long they have known each other; where the friend lives, and how often the respondent and friend are in touch with each other; and, of course, the ethnic background (and sex) of the friend. Additional information relevant to the ethnic role of friendship includes whether the friend is aware of the respondent's ethnic background, and whether this is ever a topic of discussion between them.[4]

The friendship data seem to provide ample information about the close social contacts of respondents (see table 6.1). About 80 percent of native-born whites named at least four people as close

Table 6.1   Some characteristics of the
friendship circles of native-born whites

Number of friends named:	
Zero	3.5%
1–3	15.9
4	18.5
5	62.0
Length of acquaintance[a]	
1 year or less	4.2%
2–4 years	13.8
5–9 years	18.8
10 or more years	63.1
Frequency of contact[a]	
Daily	25.1%
One or more times a week	36.4
One or more times a month	24.1
One or more times a year	12.7
Less than yearly	1.7
Friendship origin[a]	
Kinship	14.8%
Childhood	5.8
School	12.6
Work	20.8
Neighborhood	14.0
Organization	9.4
Through another friend	9.9
Through spouse or child	6.2
Other	6.5

[a]Each of these distributions is based on the total
number of friendships (N = 1922, a total which may
be reduced in a specific tabulation by missing data).

friends, and more than 60 percent named five or more. In general,
the persons named as friends appear to represent close social ties,
who on average have been acquainted with respondents for long
periods of time and are in regular contact with them. Nearly two-
thirds have been known to respondents for at least ten years, and
another 20 percent for periods between five and nine years. About
60 percent are friends with whom respondents are in touch at least
once a week (and a quarter represent daily contacts). The friendships also have very diverse origins. The answers of respondents to
our question about how they first met each friend spread across a
number of settings, mixing relationships originating in kinship[5] or

childhood with others stemming from adult activities. Most frequently cited are friends met through work, who account for a fifth
of all the friends named. But next most frequently named are relatives (spouses not included[6]), who represent 15 percent of all
friends. Following closely behind these two are neighbors and
friends met in school.

Ethnic Commonality in Friendship
There are some basic demographic constraints on friendship (see
Fischer, 1982), which have ethnic ramifications. The ethnic match
between friends can be influenced by a great variety of factors.
Obviously, it can be influenced in part by preferences, should they
exist, to be with people who are ethnically similar. But preferences
alone cannot tell the whole story, because the ethnic composition of
friendship groups is shaped importantly by the relative availability
of people from different ethnic backgrounds, the degree of ethnic
variety in chance, everyday contacts, some of which eventually
flower into friendship. Hence, the composition of informal groups is
influenced by the degree of segregation between groups in residence, workplaces, schools, and other social spheres. Where segregation is high, the ordinary contacts of individuals will be dominated by others of their own ethnic background, and their friendships are likely to be ethnically homogeneous, regardless of their
preferences on this matter. Where segregation is low (and this is
increasingly true for the situations of whites of European background) then ordinary contacts will include persons from a number
of backgrounds. In a situation of low segregation, the latitude af-
forded ethnically related preferences is greater. Nevertheless, the
influence of a preference to be with coethnics may be limited if there
are few suitable group members around or if compatibilities based
on nonethnic criteria (similar leisure-time interests, say) exert a
stronger pull.

   Segregation is not the only factor capable of influencing the
structure of opportunities for contacts within or across ethnic
boundaries. Another is the size of groups, or the ethnic mix in the
general population. Members of large ancestry groups are more
likely to encounter and form friendships with their ethnic peers, as
larger size means greater availability of potential partners of the
same background (Blau, 1977). Groups that are small face difficul-

ties in maintaining in-group interaction. Their members may be driven into cross-ethnic contacts by the rarity of fellow group members. The principle of group size implies that individuals from the largest old-stock backgrounds are likely to have at least some friendships with others from these backgrounds, simply because their representation in the Capital Region's population is so large; strong preferences for coethnics are not required.

Type of ancestry is a further influence on the degree of ethnic match among friends, because persons of mixed ancestry, and particularly those with complicated ancestry mixtures, have a greater chance of having friends whose ancestries share something in common with their own; their ancestries present greater opportunity for some kind of match (this same principle was found at work in marriage patterns). This principle also affects differentially the largest old-stock ancestry groups because they are the most likely to be found in ancestry mixtures.

The appearance of ethnic homogeneity in friendship is also affected by the way in which ethnicity is socially perceived. The friendship data display two relevant features in this respect. First, even though it appears in general that respondents readily answered our questions about their friends' backgrounds insofar as they could, the proportion of friends whose ethnic backgrounds were unknown to respondents was rather high—almost exactly a quarter. (Counted among the unknowns are friends whose backgrounds are described only as "American.") The magnitude of this figure is to be expected. For many individuals, ethnic considerations are not salient in friendship, and so the ethnic backgrounds of friends may not be discussed and may also not be apparent from such usual indicators as names, accents, or other behavioral cues. Even though some of these friendships may involve some degree of ethnic commonality, one cannot regard them as relations between coethnics inasmuch as whatever shared ethnicity exists is not recognized by the participants. Therefore, in an assessment of the degree of ethnic relatedness, it is appropriate to count relations to friends of unknown ethnic background as not involving ethnic overlap.

The second feature is that the vast majority of friends whose backgrounds are known are described by respondents in terms of a single ethnicity. Since there is every reason to believe that the ethnic ancestries of friends are as complex as those of respondents, it is obvious that respondents think about their friends' backgrounds in simplified terms. Whether this occurs because ethnicity tends in general to be simplified in its social presentation or because friends' backgrounds are not known in any depth cannot be inferred from the data. This simplification may reduce occurrence of ethnic commonality in friendship, for a shared ethnic element may not be recognized. It also has ramifications for the analysis of the friendship data, implying that the distinction between partly and completely overlapping ancestries, so central in the analysis of marriage patterns, cannot be applied meaningfully here. Given the rarity of reports of mixed ancestry among friends, there is little practical chance of completely overlapping ancestries between respondents of mixed ancestry and their friends (except in the case of relatives). Hence, the distinction between partly and fully overlapping ancestries degenerates into one between respondents of single ancestry, whose friends' ancestries can only overlap completely with their own, and those of mixed ancestry, whose friends' ancestries usually overlap just partly. Accordingly, I distinguish only between friends whose backgrounds overlap with those of respondents, regardless of whether the overlap is partial or complete, and friends whose backgrounds do not overlap (or are unknown to respondents).

These considerations draw our attention to the necessity of evaluating carefully the ethnic significance of friendships between persons of the same ethnic backgrounds and equally that of friendships between persons of different backgrounds. The mere occurrence of similar ethnic backgrounds cannot be taken as direct evidence for ethnic preferences in friendship or for other ethnic loyalties. The demographic constraints on friendship formation, however, may check the effects of preferences for coethnics that do exist.

The survey data show that approximately a third of the top five friendships of native-born whites involve some degree of ethnic overlap (see table 6.2).[7] In all probability, this figure is greater than it would be if friendships were formed without regard for ethnicity.[8] It indicates, nevertheless, that the clear majority of friendships (two-thirds) do not involve a *recognized* common ethnic element. As already noted, the ethnic backgrounds of friends are unknown to respondents in a quarter of friendships. For approximately 40 per-

Table 6.2   Ethnic overlap in friendship by friendship origin

	Full or partial overlap	No overlap	Friend's ancestry unknown	N
Friendship origin:				
kinship	72.9%	17.2%	9.9%	273
childhood	53.2	29.4	17.4	109
school	31.8	47.3	20.9	239
work	23.8	48.7	27.4	390
neighborhood	23.8	46.1	30.1	256
organization	25.3	42.1	32.6	178
through another friend	27.0	42.7	30.3	185
through spouse or child	17.9	50.4	31.6	117
other	21.7	55.0	23.3	120
Total	33.7	41.7	24.6	1867

Overall significance level: $p < .001$

Note: Tabulated are all friendships of native-born white respondents of known ancestry.

cent of friends, then, ethnic backgrounds are known and are different from those of respondents.

Relationships to relatives and to persons known from childhood occur disproportionately among friendships involving some degree of common ethnic background. Nearly three-quarters of kin who are named as friends are described by respondents as having some ethnicity in common with them; this figure can hardly be viewed as surprising given that most of the kin so named are parents, siblings, and grown children. In the case of friendships from childhood, about half involve some common ethnicity. Characteristic of both types of friendship, for obvious reasons, is that the ethnic backgrounds of friends are usually known.

More contemporaneous friendships, that is, ones that typically originate in adulthood, are less likely to involve common ethnicity. The contrast with friendships from childhood is particularly intriguing for it suggests that friendships among whites were more ethnically structured in the past, perhaps as a function of greater ethnic segregation among neighborhoods. (An alternative explanation would be that childhood friendships involving shared ethnicity are more likely to survive the passage of years.) Just a quarter of friendships that started in the workplace, for example, involve any degree of ethnic overlap; similar proportions are found for friendships with neighbors and for those having their origin in an organizational affiliation. For these types, friends of unknown background are also more common than is the case with kin and friends from childhood, accounting for between a quarter and a third of friendships.

Even though only a minority of friendships involve some degree of common ethnic background, most whites have one or more such friendships as part of friendship circles, which typically encompass considerable ethnic diversity. At issue here are the patterns that arise when friendships are considered not one by one, but as groups reflecting the social milieus of individual respondents. Viewed in this light, 70 percent of native-born whites have at least one close friend of overlapping background (see table 6.3).[9] Nevertheless, such friends usually form a minority even in those friendship groups where they are present. In roughly 40 percent of friendship groups containing at least four friends, just one or two friends have backgrounds that overlap with respondents'; and in another 30 percent, there are no friends of this type. Hence, only in approximately 30 percent of the groups is there a majority (three or more friends) composed of persons who share some ethnic ancestry with respondents. Even in these friendship circles there may be considerable ethnic diversity. Not only do they often contain some friends whose backgrounds bear no resemblance to respondents', but even those friends whose backgrounds do may differ ethnically from each other. In particular, this can happen in the friendship circles of persons of mixed ethnic ancestry (for example, a person of French-German-Irish ancestry can have friends of French, German or Irish ancestry).

Friendships involving common ethnicity are not distributed at random in the social milieus of native-born whites but cluster in some patterned ways. There are more friendship circles characterized by a high degree of common ethnicity than one would expect by chance; there are also more friendship circles where common ethnicity is absent. These observations follow from a comparison of the empirical distribution of ethnically overlapping friendships with the distribution that would occur from chance alone.[10] At the high end, one would expect by chance that only 4 percent of friend-

Table 6.3   The number of friends of overlapping
ancestry by respondent's ethnic identity status

	One or more friends of overlapping ancestry	Three or more friends of overlapping ancestry
ALL FRIENDS		
Overall	70.1%	28.2%
By ethnic identity status		
(ancestry/identity type):		
single/single	70.3	35.2
multiple/single	85.7	36.4
multiple/multiple	69.1	27.2
single/none	48.0	12.0
multiple/none	63.0	18.5
Significance levels:	p < .01	p < .05
NONKIN FRIENDS ONLY		
Overall	55.5%	16.3%
By ethnic identity status		
(ancestry/identity type):		
single/single	51.6	17.6
multiple/single	77.9	24.7
multiple/multiple	49.4	14.8
single/none	40.0	8.0
multiple/none	49.4	11.1
Significance levels:	p < .001	N.S.

Note: The table includes only respondents of known ancestry who
have at least four close friends (N = 355).

ship groups would contain four or more friends of overlapping background, whereas this occurs in fact for 13 percent of friendship
groups. At the other end, one would expect by chance that just 14
percent of friendship groups would contain no friends of overlapping background, whereas 30 percent do.

The choice of relatives as close friends is part of the explanation
for this clustering. But the presence of relatives complicates any
attempt to determine the ethnic implications of friendship circles.
Friendship with relatives may be more an indicator of familism
than of any ethnic tendency (although familism may itself be linked
with ethnicity); given the lack of control individuals have over the
ethnic backgrounds of their relatives (except for those created by
their marriages), friendships with nonrelatives are, arguably, a bet-

ter indicator of the ethnic character of the social milieu (Fischer, 1982). The proportion of friendship groups that include nonrelatives having ancestry in common with respondents is substantial— more than half (56 percent; see table 6.3). And a sixth (16 percent) of friendship groups contain majorities made up of such friends. These friendships, too, can be shown to cluster in nonrandom ways.

Clearly, some native-born whites are more likely than others to be in social milieus that include individuals of their own ethnic background. One reason is that such milieus are correlated, although not strongly, with ethnic identity status (see table 6.3). The pattern is complicated by the relation of ancestry type to friendship involving shared ancestry. Individuals of mixed ancestry have in general more of such friendships because they have more possibilities for ancestral overlap. With this complication in mind, it is apparent that two categories of identity status stand out: ethnic identifiers of single ancestry (in comparison to nonidentifiers of the same ancestry type) and persons of mixed ancestry who identify with a single group. Regardless of whether one looks at all friendships involving shared ancestry or only at such friendships with nonrelatives, members of the latter category have the highest probability of friendship with fellow ethnics.

The distinctiveness of mixed-ancestry individuals who identify with a single group is intriguing, for it suggests that there exists a social-structural support for their identities in many cases. Inspection of the data indicates that most of the friends of overlapping ancestry are from the same ethnic background that respondents identify with. The pattern implies that the choice of a single identity from a mixed ancestral background may be associated with a social milieu that reflects to some extent the identity chosen. Whether this occurs because such identifiers seek out others of the "right" ethnic background, or because the ethnic character of their milieus influences their identity, cannot be established from cross-sectional data. Nevertheless, it must be kept in mind that only a minority of the members of this identity category have friendship circles dominated by fellow ethnics.

The subjective importance attached to ethnic background is also related to friendship involving shared ancestry. Individuals whose identities are more salient are more likely to have friends with their background, to have friends of this type who are not relatives, and, finally, to have friendship circles dominated by ethnically similar friends. Among the ethnically identifying who attach great importance to their backgrounds, for example, about 85 percent have at least one friend of overlapping background[11], and more than 40 percent indicate that a majority of their close friends share some ethnic background with them (see table 6.4). By way of comparison, among the ethnically identifying who attach little or no importance to their backgrounds, the proportion who lack any friend of overlapping ancestry is twice as high as among the strongly identifying; and the proportion with a majority of friends of overlapping ancestry is reduced to 25 percent. In these respects, there is little difference between identifiers who attach little importance to their backgrounds and nonidentifiers.

But the relationship between the individual's ethnic identity and the ethnic composition of his or her friendship circle is more complex than this quickly sketched picture shows. For one thing,

Table 6.4   The number of friends of overlapping ancestry by respondent's ethnic identity status and subjective importance of background

	Subjective importance		
	very important	*somewhat important*	*not important*
% with one or more friends of overlapping ancestry			
Ethnically identifying	85.5	74.8	66.2
Nonidentifying	58.3	61.8	60.6
Significance levels:	identity status X 1+ friends, p < .05 importance X 1+ friends, N.S.		
% with three or more friends of overlapping ancestry			
Ethnically identifying	43.6	33.0	24.7
Nonidentifying	20.8	23.5	12.1
Significance levels:	identity status X 3+ friends, p < .01 importance X 3+ friends, p < .05		

Note: The table includes only respondents of known ancestry who name at least four close friends (N = 355). Given the small sizes of some cells, the detailed categories of ethnic identity status have been collapsed for presentation.

the relationship occurs in part because of the greater attentiveness of the ethnically identifying, and especially of those with salient identities, to the facts of ethnicity in the first place. This aspect of the relationship is easily demonstrated by the extent of respondents' knowledge about their friends' backgrounds. About two-thirds of respondents with salient identities know the backgrounds of all of their friends, compared to just one-third of those with weak identities. The latter figure approximately characterizes nonidentifiers as well. Not knowing the backgrounds of many of their friends reduces the chances of overlap for the nonidentifying and those with weak ethnic identities.

A second complication is the degree of ethnic diversity in the friendship circles of mixed-ancestry individuals, even when they include many friends of overlapping ancestry. This feature is potentially of consequence, since the ethnic reinforcement of an ethnically diverse milieu could be less than that of a homogeneous one. When the friendship circles of persons of single ancestry contain many friends of overlapping background, it is obvious that they must be homogeneous as well—the backgrounds of these friends must be the same. But this need not be the case for persons of mixed ancestry because of the multiple possibilities for ancestry overlap. That such a difference occurs in fact is demonstrated by an index of ethnic diversity calculated for each friendship circle. The index is created by counting the number of different ethnic backgrounds present among a respondent's friends.[12] For respondents of single ancestry whose friends mostly have the same ethnic background as themselves, diversity is low, as more than 60 percent of those with three or more friends of overlapping ethnic background describe just one or two ethnicities among their friends. This degree of homogeneity is much less common in the friendship circles of persons of mixed ancestry, for just 32 percent of those containing three or more friends with backgrounds overlapping those of respondents have low ethnic diversity, that is, just one or two ethnicities represented. Moreover, a substantial number of these friendship groups include a great deal of ethnic diversity, for instance, more than 40 percent contain friends representing four or more ethnic backgrounds. Diversity is particularly large for persons of mixed ancestry who identify in a mixed fashion, but it occurs also for those who identify with a single group.

In addition to ethnic identity, geographic immobility appears to affect the ethnic character of the friendship circle, to enhance the prospects that it will contain fellow ethnics. Specifically, individuals who live near relatives or who have lived in the same community for twenty or more years have more friends of overlapping ancestry. (These effects appear in regression analyses in which the numbers of friends and nonkin friends of overlapping ancestry are taken as the dependent variables; see table 6.5.[13]) Proximity to relatives is undoubtedly an indicator of embeddedness in family networks; accordingly, those who live near relatives are more likely to name relatives as friends. This explanation is supported by the fact that the proximity variable is significant only in the equation where friendships with relatives are counted among those involving common ancestry. As for length of residence in the community, two sorts of effects are probably compounded in it.[14] One is that prolonged residence in the same community is a partial proxy for lifelong residence in or near the Capital Region, which increases the chance of having adult friendships that originated during childhood; these are likely to involve some degree of ethnic commonality. In addition, stable residents of a community, whether they have lived there for their whole lives or not, are likely to have greater depth of knowledge about the backgrounds of their friends and thus to recognize any existing degree of ethnic connection.

Other influences on the ethnic character of the friendship circle are education, gender, and confidence in knowledge of one's own ancestry. The gender and ancestry-knowledge effects seem inherently less interesting: both appear only in relation to the total friendship circle and disappear when relatives are no longer considered. In the case of gender, the effect is easily explained, since women are more likely than men to name relatives as close friends; this commonly found difference between the sexes (Fischer, 1982; Wellman, 1985) accounts for women's greater tendency to have friendships involving shared ethnicity.

Education's effect, however, only matters for friendships to nonkin and seems noteworthy because it offsets the role of education in lifting friendship out of the context of the family. In fact, other analyses show that the highly educated are less likely to name kin among their close friends, which ought to decrease the ethnic commonality of their friendships. But, while more education leads to fewer friends drawn from the family circle, it also leads to more unrelated friends who share one's ethnic background. The latter effect can be shown to be connected with the greater knowledge of their friends' backgrounds possessed by the highly educated. This explanation is compatible with the notion that ethnicity functions as a form of cultural capital for many whites. Since the highly educated are more prone to employ symbolic systems in their contacts with others, they are more likely to know about the ethnic backgrounds of their friends.

The multivariate analyses also modify the apparent relationship of ethnic identity to the ethnic character of the friendship circle. Specifically, they diminish in prominence the role of identity salience, that is, the subjective importance of background. Throughout the analyses presented in this book, this has been the single most important variable in accounting for ethnic behavior. Although the subjective importance of background is related to the ethnic character of the friendship circle when other variables are controlled, the relationship does not have a magnitude on a par with its effects in previous analyses.[15] In the analysis for the overall number of friends of overlapping ancestry (that is, with relatives included), for example, the expected difference between those attributing a lot of importance to their backgrounds and those attributing none (this difference is twice the unstandardized coefficient in table 6.5) is about the same as the effect of living near relatives or that of residing in the same community for twenty or more years, even though in other analyses it usually overshadows such variables. It is difficult to pin down definitively why identity salience should be less powerful here than elsewhere, but the difference does suggest that the correspondence between friendship and identity is only modest in strength (except for the category of mixed-ancestry individuals who identify with a single group). The friendship circle is constrained by the availability of compatible coethnics in everyday life.

Finally, the variation in friendship patterns among ethnic groups must be noted. This variation, which is considerable, has potential significance, insofar as such ethnic characteristics as cultural patterns may hinge on supportive social structures, and these are evidently more available to the members of some groups than others. In the Capital Region, the groups most conspicuous in terms

Table 6.5 Regression analysis of the number of friends of overlapping ancestry

	ALL FRIENDS			NONKIN FRIENDS		
	Regression coefficients		*Statistical*	*Regression coefficients*		*Statistical*
	unstandardized	*standardized*	*significance*	*unstandardized*	*standardized*	*significance*
Ethnic identity status:						
single/single	—[b]	.228[a]	p < .001	—[b]	.227[a]	p < .01
multiple/single	.523			.605		
multiple/multiple	-.094			-.000		
single/none	-.865			-.350		
multiple/none	-.174			.010		
Subjective importance of background	.207	.111	p < .05	.183	.113	p < .05
Generation			N.S.			N.S.
Age			N.S.			N.S.
Gender:			p < .10			N.S.
male	—[b]					
female	.283	.100				
Educational attainment			N.S.	.157	.153	p < .05

222

	Model 1		Model 2	
Confidence in ancestry knowledge:				
confident	—[b]			
not confident	-.436			
	.092	p < .10		N.S.
Proximity to relatives:				
no	—[b]			
yes	.486			
	.146	p < .01		N.S.
Length of residence in community:	.166[a]	p < .05	.195[a]	p < .05
less than 1 year	—[b]		—[b]	
1–5 years	-.025		-.232	
6–20 years	.050		-.021	
20+ years	.484		.383	
R^2	.188		.172	
Adjusted R^2	.141		.123	

Note: The analysis includes only respondents of known ancestry who name at least four friends ($N = 355$). The total number of friends named (four or five) is also included as a control.
[a]The standardized coefficient is the sheaf coefficient.
[b]Indicates omitted category.

223

of friendship with fellow group members are the Irish and Italians among large groups (and Jews among smaller ones). For what are probably somewhat different reasons, high percentages of the members of each of these ancestry groups report having at least one close friend of this background—this is especially true for individuals who identify with the group—and significant proportions draw a majority of their friends from it. In the case of the Irish, 70 percent of the members of the ancestry group report having at least one friend of Irish ancestry,[16] and 22 percent have a majority of their friends from the Irish group; when the percentages are restricted to those who identify with being Irish, then 80 percent have an Irish friend, and 30 percent have a majority of Irish friends. The figures for the Italians are about the same, although the proportion with a majority of Italian friends is slightly higher. In the very small Jewish sample, the figures are higher still: nearly everyone has at least one Jewish friend, and half have a majority of Jewish friends.[17]

Different influences appear to lie behind these similar patterns. The Irish are one of the largest ancestry groups in the region, and thus one would expect that simply by chance many people of Irish background would have one or more friends who also have some Irish ancestry. But numerical considerations alone do not explain the Irish pattern. The German ancestry group, also among the region's largest, provides an instructive comparison. Only 44 percent of persons of German ancestry have one or more German friends, and just 14 percent have a majority of friends of German ancestry. The figures are raised only slightly when they are restricted to those who identify with the German group. Thus, if one takes the Germans as a baseline, it is evident that other factors must be at work in the Irish pattern. Among these may be stronger group loyalty and the effects of some institutional structures, particularly those connected with Catholicism. In the Capital Region, the parochial school system, for example, has brought together many students of Irish Catholic ancestry.

Among the Italians, the purely numerical explanation carries less weight, because Italians constitute a much smaller proportion of the general population of the Capital Region than the Irish do. But the Italian pattern is assisted by the still strong tendency to name relatives as close friends. Almost half of the Italians named at least one relative among their close friends (compared to a third of all native-born whites), and about 30 percent named two or more.

The Italian pattern of friendship is also shaped by the existence of some Italian neighborhoods. The Italians are one of the most residentially concentrated of the major white ancestry groups, although this is changing. Finally, the Italians display even stronger feelings of attachment to their ethnic background than the Irish do, and no doubt these have some influence on friendship (though they are possibly affected by friendship, as well).

In the Jewish case, numerical support for a high level of in-group friendship is entirely lacking, because Jews represent only a very small portion of the region's population. Nor are Jews as likely as the Italians to draw close friendships from the family circle. Hence, greater weight must be placed on feelings of attachment or loyalty to the group and a largely voluntary social segregation in some spheres in explaining the Jewish pattern. Obviously important in this last respect are participation in religious institutions that are also ethnic, bringing together people of the same ethnic background, and involvement in Jewish community affairs and organizations. (On a national plane, Silberman, 1985, describes in considerable detail the frequently intense organizational and philanthropic involvements of many American Jews.)

For the Irish and the Italians, there are signs of change in these friendship patterns (the Jewish group is too small in our data to examine in this way), suggesting further ethnic diversification in the social milieus of group members. This is evident in a comparison between persons of single and mixed ethnic ancestries, for homogeneous friendship circles are concentrated among persons of single ethnic ancestry, who represent declining shares of these and other ancestry groups. Consider the pattern among the Irish as an example. Among ethnically identifying persons of single ancestry from this group, half have friendship circles containing a majority of persons with Irish ancestry; by comparison, among persons of mixed Irish ancestry who identify with the Irish group, just a quarter have Irish-dominated circles. Within the mixed ancestry group, there appears to be a further difference between persons who identify solely with the Irish part of their background and those who identify with Irish as part of a mixture; the former are somewhat more likely than the latter to have an Irish-dominated friendship circle, although the numbers are too small to draw this conclusion with statistical confidence.

The evidence of decline in the ethnic homogeneity of Irish and

Italian friendship circles stands in contrast to the implications of the regression analyses, and the contrast suggests a direction for the evolution of friendship circles more generally. Pointedly, the regression analyses of table 6.5 did not turn up any of the usual traces of decline in an ethnic indicator: the number of ethnically overlapping friendships is not, for example, related to generational status, and such friendships are more common among persons of mixed ethnic ancestry than among those from an unmixed background, reversing the pattern just described among the Irish and the Italians. Nor is there any sign of decline when friendships to relatives are removed from consideration. It would appear, then, that the overall level of friendships involving some degree of common ethnic background is fairly stable. In any event, there is a floor—admittedly difficult to estimate in precise terms—below which this level cannot plunge. For even if friendships were formed without any recognition of ethnic factors and were not shaped by remaining ethnic concentrations in neighborhoods, schools, and workplaces, there would still be many friendships between people sharing some ethnic background, resulting from chance encounters reflecting the ethnic mix in the population.

But what appears to be declining is the ethnic homogeneity of social milieus. It is certainly not at a very high level among native-born whites in general. Moreover, it is declining among the very groups where it is at its zenith. But as friendship circles dominated by a single ethnic background fall in number, other circles encompassing diverse, overlapping backgrounds are on the rise. This rise is obviously associated with the growth in the number of persons of mixed ethnic ancestry, since mixture makes possible the peculiar combination of ethnic diversity with elements of common ancestry. In sum, friendships involving some degree of common ancestry are here to stay, but social milieus dominated by single ethnic colorations are continuing to fade.

Mutual Recognition of Common Ethnicity
The potential role of friendship for ethnicity is not exhausted by the extent to which friendships involve shared ethnic background. A variety of incidental reasons, such as the sizes of ancestry groups and the multiple matching possibilities associated with mixed ancestry, affect the likelihood that one or more of an individual's

friends will have ethnic backgrounds related to his or her own. Thus, the circumstances under which shared ethnic background is supportive of ethnic behavior and identity are, at this point, still open to question.

Insofar as mutual recognition exists, a friendship would seem more likely to have a wider ethnic significance, the shared background less likely to be merely incidental. Our survey provides two pieces of information relevant to this issue: one is whether the respondent believes a friend knows the respondent's ethnic background; the other, whether the respondent and friend ever discuss the respondent's ethnic background. Obviously, each knowing the ethnic background of the other, or *mutual awareness,* is a minimal requirement for mutual recognition. The respondent can, of course, be incorrect in his or her perception of the friend's knowledge, but one type of error seems irrelevant to the issue of mutual recognition: namely, if the respondent erroneously believes that his or her background is not known to the friend (when, in fact, it is), it is still reasonable to conclude that the minimal requirement for mutual recognition is not satisfied; the shared ethnic background is not mutually understood as part of the relationship. The potential significance of shared ethnic background is further enhanced when that background is a topic of discussion between friends. Such discussions may contribute to a sense of solidarity based on common ethnicity, although this need not always be the case; many discussions of ethnic background have an introductory character and are part of the complex signaling by which people, who may or may not have any ethnic background in common, get to know each other better.

In general, native-born whites believe that their ethnic backgrounds are known to most of their close friends. Nearly 80 percent of friends were described as knowing the backgrounds of respondents. The likelihood of this knowledge is influenced by several aspects of a friendship relation, as well as by the respondent's own ethnic identity (and, presumably, by the state of the friend's ethnic identity, but we have no measure of this). (See table 6.6.)

Some of the influences are self-evident. Recent friendships (of five years or less) are less likely to involve knowledge of the respondent's background, and so are relationships where frequency of contact between friends is low.[18] The origins of a friendship also leave

Table 6.6 Logistic regression analysis of mutual recognition of ethnicity as an aspect of friendship

% of friendships where present	Mutual knowledge[a] 78.6		Discussion of ethnic background 27.7	
	Regression coefficients	% change at mean	Regression coefficients	% change at mean
Friendship characteristics				
Length of acquaintance:	p < .01		N.S.	
under 5 years	−.362	−6.7		
5–9 years	+.191	+3.0		
10+ years	+.171	+2.7		
Frequency of contact:	p < .01		p < .10	
daily	+.412	+6.1	+.229	+4.8
weekly	+.124	+2.0	+.063	+1.3
monthly	−.163	−2.9	+.001	+0.0
less than monthly	−.373	−6.9	−.293	−5.5
Friendship origin:	p < .001		N.S.	
kinship	+.762	+10.1		
childhood	+.450	+6.6		
school	+.433	+6.4		

	(1)		(2)	
work	−.145	−2.6		
neighborhood	−.227	−4.1		
organizations	−.647	−12.8		
through other friends	−.385	−7.2		
through spouse or child	−.155	−2.7		
other	−.086	−1.5		
	p < .001			
Ancestry overlap:				
full or partial	+1.026	+12.5	+.511	+11.3
none	+.037	+0.6	+.446	+9.7
friend's ancestry unknown	−1.063	−22.7	−.957	−14.9
	p < .001		p < .001	
Respondent's identity characteristics				
Ethnic identity status:	p < .001		p < .001	
single/single	+1.072	+12.9	+.358	+7.7
multiple/single	−.024	−0.4	+.303	+6.5
multiple/multiple	−.257	−4.6	+.320	+6.8
single/none	−.243	−4.4	−.790	−12.9
multiple/none	−.548	−10.6	−.191	−3.7
Subjective importance of background	+.486	+7.1	+.706	+16.0
χ^2	395.62 with 20 degrees of freedom (p < .001)		257.90 with 20 degrees of freedom (p < .001)	

Note: The analysis includes all friendships of respondents of known ancestry (N = 1867).
[a]The indicator analyzed is whether the friend is believed to know the respondent's background.

their stamp on mutual awareness. For obvious reasons, relatives are highly likely to be knowledgeable about an individual's background, as are those friends whose acquaintance extends back to childhood or to school years. Friendships formed in other contexts are less likely to include awareness of backgrounds, with those originating in organizations the least likely. The differences between the two sets of contexts are on the order of 10 to 15 percentage points, which are large differences considering the high overall probability that friends possess knowledge of respondents' backgrounds.

Further, ethnic commonality contributes to mutual awareness. The effect provides a hint that shared ethnic background is something noteworthy to many respondents and their friends, for friends whose ancestries have something in common with respondents' are 13 percentage points more likely than average to know respondents' backgrounds. At the other extreme, friends whose backgrounds are unknown to respondents are frequently perceived to be unaware of respondents' backgrounds as well. According to respondents' perceptions, the probability of these friends' knowledge is 23 percentage points below average. Lastly, friends whose backgrounds are known to be different from respondents' are just about average in their perceived knowledge.

Clearly in evidence, too, is the impact of ethnic identity and ancestry. Ethnically identifying respondents from undivided ethnic backgrounds are considerably more likely (13 percentage points greater than average) than others to believe that their ethnic backgrounds are known to their close friends; least likely to believe this are nonidentifiers of mixed ancestry (11 points less than average). This impact presumably results from respondents' sense of the visibility of their ethnic backgrounds to others; these backgrounds are more visible to the extent that they are simple rather than complex, and to the extent that respondents identify with them and hence acknowledge them in a variety of ways. Also influential is the subjective importance attached to them. Respondents who attach greater importance to their backgrounds are more likely to believe that their friends know about them.

Discussion of ethnic backgrounds is much less common than mutual awareness of them. Respondents indicated discussing their ethnic backgrounds with just 28 percent of their close friends.[19] In further contrast to mutual awareness, discussing one's ethnic background with a close friend is not much affected by the characteristics of the friendship itself. Net of other factors, for instance, the probability that such discussions take place is not affected by the length of time a friendship has been in existence; and it is but minimally affected by the frequency of contact. There is also no net effect of a relationship's origin. Although respondents are more likely to discuss their ethnic backgrounds with relatives and childhood friends than they are with other friends, these differences disappear in a multivariate analysis.

The only relational characteristic with a pronounced influence on discussion of ethnic background is mutual awareness. The causal ordering must be viewed as uncertain here, for while mutual awareness may facilitate discussion, discussion may be the source of awareness. Mutual awareness enters into the analysis in the guise of the degree of ethnic overlap in a friendship. In this case, the key distinction does not revolve around ethnic commonality but around knowledge. Discussion is much more likely when the background of a friend is known to the respondent, regardless of whether it is the same as or different from the respondent's own. The effect is substantial, on the order of 25 percentage points, and the absence of an effect of ethnic commonality per se seems to corroborate that discussion of ethnicity takes place just as easily between friends of different ethnic backgrounds as between those who have the same.

Also consistent with earlier findings is the powerful influence of ethnic identity. Individuals who identify with their ethnic background and view it as important are more likely to talk about it. This is evident in two ways. First, ethnic identity status has a direct impact on the likelihood of discussing background. Ethnic identifiers are more likely to engage in such discussions than are nonidentifiers; and in this case, unlike mutual awareness, there is no difference among identifiers according to type of ancestry: identifiers of mixed ancestry are as likely to discuss their backgrounds as those of undivided ancestry. Second, the subjective importance of background, that is, the salience of identity, has a big impact. The net effect of a one-step increase in importance is a rise of 16 percentage points in the probability of discussing one's ethnic background with a close friend.

Of these two possible forms of mutual recognition of ethnic background, discussion of ethnic background would seem, in principle, more weighty in its ethnic implications. Mutual awareness of common ethnicity implies only bare knowledge of the facts of ancestry, whereas discussions of ethnicity can lead to shared understandings about it, which build on common childhood experiences, values, and ways of behaving. Discussions can thus engender feelings of ethnic solidarity. But this distinction in principle does not mean that discussion of ethnicity must be taken in every instance as evidence of solidarity. The findings so far give ample reason for caution: that discussion is little influenced by characteristics of the relationship itself; that it occurs as readily between friends of different backgrounds as between those of the same; and that it is largely an outgrowth of ethnic identity. These findings seem consistent with the notion that discussion of ethnic backgrounds is frequently a part of introductory signaling between people. It is, in fact, hard to understand the frequent discussions between people of different ethnic backgrounds in any other way, for these can hardly develop feelings of solidarity based on common ethnicity. Presumably, discussion of ethnicity is so closely related to ethnic identity because individuals whose identities are salient are more likely to employ ethnic symbols in this signaling process.

Nevertheless, if discussion need not imply solidarity, solidarity almost certainly implies discussion. Friendships involving some degree of ethnic solidarity, of special empathy and warmth derived from shared ethnic background, are very likely to be those where there is also discussion of ethnicity. This justifies giving special attention to friendships where both overlapping ancestry and discussions of ethnicity are present—*ethnically conscious* friendships. These friendships, which can be measured in the data, place a reasonable upper bound on friendships involving ethnic solidarity, which cannot be measured.

By this measure, it would appear that ethnically solidary friendships are not very widespread, and unusual indeed are individuals whose social milieus are dominated by this form of friendship. In numerical terms, the findings are on a par with those concerning relationships involving a special feeling derived from shared ethnicity (see chapter 4). About 30 percent of native-born whites have one or more ethnically conscious friendships; but only 10 percent have a majority of their friendships of this type (see table 6.7).

Given the close connection between ethnic identity and the act of discussing ethnic background, the profile of ethnically conscious friendship in relation to other variables is quite predictable and does not need to be described at great length. Individuals who, for instance, identify ethnically are considerably more likely to have friendships of this type than are those who do not identify in ethnic terms. Almost none of the latter have social milieus in which such friendships are the predominant element, compared to 13 percent of identifiers (see table 6.7).[20] Likewise, ethnically conscious friendship varies strongly with the salience of identity (this is not shown in a table). Friendships of this type reach their high-water mark among individuals with intense identities (that is, who identify and hold their backgrounds to be very important). Half the members of this group have one or more such friendships, although even here this type of friendship predominates in the milieus of just a small minority (about 20 percent). There is also a predictable variation by ethnic group, with Italians (among large ancestry groups) and Jews (among smaller ones) leading the pack. Among old-stock groups, the

Table 6.7   The number of ethnically conscious friendships by respondent's ethnic identity status

	One or more such friends	Three or more such friends
Overall	29.0%	10.4%
By ethnic identity status (Ancestry/identity type):		
single/single	37.4	16.5
multiple/single	32.5	11.7
multiple/multiple	33.3	11.1
single/none	8.0	0.0
multiple/none	18.5	4.9
Significance levels:	p < .01	p < .10

Note: The table includes only respondents of known ancestry who name at least four close friends (N = 355).

Irish have relatively more ethnically conscious friendships than others.

Do Friendships Involving Common Ethnicity Provide a Social Context Supportive of Ethnicity?
The most critical issue is whether friendships to people of the same ethnic background can be seen as forming an ethnic social structure, that is, a social context supportive of cultural and other expressions of ethnicity. From the evidence so far, one would have to judge that they have the effect to a modest degree. On the positive side is the consistent relationship between ethnic identity and friendship involving common ethnicity. Cross-sectional survey data cannot establish causal order, but it seems plausible that this relationship is reciprocal in nature; that is, ethnically identifying individuals to some extent seek out and prefer friendships with people ethnically like themselves. They also find themselves with some friendships of this type from childhood on and these help to make their ethnicity more salient to them. The strength of this mutuality must not be overstated. Even among the most strongly identified, a majority have just a few friends who are coethnics, and they have other close friends with whom they do not share any common ethnic background.

On the other side is the limited extent to which common ethnicity is openly recognized as part of friendships where it is present. In many friendships involving common ethnicity, there is little or no discussion of ethnic background. Indeed, common ethnicity apparently does not even make such discussions more likely. Those who identify ethnically discuss their backgrounds as readily with friends who are not coethnics as with friends who are.

But what is the relationship of friendship involving common ethnicity to other experiences that are ethnic in character? Do friendships of this type help to sustain ethnic behaviors, such as eating ethnic foods, practicing customs, and becoming involved in ethnic political issues? Here, too, one must recognize that the direction of causality remains ambiguous. Ethnic experiences can be seen as drawing an individual into ethnically based networks. The person who takes an interest in ethnic cultures is likely to find friends among people with similar interests, just as membership in a friendship circle where ethnic commonality is present can be seen as supportive of such experiences. But even if the direction of causality remains problematic, it is still relevant to examine the relationship between ethnic experiences and friendship. To this end, I have carried out a number of regression analyses with a modified index of ethnic experiences[21] as the dependent variable and various ways of looking at the ethnic character of friendship circles among the independent variables (see table 6.8).

The overall number of friendships involving overlapping ancestry is related, net of other factors, to the level of ethnic experience. As reflected in its standardized regression coefficient, the relationship is not powerful, but it is of moderate strength. In specific

Table 6.8   Regression analysis of index of ethnic experience on ethnic characteristics of friendship groups and other variables

	Regression coefficients		Statistical significance
	unstandardized	standardized	
From equation I:			
Number of friends of over-lapping ancestry	.281	.167	p < .001
From equation II:			
Number of relatives named as close friends			N.S.
Number of nonkin friends of overlapping ancestry	.378	.196	p < .001
From equation III:			
Number of nonkin friends of overlapping ancestry with whom background is discussed	.554	.200	p < .001
Number of other nonkin friends of overlapping ancestry	.349	.157	p < .01
Number of other friends with whom background is discussed	.313	.184	p < .001

Note: All equations are based on respondents of known ancestry who name at least four friends (N = 355). The index of ethnic experiences has been modified by removing the four experiences connected with sensitivity to ethnicity in the social world. Each equation includes as controls: ethnic identity status, subjective importance of background, generation, age, gender, educational attainment, and confidence in ancestry knowledge.

terms, each friendship adds approximately .3 to the number of experiences. Thus, the expected difference between someone with no ethnically overlapping friendships and another who has a majority of friendships of this type (that is, three) is on the order of one experience. By this measure and also that of its standardized regression coefficient, the number of ethnically overlapping friendships trails in magnitude of effect the subjective importance of ethnic background, by far the most powerful predictor of the level of ethnic experience. But it is comparable to education and generation (not shown in the table), two rather consistently important variables.

The number of ethnically overlapping friendships is but a crude index of the ethnically relevant characteristics of a friendship group. Hence, it is of interest to take this index apart in some different ways to determine which features of friendship circles are most critical for ethnic experience. One significant distinction is between relatives and other friends of ethnically overlapping background. For, despite the plausibility of the notion that family networks are likely to be supportive of ethnic behavior, the number of relatives named as close friends has, net of other factors, no relation to the index of ethnic experiences. Rather, the number of nonkin friends of overlapping background turns out to be a critical feature of the friendship group. The net influence of each addition to the number of such friends is almost .4 experiences.[22] The difference between a person with no nonkin friends of overlapping background and someone with a majority of friends of this type is more than one experience—a sizable difference, although an uncommon one, since there are few people who have such a majority made up of nonkin friends.

This effect does not seem to be reduced by the ethnic diversity of the friendship circle. That it holds up when diversity is taken into account may prove important in the long run, since the diversity of friendship circles is increasing even when they include friendships involving ethnic commonality. Incorporating diversity as an independent variable in the analysis of ethnic experience changes nothing; the variable is not significant, and the coefficient for nonkin friends is not affected (the results from this model are not reported in table 6.8).

Another way of viewing the friendship group is in terms of the mutual recognition accorded friendships involving common ethnicity. It is plausible that friendships where mutual recognition is present should have a larger ethnic impact, but the evidence for this turns out to be equivocal. Recognition, as reflected in discussions of ethnicity between friends of the same background, seems at least as much a function of the respondent's ethnic identity as it does a property of the friendship relation. Consequently, an effect similar to that of mutual recognition appears even when friendships possess no shared ethnic element.

This ambiguous result is seen when discussions of ethnic background are factored into the analysis. This is accomplished by dividing the number of nonkin friends of overlapping background into two components—one for those friends with whom such discussions take place and the second for the remainder. Also entered into the equation is the number of other friendships involving discussion of ethnic background. With the distinction between the two types of nonkin friendships made, there is a noticeable difference between their impacts. The friendships involving both common ethnicity and the discussion of ethnic background are associated with higher levels of ethnic experience than are the friendships involving common ethnicity only. Also significant in effect, however, are other friendships involving discussion of ethnic background. These are friendships where common ethnic ancestry is generally not present,[23] and their effect is just about equal to the difference between the two types of nonkin friendships. Consequently, there appears to be a general heightening of ethnic experience associated with discussing one's ethnic background, whether one discusses it with friends of similar or different backgrounds. The occurrence of such discussions thus serves as another indicator of salient ethnic identity, one not fully captured in the explicit measures of identity. It seems inappropriate to attribute its effects to friendship.

Nevertheless, some friendships do have ethnic reverberations, and some kinds of experience are more susceptible to the influence of ethnic networks. Analysis of the most important ethnic experiences discussed earlier (chapters 3 and 4) reveals that the effect of the number of nonkin friends of overlapping background, the critical feature of the friendship circle, is variable, both in existence and magnitude. The cultural experiences are most consistently affected by the ethnic character of the friendship circle. Thus, the probabilities of eating ethnic foods at all, of eating them at home, and of using them to celebrate special occasions are related to the number of ethnically similar, nonkin friends (this statement holds with other relevant variables controlled). So, too, are the probabilities of knowing and using a mother tongue. Of the cultural experiences, only that of attending ethnic festivals does not show the influence of the friendship circle.

Other experiences display greater variability in relation to ethnic friendship networks. On one side are the experiences connected with prejudice and discrimination, in particular, hearing about discrimination against fellow ethnics and coming into contact with stereotypes about one's group. Both are influenced by the number of nonkin friends of overlapping background. On the other side is the political manifestation of ethnicity, being concerned with ethnic political issues and taking some action with respect to them (cf. McAdam, 1986). Neither appears to be influenced by the ethnic character of friendship, nor does the desire to transmit an ethnic identity to children.

Despite this variability, what has been clearly demonstrated is that friendships involving common ancestry, especially those to nonrelatives, provide elements of an ethnic social structure associated with stronger ethnic identities and higher levels of ethnic experience. One must be careful not to overstate the linkages involved. After all, most friendship circles are not ethnically homogeneous, and most friendships involving common ethnicity are found in social milieus encompassing considerable ethnic diversity. Nevertheless, it is in friendship, not in marriage, that one must seek for the remnants of ethnic social structure.

Organizations

The Ancient Order of Hibernians helps you hold on to your glorious Irish past, and to hand it down to your children.
Through the A.O.H. you'll meet people interested in and knowledgeable about Irish Culture and History . . . Proud of your Irish heritage? And Catholic faith? Concerned about Human Rights Violations in Northern Ireland? Join the A.O.H. today.
—AD PLACED BY THE ALBANY CHAPTER OF THE ANCIENT ORDER OF HIBERNIANS IN THE 1988 PROGRAM FOR THE CAPITAL REGION'S SCOTTISH GAMES.

Voluntary organizations can also be seen as a potential haven for ethnicity in a society where ethnic lines are crossed so easily, where interethnic contacts occur without great notice in neighborhoods, marriages, schools, and on the job (Olzak, 1983; Yancey et al., 1985). In many parts of the country, such organizations include a stratum of avowedly ethnic organizations, such as the Ancient Order of Hibernians, the B'nai Brith, and the Polish National Alliance Club. Avowedly ethnic organizations presumably come into being to serve ethnic purposes, which frequently include the preservation of ethnic identities and cultures and the representation of ethnic interests. They are places where people who identify with a group can come together, inter alia, to socialize with fellow ethnics, to discuss matters of common concern, and to introduce the next generation to an ethnic social circle and to ethnic ways. In addition to such explicitly ethnic organizations, there are many other organizations that are ethnically homogeneous, or at least relatively so, as a matter of fact rather than design. These organizations have memberships that are drawn largely from one ethnic group, even though their founding purpose is not ethnic in character.[24] Organizations of this type, which can range from neighborhood athletic teams to veterans' groups, can serve some of the same purposes as avowedly ethnic organizations.

The question to be addressed is whether either type of organization actually functions in a significant way as a component of ethnic social structure, contributing to the maintenance of ethnic identity and behavior in a manner paralleling that of ethnically based friendship. Were this to prove the case, then such organizations might be even more powerful as reservoirs of ethnicity than friendship. For friendship circles are extensively populated by people of unrelated ethnic backgrounds and generally quite circumscribed as ethnic social structures—it is probably infrequent that they link individuals to much larger, ethnically based networks—whereas avowedly ethnic organizations, almost by definition, are constituted by extensive ethnic networks and are often connected to national parent organizations. Thus, they can serve as spheres in which ethnic issues are discussed and through which ethnic outlooks are disseminated; and they bring together individuals on the basis of a shared ethnic bond who may then meet in other social contexts (in business, say) and be better able to cooperate because of the preexisting, solidary tie.[25]

In order to examine the extent and effects of memberships in ethnic organizations, we collected extensive organizational data, going far beyond our immediate purpose in order to make sure that ethnic organizations of either type were not overlooked. We asked our respondents to name the organizations they belonged to (including the church or synagogue they attended), and we provided them with a list of different types of organizations to make sure that none were overlooked.[26] They gave us memberships in voluminous detail (see table 6.9). Only 9 percent of native-born whites failed to name at least one organization, while more than 60 percent named more than one. There were also a substantial number of respondents who might fairly be called "joiners," persons with many memberships; for example, 22 percent listed four or more organizations, and one of every thirteen belonged to six or more.

Most important among these memberships are not ethnic organizations but religious ones: churches, synagogues, and other religious organizations account for 36 percent of all organizations listed. No other organization type rivals religious organizations in importance. Otherwise, our respondents were most likely to belong to social clubs (10 percent of memberships), professional societies (8 percent), labor unions (7 percent), fraternal and veterans' organizations (6 percent), and sports teams (5 percent). None of the remaining organization types we inquired about, which included civic groups, country clubs, neighborhood groups, and political clubs, accounted for as much as 5 percent of the memberships.

Included in the list of groups presented to respondents was the category "ethnic, racial, nationality" organizations. Our intent was that this category would include avowedly ethnic organizations, that is, those organized *in principle* on the basis of common ethnic background. In fact, there are quite a fair number of such organizations in the Albany region (for example, the Sons of Italy, the German-American Club, and the Polish Community Hall), and so it was plausible that this category should account for a significant fraction of organizational memberships. Moreover, close scrutiny of the organizations respondents put in the category, as well as of the organizations they placed in other categories, indicates that, generally speaking, they understood our intentions. Only a trivial number of organizations needed to be reclassified.[27]

Yet such ethnic organizations appear to represent no more than a tiny part of the organizational affiliations of native-born whites.

Table 6.9   Some characteristics
of the organizational
memberships of native-born
whites

Number of memberships:

zero	9.1%
one	28.3
two	23.9
three	16.5
four or five	14.3
six or more	7.8

Organization type[a]:

business or civic	4.8%
charity or welfare	3.8
cooperative	0.5
country club	1.5
ethnic, racial, or na- tionality	1.1
farm	0.7
fraternal or veterans'	5.8
special interest	4.4
labor unions	6.8
neighborhood	1.9
PTA or school	4.2
political	1.9
professional	7.5
religious	36.4
social club	10.0
sports team	5.2
youth group	2.9
other	0.5

[a]Based on total number of organization
memberships (N = 1154).

Our respondents cited scarcely more than a handful (thirteen *altogether*) of memberships in such groups. Only 2 percent of native-born white respondents were members. In terms of frequency, membership in avowedly ethnic organizations is roughly of the same order of magnitude as membership in country clubs, and far less common than memberships in virtually all other organization types. The low level of membership among native-born whites can be contrasted to the levels of membership in such organizations among non-whites and the foreign born. While not high in an absolute sense, they are four to five times as large as among native-born whites—about 10 percent of non-whites and immigrant whites belong.

The native-born whites in our sample who belong to ethnic organizations are too few in number to justify a formal statistical analysis, but an examination of their characteristics suggests that membership is typically associated with a strong ethnic identity, a great deal of ethnic experience, closeness to the immigrant generation, and numerous ethnically based friendships. Virtually all of these individuals identify in ethnic terms (just one does not). All of them also attach at least some importance to their ethnic backgrounds, and half say their backgrounds are very important to them—a fraction well above that found among native-born whites as a whole. Also overrepresented in this group are members of the second generation, while few are members of the fourth and later generations.

The strong correspondence between membership in ethnic organizations, on the one hand, and high levels of ethnic experience and of ethnically based friendships, on the other, offers further evidence that members of such groups are embedded in unusually ethnic social worlds. All of the native-born whites with such memberships reported at least four ethnic experiences, in contrast to just a third of native-born whites as a whole. Most are found in the highest level of ethnic experience, six or more (only a quarter of all native-born whites are at this level). About half of the members of ethnic organizations have friendship circles in which nonkin co-ethnics constitute a majority. Among native-born whites as a whole, this is a comparatively infrequent occurrence.

If few native-born whites appear to belong to organizations that are ethnic in purpose, another form of ethnic membership is more widespread, namely, in organizations that are ethnic in fact, having members who are largely of the same ethnic background. To obtain information about such ethnically homogeneous (or ethnic-membership) organizations, we asked respondents which of the organizations they belonged to had many members of the same ethnic background as themselves. (Specifically, they were asked to identify organizations at least half of whose members were from their own ethnic background.) Similar questions were asked in terms of re-spondents' community and religion.

Although membership in ethnically homogeneous organiza-tions is more widespread than membership in organizations dedi-cated to ethnic purposes, it is still not the experience of the majority. Overall, about one in six organizations to which our respondents belong are ethnically homogeneous (see table 6.10), and it is likely that this figure is somewhat inflated. A close examination of the organizational lists reveals that some respondents who thought of themselves only as Americans indicated that the organizations they belong to are ethnically homogeneous, probably meaning that the members are also Americans. It is not really feasible to eliminate these "erroneous" specifications (too much guesswork is involved), but their presence suggests the need for caution in interpreting the percentage of organizations with ethnic memberships.

The degree of ethnic homogeneity in organizational mem-berships is considerably less than that of homogeneity in terms of

Table 6.10   Ethnic-membership organizations
by organization type

		N
Overall	16.9%	1154
By organization type:		
business or civic	9.1%	55
charity or welfare	13.6	44
cooperative	16.7	6
country club	23.5	17
ethnic, racial, or nationality	84.6	13
farm	0.0	8
fraternal or veterans'	13.4	67
special interest	9.8	51
labor union	7.7	78
neighborhood	13.6	22
PTA or school	10.2	49
political	4.5	22
professional	6.9	87
religious	24.8	420
social club	14.8	115
sports team	11.7	60
youth group	11.8	34
other	16.7	6

residence and religious background. Nearly 60 percent of organizations had primarily local memberships, according to our respondents, and more than 40 percent had memberships that were more or less homogeneous in religious terms. The religious homogeneity of organizations is, in large measure, due to the frequency of religious organizations on the membership lists of respondents. But even when churches and synagogues are discounted, it appears that organizations are more religiously homogeneous than they are ethnically, although the margin of difference is not great.

Religious groups also account for a very substantial portion of ethnically homogeneous organizations. Religious organizations, principally churches, made up more than half of such organizations cited by respondents. This figure is disproportionate to the overall representation of churches and synagogues in the organizational lists of respondents, because religious organizations are apparently more likely than other types to have ethnically homogeneous memberships. There is a reality here, as well as perhaps some confusion in the application of the word *ethnic*. Many religious organizations are also ethnic in character; the Capital Region has Ukrainian, Armenian, and Greek Orthodox Churches, as well as some remaining nationality parishes of the Catholic Church. Even when churches do not have a specifically ethnic base, they generally overrepresent specific ethnic groups because of the historical association between ethnicity and denomination (for example, Italians in the Catholic Church). But the disproportion in the number of religious organizations described by respondents as having ethnic memberships suggests that some respondents did not distinguish clearly between ethnicity and religion. This may be another instance of the confusion over what is ethnic and what is not.

Only a small proportion of nonreligious organizations have ethnically homogeneous memberships (12 percent). Only a few of the major categories of organization types contain a greater-than-average number of ethnic-membership organizations (table 6.10), specifically, social clubs (15 percent), neighborhood groups (14 percent), and fraternal and veterans' organizations (13 percent). Also unusually homogeneous in ethnic terms are country clubs (24 percent), but our respondents belong to few of these. (And, of course, there are avowedly ethnic organizations; as noted, membership in them is rare.)

The majority of native-born whites do not belong to any ethnically homogeneous organizations (table 6.11). Specifically, almost three-quarters of respondents do not (and this fraction is calculated on the basis of only those individuals with at least one organizational affiliation). Of those who do belong to such organizations, about two-thirds belong to just one, and for most, this organization is a church or synagogue. Only a small fraction of native-born whites (10 percent) might be considered "ethnic joiners," persons who belong to two or more ethnically homogeneous organizations (and small as it is, the percentage is inflated by the inclusion of some persons with an "American" identity who checked all of their organizations as being ethnically homogeneous).

Membership in an ethnically homogeneous organization is only weakly related to indicators of ethnic identity. On the one hand, this weakness is partly the product of measurement difficulties. There was not consistency among respondents in applying the word *ethnic* to organizations, and this weakens in the data the patterns that may exist in reality. On the other hand, there may be some reality reflected here as well. Some memberships in ethnically homogeneous organizations do not so much reflect active searches on the part of ethnically identifying whites for organizations that

Table 6.11   Memberships in ethnically homogeneous organizations by ethnic identity status

	% with one	% with two or more	Sum (% with any)
Overall	17.9	10.0	27.9
By ethnic identity status (ancestry/identity type):			
single/single	23.9	8.0	31.9
multiple/single	17.3	7.4	24.7
multiple/multiple	17.0	8.0	25.0
single/none	10.3	13.8	24.1
multiple/none	13.8	14.9	28.7
unknown/none	23.1	15.4	38.5

Overall significance level: N.S.

Note: Only native-born white respondents with at least one organizational membership (N = 418) are included in the tabulation.

match their ethnic sentiments as they do religious and communal attachments. The person who grows up in a French Canadian parish, for example, may continue to attend services there, even after forsaking the old neighborhood for a nearby suburb. While the motivating force may be loyalty to the religious expression one knew as a child, the consequences for ethnicity of such attachments may be significant. Ethnically homogeneous organizations thus may still constitute a kind of ethnic social structure that is almost independent of ethnic identity.

The weakness in relation to ethnic identity is readily apparent. There is no difference between the ethnically identifying and nonidentifying in likelihood of belonging to an ethnic-membership organization (see table 6.11). And the subjective importance of ethnic background, elsewhere the most powerful predictor of ethnically related behavior, does not make a large difference, even among the ethnically identifying (this is not shown in a table). Among those who identify and feel their background are very important, 38 percent belong to one or more ethnically homogeneous organizations; among those who identify but feel their backgrounds hold little or no importance, the comparable figure is 23 percent. The difference is statistically meaningful, but the figures make clear that even among those who identify strongly with their ethnic background, membership in ethnically homogeneous organizations remains a minority phenomenon. Although the relationship of membership to ethnic identity might be strengthened if the inconsistencies in the data could be corrected, the fact that membership characterizes only a minority of the strongest identifiers would not change, for the corrections would lower the overall frequency of membership.

Nor is membership in ethnically homogeneous organizations much explained by the demographic and socioeconomic factors, such as generational status and education, that have played a prominent role in explaining ethnic identity and experience. When the number of such memberships is analyzed by regression analysis as a function of these factors, the explanatory power of the resulting equation is principally attributable to the inclusion of the total number of organizational memberships among the independent variables[28] (see table 6.12). Otherwise, only gender, ethnic identity status and subjective importance, and confidence in ancestry knowledge are statistically significant, and none is associated with

Table 6.12   Regression analysis of the number of memberships in ethnically homogeneous organizations

	Regression coefficients		Statistical significance
	unstandardized	standardized	
Ethnic identity status:		.158[a]	p < .10
single/single	—[b]		
multiple/single	−.134		
multiple/multiple	.057		
single/none	−.003		
multiple/none	.275		
Subjective importance of	.109	.093	p < .10
background			
Generation			N.S.
Age			N.S.
Gender:		.093	p < .10
male	—[b]		
female	.167		
Educational attainment			N.S.
Confidence in ancestry			
knowledge:		.133	p < .05
confident	—[b]		
unconfident	.400		
Number of relatives among	.082	.108	p < .10
close friends			
Number of nonkin friends of	.117	.160	p < .01
overlapping ancestry			
Total number of organiza-	.146	.295	p < .001
tional memberships			
R^2		.171	
Adjusted R^2		.125	

Note: Because of the inclusion of friendship variables, the regression is limited to respondents who satisfy the criteria: their ancestry is known; they name a minimum of four friends; and they belong to at least one organization (N = 331).
[a]The standardized coefficient is the sheaf coefficient.
[b]Indicates omitted category.

substantial differences in membership. (Note, too, the effect of confidence in ancestry knowledge, which seems in the wrong direction since those with less confidence are more likely to be members, and almost certainly reflects the measurement difficulties in the organization variable.)

This type of membership is, however, associated with ethnic homogeneity in friendship, confirming again that membership in ethnic organizations is associated with embeddedness in ethnic social structures more generally (see Yancey et al., 1985). The association is not very strong, but it appears to be stronger than the effect of subjective importance of background, for instance. When the number of relatives named as friends and the number of nonkin friends of overlapping background are entered into the regression equation (as independent variables), both are significant. The number of nonkin friends makes the larger difference: net of other factors, each such friend is associated with a difference of .12 memberships. Consequently, the expected difference between someone with no friends of this type and another with a majority of them translates into approximately a third of a membership, which is larger than the difference to be expected between people at the extremes of the subjective importance scale.

Like ethnically based friendship, membership in ethnically homogeneous organizations has an impact on the level of ethnic experience. Indeed, the net effect of both types of ethnic social structure is considerable (see table 6.13). When added to an equation predicting the index of ethnic experience (minus the experiences of sensitivity to ethnicity in the social world), both the number of mem-

Table 6.13   Regression analysis of the index of ethnic experience on memberships in ethnically homogeneous organizations, ethnic characteristics of friendship groups, and other variables

	Regression coefficients		Statistical significance
	unstandardized	*standardized*	
Number of memberships in ethnically homogeneous organizations	.244	.091	p < .10
Number of relatives named as close friends			N.S.
Number of nonkin friends of overlapping ancestry	.389	.198	p < .001

Note: The analysis includes only respondents of known ancestry, who belong to at least one organization, and who name at least four friends (N = 331). The index of ethnic experiences has been modified by removing the four experiences connected with sensitivity to ethnicity in the social world. Each equation includes as controls: ethnic identity status, subjective importance of background, generation, age, gender, educational attainment, and confidence in ancestry knowledge.

berships and the number of nonkin friends of overlapping ancestry make significant differences. Each membership is associated with a difference of .24 experiences, and each friend with a difference of .39 experiences. To put this in perspective, the net effect of one membership and one ethnically based friendship is about the same as that associated with each further generational remove from the point of immigration. Nonetheless, the most powerful predictor of the level of ethnic experience remains the subjective importance of ethnic background.

In summary, ethnic-membership organizations constitute, along with ethnically based friendship, a kind of ethnic social structure that helps to maintain ethnic behavior. Membership in organizations of this type is not very widespread, but it is far more extensive than membership in organizations formed explicitly to serve ethnic purposes. Moreover, it is spread rather evenly among the major ancestry groups—about a quarter of each group belongs to one or more ethnically homogeneous organizations.

Also significant is that religious organizations are prevalent among organizations of this type. Because of evident problems of measurement, the data are somewhat uncertain, but they do hint at a special role for religious groups in sustaining ethnicity, a notion supported by other considerations as well. Religious organizations tend to draw selectively from ethnic groups, thus engendering greater ethnic concentrations in their memberships than can be found in the general population. And they provide an institutional and ritual framework that, if genuinely associated with ethnicity, can substitute to some degree for the ethnic communities, institutions, and traditions eroding under the force of assimilation.

Yet one must be wary of drawing too strong a conclusion about the linkage between religious organizations and ethnicity. By itself, the effect of ethnically homogeneous organizations on ethnic experience is not strong. It is likely that some of this effect is due to churches and synagogues in a dwindling number of ethnic neighborhoods. This inference is exemplified in the Italian pattern, given the continued existence in the region of largely Italian parishes in once heavily Italian neighborhoods. Accordingly, an unusually high rate of membership in ethnically homogeneous organizations is found among Italians of unmixed ancestry who identify as Italians, a group whose attachment to ethnic parishes is likely to be strong.

But once church and other religious memberships are removed from consideration, Italian participation in ethnic-membership organizations falls off considerably and is scarcely different from anybody else's.

Summary

The picture is mixed, but it does contain some elements that help to make understandable the persistence of ethnic identities and experience at a time when the hard edge of the massive ethnic differences of the past has been blunted. On a social plane, there is great interpenetration among ethnic categories in the white population. Most native-born whites have close friendships with some persons whose ethnic backgrounds differ from their own, and many have friendship circles that encompass considerable ethnic diversity. Only a minority have ethnically based friendship circles, in which people with the same ethnic background are the predominant element. Few have circles that are truly homogeneous. Likewise, only a few belong to organizations formed around ethnic concerns. Most of the organizations to which whites belong have memberships that are ethnically diverse, at least insofar as this can be judged from the capsule, and occasionally erroneous, evaluations of respondents.

But if integration on a social level is the experience of the majority, it is an integration frequently enough perforated by the filaments of ethnic social structures. The majority of whites have one or more friendships to persons whose ethnic backgrounds overlap their own in some respect. In part, this is because relatives are often named as close friends. But even when friendships with relatives are discounted, it is still the case that a majority, albeit a bare one, has at least one nonkin friend of similar ethnic ancestry. Also notable are affiliations with organizations whose memberships are largely homogeneous in ethnic terms, although this remains the experience of only a minority of whites.

These findings about ethnic social structure stand in marked contrast to those in which intermarriage was so extensive that only a small minority could be considered to have avoided it. How can one account for this discrepancy? Perhaps the critical factor lies in the multiple relations found in an individual's everyday social world, in contrast to the singularity of a marital partner. For most people, there are numerous criteria of compatibility that must be considered in the choice of a spouse—age, educational background, intentions with regard to children, and cultural tastes, to name just a few. Given the rigorous filtering of the field of eligibles produced by these criteria, ethnic background tends to lack in weightiness, especially when everyday contacts among whites routinely bring together people of different European ancestries. Multiple friendship relations and organizational affiliations, however, offer more latitude for satisfying a taste to have some contact with persons of the same, or similar, ethnic background. Satisfying this taste need not contradict the basic integration that characterizes the social milieus of most whites of European background. But this taste, if that is indeed what it is, seems to be for ethnicity in a mild form, without strong commitments to ethnicity as a social bond. In this respect, it is noteworthy that so few whites belong to avowedly ethnic organizations and also that discussions of ethnic background play such a minor role in friendships involving shared ethnic ancestry.

Thus, the portrait that emerges from the ethnic social affiliations of many whites seems far removed from the more thoroughly ethnic milieus that were common in the past. Nevertheless, these affiliations are not without effect, for they do have some relationship to the ethnic character of the contemporary experiences of whites. The effects can easily be overstated, but they are there, especially for elective affiliations as opposed to those determined by birth, reflected particularly in the number of nonkin friends of overlapping ancestry. The analysis thus indicates that some friendships and organizational memberships can function as ethnic social structures, supportive of ethnic experience and, to a lesser extent, of ethnic identities.

There is good reason to believe that some ethnic affiliations, at least those rooted in friendship, will not erode to the same depth as many other social anchors of ethnicity. To be sure, there is evidence of continuing decline in the ethnic homogeneity of social milieus, for instance, in the friendship circles of the Irish and Italians, where homogeneity is now relatively high. (The disproportionate number of coethnic friendships originating during childhood also suggests some ongoing decline.) But sound reasons, structural ones, indicate that friendship involving some shared ancestry will continue to be widespread. Whatever their preferences on the matter may be, members of many ethnic groups, especially large ones, are likely to have friendships where common ethnic elements are present, simply as a result of the ethnic mix in the population. Bolstering this notion is the absence of any generational or cohort effects to indicate further large-scale, demographically driven decline in friendships of this type.

Yet one has to remain skeptical about the long-run potential of such structures to maintain ethnicity among whites. One doubt creeps in with respect to the growing complexity of ancestry. As ancestries become increasingly mixed, the probability rises that friendship involves a common ethnic element. But what will happen to the significance of any common ethnicity when it is but a limited part of a complex mixture and when the friendship it characterizes occurs in an ethnically variegated social milieu? A greater doubt appears when friendships involving common ethnicity are juxtaposed with other ethnic trends. Can such partial and informal social structures compensate for the steady erosion of ethnicity's moorings in families, communities, and workplaces? The findings, for example, offer no evidence that ethnically based friendships or organizations that are more or less ethnically homogeneous can carry out the function of socializing a new generation to be ethnic, as ethnically unified families once did. Perhaps if the ethnic aspect of these friendships and organizations was more self-consciously cultivated, they could fulfill this function. But this possibility seems to fly in the face of their informal, unself-conscious qualities, presumably the very qualities valued by the many whites who participate in them. The effect of such informal social structures may be one thing when there are still many whites who, belonging to the second or even third generations, have been brought up in ethnic ways, but something else again when these generations have shrunk.

The Changing Map of Ethnicity: Ethnicity and Neighborhood

One of the most visible signs of ethnic difference is the ethnic neighborhood. Such neighborhoods can be found in both large and small cities throughout the United States, although they are concentrated in those places that have served as the historical receiving grounds for immigrants—in the Northeast and industrial Midwest and along the Pacific Coast and the Rio Grande. The ethnic character of neighborhoods is often quite prominent, visible in the names and nature of their small businesses, in the style and exterior decoration of their housing, and of course in the skin color, speech, and surnames of their residents. Given the non-European sources of contemporary immigration, ethnic neighborhoods are today as frequently populated by Asian, Caribbean, and Latin American immigrants as they are by the children and grandchildren of earlier European ones (and in many cities, the largest areas of all are those occupied by descendants of formerly rural African Americans). But the remarkable fact is the continued existence of neighborhoods whose ethnic character derives from the immigration of the nineteenth and early twentieth centuries.[1]

To the casual observer, the presence in American cities of neighborhoods of white ethnics, long after the cessation of mass immigration from Europe, seems tangible proof of the enduring viability of ethnicity, even in a rapidly changing, advanced industrial society. In their classic statement on the urban role of ethnicity, Glazer and Moynihan (1970) chart some of these neighborhoods as they existed in the New York City of the 1950s and 1960s. They describe the ethnic atmosphere of Italian neighborhoods, for example, as a transplantation of village-centered Southern Italian culture. Their portrait, dominated by an image of stable, well-kempt neighborhoods and watchful family-based networks, seems compelling as evidence of the power of ethnicity to mold the social contours of urban space.

Ethnic neighborhoods are important not merely as visible manifestations of ethnicity, but also for their capacity to concentrate the institutions and cultures of an ethnic group, thereby keeping alive the sentiments and loyalties associated with ethnicity in adult residents and socializing a new generation to ethnic ways.[2] Ethnic neighborhoods typically house the small businesses that cater to special ethnic needs, such as those connected with a group's cuisine, and often serve as sites for such events as ethnic and religious festivals, which celebrate ethnicity and perpetuate its traditions. Accordingly, they expose their residents to ethnicity in its most unadulterated form (however altered that may be from the culture and ways brought by immigrants). These effects need not be limited to residents, although the impact on them is deepest. Ethnic neighborhoods can serve as beacons of ethnicity for those group members who reside in more assimilated settings. Outlying ethnics can travel to these neighborhoods in order to visit with relatives and old friends, to purchase the needed ingredients for ethnic dishes or other kinds of ethnic supplies, and to attend traditional celebrations. Ethnic neighborhoods are thus likely to fuel a sense attachment to the group. Fainter effects may even be felt by those who do not make such visits. Merely by existing as undeniable embodiments of ethnicity, ethnic neighborhoods can rekindle some of the memories and feelings of those whose identities have weakened or lapsed.

The impact of an ethnic neighborhood on its residents does not end with its explicitly ethnic features. In such a neighborhood, any social structure that draws primarily on community residents is also ethnic to a degree. Institutions such as schools and churches tend to be disproportionately ethnic, if not homogeneous, as do sports teams, youth clubs, and other local groups. While this ethnic composition can be seen as incidental, it may not be without effect, since the solidarity predicated on common membership in an organization is fused inextricably with consciousness of shared ethnicity.

In sum, ethnic neighborhoods can be seen not merely as physical settings, but also as ethnic social structures. But the critical question is, to what extent is this role still consequential for Americans of European ancestries? Despite the survival of some ethnic neighborhoods originating in mass immigration during the nineteenth and early twentieth centuries, it is apparent that the urban neighborhoods of European-ancestry groups generally have been declining, as a result of such forces as educational and occupational mobility and competition with newly arriving groups for space and housing. Indeed, the readiness of immigrants and their children to forsake initial areas of settlement, often located in rundown, congested districts near the central business and industrial zones, once they had achieved some economic security was observed quite a long time ago by sociologists of the Chicago school, who used it as a premise for their ecological model (Massey, 1985). In the post-World War II era, the outward migration from inner-city ethnic neighborhoods has been stimulated by the more general exodus to the suburbs and the growing popularity of the suburban life-style as well as by the in-migration of Southern blacks and, in some cities, of new immigrants.[3]

The first issue to be addressed is the condition of ethnic neighborhoods: to what extent do they still exist, and what portions of ethnic groups still reside in them? These questions are connected with the decline in objective indices of ethnicity among whites. Educational and occupational differences among groups have attenuated to a substantial degree, especially for the younger members of the third and later generations, and intermarriage has soared. If social mobility and social assimilation (as reflected in intermarriage) are accompanied by movement out of ethnic neighborhoods and to more ethnically diverse areas, then the viability of ethnic neighborhoods, at least on a mass scale, must be called into question. (Indeed, the scale of intermarriage alone makes the viability of these neighborhoods doubtful, since if families are ethnically integrated, neighborhoods must be as well.) Yet these seemingly obvious implications of well-established patterns of ethnic change among whites are themselves challenged by data on residential patterns that suggest persisting segregation along ethnic lines (for example, Guest and Weed, 1976) and by the fact that ethnic neighborhoods can still be found in many American cities. What, then, is the true state of these neighborhoods?

The location of ethnic neighborhoods presents a second vital issue. They are often visualized as a feature of the urban landscape, and the word *neighborhood* conjures up urban imagery, but the conventional equation between ethnic neighborhoods and cities is problematic. Claude Fischer (1975) presents the strongest case for the conventional view, asserting that urban environments are best able to shelter subcultures that deviate from the mainstream. But this argument runs up against the fact that many ethnic areas in the United States were never in cities in the first place. Immigrant settlement in rural hinterlands from the seventeenth to the nineteenth centuries created ethnically homogeneous regions with some of the same potential for the perpetuation of ethnic patterns as is generally ascribed to urban ethnic neighborhoods. Indeed, the counterargument is sometimes made that rural places insulate ethnic subcultures from assimilatory pressures, because they do not promote cross-ethnic contacts to the same degree as ethnically diverse cities. (The example that comes readily to mind is that of Germans in the rural Midwest during the nineteenth century, who successfully maintained German as a language of everyday life, even to the extent of establishing public school systems in which it was the sole or a primary language of instruction [Fishman et al., 1966].)

An important application of this issue is to the urban-suburban divide. If urban ethnic neighborhoods are being forsaken, it is primarily for suburbs, not rural hinterlands. Thus, an intriguing question is whether ethnic neighborhoods are being reestablished in the suburbs by upwardly mobile migrants from cities. (Perhaps in some cases, the nuclei of such neighborhoods existed prior to any large-scale migration, in the form of ethnics who settled in these areas before they were suburbs in order to take advantage of nearby farming or industrial opportunities.) In order to infer that suburban ethnic areas have some ethnicity-maintaining effects, it may not be necessary to demonstrate that they replicate all the features of urban ethnic neighborhoods, especially if the latter also exist to meet certain ethnic needs (for example, food shops). Nor is it necessary to find that they are as ethnically homogeneous as their urban equivalents. But if suburban ethnic neighborhoods exist, then migration to suburbs, which frequently accompanies social mobility, may not have the ethnicity-diluting impact that is often assumed for it. Although the questions surrounding ethnicity in suburbia seem obvious the moment they are stated, there has been remarkably little research attention to them.[4]

The final issue may be the most important: What is the impact of ethnic neighborhoods on their residents? Although the link between residence in such neighborhoods and a more intense ethnicity seems plausible, it should not be left unexamined. In particular, it is relevant for any assessment of the long-run significance of ethnic identity, which hinges on the relationship of identity to ethnic social structures: if this relationship is weak or negligible, then identity is likely to lead to increasingly private forms of ethnicity. If this relationship is strong, then the way is open to the elaboration of widely shared cultural and other expressions of ethnicity, which can further promote bonds of solidarity between group members.

The impact of ethnic neighborhoods has rarely been studied. Although a great deal of research effort has been invested in the study of ethnic residential patterns, the linkages between these patterns and other aspects of ethnicity have been far more presumed than subject to direct examination (for a rare exception, see Yancey et al., 1985). The reason does not lie in the negligence of scholars, but in the difficulty of assembling relevant data. The problem is rooted in the difficulties of combining data about the ethnic characteristics of individuals, as collected by surveys or other means, with objective information about their residential contexts. The Capital Region study offers an almost unique opportunity, for it not only provides extensive data about the ethnicity of respondents, but respondents can be linked through their addresses to census data about the ethnic character of their neighborhoods.[5] Hence, it is possible to establish the relationship between neighborhood and the ethnic identities and behavior of individuals.

Ethnic Residential Concentrations

The basics concerning the existence and locations of ethnic neighborhoods in the Capital Region are entangled with a set of questions that sociologists have usually addressed under the rubric of "residential segregation." Because many are likely to approach the topic with mental prototypes established by the conventions of segregation research, it is essential to examine closely the concept of segregation (as traditionally employed) and the strategies for measuring it. Only then will we be in a position to assess accurately the state of ethnic neighborhoods.

Two sorts of phenomena, with rather different implications, are often confounded in the measurement of residential segregation. One phenomenon is the ethnic neighborhood, which is an area that is ethnically homogeneous, or at least so disproportionately composed of the members of one ethnic group that it has a manifest ethnic character, visible for example in its small businesses.[6] Segregation in the form of an ethnic neighborhood may be voluntary or involuntary. It is often difficult to decide whether ethnics cluster in the same neighborhoods because they are excluded from residence in other areas or because they want to live near each other. But in either case, such neighborhoods have evident implications for ethnicity.

This is much less true for the second phenomenon: some ethnic distinctiveness in residential patterns arising from incidental features associated with ethnicity, such as the historical moment of a group's arrival or the preferences of its members for a certain type of housing. An ethnically distinctive residential pattern is created whenever a greater than average number of a group move into an area for whatever reason, even if they settle in the midst of people of other ethnic backgrounds and in concentrations well short of those of an ethnic neighborhood. The dividing line between this phenomenon and an ethnic neighborhood is not easy to fix with precision: "Incidental" factors may lie behind the emergence of some ethnic neighborhoods. Nevertheless, at its extreme this is clearly a separate phenomenon. Broadly speaking, the forces behind ethnic distinctiveness in residential patterns can be viewed as by-products of the interaction between residential opportunities at a given moment in time and the stages of ethnic mobility and assimilation; for instance, if an area's housing expands at a time when the members of one group are more ready than others for residential mobility, an ethnically distinctive residential pattern is created. Such patterns can be expected in many suburbs, since suburbs frequently develop in spurts of housing construction and therefore may draw greater than average numbers from those central-city ethnic groups with many members at the appropriate stage of mobility. They can also be expected in cities, which develop in patchwork fashion, with the result that in any given moment the opportunities to find new or better housing are clustered, not spread uniformly.

Recent research on residential segregation has tended to employ several different measures that help to separate out ethnic concentrations in the form of ethnic neighborhoods from other kinds of ethnic residential distinctiveness (see Massey and Denton, 1987; Stearns and Logan, 1986). One is the index of dissimilarity, which used alone can be extremely misleading. The index compares the residential distributions of any two groups, arriving at a measure of their difference or dissimilarity which can be interpreted as the proportion of the members of either group who must be moved to make the distributions identical.[7] Accordingly, the index is influenced by any factor that makes ethnic residential patterns different, whether or not these patterns include ethnic neighborhoods. The second measure is the so-called exposure index, P^* (Lieberson and Carter, 1982). For any two groups, this index can be defined as the proportion of residents belonging to group j in the average residential area of group i's members.[8] Although the wording of the definition is cumbersome, the implications are more straightforward, for the index reflects the likelihood that the members of one group (group i) have members of the other (group j) as neighbors. The third measure, the isolation index, is a variant of the second. It is defined for any single group, by measuring the group's "exposure" to itself, reflecting the extent to which the average group member resides in areas containing coethnics. Thereby, it provides a direct reading of the average extent of ethnic homogeneity in neighborhoods.

All of these measures provide useful assessments of the residential patterns of ethnic groups in the aggregate, but this is also a serious limitation. In a period when ethnic social structures, including residential concentrations, may be weakening, if not breaking down, the significance of aggregate measures may be open to challenge because they mix together in unknown proportions the residential characteristics of quite disparate kinds of group members: at one extreme, those whose locations betray no ethnic influences; at the other, those who live in ethnic neighborhoods. Because this study is a regional one, it is possible to overcome this limitation, by searching for specific areas that contain disproportionate numbers of an ethnic group—*areas of ethnic concentration*—and investigating their characteristics. Such an approach, instead of relying on global comparisons among different ethnic groups, inevitable when only aggregate measures are available, focuses on comparisons among residential areas. Once areas of ethnic concentration are identified, it becomes possible to address questions that cannot be answered in terms of aggregate measures alone; for example, what is the degree of ethnic homogeneity in areas of ethnic concentration (and, thus, are they plausibly viewed as ethnic neighborhoods)? in which kinds of places (urban, suburban, or rural) are these areas typically located? and what proportion of the members of a group live in its areas of concentration?

Areas of ethnic concentration can be found by straightforward comparisons of the ethnic compositions of residential areas, based on the percentages of an area's occupants constituted by various ethnic groups. Such areas are then identifiable either because their population is drawn largely from the members of a single group, which we will see is unusual in the Capital Region, or because a group's proportion in an area is noticeably larger than should be expected from its size in the region's population as a whole. A simple device for discovering areas that satisfy the latter criterion is standardization. This is the main tool I employ to locate unusual concentrations of specific ethnic groups.

The areal unit used throughout the analysis of ethnic residential patterns is the census *block group*. Because ethnic neighborhoods may involve very small areas, perhaps no more than a few blocks of dense ethnic concentration, it is essential in searching for them to achieve a fine grain of geographic detail. The block group is the closest one can come to this ideal with census data. It is smaller than the more familiar census tract, of which it represents a subdivision (the average tract of the Capital Region contains approximately four block groups). As its name implies, the block group is an aggregate of blocks,[9] typically containing between five and twenty populated blocks, and it is the smallest geographical unit for which the Census Bureau reports ethnic ancestry information. In 1980, the four counties included in this study encompassed approximately 750 block groups, averaging about a thousand people in size.[10] These are thus small population areas that approximate a neighborhood level, and in some cases a subneighborhood level, of detail.

Measured on this plane, there is not a great deal of residential separation between the major European ancestry groups and other whites. The fact that segregation is measured at such a fine level of detail should give confidence in this conclusion, for in general the smaller the areas used, the greater is the apparent segregation among groups (Taeuber and Taeuber, 1965). The limited segregation among whites in the Capital Region is shown by the dissimilarity, exposure, and isolation indices in table 7.1, which also presents comparable data for the region's blacks to serve as a point of comparison. The figures for the black population can be used to illustrate the interpretations of the different indices. The dissimilarity index shows that 70 percent of blacks would have to be moved in order to bring the group's residential distribution into correspondence with that of whites. Clearly, there is considerable residential concentration of this group. Nevertheless, because it is small in this region, representing just 4 percent of the overall population, there is also a great deal of proximity to whites, evidenced in the exposure index: the average black lives in an area that is 65 percent white. (The residential exposure of blacks to whites in the Capital Region is the second highest among the sixty largest metropolitan areas in the United States [Massey and Denton, 1987: table 1].) However, the residential area of the average black is also 33 percent black (according to the isolation index), far above what one would expect if the region's small black population were evenly distributed. In sum, the data indicate considerable racial segregation, ameliorated to a degree by the small size of the black population, which precludes the sort of extensive, racially homogeneous neighborhoods found in many cities and metropolitan regions.

In general, the separation of European ancestry groups from the rest of the region's whites is much less than the degree of separation between blacks and whites. Consider the residential picture for single-ancestry categories, which in some cases, such as the Ital-

Table 7.1   Dissimilarity, exposure, and isolation indices for blacks and European ancestry groups in the Capital Region

	Dissimilarity from other whites[a]	Exposure to other whites[a]	Isolation index	Group proportion of regional population
Blacks	.696	.654	.325	.039
Single ancestry groups:				
Dutch	.426	.942	.025	.010
English	.239	.877	.084	.062
French	.368	.895	.065	.030
German	.227	.888	.071	.053
Greek	.732	.929	.024	.003
Hungarian	.669	.941	.013	.003
Irish	.240	.852	.106	.080
Italian	.310	.818	.144	.085
Polish	.328	.890	.065	.035
Russian	.577	.918	.035	.008
Scottish	.468	.953	.017	.006
Swedish	.637	.952	.014	.003
Ukrainian	.593	.935	.031	.005
Other	.411	.620	.192	.072
Mixed ancestry groups:				
English	.183	.788	.181	.154
French	.229	.825	.140	.108
German	.175	.779	.185	.161
Irish	.149	.747	.218	.196
Italian	.223	.875	.089	.070
Polish	.263	.900	.065	.045
Combined (single & mixed) ancestry groups:				
English	.181	.719	.248	.216
French	.241	.781	.183	.137
German	.178	.720	.243	.215
Irish	.158	.660	.303	.276
Italian	.247	.755	.209	.155
Polish	.248	.850	.111	.081

Note: The residential concentration indices are computed across the block groups of the counties of Albany, Rensselaer, Saratoga, and Schenectady. (Block groups with fewer than 30 residents are not included.) The ancestry categories are those reported in Summary Tape File 3 of the 1980 Census, the data source for the calculations. (Ancestry groups with fewer than 1,000 members in the region's population have been dropped from consideration.)

[a]For European ancestry categories, the dissimilarity and exposure indices represent comparisons to *all other* whites; for blacks, the indices present comparison to *all* whites.

ians, Poles, and Ukrainians, still contain substantial numbers of the foreign-born and thus are influenced by the distinctive settlement patterns of immigrants and their children.[11] Of the major ancestry groups (according to size), the largest dissimilarity indices are found for the French, Italians, and Poles. They are each within range of .33, indicating that approximately a third of each category's members would have to be moved to make its residential distribution the same as that of other whites. But, even though these ancestry categories show clearly distinctive residential patterns, they are not very segregated from the rest of the white population. According to the exposure indices, the average person of single French or Polish ancestry lives in an area 90 percent of whose residents belong to other white ethnic categories (which may, it should be acknowledged, include persons of mixed French or Polish ancestry); only 7 percent of the residents, in either case, belong to the ancestry category in question. By the measure of the exposure and isolation indices, the degree of Italian residential concentration is somewhat greater, largely because the Italian category is bigger and thus one would expect the average residential area to contain a larger proportion from this group. Even so, the average person of single Italian ancestry lives in an area that is only 14 percent (single) Italian.

Aside from the French, the old-stock groups exhibit fairly weak residential distinctiveness. Consider the Irish as an especially pertinent case, since Irish ethnic distinctiveness has emerged in other ways. About a quarter of persons of single Irish ancestry would have to be moved to make the group's residential distribution match that of other whites. Moreover, the average such person lives in an area that is just 11 percent (single) Irish. The residential concentrations of persons of single English and single German ancestries are even a bit lower.

Among whites, only very small ancestry categories exhibit residential distinctiveness on a par with that of blacks; but because these categories are so small, their degree of residential intermixture with other whites is far greater than is the case for blacks. (Moreover, the close correlation between values of the dissimilarity index and group size suggests that there may be an artifactual numerical phenomenon behind the highest dissimilarity values among whites.)[12] The pattern is exhibited by such single-ancestry categories as Greek, Hungarian, Russian, and Ukrainian, with Dutch and Scottish not far behind. The dissimilarity indices of these groups are generally in the range .5 to .7, meaning that a majority of their members would have to move to produce residential distributions equaling that for other whites. These index values indicate clearly that there are some block-group areas that contain disproportionate numbers of the members of these groups. Nonetheless, the type of area in which the average group member lives contains few others of the same background; the great majority of its residents are ethnically different. Even though the dissimilarity index for persons of single Greek ancestry, for example, .732, is the highest of all the index values, the average person of Greek ancestry lives in an area that is only 2 percent Greek, while 93 percent of its residents belong to other white groups (and the rest to other, non-white groups). Although the isolation and exposure indices for the group are based only on persons of single Greek ancestry (the residential patterns of persons of mixed Greek ancestry are not reported by the Census Bureau), it is obvious that this picture of residential intermixing could not be changed greatly by the inclusion of persons of mixed Greek ancestry, since their numbers cannot be large enough to alter radically the balance between Greeks and non-Greeks in the average area. A similar conclusion applies to the other white ethnic groups exhibiting high dissimilarity values.

Moreover, persons of ethnically mixed ancestry generally are less residentially distinctive than are those of single ethnic background. This, in fact, is a major finding, demonstrating that basic demographic trends—specifically, the rising proportion of whites with ethnically mixed ancestry—favor further reduction in ethnically distinctive residential patterns. Two explanations probably account for the lower distinctiveness of mixed ancestry categories. The more obvious one is that adults of mixed ancestry have fewer reasons to live in areas of ethnic concentration. They have less loyalty to the group, fewer social ties with the residents of ethnic areas, and so forth. In addition, children of mixed ancestry are tracers for the residential patterns of intermarried couples; because these couples are more residentially integrated than endogamous couples, their children are as well.

Given the reporting of the Census Bureau, a comparison between persons with single and with mixed ancestry is possible only for six large ancestry groups: English, French, German, Irish, Italian, and Polish, all of which are important in the Capital Region. In every case, the dissimilarity index of the mixed-ancestry category is lower than that for the corresponding single ancestry category, and in some cases, the drop is substantial. For example, 37 percent of persons of single French ancestry would have to be moved to produce the residential distribution of other whites, but only 23 percent of persons of mixed French background would have to be moved to do this. A reduction of almost the same magnitude occurs among the Italians. Even for those groups whose single-ancestry categories have low dissimilarity values (the English, Germans, and Irish) there is a further fall-off among persons of mixed ancestry.

Given the disparate patterns for persons of single and mixed ancestry from the same group, it is worthwhile to examine the residential concentrations of composite ancestry categories, which combine persons with single and mixed ancestry from the same group.[13] Although these composite categories can only be constructed for the largest ancestry groups, they allow one to make strong statements about how members of a given ethnic group differ residentially from all other whites, because they do not artificially separate persons of single ancestry from their compatriots of mixed heritage, who may also feel some identity with the group. The overall picture yielded by the composite categories is one of a low level of residential distinctiveness by the measure of the dissimilarity index, especially for the English, Germans, and Irish. Only 16 percent of persons of Irish ancestry, for example, would have to be moved in order to make the group's residential distribution equal that of non-Irish whites. Even the groups that are more distinctive in residential pattern (the French, Italians, and Poles) are highly dispersed. In each case, about a quarter of a group's members would have to be moved to bring about residential equality.

Yet, because these are large groups, the average group member still lives in an area with many other coethnics. The overall picture for residential concentration thus parallels what we have already found for friendship circles: a great deal of interpenetration among different ethnic groups coexisting with a limited degree of close contact between people of the same ethnic background. The Irish exhibit the lowest distinctiveness according to the index of dissimilarity, but, because this group is so large a portion of the region's population, its average member lives in an area that is 30 percent Irish. This surely means that the average person of Irish ancestry has some neighbors who are also of Irish ancestry (of course, the ethnicity of these neighbors need not be obvious, since in most cases the Irish ancestry is mixed with other ethnic elements, and Irish surnames may have been lost through marriage). Yet most neighbors are non-Irish whites, as the average member of the Irish group lives in an area two-thirds of whose residents are non-Irish whites.

The indices discussed so far "average" the residential situations of the members of a given group. But these averages can hide considerable residential variation within a group, mixing together persons living in ethnic neighborhoods with others who live in very intermixed settings. Where, then, are the areas of ethnic concentration? How homogeneous are they? And what proportion of the members of a group live in them?

In principle, there are two ways of locating such neighborhoods in census data. The more obvious is to look for areas whose residents come largely from a particular ethnic background. This means defining a criterion in terms of the percentage of an area's residents who belong to an ethnic category (say, 50 percent or more of residents are from the same group). The difficulty with a definition of this sort is that larger groups will have an easier time meeting any such standard than smaller groups will. For this reason, it is useful to employ a second way of locating ethnic areas, namely, to look for areas whose residents come disproportionately from a given ethnic group. The criterion here is defined relative to a group's overall size in the region's population. There are different ways such a criterion might be implemented, but I have chosen one based on standardization. A group's proportion in an area is transformed into the appropriate number of standard deviation units above or below the group's mean proportion. When the proportion is sufficiently greater than the mean (say, two standard deviation units) then an area is defined as one of ethnic concentration. The disadvantage with this strategy is precisely the reverse of the first: for very small groups, there is a danger of defining areas as ethnic neighborhoods that in fact contain only a small proportion of residents from that background. As a practical matter, both sorts of criteria have to be used in evaluating the ethnic character of neighborhoods.

A close examination of the areas of ethnic concentration (which are statistically summarized in table 7.2 for blacks and major white

Table 7.2 Characteristics of areas of ethnic concentration of blacks and major white ethnic groups[a]

	Size of entire group	Block groups where group is in the majority				Other block groups 2 standard deviations above mean				Block groups between 1 and 2 standard deviations above mean			
		Total # of block groups	# in rural/ suburban areas[b]	Range of group share of residents	% of entire group in these areas	Total # of block groups	# in rural/ suburban areas[b]	Range of group share of residents	% of entire group in these areas	Total # of block groups	# in rural/ suburban areas[b]	Range of group share of residents	% of entire group in these areas
Blacks	28,965	14	0/0	53.6–91.2%	24.9	23	0/1	28.7–49.8%	23.3	23	2/0	16.4–27.5%	14.1
English	160,157	5	4/0	51.6–61.8	0.3	23	18/5	41.1–49.2	3.7	84	53/26	31.1–40.3	17.0
French	101,722	4	3/1	55.1–61.2	0.1	35	5/7	32.5–49.8	10.1	59	31/12	23.1–31.8	16.1
German	159,299	2	2/0	52.9–63.3	0.1	12	9/3	38.3–48.7	2.3	99	51/38	29.4–38.0	22.4
Irish	204,476	14	3/2	50.4–91.3	1.8	3	0/1	48.0–49.8	0.6	91	15/30	37.7–47.8	14.4
Italian	114,587	7	0/1	51.8–70.2	2.8	27	3/3	36.9–49.2	7.2	66	5/12	25.8–36.0	15.7
Polish	59,689	0	—	—	—	29	5/4	19.9–39.7	7.5	68	16/18	13.9–19.6	16.8

[a] The major white ethnic categories are composites, containing persons with both single and mixed ancestry.
[b] Rural areas are defined as block groups outside of urbanized areas as identified by the Census Bureau; suburban areas are defined as block groups not in the region's major cities (Albany, Schenectady, Troy) or its smaller industrial ones (e.g., Cohoes, Rotterdam, Watervliet). (See footnote 17 for further details.)

ethnic groups) suggests explanations for much of the ethnic distinctiveness indicated in the aggregate measures of residential patterns in terms of the region's ethnic and industrial history. The detailed data reveal a complex layering of ethnic residential concentrations in accordance with patterns of settlement and occupational concentration having roots extending in some cases centuries into the past.[14] Thus, in residence one can see the long-run impact on ethnic social structures of events occurring at the time of a group's early settlement in the region. By any standard, these concentrations represent ethnic patterns. They are, however, eroding among major white ethnic groups and are already very weak for some, and newer residential concentrations on the scale of the older ones do not appear to be arising.

Once again, the residential concentrations of the region's relatively small black population can serve as a revealing counterpoint for the patterns among white ethnic groups. The black population is considerably more concentrated than any of the large white ethnic groups. Some indications of this are the number and contiguous location of block groups that have black majorities, as well as the proportion of the total black population residing in areas that are disproportionately, but not necessarily predominantly, black. Fourteen block groups have black majorities, all located in downtown Albany, and a number of them have very high black proportions, ranging from two-thirds to nine-tenths of all residents. Many adjacent areas also contain large black proportions, which fall just short of majorities. In this context, it should be recognized that any group's proportion in a block group is an average that conceals some variation within the area described. Thus, block groups 70 or 80 percent of whose residents are drawn from a particular group are likely to contain blocks that are almost exclusively made up of members of this group. And when bordering block groups also contain unusually large proportions from the group, it is a reasonable presumption that these proportions are even higher for the blocks on the immediate border and drop off as one moves away. What the census data describe, somewhat imperfectly, is an extensive area of downtown Albany made up of largely black neighborhoods.

Smaller and less homogeneous black concentrations exist in the region's other major cities, Schenectady and Troy. These areas are disproportionately black in the sense that their black proportions are at least two standard deviations above the black mean for the entire region (this criterion requires that at least 28 percent of an area's residents be black). There are four such block groups in Schenectady and also four in Troy; in each city, these disproportionately black areas are contiguous and typically have residential populations which overall are one-third black.[15]

A relatively high proportion of the region's entire black population resides in heavily black areas. Approximately a quarter of blacks live in block groups with black majorities, and almost half of all the Capital Region's blacks live in areas that are disproportionately black (in the sense defined above). If one extends the definition of a disproportionately black block group to include block groups with black proportions one standard deviation above the mean, then more than 60 percent of blacks reside in such areas. Virtually all of the additional areas designated as disproportionately black by the new, less stringent criterion border on the heavily black areas already identified in Albany, Schenectady, and Troy. Only a very few areas of black concentration lie outside of the region's three major cities.

Thus, the pattern of settlement of blacks is one of fairly intense concentration in heavily black neighborhoods in major urban centers. Even though the black population of the Capital Region is small and therefore has more residential "exposure" to whites than is typical elsewhere, this pattern of black settlement is quite similar to that found in many other northern metropolitan regions. Undoubtedly, too, it has similar origins in the post-World War II history of urban change and black migration. Although blacks have been continuously present in the region since its earliest days of European settlement (when they served as slaves to Dutch farmers and accounted for 10 to 15 percent of Albany's population [McEneny, 1981]), contemporary patterns were laid down after World War II. Then, drawn by northern industrial opportunities and following routes established by preceding white migrants into cities, southern blacks settled in densely populated, inner-city neighborhoods, close to industrial jobs and often close to white ethnic neighborhoods. But, in the immediate postwar period, many of these white ethnic neighborhoods entered periods of stagnation, if not decline, as socially mobile second- and third-generation ethnics joined the streams of migrants to the suburbs. While this movement opened up additional residential areas for blacks, it also meant that central cities became increasingly non-white, in tandem with the growth of their surrounding suburbs. The racial cleavage between city and suburb is not as deep in the Capital Region as it is in larger metropolitan areas, such as Detroit, Newark, and even New York City; but it is nonetheless a detectable pattern.

The residential patterns for all of the major white ethnic groups present a strong contrast to the black pattern. Each of these groups has areas of concentration, but only rarely do these areas approach the most heavily black districts of Albany in degree of homogeneity. Far smaller proportions of these groups, moreover, reside in the areas of ethnic concentration. Thus, there is a great deal of inter-mixing among whites of different ethnic backgrounds. Yet the patterns of concentration of white ethnic groups also vary from one another in ways that lend themselves to interpretation in terms of the histories of these groups in the region. These variations appear to go far in explaining the remaining ethnic distinctiveness in residential distribution.

One kind of pattern is shown by the English (and also by the Germans and, to a lesser extent, the French).[16] Owing to the group's settlement in the region during the seventeenth and eighteenth centuries, its areas of concentration are mostly in rural places, or in formerly rural places that have become suburban by encroachment.[17] There are only occasional areas of concentration in cities. Even though the English ancestry group is quite a large part of the region's population, the most heavily English areas are not ethnically exclusive (in pointed contrast to the black pattern): only five block groups have English majorities. And there is no extensive area, composed of many contiguous block groups, that is heavily English. The block groups with English concentrations are scattered through the rural parts, and to a lesser extent the suburban ones, of the region.

The low degree of concentration of the English is demonstrated by the small proportion of the group residing in its areas of concentration. All of the majority English block groups have small populations, and accordingly just .3 percent of the ancestry group resides in them. Looking more broadly to areas that are disproportionately English in the strong sense (that is, the proportion of their residents who have English ancestry is two standard deviations above the mean), one finds that they contain only 4 percent of the entire ancestry group. In stark contrast, the equivalent areas contain almost half the region's black population. If the definition of an ethnic concentration area is extended down to those block groups with English-ancestry proportions at least one standard deviation above the mean, then a considerably larger proportion of the entire ancestry group is included, but still it remains a small minority of the group as a whole. This expanded criterion simply identifies a scattered set of block groups, with little contiguity; there is no sense, as there is in black residential patterns, of extending outward the boundaries of core ethnic neighborhoods.

Quite a different pattern of concentration is shown by the groups that entered the region in the nineteenth and early twentieth centuries as industrial immigrants and therefore settled initially in neighborhoods in the region's major industrial cities of the time. Groups exhibiting this pattern include the Irish, Italians, and Poles. Except for the Irish, they are moderately more concentrated in ethnic areas than the English, but far less concentrated than blacks.

In spite of the fact that the Irish constitute the largest ancestry group in the region, there are very few block groups in which they are in the majority. Just fourteen can be found in the 1980 census. In contrast to the English pattern, these are predominantly in cities rather than rural and suburban areas, but in contrast to the black pattern, they are as much in the region's smaller, and once heavily industrial cities, as in the three largest ones.[18]

In most of these areas, the Irish are just barely in the majority, representing between 50 and 60 percent of the residents. (There is one area that is nine-tenths Irish, but it is something of a statistical oddity, having a population far below average in size, with fewer than a hundred residents.) Just a small part of the entire Irish ancestry group (less than 2 percent) lives in majority Irish areas. Since these areas are virtually coterminous with areas that are disproportionately Irish in the strong sense of having Irish proportions two standard deviations above the group mean, the proportion of the group in heavily Irish areas is not much altered by including areas of the latter type.

The picture is changed by the consideration of areas that are disproportionately Irish by a weaker criterion. But the conclusion that the Irish group is not greatly concentrated residentially remains unaltered. There is a large number of areas that contain Irish proportions between 38 and 48 percent, that is, between one and two standard deviations above the group mean. In spite of this number, however, it remains true that only a small portion of the entire ancestry group (about one-sixth) resides in areas of Irish concentration, even as stretched by the weaker standard.

The weaker criterion uncovers, for the first time, a sizable number of rural and suburban areas with large Irish populations.[19] Nevertheless, the primary locale for Irish areas is still urban. About half of the newly identified areas are in cities; for example, about twenty of them are in Troy, the city with the most extensive Irish section. But these areas are more widely scattered among different cities than are the block groups of more intense Irish concentration. The weaker standard turns up the first Irish concentrations in the city of Albany, which typically fall at the lower end of the range of concentration. In contrast to this city's black concentrations, however, the Irish areas do not constitute a single, extensive section but exist as patches scattered throughout Albany's center and its southern and western reaches, and thus intermixed with areas having fewer Irish and more whites of other ethnic backgrounds.

In comparison to the Irish, a moderately greater degree of ethnic concentration is found for the Italians and Poles, whose entry into the Capital Region dates to the last decades of the nineteenth century and continued through the early decades of the twentieth. This comparative recency is the likely explanation for the relatively greater concentration of these groups: that is, their residential distributions are influenced by the neighborhood concentrations of immigrants, still present in significant numbers (especially among the Italians), and by the large portions of the groups who belong to the second generation and stem from unmixed backgrounds. Like the Irish, the areas of concentration of these groups lie primarily in cities, and are often connected with early economic opportunities in the region. But because of the smaller sizes of these groups, there are very few areas in which either group can claim to be in the majority.

The Italians illustrate the residential patterns of both. There are just seven block groups in which persons of Italian ancestry are in the majority (the Poles, a much smaller group, have none). These are scattered, with some in the cities of Schenectady and Troy, and others in a small industrial city (Mechanicville), which still contains a large Italian-ancestry population tracing its origins to immigrants who came to work at a paper plant. But less than 3 percent of the Italian ancestry group lives in majority Italian areas.

A less stringent criterion, an Italian proportion at least two standard deviations above the group mean, brings the Italian areas of concentration into sharper focus. More than thirty block groups (including the majority Italian areas) meet this test, and each contains a population at least 37 percent Italian. The areas of concentration lie primarily in small industrial cities and in the cities of Schenectady and Troy. In Schenectady, which only developed into a major industrial city late in the nineteenth century and hence attracted mainly southern- and eastern-European immigrants rather than earlier groups such as the Irish, a fairly extensive section with a disproportionately large Italian population comes into view. There are also a few areas of concentration outside of cities, which generally are of long-standing Italian settlement (for example, just north of Albany, around former railroad and stock yards where immigrants found work). Weakening the criterion for consideration even further, by including areas with Italian proportions one standard deviation above the group mean, extends the apparent areas of concentration, but does not fundamentally alter the map of heavily Italian areas.

As a group, the Italians are more concentrated in such ethnic neighborhoods than are some of the old-stock groups, but they are much less so than blacks. Ten percent of the ancestry group resides in Italian areas as defined by the strong criterion (that is, two standard deviations from the mean), and another 16 percent are in those areas added by the weaker criterion. The proportions of the entire group living in ethnic areas are plainly above those for the Irish, but still fall well short of the extremes attained by blacks.

There is also strong evidence of an ongoing dilution of Italian residential concentrations, which is likely to lead in the future to levels of concentration approximating those for the Irish. This can be seen by tracing the evolution of historically Italian neighborhoods, for most of the contemporary areas of concentration of the group have had a strong Italian presence for decades; few new areas of concentration have emerged. Thus, the historic neighborhoods are barometers for the residential concentration of the group as a whole. Looking backward a few decades, one finds that Italians were more residentially concentrated than they are today, although it is probably the case that they, like other Europeans, were never as segregated as blacks (the different treatment accorded blacks is amply demonstrated by historical analyses from other cities; see Spear, 1967, on Chicago or Zunz, 1982, on Detroit). Admittedly, a precise comparison of the past to the present is made difficult by changes in census definitions. Censuses prior to 1980 relied on a foreign-stock definition of ethnicity, which limits the identifiability of ethnic populations to the first two generations.[20] But even as late as 1960, the map showed large Italian populations in historically Italian neighborhoods, such as Albany's South End and Schenectady's Mount Pleasant. In that year, more than 35 percent of the foreign-stock Italian group resided in these neighborhoods.

By 1970, some of the Italian concentrations were beginning to disperse. In Albany, the South End area in particular, which held about eighteen hundred Italians in 1960, now provided home to just one-third as many, although some Italian businesses, including a landmark restaurant still in existence, survived the exodus of their local clientele. Many of these Italians appear to have moved immediately westward, where another Italian concentration emerged. Other areas, especially those in Schenectady, appear to have held their own during the 1960s. Even so, the group was not as concentrated as it had been ten years before, and the portion residing in its historic neighborhoods had dropped by 5 percentage points.

Although most of the same neighborhoods were still identifiable as Italian in 1980, exhibiting what might seem an impressive degree of continuity, they were not home to as much of the group as in the past. The proportion of the group in these areas was declining, for they held just 23 percent of persons of single Italian ancestry, the subgroup most comparable to the foreign-stock population identified in earlier censuses. Moreover, the Italians residing in the historic neighborhoods were increasingly limited to older members of the immigrant and second generations. These areas were not undergoing a demographic renewal of their Italian population and were failing to retain younger Italians. One indicator is that the areas of high Italian concentration also contained many immigrants, demonstrating the disproportionate role of the first generation.[21] A more telling indicator is that the historic neighborhoods encompassed only 12 percent of mixed-ancestry Italians. Thus, younger Italians of later generations, who mainly compose the mixed-ancestry subgroup, have generally moved elsewhere.[22] Indeed, as table 7.1 shows, persons of mixed Italian ancestry are not very concentrated in residential terms and are not much different from other whites. Consequently, as the proportion of the group with unmixed ancestry declines because of intermarriage, the Italian neighborhoods will be eroded further.

One can continue the story of ethnic residential distinctiveness for as many groups as are represented in census data, but the basic outlines would remain intact. The French, for example, display a pattern of concentration that resembles that of the English and Germans and also that of the Irish and Italians. Because of the long history of French-speaking people in the region and the entry of many to work in the forestry and tanning industries, there are many French areas of concentration in rural places. But others are intertwined with the region's early urban, industrial history. This is true of the important French concentrations in the former mill city of Cohoes, for instance.

For the small groups, this story is thwarted by the absence of data for their mixed-ancestry members. Nevertheless, the single-ancestry data still allow one to pinpoint some ethnic concentrations. Because of the small size of these ancestry groups, their areas of ethnic concentration are in fact quite dilute when measured by the standards set by the largest ancestry groups. Greeks, for example, appear to be one of the most residentially distinctive groups according to the index of dissimilarity. It follows that there must be areas with *relatively* high proportions of Greek residents when compared to the group's overall proportion in the region's population. But even in their few areas of concentration, Greeks are sparsely represented. The most intensely Greek area is in Albany and has a population that is almost 10 percent Greek. Two other block groups in other cities have populations that are 8 percent Greek (although one of these areas is tiny). Otherwise, the typical Greek proportion in the group's areas of concentration is in the 2 to 3 percent range, and the numbers of Greeks these areas contain are generally quite small, on the order of 20 to 60. The Greek areas are for the most part scattered throughout the Capital Region (Albany is an exception), and they do not add up to an extended section capable of making up for its low Greek proportion by a sizable absolute number of persons of Greek ancestry living within proximity of each other. The details differ, especially with respect to the locations of ethnic concentrations, but the story is much the same for groups such as the Dutch, Russians, and Ukrainians. (The Russian concentrations are of particular interest because the Russian ancestry category in census data is generally thought to reflect Jewish patterns, which cannot be directly measured by the census as it is forbidden by law from collecting information about religion.[23])

For white ethnic groups, then, there are few areas of concentration worthy of being considered as ethnic neighborhoods, unless one is willing to regard as an ethnic neighborhood almost any area with a greater than average number of members of a group. The contrast to the black pattern is strong, even though the blacks of the Capital Region have an unusually high level of residential exposure to whites and thus are less residentially segregated than in most of the nation's other major metropolitan areas. In general, there are few residential areas in which the members of any European-ancestry group are in the majority. Still, one can identify areas of concentration for the various major white ethnic groups that contain a plainly disproportionate number of residents from a given group but generally less than a majority. But these areas do not typify the residential situations of these ethnic groups, as only small proportions of each reside in its areas of concentration. The great majority is residentially intermixed, and quite thoroughly so, with whites of other ethnic backgrounds.

As weak as the residential concentrations of white ethnic groups appear to be, there are also signs of their ongoing dilution, and the downward trend of residential concentration thus resembles the trends for other objective indicators of ethnic difference among whites. In general, areas of concentration are connected with the pre-World War II history of the various European-ancestry groups in the region—many are areas of initial, or at least early, settlement by incoming immigrants, and others are areas of second settlement created by internal movements to take advantage of residential opportunities opened up by the expansion of cities (such movements have also been spurred, of course, by the desire to gain some distance from newer groups, first from the southern and eastern Europeans and subsequently from blacks). That these ethnic concentrations are gradually weakening is demonstrated by the lower residential distinctiveness exhibited by persons of mixed ancestry from all major groups (and also by the decline of the historic neighborhoods of one of the most residentially concentrated of the major groups, the Italians). Among the Irish and the southern and eastern Europeans, one of the most significant forces eroding residential concentration has been movement to the suburbs, which in this region have grown rapidly during the postwar period. But relatively few areas of concentration of these groups are located in suburbs (especially when a strong criterion of group concentration is employed), demonstrating anew that postwar residential changes are working against pronounced ethnic residential concentrations among whites.

Ethnic Areas and Ethnic Characteristics

How ethnic are the residents of areas of ethnic concentration? Are they likely to identify with their backgrounds or to maintain ethnic traditions? These questions can be addressed by combining the survey data with census data about the ethnic composition of neighborhoods. Such a linkage makes it possible to identify those respondents who live in areas containing many residents of their own ethnic background and to compare their characteristics to those of other respondents who live in areas with few residents who are ethnically like themselves. Thereby, we can determine whether ethnic identifiers are found in areas of ethnic concentration, whether the residents of these areas have on average more ethnic experiences than others, and whether they are more likely to be enmeshed in ethnic social structures.

First, some technical problems must be addressed. One arises because the widely divergent sizes of the ethnic categories represented among respondents make the use of a specific percentage criterion of residential concentration impractical, since larger groups will more easily meet a criterion of this type. Therefore, I have relied on standardization to identify in a fair way the ethnic areas of large and small groups. As explained earlier, a standardization criterion identifies areas with disproportionate numbers of a group, and can be satisfied even when the proportion of an area's residents belonging to the group is small (as the example of the Greeks illustrates). A related problem is whether to employ standardized values based on single-ancestry categories or on composite ones, containing persons with both single and mixed ancestries from specific groups. Since either could be argued to have some merit, I generally present both (except for table 7.3). But because the mixed-ancestry data for block groups are reported by the Census Bureau only for the largest ancestry groups, I limit the neighborhood analyses to persons whose ancestries are English, French, German, Irish, Italian, Polish, or some combination of these.[24]

Table 7.3   Neighborhood ethnic concentration by ethnic identity status and by the subjective importance of ethnic background

| | Distance from group mean | | | |
	0 to +1 std. dev.[a]	+1 to +2 std . dev.	+2 or more std. dev.	Total
Total	71.9%	16.8%	11.3%	100.0%
Ethnic identity status (Ancestry/identity type)				
single/single	79.6	11.7	8.7	100.0
multiple/single	75.0	16.7	8.3	100.0
multiple/multiple	70.5	13.6	15.9	100.0
single/none	80.0	10.0	10.0	100.0
multiple/none	52.8	32.1	15.1	100.0
Overall significance level: p < .10				
Subjective importance of background[b]				
very important	79.6	12.2	8.2	100.0
somewhat	81.1	12.2	6.8	100.1
not	67.2	15.5	17.2	99.9
Overall significance level: N.S.				

Note: The standardized value in the table has been calculated for neighborhood concentrations of composite groups, combining persons with single and mixed ancestries. Since these concentrations are reported only for English, French, German, Irish, Italian, and Polish ancestries, the table is limited to native-born respondents with ancestries derived entirely from these groups (N = 256).
[a]Neighborhood concentrations less than the group mean are reported as zero.
[b]Among ethnic identifiers only.

Another problem concerns respondents of mixed ancestry, since it is not obvious which of the multiple ethnic elements in their ancestries should be used for the purpose of measuring the ethnicity of their neighborhoods.[25] On empirical grounds, it does not appear useful to average the standardized values for these different elements; since few neighborhoods contain disproportionate numbers for more than one or two groups, averaging tends to produce low values for the neighborhoods of mixed-ancestry respondents and is virtually guaranteed to do so when the number of elements in an ancestry rises above two. Accordingly, I have resorted to the maximum standardized value for any group in a respondent's ancestry to measure the ethnicity of his or her neighborhood. This has the consequence that the standardized values for the neighborhoods of respondents of mixed ancestry are slightly larger on average than their equivalents for persons of single ancestry (see table 7.3), because persons with mixed ancestry have more than one chance to achieve a high score whereas those of single ancestry have only one.

The survey data, when merged with information about the ethnic composition of neighborhoods, demonstrate again that few native-born whites live in neighborhoods with a strongly ethnic flavor (see table 7.3).[26] Only 11 percent of whites live in areas with ethnic concentrations (of one of their own groups) two or more standard deviations above the group mean. Another 17 percent live in areas of milder ethnic concentration, between one and two standard deviations above the mean. The great majority of whites, nearly three-quarters, live in areas where the representation of their ethnic group is close to its average. Such areas lack, at least in terms of their population if not also their institutional fabric, a definite ethnic character corresponding with the backgrounds of respondents.

Not only is residence in areas of ethnic concentration infrequent among whites, but it has no substantively meaningful relationship to ethnic identity (see table 7.3). There is no significant difference in the probability of living in a disproportionately ethnic area (two or more standard deviations above the mean) between those who identify with their ethnic background and those who do not. Nor does any meaningful difference appear when the focus expands to include neighborhoods with weaker ethnic concentrations (although a difference exists between single- and mixed-ancestry categories due to the method of scoring the neighborhoods of those with multiple ancestries). People who identify ethnically, then, are not concentrated in ethnic neighborhoods and are as likely to be found living with relatively few others of their group as they are with many others. Put conversely, the residents of ethnic areas are not more likely than others to identify in ethnic terms. The absence of any relationship between neighborhood and identity also carries over into the subjective importance attached to ethnic background. The residents of areas of ethnic concentration are not discernably more likely to view their ethnic backgrounds as important than anybody else.

If the link between neighborhood and ethnic identity is missing, one may still ask about the distribution of ethnic identifiers across urban, suburban, and rural places. Given the long history of a connection between cities and immigrant settlement, it is easy to imagine that urban residents might be more prone to identify with their ethnic backgrounds than the residents of either suburbs or rural areas. Even if they are not themselves living in an ethnic neighborhood, city dwellers are more likely than residents of other places to come into contact with identifiable ethnic neighborhoods and their street-level facades of restaurants, stores, and social clubs, and perhaps therefore to be reminded of the potential significance of their own ethnic backgrounds. But however plausible this reasoning may appear to be, it does not apply to native-born whites, at least in the Capital Region.

Table 7.4 shows the relationship between type of place[27] and ethnic ancestry and identity. There are minor variations among specific ancestry/identity categories, but there is no overall difference between identifiers and nonidentifiers in terms of urban residence. Ethnic identifiers are thus as likely to be found in suburbs and rural places as is the population at large. Perhaps they are even a bit more likely in the suburbs—the most intriguing feature in the table is high rate of suburban residence (44 percent) among persons of mixed ancestry who identify with a single group.[28] There is no reason to think that ethnic consciousness hinges on the ethnic concentrations to be found in cities or to believe that such consciousness is extinguished by the middle-class and largely nonethnic character of suburbs.

Residence in an area of ethnic concentration is not predicted well by the basic demographic and socioeconomic variables that

Table 7.4   Type of place of residence by ethnic identity status

	Large city[a]	Small city[a]	Suburb[b]	Rural	Total
Ethnic identity status (Ancestry/identity type):					
single/single	47.9%	14.0%	23.1%	14.9%	99.9%
multiple/single	28.4	13.6	44.3	13.6	99.9
multiple/multiple	40.6	10.9	24.8	23.8	100.1
single/none	46.9	21.9	18.8	12.5	100.1
multiple/none	38.8	11.7	29.1	20.4	100.0
unknown/none	47.6	20.0	13.3	20.0	100.0
Total	40.4	13.5	28.3	17.8	100.0

Overall significance level: p < .10

Note: The table includes all native-born whites (N = 460).
[a] The large cities are those with more than 50,000 in population—Albany, Schenectady, and Troy. The small cities are typically older industrial places.
[b] The suburban category includes any urbanized area (as classified by the Census Bureau) that is not in a city.

have been used in previous analyses. Residence in such an area, then, appears to represent an aspect of ethnic social structure that is largely, albeit not wholly, independent of the individual-level factors connected with ethnic identity, such as generational position. This is a somewhat surprising finding, but it may be important to recognize that areas of ethnic concentration are being discussed, only some of which would be recognized as ethnic neighborhoods, having ethnic majorities, ethnic businesses, and other ethnic institutions. Presumably, residence in an ethnic neighborhood is more closely tied to such factors as ethnic identity and generational position. (In addition, the analysis is restricted to United States-born whites, and it is possible that, with the inclusion of the foreign-born, these relationships would appear.)

The near independence of residence in ethnic concentrations is established by regressions of the sort that have been used earlier to predict many ethnic characteristics (see table 7.5). The dependent variables in this case are the two standardized values for block-group neighborhoods.[29] The independent variables are the demographic and socioeconomic variables in the standard model, including, among other things, generation, education, and the subjective

Table 7.5 Regression analysis of neighborhood ethnic concentration

Dependent variables:	Standardized neighborhood values					
	1. based on single-ancestry groups			2. based on combined single- and mixed-ancestry groups		
	Regression coefficients			Regression coefficients		
Independent variables:	Unstandardized	Standardized	Signif.	Unstandardized	Standardized	Signif.
Ethnic identity status			N.S.			N.S.
Subjective importance of background			N.S.			N.S.
Generation			N.S.			N.S.
Age			N.S.			N.S.
Gender			N.S.			N.S.
Educational attainment	−.198	−.218	p < .01	−.143	−.182	p < .05
Confidence in ancestry knowledge: confident			N.S.	—[a]		
not confident				−.390	−.127	p < .05
R^2		.093			.101	
Adjusted R^2		.039			.047	

Note: Only U.S.-born respondents whose ancestries are English, French, German, Irish, Italian, Polish, or some combination of these (N = 256) are included in the regression analyses.
[a]Indicates omitted category.

importance of ethnic background. Only two independent variables are significant, and the overall explained variance (R-squared) of the equations is the lowest among all the equations examined to this point, indicating the low predictability of residence by the standard model.

Nevertheless, the two statistically significant variables imply relationships of the sort that should be expected if residence in an area of ethnic concentration is linked to broader, individual-level processes of assimilation. One relationship is that more highly educated individuals tend to reside in areas of lower ethnic concentration, affirming that social mobility is connected to movement out of ethnic areas. The other (which appears only in one of the two equations) is that persons who lack confidence in their knowledge of their ancestry are less likely to live in areas of ethnic concentration. The causal direction of this relationship is debatable: on the one hand, people whose knowledge of their ancestry is hazy and uncertain might be less likely to look for residence near others of their ethnic background; on the other, people who live outside of such areas may lack the social reinforcement to remind them of their backgrounds and thus end up less sure about it. In either case, a correlation is implied between ethnic drift in knowledge of ancestry (see chapter 2) and residence outside of ethnic areas.

But what are the repercussions of areas of ethnic concentration for the ethnicity of their residents? The weak relationship of living in these areas to ethnic identity and to standard socioeconomic and demographic indicators might lead to the suspicion that there are none, or at least none powerful enough to have a claim on our attention. But this is demonstrably untrue: areas of ethnic concentration support other ethnic social structures, and are linked to higher levels of ethnic experience (see table 7.6).

A connection between ethnic experience and residence in ethnic areas is visible in the top part of the table, which shows that the standardized value of neighborhood (in either single- or mixed-ancestry form) has a significant impact on the index of ethnic experience[30] when it is added to the standard model, previously employed to analyze ethnic experience. The influence of residence is not large. A difference of two standard deviations in the ethnic composition of a neighborhood, quite a large difference in residential terms, is associated with an increase of just half an experience, but

Table 7.6   Regression analyses of ethnic experiences, friendships, and organizations on neighborhood ethnic concentrations and other variables

	Standardized neighborhood values					
	1. based on single-ancestry groups			2. based on combined single- and mixed-ancestry groups		
	Regression coefficients			Regression coefficients		
Dependent variables:	Unstandardized	Standardized	Signif.	Unstandardized	Standardized	Signif.
Modified index of ethnic experiences	.247	.114	p < .05	.252	.100	p < .10
Number of friends of overlapping ancestry	.260	.204	p < .01	.388	.259	p < .001
Number of nonkin friends of overlapping ancestry	.202	.182	p < .05	.302	.232	p < .01
Number of memberships in ethnically homogeneous organizations	.139	.200	p < .01			N.S.

Note: Only U.S.-born repondents whose ancestries are English, French, German, Irish, Italian, Polish, or some combination of these are included in the regression equations. Further, respondents with fewer than four close friends are excluded from the friendship equations; those with no organizational affiliations are excluded from the organization equations. Each equation also includes other relevant identity, demographic, and socioeconomic controls (e.g., ethnic identity status, generation, and education).

it is statistically significant even after controls for such variables as education, generation, and ethnic identity. It demonstrates that residents of areas with many others of their own ethnic background tend to have more ethnic experiences than residents of nonethnic areas. Moreover, other analyses reveal that residence has a more powerful impact on the level of cultural experiences (for example, eating ethnic foods or practicing customs) than on other experiences.

The effect of ethnic residential concentrations on levels of ethnic experience does not appear to be an incidental by-product of some other characteristics of these areas. It might be argued, for instance, that the effect here is really one of residence in urban areas, which provide a shelter for subcultures of various kinds, including ethnic ones, and therefore are linked to ethnic experience (Fischer, 1975). But further analysis (not presented) shows that the type of place in which a person resides (urban, suburban, or rural) has no relationship to the level of ethnic experience when added to the standard model. In another argument, the effect ascribed to neighborhood ethnic concentrations might be viewed as a function of the social-class character of these areas. The view that ethnic subcultures are most robust in working-class ethnic enclaves is widespread among scholars of ethnicity in the United States and gains support from many ethnographic studies of ethnic neighborhoods (for example, Gans, 1982). But it finds no support here. To measure the social class character of a block group, I have used the proportion of its adult residents (persons twenty-five and older) who have attended college. This variable also has no relationship to ethnic experience when it is added to the standard model.

The social structural implications of ethnic residential concentrations are made plainer when friendship circle and neighborhood are brought into direct relationship. To do this, I have taken the final models for key friendship variables (see chapter 6) and added the standardized value of neighborhood to the list of independent variables (see the middle sections of table 7.6). There are two sets of equations: one for friendships to persons of overlapping background and the other for such friendships with nonrelatives. In both, the influence of residential area is significant. In neither case can the effect of living in an area of ethnic concentration be described as very large, and it is far from true that residence largely determines the ethnic character of friendship circles. But compared to other prominent factors, the effect of residence is noteworthy. By the measure of its standardized coefficients, residence in areas of ethnic concentration is among the most influential variables considered in the equations. It is more influential, for instance, than the subjective importance attached to ethnic background, which is elsewhere such an important predictor of ethnic traits.

Residence in an area of ethnic concentration also corresponds to a significant degree with memberships in ethnically homogeneous organizations (see chapter 6 on these organizations, which have members largely drawn from the same backgrounds as respondents but are not typically formed to serve ethnic purposes). In this case, the relationship shows up for only one of the two standardized neighborhood variables—specifically, for the one based on single ancestry categories. The fact that the effect holds for this neighborhood variable, and not for the one incorporating mixed ancestry information, seems to bolster the conclusion that ethnically homogeneous organizations are frequently churches and synagogues located in once heavily ethnic neighborhoods (such neighborhoods are better indicated by a disproportionate number of persons of single ancestry from a group). As for friendship, the relationship between residence and organizational membership is stronger in a relative than in an absolute sense. Residence, then, cannot be said to determine organizational affiliation (for instance, a difference of two standard deviations in residence translates into only a quarter of a membership). But its influence is on a par with the strongest predictors in the equation.

In sum, areas of ethnic concentration are another form of ethnic social structure. Residence in such areas is linked to other kinds of ethnic social structure, to tendencies to have fellow ethnics among one's close friends and to belong to organizations that are more ethnically homogeneous than average. Since both of these other forms of ethnic social structure promote higher levels of ethnic experience, it is not surprising that residence in ethnic areas of concentration does also. The question is whether the effect of residence on experience is merely a function of its association with other forms of ethnic social structure or, instead, whether residence has additional independent effects. The question, unfortunately, cannot be answered with the data at hand; when all three forms of ethnic social structure are entered as independent variables in an equation predicting the level of ethnic experience, the results are indeterminate.[31]

Summary

The ethnic neighborhood has long been viewed as a bulwark of ethnicity, although there have been almost no systematic quantitative attempts to assess its impact on residents. The concept, however, must be applied cautiously to contemporary whites. In the Capital Region, whites do not reside in extensive ethnically homogeneous areas (they do reside in racially homogeneous areas, however). Rather, there is a great deal of ethnic intermixture in neighborhoods, combined with some variation in the degree of ethnic concentration for the groups represented among inhabitants.

It is in the degree of ethnic concentration that one can find usable remnants of the ethnic neighborhood concept. These concentrations generally fall short of any plausible numerical criterion for an ethnic neighborhood. Except for its black neighborhoods, few areas of the Capital Region have, for instance, a majority of their residents drawn from a particular ethnic background. But the existence of ethnic concentrations can be established by a relative standard, which measures the proportion of residents of a given ethnic background against the overall residential distribution for the group, as a number of standard deviations from the group mean. The areas of ethnic concentration located in this way make historical sense, as most can be identified as areas of ethnic settlement that date back to the early period of a group's stay in the region and are intertwined with its early work opportunities.

Even so, few native-born whites reside in areas of concentration of their group; in this respect, the findings mirror those establishing that only a minority of whites are enmeshed in strongly ethnic friendship circles. When the criterion of neighborhood concentration is drawn stringently (at, say, two standard deviations from the mean), 10 percent or less of a group's members typically reside in its areas of concentration. Obviously, this proportion increases as the criterion is weakened, but only a small minority of group members reside in such areas, no matter how generously they are defined. Only blacks are an exception to this generalization, but they are the type of exception that proves the rule, demonstrating that the high degree of residential integration among white ethnic categories is not a universal feature of residence in the United States. It is probably true that ethnic whites were never as segregated as blacks, but this simply shows that they were subject from early on to an assimilatory dynamic not present for African Americans (Lieberson, 1963, 1980).

Indeed, it seems likely that the current level of residential integration among whites is greater than it was in the past and will be higher still in the future, as a consequence of the demographic and socioeconomic leveling of differences among ethnic categories. In census data, some continued decrease in residential segregation is foreshadowed by the lower residential distinctiveness of persons with mixed ancestry, who in the future will make up larger shares of European-ancestry groups. The omens of decline in residential concentration are not as striking in the individual-level analyses of the survey data. Nevertheless, the tendency of more highly educated individuals to reside outside of areas of ethnic concentration is consistent with a general trend of decline.

Residence in areas of ethnic concentration interweaves with other forms of ethnic social structure, but it is independent of ethnic identity. The correlation with other aspects of ethnic social structure demonstrates that residence in ethnic areas does enhance some ethnic characteristics; thus, it is evidence for the common view of ethnic neighborhoods as perpetuators of ethnicity. Ethnic areas of concentration help to sustain ethnically based friendship networks as well as organizations with ethnic memberships. They also raise the levels of ethnic experience of their inhabitants. But these effects are not very strong, probably because most areas of ethnic concentration do not resemble old-fashioned ethnic neighborhoods, which were more homogeneous and where layers of local institutions matched and reinforced the ethnic backgrounds of residents. The analysis implies that the role often ascribed to ethnic neighborhoods needs rethinking as far as contemporary ethnicity among whites is concerned.

The effects of ethnic concentration do not appear to be side effects of other features of these areas. I find little support in this analysis for well-known theses about urbanism or working-class enclaves. Many areas of ethnic concentration are still located in cities, both large and small, reflecting the immigrant industrial history of the region, since many nineteenth- and early-twentieth-century immigrant groups were first drawn into the region by specific labor-market opportunities available in emerging urban areas and settled in the vicinity. Even so, many other areas of concentration, especially for the region's oldest European groups, such as the English and French, are located in rural areas or in rural places that have gradually become suburban. But apart from the presence of many ethnic concentrations, urban areas appear to have no special ethnic effects, despite the frequent view that they are better able than suburban and rural places to shelter ethnic subcultures. Likewise, there is only limited support for the view that the character of ethnic residential concentration owes something to working-class traits. Education is a statistically significant but weak predictor of residence in these areas at an individual level, but at an aggregate level the educational attainment of an area's residents, an index of their social-class position, has no reflection in their ethnic characteristics.

Perhaps the most theoretically significant finding lies in the absence of any relationship of neighborhood to ethnic identity. This finding underscores the distinction between social structure and identity. On the one hand, individuals can be embedded in ethnic social structures without necessarily thinking of themselves as especially ethnic (perhaps it is less essential for such individuals to think of and present themselves as ethnic because their surroundings are ethnic). On the other hand, strong identifiers apparently do not need ethnic social surroundings in order to maintain a sense of themselves as ethnic. These findings point up the individualism that lies behind much of the widely proclaimed revival of ethnicity in the contemporary United States.

Conclusion:
The Emergence of the
European Americans

Although human phenomena—whether attitudes, wishes, or products of human action
may be looked at on their own, independently of
their connections with the social life of men,
they are by nature nothing but substantializa-
tions of human relations and of human behavior, embodiments of social and mental life.
—NORBERT ELIAS ([1939] 1978: 117)

The examination of ethnicity among whites has produced a paradoxical divergence: between the long-run and seemingly irreversible decline of objective ethnic differences—in education and work, family and community—and the continuing subjective importance of ethnic origins to many white Americans. This divergence casts a shadow of uncertainty over the ultimate significance of the transformation of ethnicity among whites.

The objective decline of ethnicity has not been my main focus, but it has been glimpsed throughout and appears undeniable on the face of the evidence. Among whites, ethnicity has been in the past a powerful determinant of life chances—to attain a high level of education, to get a good job, and to choose a marital partner of a different background, among others. This past role is obvious to all who observe the American scene, but recent research reveals enormous changes that are largely leveling the once important social distinctions deriving from European origins. These changes represent an ongoing process, not one that has already reached its culmination,

290

and therefore one can still find significant differences among aggregate ethnic categories in the white population. But the trajectory of change is evident when one decomposes ancestry groups, in particular, when one examines shifts among different generational groups and among birth cohorts.

The objective ethnic changes among whites can be traced in terms of the convergence of life chances in education and employment and the decline of cultural indicators such as language, but the most compelling evidence of change is undoubtedly the great extent and ease of intermarriage. Because of the intimacy of marriage and its implications for family networks and children, it remains a sensitive device for detecting ethnic boundaries, or social boundaries of any sort. Among whites in the United States, a long-term trend of rising intermarriage has reached the point that marriage between people having different ethnic ancestries could be described as the rule rather than the exception. According to the 1980 census only one in four marriages of native-born whites unites partners of identical ancestry. This is an intermarriage that is still contained within some ethnic boundaries (Alba and Golden, 1986), for marriage of non-Hispanic whites with Hispanics or non-whites is still fairly uncommon (and marriages between whites and blacks are downright rare). Thus, the spread of intermarriage reveals the growing extent of social integration among persons with European ancestry in particular. The commonness of intermarriage, moreover, is directly altering the recognizable social contours of ethnicity by giving rise to a population with mixed, and increasingly with complex, ethnic ancestry. It is likely that a majority of native-born whites today have mixed ethnic ancestry, and whatever the proportion may be, it is increasing over time, as pre-World War II cohorts and early generations, where persons with unmixed ancestry are concentrated, are steadily reduced in numbers by mortality.

Yet these seemingly clear-cut patterns in the decline of objective ethnic differences do not seem to be matched as yet by an equally clear fading of ethnic identities constructed on the basis of the European origins of ancestors. I have presented no data over time, and thus any direct assessment of the trend of ethnic identity is impossible. Nevertheless, one has to be impressed by the large number of American-born whites who are willing to describe themselves in terms of ethnic labels and who attach some importance to these, even though in many cases the points of origin of the labels lie two, three, or more generations back in time. In the Capital Region, two-thirds of whites present themselves in terms of an ethnic identity, and about half view their ethnic backgrounds as of moderate importance at least. And most of the identifying group can point to at least some ethnically relevant experiences as confirmation of the role of ethnicity in their lives.

There is no reason to believe that this disparity is idiosyncratic to the locale of the study. Certainly, in comparison to the nation, a distinguishing feature of the locale is the large number of its native-born whites who are children or grandchildren of immigrants and thus within living memory of the immigration experience. This may predispose them to identify with their ethnic backgrounds more than the average white American does. Although whites in this region are more concentrated in the second and third generations than white Americans as a whole, the region is not unusual in this respect compared to other metropolitan areas of the Northeast and Midwest, which developed with the same flow of immigration during the nineteenth and twentieth centuries. The Capital Region has large numbers of white ethnics, as do Boston, New York City, Philadelphia, and their surrounding suburbs.

What, then, is one to make of the puzzling divergence between the objective and subjective courses of ethnicity? Why do many Americans continue to identify themselves with countries and an immigration experience that has little direct relevance for their lives and recedes ever further into the past? Is it merely that ethnic identities are lagging behind other kinds of ethnic difference, and that eventually they too will subside? Or are there forces at work that tend to sustain these identities, even in the face of other assimilatory trends? And, if so, what is the nature of these forces? I attempt some answers, admittedly speculative, arguing that the divergence is itself a symptom of the underlying transformation of ethnicity in the lives of white Americans. Ethnic distinctions based on European ancestry, once quite important in the texture of American social life, are receding into the background. Yet this development does not imply that ethnicity is any less embedded in the social fabric, but rather that the ethnic distinctions which matter are undergoing a radical shift. The transformation of ethnicity among whites does not portend the elimination of ethnicity but instead the formation of a new ethnic group: one based on ancestry from anywhere on the European continent. The emergence of this new group, which I call the "European Americans," with its own myths about its place in American history and the American identity, lies behind the ethnic identities of many Americans of European background. The persistence of ethnic identities can thus be understood as an outcome of assimilation in a societal context that remains fundamentally multiethnic and multiracial, and where, therefore, competition between groups defined in ethnic terms remains a powerful force.

The Nature of Contemporary Ethnic Identities

Before delving into the long-run significance of ethnic identities, it is necessary to grasp hold of their nature more firmly, by synthesizing some of the key findings into a composite portrait. These findings pertain to an overall ethnic situation that is still in flux: Even in terms of diminishing objective differences, the transformation of ethnicity has not run its full course among Americans of European ancestry. Therefore, a survey of the population turns up varied stages in the long-term process of ethnic change, including some individuals who are still close to an older form of ethnicity as lived typically by that part of the second generation which remains firmly embedded in a communal matrix of ethnicity; some who have grown up in families of this type and retain indelible and attractive memories of this older ethnicity, even though they have moved away from ethnic social attachments; and some whose lives and upbringing are remote from ethnicity as a social form. In the aggregate, the ethnic identities of whites mirror this complex amalgam. Therefore, in deciding on the features to go into the portrait of ethnic identity, it seems wise to be selective and to attempt to delineate the kind of identity that is observable today but is likely to be even more fully realized in the future by accumulating layers of ethnic change (exemplified in the increasing complexity of ancestry and the growing generational distance from immigration). In short, my attempt is to capture the essential features of an ethnic identity that, in light of the forces eroding the older form of ethnic solidarity, is now emerging as a prevalent form of ethnicity among whites. I see these features in the four following ways:

1. Ethnic identities vary widely in salience, or intensity. This includes the very fact of identifying oneself in terms of ethnic categories in the first place. Our survey's test of the willingness to identify was a simple one, but not all-encompassing. It amounted to whether respondents were willing to describe themselves with ethnic labels to a courteous stranger, the interviewer. Since virtually all respondents knew something about the ethnic origins of their ancestors, those who refused to respond in ethnic ways were, in essence, denying the relevance of ethnic categories for this situation, and they were revealing the low salience of ethnic background for themselves, as some in fact told us, stating that they never think about their backgrounds or are just Americans and nothing else. Of course, among those who did not respond ethnically to our question are undoubtedly some who use ethnic labels on other occasions—for example, with some social intimates. This fact makes the precise dividing line between identifiers and nonidentifiers unclear, but it does not deny that there is ultimately some spectrum of intensity on which individuals can be arrayed. Those who are unwilling to describe themselves in ethnic terms to an interviewer generally belong toward the low end, while identifiers as a group are placed higher, ranked according to the importance ethnicity holds for them.

The wide variation in intensity seems one of the most outstanding properties of ethnic identity. No matter how generously one counts, there is only a small minority, amounting at best to no more than one-fifth of native-born whites, who hold intensely to an ethnic identity. An equally small group denies any importance for ethnic background, refusing to identify ethnically and proclaiming that ethnic background is of no importance. In between these extremes is a large group, containing the majority of whites in the Capital Region, for whom ethnic identity is of middling salience. This group can be further differentiated; many in it describe their ethnic backgrounds as somewhat important to them, while others are merely willing to identify their ethnic backgrounds to others but personally ascribe little or no importance to the facts of ethnic ancestry.

Evident in this variation is that, for Americans of European background in general, ethnic identity is a choice. In contrast to many parts of the world—for example, the Soviet Union, where ethnic origins are recorded in passports—no governmental recognition is accorded the ethnic identities of American-born whites (Lieberson, 1985). (In the United States, the principal official use of ethnic categories to make distinctions among citizens is for the purpose of affirmative action, but this does not create distinctions based on European origins, except for the small group from Spain, who can claim to be Hispanic.)[1] The absence of official sanction for ethnic identities eliminates one source of their standardization, particularly important at a time when intermarriage and mixed ancestry are widespread. Nor, in the face of the variability in the manner of response to questions about ethnic identity and its intensity, does it appear that there are widely accepted norms governing this identity. (It is unclear how such norms would arise or be enforced, given the very limited integration of the great majority of whites into ethnic social structures, such as ethnically based friendship networks.) This does not mean that the identities of whites are wholly unconstrained or without any social patterning whatsoever; for instance, when asked to identify themselves in their own words, most of our ethnically identifying respondents framed their answers in terms of recognizable categories of ethnicity (for example, Italian or German) rather than idiosyncratic ones. But within the limits of this vocabulary of ethnicity, whites are largely free to identify themselves as they will and to make these identities as important as they like. This is especially true of the emerging majority of white Americans who come from mixed ethnic backgrounds, who can present and think of themselves in terms of a hybrid identity, or emphasize one ethnic component while recognizing the other (or others), or simplify their background by dropping all but one of its components, or deny altogether the relevance of their ethnic background.

The volitional nature of ethnic identity means that this form of identity cannot be regarded as a fixed attribute of an individual in the same sense that his or her ancestry is. Hence, as others have pointed out (for example, Lyman and Douglas, 1973), ethnic identity can be situationally specific. This description covers not only the willingness to express an identity, but increasingly, because of the growing complexity of ancestries, the nature of the identity that is presented. Thus, a person with German-Irish-Italian ancestry (one of the most common three-ancestry combinations, according to the 1980 census) can find something in common with others of German, Irish, or Italian ancestries, or even combinations of these. But the malleability of ethnic identity can be pushed even further, for this imagined person may be capable of finding something ethnic in common with someone whose ancestry is far afield—Polish, say. The commonality, which obviously could not lie in the ethnic points of origin themselves, can lie in similarities in the immigrant experiences endured by grandparents or parallels in the manner of growing up. That this is not a fanciful supposition is indicated by the frequency with which whites have discussions of ethnicity with friends whose backgrounds have nothing in common with their own; this happens about as frequently as discussions with co-ethnics. Our data do not establish that these discussions generally revolve around commonalities, but it is not unreasonable to presume that this is often the case. The point, however, is that any sharing of ethnicity between persons of seemingly dissimilar backgrounds is made possible by the lability of ethnic identity, and this in turn hinges on the absence of a rigid social definition of how people ought to identify in ethnic terms.

But even if ethnic identity is a choice, whose degree of commitment is subject to some fluctuation, it is a meaningful choice.[2] Throughout my analyses, the strongest and most consistent correlate and predictor of ethnically related phenomena has been the subjective importance attached to ethnic background, a measure of the salience of identity. No other variable entertained in the analyses comes close to matching the role of subjective importance, which has a strong relationship to phenomena as diverse as eating ethnic foods, perceiving ethnic discrimination, desiring an ethnic identity for one's children, and discussing one's ethnic background with others.

2. Ethnic identities tend to be reflected in some experiences that are seen as ethnic, but the kinds and qualities of these experiences are highly variable. Most white Americans have some experiences that they view in ethnic terms, but few have many such experiences or experiences that occur with great regularity. Since experiences of this sort are not subject to absolute personal control—an aunt may always prepare an ethnic dish to celebrate Christmas (or even Thanksgiving)—ethnic experiences occur even

to people who do not identify as ethnics or who view their backgrounds as of no practical consequence. But, in general, these experiences are most common and most intense among persons who identify ethnically and who view their identities as important.

The nature of the most common ethnic experiences seems to fit with the social milieus in which most whites find themselves, which involve continual contact among persons of varied ethnic ancestries (and where, moreover, these ancestries may not even be readily discernable, as shown by the high proportion of *close* friends whose ethnic backgrounds are unknown to respondents). In general, the common ethnic experiences are unlikely to generate conflict with people of other backgrounds and, in most cases, are capable of being shared across ethnic lines. This seems true for the most frequently cited experiences of eating ethnic foods, discussing one's ethnic background with others, feeling curious about the backgrounds of others, and attending ethnic festivals. These are mainly experiences in private rather than public realms; they are innocuous, unlikely to give offense or even attract negative comment; and they need not be ethnically exclusive (ethnic foods can be, and no doubt frequently are, shared with people of other backgrounds, and discussions of ethnicity can be little more than exchanges of information about family background between persons of different ethnic origins). Much less common are experiences without these characteristics, having instead aspects of ethnic exclusion, favoritism, or conflict—experiences such as receiving business or professional help from a coethnic, suffering from ethnic discrimination, and being involved in ethnic political issues.[3] (The principal exception to this scheme is the experience of encountering stereotypes, which seems by virtue of its character to belong to the second set, but by virtue of its frequency to vault almost into the first one. Yet this experience often seems rather mild in the reports of our respondents, lacking the sting of denigration applied to the person. In a society such as the United States, where ethnicity has had such a paramount role as a basis for social division, stereotypes of course exist, but increasingly among whites, they are detached from application to the interethnic contacts of the ordinary social world.)

It is hard to avoid the conclusion that ethnic experience is shallow for the great majority of whites and, in the critical domain of culture, being eroded by the churning of large-scale demographic forces. Many of the experiences checked by our respondents turn out to be quite occasional in frequency. The experiences of sensitivity to ethnicity in the social world exemplify this. Although relatively common among native-born whites, they are mostly indicated as occasional or infrequent; few respondents seem to view their daily social round through ethnic lenses. Maintaining ethnic customs and attending ethnic festivals are other examples; these experiences seem rigidly limited in frequency, since few respondents attend festivals more than once a year, and most of the customs reported to us are linked to such annual holidays as Christmas, Easter, and Passover. The shallowness of much ethnic experience is revealed in still another way by customs, which seem only hazily defined to many: A large number of respondents claiming this experience pointed to religious or family observances, rather than ethnic customs, revealing their uncertainty as to what practices are or are not ethnic customs (see also Waters, 1990). Behind such cloudy notions lies a lack of contact with a vital ethnic community whose practices would sharpen the perception of the group's traditions.

Further, the experiences that in principle seem most central to defining a positive content for ethnicity are being weakened by such demographic forces as generational change. This holds for the knowledge and use of a mother tongue, which turn out to be quite limited in extent. Knowledge and use are concentrated among persons of single ancestry and in the second generation, and both groups are declining as part of the white population. Thus, the important cultural preserve of ethnic language will be whittled down further in the future, all the more so as the decline in the number of speakers will further decrease the opportunities and incentives to learn and use a language.

The phenomenon of demographically spurred decline is also apparent for the eating of ethnic foods, an experience that deserves special consideration. It is, by a good margin, the most widespread of ethnic experiences. But some decline in its preeminence appears to be foreshadowed by its decrease in regularity among the members of the fourth and later generations and the sense of many respondents that the ethnic foods of today are not equal in quality to those they remember from their childhoods. Yet any decline may be cushioned by American culture. Ethnic cuisines have earned an accepted, even an honored, place among American foods, and variants unknown to immigrant ancestors, such as "high-brow" northern Italian cuisine, can make ethnic cooking appealing at all social-class levels. Thus, while the authenticity of ethnic foods and the frequency with which they are consumed may be diminishing over time, there is no reason to think that the survival of ethnic cuisines is in danger (see van den Berghe, 1984). Many white Americans will, no doubt, continue to eat foods connected with their ethnic backgrounds (even if these are not necessarily the same as the dishes enjoyed by immigrant ancestors).

But the experience of eating ethnically, which is likely to remain the most common of ethnic cultural experiences, seems a paradigm for the emerging role of ethnic experience in general. It is very unlikely to arouse controversy or conflict and is capable of being shared across ethnic lines (as indicated by the minimal impact of intermarriage on ethnic cuisine). And it is a largely private experience geared to the family circle. In light of the deterioration of forms of ethnic community larger than the family, ethnic commensalism seems far more suited to bring about family communion, especially for families bringing several different ethnic backgrounds to the dinner table, than to foster ethnic cohesion.

3. Ethnic identities are bound up in the minds of many with family history. For many whites ethnicity is inseparable from their notions about their families, and a larger social group is only hazily discerned at best. The frequent equation of ethnicity with family emerges in different ways in our interviews; for example, in the reasons respondents give for the importance they ascribe to ethnicity. A large number of respondents attaching middling importance to ethnicity viewed it as providing a sense of family origins. This equation also comes up in connection with the topics respondents discuss when they do in fact discuss their ethnic backgrounds with friends and others. Once again, family experiences—notably, where ancestors came from, their experiences as immigrants, and how the respondents themselves grew up—are important on the list. Perhaps most revealing is the kind of ethnic identity many respondents appear to imagine for their children (insofar as they imagine one at all). Frequently it seems little more than a sense of family background, as when intermarried respondents tick off a list of ethnic elements that honors the complexities on both sides of the

family or simply say, "All of their background," as if the individual ethnic elements are of little importance.

This amounts to a privatization of ethnic identity—a reduction of its expression to largely personal and family terms. As such, it seems an inevitable outcome of the broad changes to ethnicity. Put quite simply: The zone of common experiences that can be presumed for the members of any group has been steadily narrowed by such processes as acculturation, large-scale social mobility, intermarriage, and movement out of ethnic neighborhoods. This means that when two persons with similar ethnic ancestries meet for the first time, there is little they can assume is common to them both solely on the basis of ethnic background. The effects of these processes have been enhanced by the fact that they correspond with important fault lines within ethnic groups—notably, those of generation and birth cohort—which in combination lead to sharp differences between older and younger members of the same group (Alba, 1988). The erosion of characteristics common to the members of a group—be they cultural, such as language, or socioeconomic, or something else—takes away from any larger meaning that group membership may have for persons with a given ancestry. With such a meaning unclear, if not absent, it is understandable that many whites fall into the view that ethnicity is no different from the facts of their own family history—that it means having, say, grandparents who were immigrants from particular European places, faced particular obstacles after their arrival in the United States, raised their children in particular ways, and so forth.

This privatization is related to what Herbert Gans (1988) has called "middle American individualism." This quintessentially American phenomenon, first identified by de Tocqueville more than 150 years ago, insists on the autonomy of the individual within his or her social milieu of friends and family, on the freedom to be different, an absolutely unique individual, within this private sphere. Ethnic identities are quite compatible with this individualism. They offer additional ways of defining one's distinctiveness in regard to others (Waters, 1990). They are also shaped by the ethos of individualism: This influence is reflected in the belief, evident throughout our interviews, that there is little obligation to identify in ethnic terms and also little obligation to behave in specific ethnic ways. Most whites who identify ethnically can point to certain patterns in their behavior or certain experiences that are ethnic; however, there is a great deal of latitude for the individual when it comes to such behaviors and experiences.

The individualism at the heart of ethnic identity deeply constrains the parents' transmission of their ethnic identities to their children and thus interferes in a critical way with the continuity of ethnicity. Only a minority of whites care whether their children identify, and an even smaller minority take actions to inculcate a sense of identity. These are remarkable findings, given ethnicity's traditional dependence on the family for nurturance. But equally remarkable is that even those parents who desire their children to identify frequently express little concern over the children's interest (or lack of it) in their ethnic backgrounds. This is apparently owing to the belief of many parents that their children's ethnic identities are ultimately a matter for the children to decide (just as, implicitly, the parents' identities are their own affair and no one else's). To attempt too strongly to instill an ethnic identity is, therefore, to impose on their children's embryonic individualism, on what is properly a prerogative of the children.[4]

4. Ethnic identities are not typically anchored in strongly ethnic social structures. Such structures still do exist, although they have been weakened by powerful currents of assimilation. But they seem rather independent of identities. This important finding offers another clue to the emerging role of ethnic identity. The weight of ethnic social structures is necessarily limited by the erosion they have suffered over past decades. Intermarriage is widespread; friendship circles are typically quite diverse in ethnic terms; membership in ethnic organizations is quite rare; and so forth. As a consequence, many whites who identify in ethnic terms, even intensely so, have only limited contact with persons of the same ethnic background. Their social worlds thus do not bear a deep imprint of ethnicity. The one respect in which an ethnic element commonly appears is that most have at least one fellow ethnic among their friends (often these coethnic friends are also relatives); but even here, the difference from whites with little or no sense of ethnic identity is marked only for the group with the most intense identities. Indeed, the characteristics of ethnic identity do not seem to correspond very well with those of social structures. Ethnic identity and its salience have little relationship to whether individuals are

intermarried, to whether they belong to organizations with many coethnic members, and to whether they live in ethnic neighborhoods. A relationship of this sort is somewhat stronger with respect to ethnic friendships. But, overall, what impresses is the degree of independence between ethnic social structures and ethnic identity.[5]

It may well be that we are glimpsing in these results two alternative bases of ethnicity—with very different implications—gradually sliding past each other, as one is being steadily eroded and the other perhaps not. The one undergoing unmistakable erosion is the communal basis of ethnicity, the older form of ethnic solidarity, in which members of an ethnic group regularly encountered each other, because they lived in the same neighborhoods, went to the same schools, worked at the same jobs, and befriended and married one another. Given the massive contact across ethnic lines among whites, this form of solidarity is in eclipse among European ancestry groups and undoubtedly is not visible in a robust state in the survey data. But the data do establish that attachment to ethnic social structures, in friendship, organization, and neighborhood, carries concrete behavioral manifestations, independent of ethnic identity. These manifestations are reflected, for instance, in the index of ethnic experiences.

In highlighting the unmistakable erosion in the communal form of ethnicity, I do not mean to imply that it is likely to disappear any time soon, if ever. On this point, there is a potential for misunderstanding which should not be left unchallenged; in my view, this misunderstanding mars the debate over the importance of ethnic differences among white Americans. The potential misunderstanding here turns on the distinction between the present conditions of ethnic communities and their future as implied by current trends. Obviously, such communities exist and are prominent in some places—one thinks of south Boston's Irish or south Philadelphia's Italians. No one should be foolish enough to predict that these communities, or others like them, will cease to exist in the foreseeable future (though some will surely disappear, as has largely happened to Manhattan's Little Italy). But what does seem predictable based on current trends is that ethnic communities, and more generally ethnically rooted social milieus, will encompass a declining share of whites.

Hence the importance of the second basis for ethnicity: ethnic identity. It, too, carries concrete behavioral manifestations, although these are almost certain to be different from those associated with the communal form of ethnicity and are likely to vary far more among individuals than is true for the manifestations of the older form. In light of the features already described, the outstanding aspect of ethnic identity as a basis for ethnicity is that it leads to a highly individualized form. Ethnic identity is, in all of its ramifications, a choice by an individual, even if there are social influences on that choice (such as growing up in an ethnic home, as most members of the second generation do). Indeed, choice is probably the key to unlocking the full implications of the transition underway from community to identity as a basis of ethnicity among whites. It is not only that individuals can choose to identify or not, and choose also precisely which elements in an ancestry mixture to emphasize and how important an ethnic identity should be for them, but they also have a wide latitude of choice when it comes to the manifestations or expressions of ethnicity. Thus, for the person who chooses to identify, an identity can be expressed by a curiosity about the immigrant experience, perhaps viewed nostalgically as having a bittersweet authenticity in which the too assimilated third- or fourth-generation ethnic American cannot share; by participation in political activities with ethnic themes concerned with the homeland or a group's standing in American society; by a fondness for ethnic cuisine; or by myriad other outlets. These choices are socially influenced—they are framed within parameters determined by class, region, and so forth, as well as by available collective expressions of ethnicity (the supply side of ethnicity). Thus, an upper-middle-class identifier will no doubt receive disapproval from family and friends if the style of his or her expression of ethnic identity is inappropriate (for example, too intense or too similar to a working-class ethnic identity). Constraint is not altogether absent, but without the normative framework provided by an ethnic community, the choices made by one individual are not likely to match those of another and the basis for any commonality of experience is likely to slip further away.

There is a useful comparison to religion, which is also affected by the deeply rooted individualism of American life. In his exploration of middle-American individualism, Herbert Gans (1988) points out how the value Americans place on personal freedom and individual choice is loosening their ties to formal religion and widening the range of acceptable religious expression (the latter exemplified by the emergence of charismatic forms of religiosity in highly bureaucratized religions, such as Catholicism). Nevertheless, the American credo still emphasizes that everyone should have a religion, even while leaving open to personal choice the specifics of religious commitment. In this respect, there is a tempting parallel to ethnicity. Even though there is no specific obligation to be ethnic, there is an acceptance of ethnic identity as a personal choice and a recognition of an individual's freedom to define the terms of his or her ethnic commitment (Glazer, 1975, identifies these elements as among the essentials of the "American ethnic pattern").

On the basis of a few of the findings, the temptation may be to press even further, to view religion as a possible haven for ethnicity (this is a classic position in the study of ethnicity, popularized by Herberg, 1955); for example, the prominent place of religious organizations among those with more or less ethnically homogeneous memberships seems to point in this direction. But except for the ethnic groups that are also religious bodies (such as Jews and Greeks), the evidence that religion can sustain ethnicity is not convincing. For one thing, religious organizations appear so high on the list of those with ethnically homogeneous memberships in part because of the existence of some dwindling nationality parishes of the Catholic Church, likely to undergo further decline along with the ethnic neighborhoods in which they are located. And the broad ethnic effects of ethnic-membership organizations appear small. Moreover, religious identities, or combinations of ethnic (that is, national-origin) and religious identities, were not very common among respondents, hardly what one would expect if religion were fusing with ethnicity. And then there is the growing frequency of interreligious marriage. All in all, a variety of indicators suggest that religion has only a weak power to support ethnicity (although the linkage between the two deserves further study).

The parallel between religion and ethnicity also breaks down in a revealing way, highlighting structural underpinnings that religions possess but American ethnic groups typically do not. For religions are generally represented by elaborate institutional structures, which identify for the believer a core of religious doctrine and practice that are obligatory. (There is often considerable leeway for individuals in what they accept from this core. Many Catholics do not accept their church's teaching on abortion, for example, but there are invariably some essentials to which the mass of believers holds firm.) Religions also have rules and rituals for accepting new members. These play an important role in delineating a boundary and, in particular, for incorporating individuals whose membership is not determined by birth, such as the children of intermarriages. Finally, religions provide regular occasions, in the form of worship services, for their members to assemble as a religious community and to recognize (and celebrate) this fact. Most Americans attend church or synagogue services several times a year (at a minimum, on such major religious holidays as Easter or Passover), and many attend far more frequently (especially during certain stages of the life-cycle, as when they have young children). In all these respects, there is no equivalent for most ethnic groups (except in those instances where religion and ethnicity are intrinsically fused). Who can say what beliefs or practices constitute being Irish or Polish? Who can define the precise membership boundaries of these groups, especially when it comes to individuals who are Irish or Polish as part of complex mixtures? What regular occasions are there for ethnic communities to assemble and recognize their common bonds? Ethnic festivals generally attract a multiethnic crowd and occur only a few times a year at most. Explicitly ethnic organizations are a more plausible forum for such occasions, but we have already seen that few Americans of European ancestry belong to them.

Some Implications of Ethnic Identity as a Basis of Ethnicity

At the beginning of this book, I raised the question of whether ethnic identity would lead to a new basis for ethnic solidarity and hence social division among whites, as many prominent scholars expect, or whether it should instead be viewed as "symbolic ethnicity," a vestigial attachment to a few ethnic symbols imposing little cost on everyday life, as Herbert Gans (1979) has suggested. This amounts to asking, What kind of ethnicity can be expected from ethnic identity? The moment for an answer has arrived. The preceding portrait indicates that ethnic identity is far more consistent with the latter possibility than with the former. The severe limits on ethnic identity as a basis for solidarity stand out: its tendency to manifest itself in private behavior and in ways that are capable of being shared across ethnic lines; its voluntary nature, extending also to the modes of its expression; and its lack of anchor in ethnic social structures. Likewise, there is little evidence of ethnicity functioning as a form of mutual assistance. Rare are the whites who claim to have received any special professional or economic assistance from fellow ethnics. Even mutual assistance in a more diffuse form, namely, involvement in political issues having an impact on the group, is surprisingly infrequent. Accordingly, the interpretations that suggest a revival of ethnicity among whites, inspired by a surge of ethnic identity, seem contradicted by the evidence. The popular notion of a third-generation return to ethnicity is incompatible with the progressive decline across the generations in the salience of ethnic identities, and the thesis that ethnic identities are reinvigorated by the increasingly political character of ethnicity in advanced industrial societies does not square with the scanty attention most whites seem to give to ethnic political issues.

The general outlines of symbolic ethnicity offer a far better fit to the emerging nature of ethnic identity—essentially in the desire to retain a sense of being ethnic, but without any deep commitment to ethnic social ties or behaviors. Symbolic ethnicity is concerned with the symbols of ethnic cultures rather than with the cultures themselves, and this seems true also of the cultural commitments of ethnic identity: the cultural stuff of ethnicity continues to wither, and thus ethnic identity tends to latch onto a few symbolic commitments (such as St. Patrick's Day among the Irish). Symbolic ethnicity makes few and intermittent demands on everyday life and tends to be expressed in the private domain of leisure-time activities. These characteristics have been amply demonstrated for the ethnic identities of most whites.

The resemblance of ethnic identity to symbolic ethnicity raises as an issue the future of this new form of ethnicity. In his classic description of symbolic ethnicity, Gans remains somewhat agnostic about its long-run outcome, although he suggests that it is an "ethnicity of last resort," the penultimate stage in the long winding down of the ethnicities set in motion in the United States by mass immigration from Europe. This suggestion stands in accord with the powerful currents of assimilation and mobility depicted in this book. Could it be, then, that ethnic identity simply lags behind some other manifestations of ethnicity and that it too will soon begin to fade, as such forces as generational change and social mobility continue to exert their effects?

In some ways, the answer appears to be yes. The impact on ethnic identity of some large-scale and seemingly irreversible demographic changes seems corrosive: mixed ancestry and particularly complex ancestry, membership in the fourth and later generations, and uncertainty about one's ethnic background all, in one way or another, reduce the probability of identifying ethnically and the felt intensity of ethnic identity. Since these characteristics are increasing in the white population as a result of such forces as advancing generational status and high rates of intermarriage, it would appear that ethnic identities will, in the future, decline in prevalence and salience.

But the picture is not all one-sided. One surprise of the Capital Region study is the absence of any decline in ethnic identity across cohorts, given the striking decline in objective ethnic differences across birth groups, from older to younger white Americans. Indeed, there have been hints in the analysis that younger individuals are in some ways more interested in their ethnic backgrounds than their elders; for example, when it comes to eating ethnic foods or being sensitive to the ethnic backgrounds of others. Age differences have not been entirely consistent, and it is not fully clear how such differences should be interpreted, as they are likely in some part to be reflections of variations over the life cycle. But there is good reason to suspect that some true cohort effects are present as well. Younger Americans have enjoyed more open attention to ethnic diversity—in schools, for example[6]—than is true for Americans brought up prior to the 1960s. It may therefore be less difficult for them to acknowledge their backgrounds and to express some interest in them. Further evidence in favor of this interpretation comes from an analysis of national surveys in which respondents of mixed ancestry are asked whether they feel closer to any one ethnic element in their background. Younger whites are more willing to answer such questions affirmatively (Alba and Chamlin, 1983).

The relationship of education to ethnic identity is also not consistent with an inevitable decline in identity. Ethnicity in the United States has often been portrayed as concentrated in the working class and undergoing progressive dilution with social mobility, and this seems to have been true to a large degree for the older, communally based form of ethnicity which emerged in the immediate aftermath of immigration. But it seems strikingly untrue for ethnic identity, which rises along with educational level, as do such manifestations of identity as knowledge of a mother tongue and social sensitivity to ethnicity. Since education, particularly past high school, leads to a broader and more sophisticated knowledge of the social world and typically to greater diversity in social contacts, this suggests not simply that increasing education tends to heighten awareness of ethnic background, but also that some natural outcomes of assimilatory processes (such as contact with ethnic diversity) may produce the same result.

Such implications flatly contradict conventional assimilation theory, and I have interpreted them throughout as consistent with a view of ethnicity as a form of cultural capital. Admittedly, this is a speculation, although it is a highly plausible one. It presumes that ethnic symbols and references can be of use in the complex signaling by which individuals establish relationships to one another. To fulfill this function, ethnic identities need not occupy more than a small portion of the identity "masks" individuals present to others, and need not be deeply felt. Moreover, it is apparent from our survey that ethnic identities can be used to establish a degree of intimacy with individuals of other ethnic backgrounds; a shared ethnicity is not required. Although the cultural capital interpretation obviously needs further confirmation, it does suggest why ethnic identities can be more salient at higher social-class levels and also why such identities may not follow in the wake of the very evident tide of assimilation.

Finally, it is impossible to discuss the future course of ethnic identity among whites without recognizing its variation across ancestry groups—in prevalence, intensity, and manifestation. For the members of some ancestry groups are much more likely to express themselves in the form of ethnic identity than are the members of others. In broad brush strokes, these variations pit the old-stock groups originating in northern and western Europe, such as the English, Germans, and Scots, against newer groups from southern and eastern Europe, such as the Italians, Jews, and Poles, with the Irish appearing to occupy an uncertain middle ground. Ethnic identity is most common, most intense, and most manifest in a variety of ways among the Italians, Jews, and Poles, although there are some members of every group who profess an identity derived from it which they view as important. The attractiveness of the ethnicities of the newer groups is firmly established by the identity patterns of individuals whose mixed ancestries combine older with newer stock. Insofar as they identify in ethnic terms, these individuals are much more likely to do so as Irish, Italians, or Poles, than as Dutch, English, or Scots, despite the higher prestige attached to early American origins. But, in the future, will the identities of these newer groups increasingly mirror the faded ethnic memories of older groups?

The prominence of ethnic identity among the newer groups does seem associated with the recency of their immigration in historical terms, thus destined to fade as a result of demographic change. Because these groups are more recent, they are still visibly present in the region and have a more bountiful supply side to their ethnicities, reflected in some neighborhoods (particularly true in the Capital Region of the Italians) and many businesses. Also because of recency, the individuals with these ancestries have typically been raised in more clearly ethnic ways, having at a minimum exposure to parents and grandparents whose lives were plainly stamped by ethnic origins; hence, when it comes to thinking of identity in terms of a family past, individuals with these ancestries have more vivid material to draw on. But, with continuing residential dispersion of groups, increasing generational distance from immigration, and the growing complexities of ancestries (including those of parents), this ethnic distinctiveness inevitably will be diminished and with it will go some of the force behind the identities of these groups.

The difficulties the newer groups will face in maintaining strong ethnic identities are suggested by the example of Jews, perhaps the outstanding instance of a group that is managing to swim to some degree against the assimilatory tide. Although the Jewish group is only thinly represented in the Capital Region survey (because of its small size in the region's population), it is so exceptional in some respects that it has emerged in the discussion despite its sparse presence in the data—for instance, in the sense of continuing discrimination against the group, in involvement with political issues, and in the extent of ethnic friendship. What is distinctive about the Jewish group in comparison to, say, the Italians is the fusion of ethnicity and religion. Thus, Jewish ethnicity benefits from the factors that in general distinguish religion from ethnicity, such as the availability of an institutional network, a social-structural carapace, for protecting and sustaining the group. Religious congregations and religious education, as well as social institutions intended to foster contacts within a religious group (for example, Jewish summer camps), create extensive social networks and a sense of ethnic distinctiveness based on shared experience that have little counterpart among groups like the Italians. (I note again the existence of some Italian parishes in the Capital Region, which are, however, tied to declining ethnic neighborhoods.) In addition, Jewish ethnicity is supported by a centuries-old tradition of survival as a minority in Gentile-dominated societies and by the intense commitment of American Jews to Israel (Cohen, 1983; Silberman, 1985).

But to suggest that the intensity of Italian and Polish ethnic identities may diminish does not mean that they will necessarily fade to resemble those of the English and Germans. Before drawing such a conclusion, one has to look more broadly than I have done so far for forces in American society that might help to perpetuate ethnic identities and ask whether these forces might differentially affect persons of different European ancestries. One needs to consider the possible reasons for whites to continue to identify themselves in ethnic terms that no longer correspond with differences in life chances or social affiliations. Implicitly, the issue has already been raised in the argument that ethnicity can be a form of cultural capital, but this argument has left unanswered why ethnicity can function in this way.

Ethnic Identities and the Emergence of the European Americans: Some Speculations on the Long-Run Outcome of Ethnic Change among Whites

Before coming to grips with the ultimate significance of ethnic identities among whites, it is necessary to dispel a persistent and deeply rooted misconception about assimilation. This misconception originates in the most important theoretical treatment of assimilation in the post-World War II era—namely, Milton Gordon's *Assimilation in American Life*. There, Gordon (1964: 71) describes the psychological aspect of assimilation under the phrase "identificational assimilation," which he defines as the "development of [a] sense of peoplehood based exclusively on [the] host society." Although there is a touch of ambiguity in these words (in particular in the phrase "sense of peoplehood"), I believe that this conception as commonly understood limits our ability to comprehend the implications of the persistence of ethnic identities among whites, because it suggests that assimilation involves the obliteration of identities cast in terms of ancestral origins, and in the extreme it can be read as requiring the fading of memories of ancestors. That the conception is still part of the intellectual tool-kit of students of ethnicity is demonstrated by Stanley Lieberson's notion of "unhyphenated whites" as the end-stage of the assimilation process (Lieberson, 1985). These are whites who cannot answer questions about ancestry other than with "American" (or confessions of ignorance). But, as Lieberson's empirical analysis shows, if the endstage of assimilation is represented by such unhyphenated whites, then Americans are gradually coming to resemble rural white southerners with limited educations. This hardly seems likely as the sole final outcome.

The other side of the same intellectual coin is the argument that the persistence of ethnic identities indicates the stability, or even revival, of ethnicity itself—for if such identities persist, then, apparently by Gordon's widely accepted standard, assimilation has become bogged down. This perception lies at the heart of much of the analysis and scholarship that claims an ethnic resurgence is occurring among American whites. One can see how tempting is this diagnosis given my findings about the wide prevalence of ethnic identities, but the difficulty is that it offers no conception of how such identities are linked to meaningful social groups. It is just such a linkage, moreover, that is called into question by the personal nature of the kind of ethnic identity that is emerging among whites.

There is a different angle of vision that I think better illuminates the significance of ethnic identities among whites and their connection to a meaningful social group. It is a perspective anchored in the recognition that the United States remains a society in which social boundaries drawn on the basis of ethnic ancestry— and I include race under this heading—remain of paramount importance; indeed, the prominence of ethnicity as a boundary may be increasing as a result of the surge of immigration from Asia, Latin America, and the Caribbean since 1965, which has imparted new vitality to some older ethnic groups, such as the Chinese, and planted many new ones, such as the Cubans, Jamaicans, and Vietnamese. But despite the continuing importance of ethnicity, the United States is an ethnically dynamic society, in which the meaningful social contours of ethnicity can be significantly reshaped within a relatively brief period of historical time.

It is precisely such a reshaping that is under way, in my estimation—a new ethnic group is emerging among whites.[7] I must reiterate that this development is still very much in process, and this accounts for some of the paradoxical character of the present. The members of this new group do not define themselves solely in terms of an "American" identity (although some do much of the time)—they are not "unhyphenated whites," to employ Lieberson's terminology. Rather, they continue to define themselves, to some extent at least, in terms of European points of origin. But, in contrast to the past, the different European ancestries are not seen as the basis for important social divisions; instead, they create the potential for social bonds having an ethnic character, founded on the perception of similar experiences of immigration and social mobility. This new group can be called, for lack of a better term, the "European Americans." (Other terms exist for this phenomenon: it has been called "pan-ethnicity" by some [see Erickson, 1975], although to my mind this term misses a key feature, the presumption of some commonality in the experiences of the descendants of immigrants from widely varying European societies; Herbert Gans suggests the alternative, "post-immigrant Americans.")[8] I have named the group based on what seem to me to be its current boundaries, but with a recognition that these are fluid and may in the future encompass additional groups, such as those from Asia, insofar as their experiences can be seen to resemble those of their European predecessors.

Some qualifications are in order. The emergence of the European-American group is not the only direction involved in the complex changes taking place among whites. There is truth also in the notion of a growing group of unhyphenated whites, since the broad thrust of demographic change is to weaken ethnic identities. Accordingly, the European-American concept cannot be applied equally to all whites (even though membership is in principle open to them all).

It may have more validity for the descendants of historically recent immigrations from southern and eastern Europe than for old-stock Americans, who can rely on the continued prestige of an older, more exclusive American identity. On an aggregate level, the outlines of the new group are more visible in some parts of the United States—in the metropolitan regions of the Northeast and Midwest, in particular—because of the continued resonance of European ethnic identities in these areas. Even in these places, membership in a European-American group is not likely to be central to the social identities of most whites, remaining frequently in the background and emerging most forcefully under special circumstances, such as the challenge of competition over residential turf and jobs with non-whites, Hispanics, and recent immigrants. Thus, this new membership is not likely to be as overriding as the ethnicity of the past.

Nevertheless, the persistence of superficially distinct ethnic identities under the umbrella of a European-American group can be understood in terms of three general aspects of an ethnic group. The first is that an ethnic group defines itself in part in terms of an account of its history, an account which typically has both factual and moral dimensions. This backward-looking aspect of ethnicity constitutes an essential component of that "subjective belief in . . . common descent," which Weber ([1922] 1968: 389) identified as the hallmark of an ethnic group, for without a larger conception of history, there can be no unifying sense of common descent larger than the family. Closely related to this sense of history is the second aspect, the inextricable linkage between ethnic membership and social honor. Weber's analysis of the ethnic group is helpful here too. He insightfully describes ethnic honor as an "honor of the masses," which is "accessible to anyone who belongs to the subjectively believed community of descent" (Weber, [1922] 1968: 391). The third aspect is the role of the ethnic group as a carrier of "interests," economic or political, which the members of an ethnic group lay claim to or defend (Glazer and Moynihan, 1970).

Running throughout the ethnic identities of contemporary whites is a diffuse sense of connection to a historical account of immigration and its aftermath, which, in spite of the considerable variation of details, displays a remarkable similarity from group to group. From every group, one hears essentially the same story of people who came poor, suffered from discrimination and other early burdens, but worked hard and eventually made their way in the new land. Stated so baldly, it is obvious that this history incorporates mythic elements, which are surely present to some degree in the histories of immigrant groups but are elevated beyond their actual role and generalized inappropriately to all members of a group. But the outlines of this history are clearly recognizable in both popular literature and social-science scholarship (Steinberg, 1981).

There is irony here, for this definition of the group's essence in terms of history amounts to a redefinition of what is quintessentially American, and perhaps in this impact on *national* identity lies the greatest achievement of the so-called ethnic revival of the 1960s and 1970s. Today, the defining American experience is seen as much to lie in immigration and its aftermath as in the eighteenth-century overthrow of the colonial yoke. This redefinition is quite visible in public symbols; for instance, the emergence and popularity on the national scene of such ethnic politicians as Mario Cuomo, Michael Dukakis, and Geraldine Ferraro, are assisted by their use of their family's recent immigration experience to validate their political personae. The redefinition is visible as well in the symbolism attached to the Statue of Liberty, as was seen in the pageantry of its 1986 centennial.

This conception of a European-American group that defines itself in terms of a history of immigration and mobility helps us to understand why ethnic identities are not disappearing to the same extent as more objective ethnic differences. Such identities are, in effect, claims of membership in this group, and they constitute assertions of participation in this history. Indeed, the point is not merely that ethnic identities are persisting beyond the life of the objective differences that once nurtured them, but it is rather that there is reason for them to persist, even if ethnic differences within the white population fade into oblivion. Identities that once separated the English, Irish, Italians, Jews, and Scots now bring individuals with these ancestries together, based on the putative memories of ancestors who contributed to this common history. Noteworthy in this respect is the desire of many of my respondents to trace their genealogical roots. For them, the sense of their ethnic background does not really extend beyond the history of their own family. That history, however, is not ethnically exclusive; it is something that can be appreciated by others from different ethnic backgrounds.

That membership in a European-American group is associated with a specific sense of social honor, the second essential feature of an ethnic group, should be obvious. The story of the immigrant ancestors of contemporary European Americans highlights heroic features of personal sacrifice for the sake of a better life for future generations and associates this sacrifice with the building of the nation; its moral claims are plain. (Whether it is true or false for specific families and groups is not at issue and can hardly be settled on the basis of historical evidence, in any event.) Moreover, by redefining the essential American experience, the historical account of this new group makes far more widely accessible the honor associated with an ethnically American identity. Relatively few Americans, after all, can lay claim to ethnic honor based on the participation of ancestors in the American Revolution or even the Civil War. But an honor that is defined in terms of the tribulations of the immigrant experience is open to all whites.

The European-American identity has not supplanted the older, unhyphenated American identity, but has emerged alongside it. Indeed, there may well be a degree of tension between the two, which surfaces especially at moments when the newer identity challenges the prestige of the older one (exemplified by the role of ethnic themes in the presidential elections of 1984 and 1988).[9] Some form of coexistence seems likely for the foreseeable future. Certainly, many respondents in our survey who trace their lineage primarily to old-stock groups claim no identity other than the American one. There may be little incentive for these individuals to identify with a specific European-ancestry label over the American one, especially when they know, or believe, that their family origins in the United States extend far back in time. But it seems an intriguing clue to shifting patterns of identification that individuals generally prefer to identify with an ethnic label when one side of their family arrived after 1800 and the other before. On this basis, it does not seem likely that the old-stock American identity will conquer the European-American one any time in the near future; if anything, further gain by the latter seems more likely.

The attractiveness of a European-American identity is also tied to the importance of ethnic interests in the political domain, broadly construed. By this I do not refer to any tendency of Americans of European ancestries to organize themselves politically along narrowly ethnic lines or to vote on such a basis; this tendency has been evident in the past and may still exist to a degree, although it is diminishing over time as ethnic communities decline among whites. The more significant political import comes in defining a prototypical American experience, against which non-European minority groups, some of long-standing on the American continent and others of recent vintage, are pressured to measure themselves. Since Americans of European ancestry constitute a numerical majority of the population and are superordinate to other ethnic groups, their view of their past is of considerable consequence for defining the nature of the American system—their justification of their superior position implied in the historical account of their ancestors' experiences amounts to a definition of "the rules of the game" by which other groups will be expected to succeed in American society. This point is echoed in the recent attempts by civil rights leaders, notably Jesse Jackson, to redefine blacks as "African-Americans."[10]

Moreover, at times of actual conflict over resources, whether these consist of neighborhoods, access to educational opportunities, or jobs, the European-American identity provides a way for whites to mobilize themselves, bridging what were once their own ethnic divisions, in opposition to the challenges of non-European groups. An attraction of finding common ground as European Americans is that it avoids the obvious pitfalls of a merely racial identity, as "whites." To give some examples, Jonathan Rieder (1985) found the Italians and Jews of Canarsie, Brooklyn, able to span a rather deep cultural gulf and cooperate in order to resist incursions by minorities. And Frederick Erickson (1975), studying interactions between counselors and students in a multiethnic, multiracial school system, discerned a tendency for these interactions to be influenced by "White Ethnic pan-ethnicity" (his terms). Noting that interactions proceeded more smoothly when a sense of ethnic solidarity existed between counselor and student, he observed that this solidarity could be evoked between participants of different European ethnicities but not between whites and non-whites.[11] In my own investigation of the conflict surrounding the open-admissions policy at the City University of New York (Lavin et al., 1981), a similar phenomenon was apparent. In a system strained by a policy intended to redress educational inequalities, white ethnics, principally Jews and Catholic ethnics, readily found commonalities that they did not share with those they perceived as newcomers, chiefly blacks and Hispanics.

On a more general level, it is relevant that the contemporary account of the so-called white ethnic experience emerged into prominence during a period when the civil rights movement was most active and racial minorities were challenging in basic respects the fairness of the American system. The self-portrayal of the white ethnics was seen at the time as a response to the challenge and the competition posed by the civil rights movement, a response that legitimated the system under which even recently arrived European-ancestry groups, such as the Italians and Poles, had surmounted early obstacles to become increasingly affluent. Indeed, it seems quite inevitable that many whites would be stimulated to think about the relevance of their own ethnic history when confronted by a challenge cast in racial/ethnic terms and justified by the historical burdens borne by a specific group. The reply of many whites, especially of white ethnics who had only recently made it out of their own ghettoes, was: our groups too faced prejudice and discrimination; we haven't made it to the top of American society, either, as is shown by our sparse representation at elite levels; and it is not fair to change the rules in midstream, after we have committed ourselves to them. (This reply is on view in much of the literature on ethnicity among whites written during the 1970s; see, for example, Novak [1971] and Glazer [1975].) The thrust of European-American identity is to defend the individualistic view of the American system, because it portrays the system as open to those who are willing to work hard and pull themselves over barriers of poverty and discrimination. Recent attitudinal research (Kluegel and Smith, 1982; Kluegel, 1985) suggests that it is precisely this individualism that prevents many whites from sympathizing with the need for African Americans and other minorities to receive affirmative action in order to overcome institutional barriers to their advancement.

In the 1980s, the civil rights movement was not as successful as it was in the previous two decades, and the problems of blacks and some other minority groups revolve around the situation of an underclass that can hardly be viewed as competition for prosperous white ethnics (Wilson, 1987). But the account of European-American history that emerged during the 1960s and 1970s continues to have political and economic implications, for social differences defined on the basis of race and recent immigration retain a fundamental importance, profoundly affecting the life chances of the members of various ethnic and racial groups. The importance of ethnicity as a general feature of American society is reinforced by the recent arrival of immigrant groups from Asia, Latin America, and the Caribbean. Their arrival, which continues without any hint of ceasing or subsiding, signals that ethnic themes are not likely to fade anytime soon in the United States and hence encourages whites to define themselves in ethnic terms. But, equally important, it challenges whites to define the nature of the American system, to set the terms by which newer groups will be expected to attain success. Will these groups establish themselves in American society along the lines of previously arrived racial minorities, or will they follow in the pathways cleared by preceding European immigrant groups? The answer will be determined in part by their response to the self-legitimating historical account of the European Americans, which defines self-sacrifice by early generations on behalf of later ones and individual mobility, assisted perhaps by informal cooperation among the members of an ethnic group, as the American pattern of "making it."

In Conclusion

There is good reason to believe that ethnic identities will continue among Americans of European ancestries, even as they become increasingly detached from ethnic structures of any sort, which are slowly succumbing to the powerful, incessant tide of assimilation. Such ethnic identities fit well with the individualism of American life, and accordingly they will become increasingly personal in nature, largely creatures of individual inclinations and tastes rather than social attachments. Yet they also bring some benefits to those who possess them. In a society where racial cleavages remain profound and where ethnicity is revitalized by new, non-European immigrations, there are incentives to retain a specifically ethnic identity, even if it has little practical consequence in everyday life. In particular, ethnic identities have become ways of claiming to be American, and this is a profound change from the past. Ethnic identity can be a means of locating oneself and one's family against the panorama of American history, against the backdrop of what it means to be American. No longer, then, need there be any contradiction between being American and asserting an ethnic identity. Increasingly, they are accepted as the same thing. Therein lies the ultimate significance of the transformation of ethnicity for white Americans.

Appendix:
The Ethnic
Identity Survey

The ethnic identity survey, whose data inform this book throughout, was carried out between May 1984 and June 1985 as a random survey of residents of the counties of Albany, Rensselaer, Saratoga, and Schenectady counties, the heart of the metropolitan region around the capital of New York State. This appendix is intended to provide interested readers with technical details about the survey.

The universe of the study consists of noninstitutionalized, English-speaking individuals eighteen years of age and older. To survey this universe, a multistage, clustered sampling strategy was employed. First, 240 blocks were selected at random (with their probabilities of selection varying according to population size). Then, starting from a randomly chosen household on each block, interviews were attempted within three consecutive households; in each, one respondent was selected based on a random procedure applied to a household census. Substitutions for selected households could be made when housing units were vacant, or no one was found home after repeated attempts to make contact, or household members were out of the universe (or ill); in any of these events, interviewers were instructed to proceed to the next housing unit down the line. Within a household, however, no substitution could be made for the selected respondent.

The sample design allowed for a possible total of 720 interviews; 524 were actually completed. Table A.1 shows the dispositions of interviewing attempts. The overall completion rate for the survey was 68 percent, which is quite good, although somewhat below the completion rates achieved by premier survey organizations (for example, completion rates for NORC's General Social Survey are in the 70 to 79 percent range [Davis and Smith, 1988: Appendix A]). The refusal rate was 22 percent. The principal other source of nonresponse was the failure to find anyone at home (typically, after numerous attempts).

Interviews were conducted face to face. The interview schedule was complex, containing approximately three hundred questions that could potentially be asked of a respondent, although no respondent was asked all of the questions. (Because of its length, the complete questionnaire is not reprinted in this book, but it is available from the author on request.) The questions actually presented depended on a respondent's answers to specific guidepost questions;

Table A.1   Dispositions of interview attempts during survey

A. Housing units included in sample[a]	803	
B. vacant		26
C. language problem		5
D. Net sample (A−B−C)	772	
E. completed cases		524
F. refusals/break-offs		173
G. never home/not available during interview period		57
H. ill		8
I. other failures to complete		10
Response rate (E/D)	67.9%	
Refusal rate (F/D)	22.4%	

Note: The format of the table and calculation of survey rates largely follows the NORC General Social Survey Codebook (Davis and Smith, 1988: Appendix A).
[a] includes substitutions.

for example, the ethnic experiences were initially presented as a list (printed on a card; see table 3.1). Each experience indicated by a respondent was subsequently followed up with a series of questions about it. As a result, the length of the interviews generally varied directly with the degree of ethnic interest of the respondent and hence with the amount of detail he or she supplied. The median length was close to forty-five minutes. Only about 10 percent of the interviews were completed in thirty minutes or less, while at the other extreme 20 percent took more than one hour.

The interview mixed together open-ended questions with others having predetermined answer categories; for instance, the basic question about ethnic identity (see chapter 2) was open-ended, whereas the question about ethnicity's subjective importance had precoded categories. Since the interview was not intended to be qualitative, open-ended answers were generally limited to a few sentences (in some cases, only the key phrases were recorded). After the survey was completed, a great deal of effort had to be devoted to coding the open-ended questions in order to make their data amenable to quantitative analysis. I have also used some material from them in illustrative quotations (and taken the liberty of changing personal details to protect the privacy of respondents).

In general, interviewers found the respondents to be cooperative and understanding of the meaning of the questions. About 85 percent of respondents were scored as "very cooperative" by interviewers, with virtually all the rest marked as "somewhat cooperative." Only 1 percent were uncooperative. The comprehension of respondents was found to be "good" in 90 percent of cases, with most of the remainder graded as "fair." Just 1 percent of respondents were believed to have "poor" comprehension of the questions.

The Adequacy of the Sample

A comparison of sample characteristics to those of the population shows reasonable accuracy, along with some predictable biases. The comparison is presented in table A.2 for some variables that play a major role in the study and are present in census data.

First, the survey is not significantly different from the population in terms of both non-white and foreign-born proportions. Among native-born whites, however, some sample-population dif-

Table A.2 Comparison of the Capital Region
sample and population for selected variables

	Sample	Population
Non-white	4.2%	4.4%
Foreign born	8.0%	6.1%
Sex*		
male	41.1%	46.2%
female	58.9	53.8
Age*		
18–29	19.6%	28.7%
30–44	31.6	26.2
45–59	18.5	22.4
60 and older	30.3	22.7
Education*		
grammar	8.9%	10.7%
some high school	16.1	14.3
high school graduate	36.8	38.3
some college	15.9	18.7
college graduate	22.2	17.9

Note: Population characteristics have been computed for non-institutionalized persons aged eighteen and older from the 5% Public Use Sample (PUMS A) of the 1980 census. For variables marked with an asterisk, the sample-population comparison is for native-born, non-Hispanic whites.

ferences are revealed by sex, age, and education. As is true for many surveys, women, the elderly, and the highly educated are more likely to respond and hence are overrepresented; young adults, however, are underrepresented. (Some biases can also be found for variables that play no role in the study. For example, occupants of single-person households are overrepresented. This is partly a function of the sample's age distribution since the elderly are more likely to be found in such households, but it probably occurs also because people living alone have more free time and are more likely to welcome intrusions.)

The most extreme differences are in terms of age. In the sample, young adults are 9 percentage points below their level in the population, while persons sixty and older are 8 points above. Smaller, but still significant, are the differences by sex and education: in the sample, women are 5 percentage points above their level in the population, and college graduates are overrepresented by approximately the same amount.

These differences are not far from those found in surveys conducted by the best survey organizations; for example, in the most recent year of the General Social Survey, 56.5 percent of sampled native-born whites were female, according to my tabulations. This is just slightly below the female share of the ethnic identity survey. Also, in that year, young adults (ages eighteen to twenty-nine) were only 22.8 percent of the native-born white sample, whereas the elderly (ages sixty and older) were 29.5 percent. Again, these figures are very close to those in the Capital Region Survey.

There may even be a danger that the underrepresentation of young adults is exaggerated by the comparison in table A.2. The Capital Region has a large number of higher educational institutions, and accordingly a sizable fraction of its young-adult population is composed of college students. Because of their schedules, these students are often hard to pull into random surveys of the population. Since many of them are only temporary residents of the region, it is not clearly desirable that they be included.

Because of the numerous complications involved, I have not attempted any weighting scheme to correct for the biases (in this, I am not alone; the General Social Survey also does not employ weights to correct for sample bias [Davis and Smith, 1988: 502]). But even if these biases are understandable, the issue of their effect on the sample arises, since some conclusions are drawn directly from overall sample magnitudes. Determining the precise effects is very difficult, but my calculations indicate that they are quite small and therefore do not jeopardize the study's conclusions.

The potential effects on the ethnic experiences, of special interest because age directly affects a number of them (see chapters 3 and 4), are possibly complex and offsetting here. Because young adults tend to have more of these experiences, the direct effect of the age bias is to lower the apparent level of these experiences in the sample. Indirectly, however, it may raise this level, because the overrepresentation of the elderly implies more members of the early generations, who report more experiences. Further, the overrepresentation of women and the college educated also implies higher frequencies of some experiences.

Nevertheless, I have carried out a "worst-case" calculation, assuming that only the age bias is of concern. Reweighting the sample to match the age distribution in the 1980 census, I find only very small differences. To give examples in terms of the index of ethnic experiences, the percentage reporting 6 or more experiences goes from 23.1 in the sample to 24.6, whereas the percentage reporting none is changed from 25.9 in the sample to 24.1. Looking at specific ethnic experiences, I find that the magnitude of change by this adjustment is typically 1 or 2 percentage points. Since the adjustment overstates the degree of bias and corrects only for age, it is clear that the net effect of the biases is quite small. (Similar calculations to correct for any possible biases in sample estimates of ethnic identification and subjective importance of background also show very small effects.)

It is also possible to compare the sample to the population in terms of ethnic ancestry, since the 1980 census collected data for the first time about ancestry. But, because of methodological differences, such a comparison would not be informative at this point or reflect on the accuracy of the study. The significance of the methodological differences is discussed at some length in chapter 2, however.

Bibliography

Abramson, Harold. 1973. Ethnic diversity in Catholic America. New York: Wiley.

Alba, Richard. 1981. "The twilight of ethnicity among American Catholics of European ancestry," *Annals* 454 (March): 86–97.

_____. 1985a. Italian Americans: Into the twilight of ethnicity. Englewood Cliffs: Prentice-Hall.

_____. 1985b. "Interracial and interethnic marriage in the 1980 census," paper presented at the 1985 meetings of the American Sociological Association.

_____. 1987. "Interpreting the parameters of log-linear models," *Sociological Methods & Research* 16 (August): 45–77.

_____. 1988. "Cohorts and the dynamics of ethnic change," in Matilda White Riley, Bettina J. Huber, and Beth B. Hess (eds.), Social structures and human lives. Newbury Park: Sage.

Alba, Richard, and Mitchell Chamlin. 1983. "A preliminary examination of ethnic identification among whites," *American Sociological Review* 48 (April): 240–47.

Alba, Richard, and Reid Golden. 1986. "Patterns of ethnic marriage in the United States," *Social Forces* 65 (September): 202–23.

Aldrich, John, and Forrest Nelson. 1984. Linear probability, logit, and probit models. Beverly Hills: Sage.

Archdeacon, Thomas. 1985. "Problems and possibilities in the study of American immigration and ethnic history," *International Migration Review* 19 (Spring): 112–34.

Banton, Michael. 1983. Racial and ethnic competition. Cambridge: Cambridge University Press.

Barth, Frederik. 1969. Ethnic groups and boundaries. Boston: Little, Brown.

Bean, Frank, and Marta Tienda. 1987. The Hispanic population of the United States. New York: Russell Sage Foundation.

Bell, Daniel. 1975. "Ethnicity and social change," in Nathan Glazer and Daniel P. Moynihan (eds.), Ethnicity: Theory and experience. Cambridge: Harvard University Press.

Bellah, Robert, Richard Madsen, William Sullivan, Ann Swidler, and Steven Tipton. 1985. Habits of the heart: Individualism and commitment in American life. Berkeley: University of California Press.

Blalock, Hubert, Jr. 1979. Social statistics, rev. 2d ed. New York: McGraw-Hill.

Blau, Peter. 1977. Inequality and heterogeneity: A primitive theory of social structure. New York: The Free Press.

Blau, Peter, Terry Blum, and Joseph Schwartz. 1982. "Heterogeneity and intermarriage," *American Sociological Review* 47 (February): 45–62.

Bourdieu, Pierre. 1984. Distinction: A social critique of the judgement of taste. Cambridge: Harvard University Press.

Breton, Raymond. 1964. "Institutional completeness of ethnic communities and the personal relations of immigrants," *American Journal of Sociology* 70: 193–205.

Cohen, Steven. 1983. American modernity and Jewish identity. New York and London: Tavistock.

———. 1987. "Reason for optimism," in Steven Cohen and Charles Liebman, The quality of American Jewish life—Two views. New York: American Jewish Committee.

Coles, Robert. 1971. The middle Americans. Boston: Little, Brown.

Cornell, Stephen. 1988. "Interests, institutions, culture: On structure and content in ethnic processes," Harvard University, unpublished manuscript.

Cortese, Charles, R. Frank Falk, and Jack Cohen. 1976. "Further considerations on the methodological analysis of segregation indices," *American Sociological Review* 61 (August): 630–37.

Crispino, James. 1980. The assimilation of ethnic groups: The Italian case. Staten Island: Center for Migration Studies.

Davis, James, and Tom Smith. 1988. General social surveys: Cumulative codebook, 1972–1988. Chicago: National Opinion Research Center.

De Vaus, David, and Ian McAllister. 1987. "Gender differences in religion: A test of the structural location theory," *American Sociological Review* 52 (August): 472–81.

De Vos, George, and Lola Romanucci-Ross. 1975. Ethnic identity: Cultural continuities and change. Palo Alto: Mayfield.

di Leonardo, Micaela. 1987. "The female world of cards and holidays: Women, families and the work of kinship," *Signs: Journal of Women in Culture and Society* 12 (Spring): 440–58.

Dillard, J. L. 1976. American talk: Where our words came from. New York: Random House.

DiMaggio, Paul. 1987. "Classification in art," *American Sociological Review* 52 (August): 440–55.

DiMaggio, Paul, and John Mohr. 1985. "Cultural capital, educational attainment, and marital selection," *American Journal of Sociology* 90 (May): 1231–61.

Elias, Norbert. [1939] 1978. The history of manners (The civilizing process, vol. 1). New York: Pantheon.

Erickson, Frederick. 1975. "Gatekeeping and the melting pot: Interaction in counseling encounters," *Harvard Educational Review* 45 (February): 44–70.

Erikson, Erik H. [1959] 1980. Identity and the life cycle. New York: W. W. Norton.

Esser, Hartmut. 1988. "Ethnische Differenzierung und moderne Gesellschaft," *Zeitschrift fuer Soziologie* 17 (June): 235–48.

Farley, Reynolds. 1984. Blacks and whites: Narrowing the gap? Cambridge: Harvard University Press.

Femminella, Francis. 1983. "The ethnic ideological themes of Italian Americans," in Richard Juliani (ed.), The family and community life of Italian Americans. Staten Island: Italian American Historical Association.

Femminella, Francis, and Jill Quadagno. 1976. "The Italian American family," in Charles Mindell and Robert Haberstein (eds.), Ethnic families in America: Patterns and variations. New York: Elsevier.

Ferdman, Bernardo. 1989. "Person perception in interethnic situations," unpublished manuscript, Department of Psychology, SUNY-Albany.

Fischer, Claude. 1975. "Toward a subcultural theory of urbanism," *American Journal of Sociology* 80 (May): 1319–41.

_____. 1982. To dwell among friends: Personal networks in town and city. Chicago: University of Chicago Press.

Fishman, Joshua, V. Nahirny, J. Hoffman, and R. Hayden. 1966. Language loyalty in the United States. The Hague: Mouton.

Fishman, Joshua, et al. 1985. The rise and fall of the ethnic revival. Berlin: Mouton.

FitzGerald, Frances. 1979. America revised: History schoolbooks in the twentieth century. Boston: Little, Brown.

Gambino, Richard. 1974. Blood of my blood. Garden City, N.Y.: Doubleday.

Gans, Herbert. [1962] 1982. The urban villagers: Group and class in the life of Italian-Americans. New York: The Free Press.

_____. 1979. "Symbolic ethnicity: The future of ethnic groups and cultures in America," *Ethnic and Racial Studies* 2 (January): 1–20.

_____. 1988. Middle American individualism: The future of liberal democracy. New York: Free Press.

Gecas, Viktor. 1982. "The self-concept," *Annual Review of Sociology* 8: 1–33.

Glazer, Nathan. 1954. "Ethnic groups in America: From national culture to ideology," in Morroe Berger, Theodore Abel, and Charles H. Page (eds.), Freedom and control in modern society. New York: D. Van Nostrand.

_____. 1975. Affirmative discrimination: Ethnic inequality and public policy. New York: Basic Books.

Glazer, Nathan, and Daniel P. Moynihan. 1970. Beyond the melting pot: The Negroes, Puerto Ricans, Jews, Italians, and Irish of New York City, 2d ed. Cambridge: MIT Press.

_____. 1975. "Introduction," in Nathan Glazer and Daniel P. Moynihan (eds.), Ethnicity: Theory and experience. Cambridge: Harvard University Press.

Goode, Judith G., Karen Curtis, and Janet Theophanos. 1984. "Meal formats, meal cycles, and menu negotiation in the maintenance of an Italian-American community," in Mary Douglas (ed.), Food in the social order: Studies of food and festivities in three American communities. New York: Russell Sage Foundation.

Gordon, Milton M. 1964. Assimilation in American life: the role of race, religion, and national origins. New York: Oxford University Press.

Granovetter, Mark. 1973. "The strength of weak ties," *American Journal of Sociology* 78 (May): 1360–80.

Greeley, Andrew. 1971. Why can't they be like us? New York: Dutton.

_____. 1972. That most distressful nation. Chicago: Quadrangle Books.

_____. 1977. The American Catholic: A social portrait. New York: Basic Books.

Greeley, Andrew, and William McCready. 1975. "The transmission of cultural heritages: The case of the Irish and Italians," in Nathan Glazer and Daniel Patrick Moynihan (eds.), Ethnicity: Theory and experience. Cambridge: Harvard University Press.

Hansen, Marcus L. 1938. The problem of the third generation immigrant. Rock Island, Ill.: Augustana Historical Society.

Hechter, Michael. 1978. "Group formation and the cultural division of labor," *American Journal of Sociology* 84: 293–319.

_____. 1987. Principles of group solidarity. Berkeley: University of California Press.

Herberg, Will. 1960. Protestant-Catholic-Jew. New York: Anchor.

Hirschman, Charles. 1983. "America's melting pot reconsidered," *Annual Review of Sociology* 9: 397–423.

Hirschman, Charles, and Morrison Wong. 1986. "The extraordinary educational attainment of Asian-Americans: A search for historical evidence and explanations," *Social Forces* 65 (September): 1–27.

Isaacs, Harold R. 1975. "Basic group identity: Idols of the tribe," in Nathan Glazer and Daniel P. Moynihan (eds.), Ethnicity: Theory and experience. Cambridge: Harvard University Press.

Kennedy, Ruby Jo Reeves. 1944. "Single or triple melting pot? Intermarriage trends in New Haven, 1870–1940," *American Journal of Sociology* 49 (January): 331–39.

Kluegel, James. 1985. "'If there isn't a problem, you don't need a solution': The bases of contemporary affirmative-action attitudes," *American Behavioral Scientist* 28 (July-August): 761–84.

Kluegel, James, and Eliot Smith. 1982. "Whites' beliefs about blacks' opportunity," *American Sociological Review* 47 (September): 518–32.

Knoke, David, and Peter Burke. 1980. Log-linear models. Beverly Hills: Sage.

Kornblum, William. 1974. Blue collar community. Chicago: University of Chicago Press.

LaGumina, Salvatore. 1989. From steerage to suburb: Long Island Italians. Staten Island: Center for Migration Studies.

Lavin, David, Richard Alba, and Richard Silberstein. 1981. Right versus privilege: The open admissions experiment at the City University of New York. New York: Free Press.

Lees, Lynn Hollen. 1979. Exiles of Erin: Irish migrants in Victorian London. Ithaca: Cornell University Press.

Lieberson, Stanley. 1963. Ethnic patterns in American cities. New York: Free Press.

―――. 1980. A piece of the pie: Blacks and white immigrants since 1880. Berkeley: University of California Press.

―――. 1985. "Unhyphenated whites in the United States," *Ethnic and Racial Studies* 8 (January): 159–80.

Lieberson, Stanley, and Donna Carter. 1982. "Temporal change and urban differences in residential segregation: A reconsideration," *American Journal of Sociology* 88 (September): 296–310.

Lieberson, Stanley, and Mary Waters. 1985. "Ethnic mixtures in the United States," *Sociology and Social Research* 70 (October): 43–51.

―――. 1986. "Ethnic groups in flux: The changing ethnic responses of American whites," *Annals*, no. 487 (September): 79–91.

―――. 1987. "The location of ethnic and racial groups in the United States," *Sociological Forum* 2 (Fall, 1987): 780–810.

―――. 1988. From many strands: Ethnic and racial groups in contemporary America. New York: Russell Sage Foundation.

Lyman, Stanford M., and William A. Douglas. 1973. "Ethnicity: Strategies of collective and individual impression management," *Social Research* 40 (Summer): 344–65.

Mangione, Jerre. [1942] 1981. Mount Allegro: A memoir of Italian American life. New York: Columbia University Press.

Marsden, Peter. 1987. "Core discussion networks of Americans," *American Sociological Review* 25 (February): 122–31.

Martinelli, Phylis. 1986. "A test of the McKay and Lewins ethnic typology," *Ethnic and Racial Studies* 9 (April): 196–209.

Massey, Douglas. 1985. "Ethnic residential segregation: A theoretical synthesis and empirical review," *Sociology and Social Research* 69: 315–50.

Massey, Douglas, and Nancy Denton. 1987. "Trends in the residential segregation of blacks, Hispanics, and Asians: 1970–1980," *American Sociological Review* 52 (December): 802–25.

McAdams, Doug. 1986. "Recruitment to high-risk activism," *American Journal of Sociology* 92 (July): 64–90.

McEneny, John. 1981. Albany: Capital city on the Hudson. Albany: Albany Institute of History and Art.

McGoldrick, Monica. 1982. "Ethnicity and family therapy: An overview," in Monica McGoldrick, John Pearce, and Joseph Giordano (eds.), Ethnicity and family therapy. New York: Guilford Press.

McGuire, William J., Claire V. McGuire, Pamela Child, and Terry Fujioka. 1978. "Salience of ethnicity in the spontaneous self-concept as a function of one's ethnic distinctiveness in the social environment," *Journal of Personality and Social Psychology* 36 (May): 511–20.

McKay, James, and Frank Lewins. 1978. "Ethnicity and ethnic group: A conceptual analysis and reformulation," *Ethnic and Racial Studies* 1 (October): 412–26.

Merton, Robert K. 1968. "Continuities in the theory of reference groups and social structure," in Robert K. Merton, Social theory and social structure. New York: Free Press.

———. [1941] 1976. "Intermarriage and the social structure," in Robert K. Merton, Sociological ambivalence and other essays. New York: Free Press.

Model, Suzanne. 1988. "The economic progress of European and East Asian Americans," *Annual Review of Sociology* 14: 363–80.

Morawska, Ewa. 1985. For bread with butter: Life-worlds of East Central Europeans in Johnstown, Pennsylvania, 1890–1940. Cambridge: Cambridge University Press.

Nee, Victor, and Jimy Sanders. 1985. "The road to parity: Determinants of the socioeconomic achievements of Asian Americans," *Ethnic and Racial Studies* 8: 75–93.

Neidert, Lisa J., and Reynolds Farley. 1985. "Assimilation in the United States: An analysis of ethnic and generation differences in status and achievement," *American Sociological Review* 50 (December): 840–50.

Nielsen, Francois. 1985. "Toward a theory of ethnic solidarity in modern societies," *American Sociological Review* 50 (April): 133–49.

Novak, Michael. 1971. The rise of the unmeltable ethnics. New York: Macmillan.

Olzak, Susan. 1983. "Contemporary ethnic mobilization," *Annual Review of Sociology* 9: 355–74.

Peach, Ceri. 1980. "Which triple melting pot? A re-examination of ethnic intermarriage in New Haven, 1900–1950," *Ethnic and Racial Studies* 3 (January): 1–16.

Petersen, William. 1979. "Ethnicity in the world today," in William Petersen (ed.), The background to ethnic conflict. Leiden: E. J. Brill.

Plotnikov, Leonard, and M. Silverman. 1978. "Jewish ethnic signalling: Social bonding in contemporary American society," *Ethnology* 17: 407–23.

Portes, Alejandro, and Robert Bach. 1985. Latin journey: Cuban and Mexican immigrants in the United States. Berkeley: University of California.

Rieder, Jonathan. 1985. Canarsie: The Jews and Italians of Brooklyn against liberalism. Cambridge: Harvard University Press.

Roche, John. 1982. "Suburban ethnicity: Ethnic attitudes and ethnic behavior among Italian Americans in two Rhode Island suburban communities," *Social Science Quarterly* 63:145–53.

Rockwell, John. 1984. Sinatra: An American classic. New York: Rolling Stone Press.

Rose, Peter. 1981. They and we: Racial and ethnic relations in the United States, 3d ed. New York: Random House.

Rosenberg, Morris. 1979. Conceiving the self. New York: Basic Books.

Rosenthal, Eric. 1975. "The equivalence of United States census data for persons of Russian stock or descent with American Jews: An evaluation," *Demography* 12 (May): 275–90.

Sandberg, Neil. 1973. Ethnic identity and assimilation: The Polish community. New York: Praeger.

Sanders, Jimy, and Victor Nee. 1987. "Limits of solidarity in the ethnic economy," *American Sociological Review* 52 (December): 745–67.

Sartre, Jean-Paul. 1948. Anti-Semite and Jew. New York: Grove Press.

Schooler, Carmi. 1976. "Serfdom's legacy: An ethnic continuum," *American Journal of Sociology* 81 (May): 1265–86.

Schuman, Howard, Charlotte Steeh, and Lawrence Bobo. 1985. Racial attitudes in America: Trends and interpretations. Cambridge: Harvard University Press.

See, Katherine O'Sullivan, and William J. Wilson. 1988. "Race and ethnicity," in Neil Smelser (ed.), Handbook of sociology. Beverly Hills: Sage.

Silberman, Charles. 1985. A certain people: American Jews and their lives today. New York: Summit Books.

Snipp, C. Matthew. 1986. "Who are American Indians? Some observations about the perils and pitfalls of data for race and ethnicity," *Population Research and Policy Review* 5: 237–52.

Spear, Allan. 1967. Black Chicago: The making of a Negro ghetto, 1890–1920. Chicago: University of Chicago.

Stack, Carol. 1974. All our kin: Strategies for survival in a black community. New York: Harper.

Stearns, Linda, and John Logan. 1986. "Measuring trends in segregation: Three dimensions, three measures," *Urban Affairs Quarterly* 22 (September): 124–50.

Stein, Howard, and Robert Hill. 1977. The ethnic imperative: Examining the new white ethnic movement. University Park: Pennsylvania State University Press.

Steinberg, Stephen. 1974. The academic melting pot. New York: McGraw-Hill.

_____. 1981. The ethnic myth: Race, ethnicity, and class in America. Boston: Beacon.

Stevens, Gillian. 1985. "Nativity, intermarriage, and mother-tongue shift," *American Sociological Review* 50 (February):74–83.

Stone, Elizabeth. 1988. "Stories make a family," *The New York Times Magazine* (January 24).

Stryker, Sheldon. 1968. "Identity salience and role performance: The relevance of symbolic interaction theory for family research," *Journal of Marriage and the Family* 30: 558–64.

Suttles, Gerald. 1968. The social order of the slum. Chicago: University of Chicago Press.

Taeuber, Karl, and Alma Taeuber. 1965. Negroes in cities: Residential segregation and neighborhood change. Chicago: Aldine.

Tajfel, Henri. 1981. Human groups and social categories. Cambridge: Cambridge University Press.

Tomaskovic-Devey, Barbara, and Donald Tomaskovic-Devey. 1988. "The social structural determinants of ethnic group behavior: Single ancestry rates among four white American ethnic groups," *American Sociological Review* 53 (August): 650–59.

U.S. Bureau of the Census. 1982. 1980 census of population and housing: User's guide, part A. Washington, D.C.: U.S. Government Printing Office.

_____. 1983a. Census tracts: Albany-Schenectady-Troy, N.Y. Washington, D.C.: U.S. Government Printing Office.

_____. 1983b. General social and economic characteristics: U.S. summary. Washington, D.C.: U.S. Government Printing Office.

_____. 1983c. Ancestry of the population by state: 1980. Washington, D.C.: U.S. Government Printing Office.

van den Berghe, Pierre. 1984. "Ethnic cuisine: Culture in nature," *Ethnic and Racial Studies* 3 (July): 387–97.

Veltman, Calvin. 1983. Language shift in the United States. Berlin: Mouton.

Waldinger, Roger. 1986. Through the eye of the needle: Immigrants and enterprise in New York's garment trades. New York: New York University Press.

Waters, Mary. 1987. "The construction of symbolic ethnicity: Sub-urban white ethnics in the 1980s," paper presented at the Hofstra University Conference on Immigration and Ethnicity.

———. 1990. Ethnic options: Later generation ethnicity in America. Berkeley: University of California Press.

Weber, Max. [1922] 1968. Economy and society. New York: Bed-minster Press.

Wellman, Barry. 1985. "Domestic work, paid work, and net work," in Steve Duck and Daniel Perlman (eds.), Understanding personal relationships. London: Sage.

Wilson, William J. 1987. The truly disadvantaged: The inner city, the underclass, and public policy. Chicago: University of Chicago Press.

Yancey, William, Eugene Ericksen, and Richard Juliani. 1976. "Emergent ethnicity: A review and a reformulation," *American Sociological Review* 41 (June): 391–403.

Yancey, William, Eugene Ericksen, and George Leon. 1985. "The structure of pluralism: 'We're all Italian around here, aren't we, Mrs. O'Brien?,' " *Ethnic and Racial Studies* 8 (January): 94–116.

Yans-McLaughlin, Virginia. 1977. Family and community: Italian immigrants in Buffalo, 1880–1930. Ithaca: Cornell University Press.

Yinger, Milton J. 1981. "Toward a theory of assimilation and dis-similation," *Ethnic and Racial Studies* 4 (July): 249–64.

———. 1985. "Intersecting strands in the theorization of race and ethnic relations," in John Rex and David Mason (eds.), Theories of race and ethnic relations. Cambridge: Cambridge University Press.

Zunz, Olivier. 1982. The changing face of inequality: Urbanization, industrial development, and immigrants in Detroit, 1880–1920. Chicago: University of Chicago Press.

Notes

CHAPTER ONE: The Transformation of Ethnicity

1. The notion of a third-generation "return" to ethnicity dates to the work of the Swedish-American historian, Marcus Hansen (1938). Although evidence for such a return has always been lacking, the popularity of the idea has never waned; and, in one form or another, it has influenced much of the writing about the so-called ethnic revival in the United States. The conviction that this revival among whites has been stimulated by emulation of the black civil rights movement, as well as the increased competition with blacks the movement brought, is also widespread (see, for example, Glazer, 1975: chap. 5, and Rose, 1981: chap. 8).

2. These views are pervasive in the American literature on ethnicity and drew strength during the 1970s from a belief that a resurgence of ethnicity was occurring on a worldwide scale. See, for example, Glazer and Moynihan (1975) and Petersen (1979).

3. In sociology, this view was spread by the writing of Robert Park and W. Lloyd Warner in particular. In recent years, the classic treatment of assimilation is Milton Gordon's (1964), although he did not herald assimilation as an inevitable outcome in American society. (For a recent review of assimilation theory and research, see Hirschman, 1983.)

4. Even normally staid scholars joined in the attack on assimilation, sometimes abandoning any appearance of objectivity or distance from their subject. One of the sharpest and most influential diatribes came from Michael Novak, who writes in *The Rise of the Unmeltable Ethnics:* "The new

ethnic politics is a direct challenge to the WASP conception of America. It asserts that *groups* can structure the rules and goals and procedures of American life. It asserts that individuals, if they do not wish to, do not have to 'melt.' They do not have to submit themselves to atomization. 'Subcultures' are refusing to concede the legitimacy of one (modernized WASP) 'Superculture'" (Novak, 1971: 270). For an incisive critique of many of the assumptions undergirding the "new ethnicity" among scholars and other intellectuals, see Steinberg (1981).

5. Strictly speaking, the qualifier "non-Hispanic" is necessary here because Hispanics constitute a sizable, non-European portion of the white population; and my thesis applies specifically to individuals of European ancestry. Nevertheless, the descendants of European immigrants make up the great majority of the white population, and in the remainder of the book, I use the term "whites" as a convenient, brief way of referring to them.

6. In their article, Neidert and Farley pursue a conventional strategy in limiting their analysis of stratification patterns to males. This may understate some aspects of ethnic differences among whites and hence the extent of recent change, as the cohort differences to follow show.

7. The south-central-east European category in the table includes anyone with ancestry from the relevant groups, regardless of whether it is mixed with other kinds of ethnic ancestry (e.g., English). This definition is necessary in order to avoid an artificial truncation of this population, by excluding individuals whose mixed ancestries represent the outcomes of long-run processes of assimilation. The British group includes only individuals whose ancestry is entirely English, Scots, Welsh, or some combination of these. In addition, it is restricted to individuals whose parents were both born in the United States.

8. To demonstrate that the average levels of educational attainment are equal in quantitative terms does not, of course, exclude the possibility of differences in the quality of the colleges attended. Nonetheless, quantitative educational measures, e.g., years of education completed, have been shown to have very strong relationships to socioeconomic position in later adulthood, as measured by income and occupational prestige. Therefore, there can be little doubt that a convergence in quantitative level of education reflects meaningful social change.

Also, a comment needs to be made about the apparent decline in college completion between the 1931–45 and 1946–60 cohorts of men. The decline is almost certainly an artifact of the youthful age of many members of the later cohort, who were in their early twenties at the time of the survey and whose educations were therefore incomplete. In light of this fact, the rise of the percent completing college in the 1946–60 cohort of ethnic women looks all the more remarkable.

9. At least into college. My argument does not imply that families had no regard for the possible economic contributions of their daughters, but only that they almost certainly saw their sons' qualifications as much more determinative of their futures than was true for their daughters'.

10. Some observers see signs of a trend in the other direction, a re-

newed interest in ethnic languages, which is often claimed as an indicator of the ethnic revival (Fishman et al., 1985). More generally, one can ask whether school language instruction could reverse the downward trend in mother-tongue knowledge and exposure. But I find it highly unlikely that self-conscious efforts at language learning, often undertaken during adulthood and without many opportunities to use a language outside of the classroom, can be the equivalent of language absorption in a childhood home. Moreover, language learning in school has itself declined in recent decades, as a result of changing academic requirements. This too contributes to the decline in knowledge of mother tongues, since previous generations of students could study ethnic languages and thereby complement the imperfect knowledge they typically acquired at home.

11. This is not to deny that intermarriage has played an important role in American ethnic shifts since colonial times. Often quoted as evidence is the late-eighteenth-century statement of the French-born American, J. Hector St. John Crevecoeur, in answer to the question of who is an American: "I could point out to you a family whose grandfather was an Englishman, whose wife was Dutch, whose son married a French woman, and whose present four sons have now four wives of different nations. *He* is an American" (quoted by Gordon, 1964: 116).

12. An additional factor in the English case may be a tendency of many persons of mixed old-stock origins to simplify their ancestry by reporting English (or British) only (note the intriguing disparity between different counts of English-ancestry Americans, commented on by Lieberson and Waters, 1988: 37). This probably exaggerates the appearance of endogamy because of the commonness of marriages involving complex old-stock backgrounds.

13. For numerical reasons, the frequency of Protestant marriage with non-Protestants has not increased as dramatically. Since Protestants form a much larger group than either Catholics or Jews, a Protestant-Catholic or Protestant-Jewish marriage has less numerical impact on the Protestant group than it does on the Catholic or Jewish one. In fact, since Protestants represent about two-thirds of the nation's population, it is not numerically possible for a majority of them to marry non-Protestants, even if all Catholics and Jews marry outside their religious group.

14. The 1980 census question found a lower proportion of persons with mixed ancestry in the general population than did another census survey employing the same question—the November 1979 Current Population Survey. Unlike the decennial census, which is conducted mostly by mail questionnaire, the Current Population Survey was executed through face-to-face interviews, which may encourage respondents to answer ancestry questions more completely. In addition, the instructions to the 1980 census encourage respondents to give a single ethnic identification wherever possible (for a general discussion of the surveys, see Lieberson and Waters, 1988). Accordingly, evidence of ancestry truncation in the 1980 census abounds (see Lieberson and Waters, 1986).

15. This definition does not mean, of course, that members of an ethnic

group have a tendency for in-group interaction under all circumstances. Such tendencies are generally channeled in specific ways in a given ethnic setting. On group characteristics in general, see Robert K. Merton (1968); and for further discussion of the importance of the relational dimension of ethnicity, see Gordon (1964).

16. For other treatments of ethnic identity, see De Vos and Romanucci-Ross (1975) and Isaacs (1975).

17. Stein and Hill (1977), however, employ an Erikson-like analysis to critique what they call the "New Ethnicity" among whites.

18. The problematic nature of ethnic labels is not limited to persons of mixed ancestry, for there is no reason to assume a priori that persons of the same single ancestry identify themselves (if they identify at all) in consistent ways.

19. It should be noted that identification with U.S. origins, as an "American" only or some related label, also constitutes an ethnic identity (Lieberson, 1985). That is, labeling oneself in this way is tantamount to distinguishing oneself from those who describe themselves with nationality, religious, or racial labels and thus amounts to making an ethnic distinction. This sort of identity is described by Michael Banton (1983) as "minus one ethnicity."

20. The data for this paragraph are from the U.S. Bureau of the Census (1983a: Tables P-9 & P-10; 1983b: Tables 113–16).

CHAPTER TWO: Fundamentals of Ancestry and Identity

1. This is tantamount to saying that the analysis will be largely restricted to native- (or U.S.-) born whites in the Capital Region sample. Since Hispanics are but a tiny presence in the region, virtually all of its whites have some European ancestry and the great majority have only European ancestry (American Indian is the most common non-European ancestry). Because of the ethnic composition of the Capital Region, native-born whites make up a large majority (N = 460) of our survey sample.

2. Adding to the confusion is that, directly below the question, the census form supplied a list of examples (e.g., "Afro-Amer. [sic], English, French, German"), which suggests by implication that a single answer is desired. Lieberson and Waters (1988) provide a thorough analysis of census procedures for measuring ancestry. That mixed ancestry is found less frequently in the 1980 census than in some other surveys is easily demonstrated, but does not establish the validity of the other surveys. In the census, some 31 percent of Americans reported having ethnically mixed ancestry (U.S. Bureau of the Census, 1983c: 1). By comparison, the NORC General Social Survey typically finds that the proportion with mixed ancestry is between 35 and 45 percent (Davis and Smith, 1988: 62). This survey in many past years, however, has itself suffered from confusion between ancestry and identity.

3. The relatively few studies that we have of ethnic identity are mostly

confined to single ethnic groups and typically use questions attuned to the specifics of identity in the groups under study (e.g., Crispino, 1980; Cohen, 1983; Martinelli, 1986). It is therefore difficult to know how to generalize from such studies to the general population. Mary Waters (1990) provides one of the rare exceptions to this narrowly ethnic limitation. Her study, which is based on in-depth interviews with third- and fourth-generation Catholics and is largely qualitative, offers a useful complement to the findings presented here.

4. Throughout the book, I move between the first person singular and the first person plural as appropriate for the context. A plural pronoun is appropriate in discussing properties of the data set, such as question wording, since the data set design and collection were very much a collaborative effort. A singular one, on the other hand, is appropriate when the discussion concerns analysis of the data or interpretation, for which I bear the chief responsibility.

5. We also of course wanted to avoid a question that seemed to carry the unnecessary baggage of social science terminology—for example, "How do you identify yourself in ethnic terms?"

The identity question, incidentally, did not immediately follow the questions about ancestry. Questions about current religion and religion during childhood occurred in between. In a certain sense, then, the stage was set for the respondent to offer an ethnic identity cast either in ancestral or religious terms. Few chose the latter course.

6. There is an asymmetry in our questions about ancestry and identity. Ancestry is an objective matter, although perhaps imperfectly known and recalled by respondents. Thus, additional questions are simply an opportunity to get the record as complete as possible. Identity is a matter of self-concept and self-presentation, which may well change from situation to situation. Our main question is a test of the respondent's willingness to answer a rather indirect and therefore fairly innocuous question about identity, and can be seen as a test of willingness to give an ethnic response in a broad range of social situations.

7. One should always bear in mind the anachronism of many contemporary ethnic identities, which impose on the past ethnic definitions that would be repudiated by those who lived it. Identities we now take for granted—e.g., German—are historically recent creations, some even products of the last century or brought into being on American soil (Glazer, 1954). All of this is to say many of us do not know how immigrant grandparents or great-grandparents defined themselves, and if we could travel back in time, we might end up with quite different definitions of our ancestry.

8. The paragraph represents a summary of the results of a logistic regression analysis, which is not presented in the form of a table. The full list of variables considered in this and many other analyses will be presented shortly.

9. A brief comment needs to be made about significance tests. In

order to avoid interrupting the flow of the text with the results of significance tests, I have usually not reported them for relationships that are discussed but not separately presented in tables (such as the relationship between generation and ancestry mixture). The reader should rest assured that I have carried out the tests. I occasionally report their results where I think a question might be raised in the reader's mind. Otherwise, I discuss only relationships (or differences) that are statistically significant, except where specifically noted.

10. There are a few ancestry combinations that can in fact represent single ethnicities rather than mixtures—French with Canadian, and Scots with Irish. The French and Canadian combination is quite important in the Capital Region, which has a sizable population of French-Canadian stock, and for this reason, I have treated all occurrences of the French-Canadian combination as a single ethnic origin (labeled "French"). Individuals with this combination can, of course, still be classified as having mixed ancestry if their backgrounds include other ethnicities. The Scots-Irish combination can be more troublesome, in the sense that it can be difficult to decide in any individual case whether the ancestry represents a single group (the Scots-Irish, persons of Scots background who were transplanted to Ireland after English conquest of the island) or a mixture. The census and other widely known surveys with ethnic data treat such combinations as mixtures (Lieberson and Waters, 1988), and I have followed this convention. From an empirical point of view, this decision poses no threat to conclusions about mixed ancestry. There are just five persons in the survey who report only the Scots-Irish combination, and the mixed ancestry of four of them is demonstrated by the fact that their Irish and Scots ancestries are on different sides of their families.

11. Very simple models account for much of the relative frequency of ancestry combinations. As one test, I estimated a log-linear model in which the frequency of occurrence of any ancestry pairing (e.g., English-French) is treated as a function of the complexity of the ancestry in which it is found and the specific ancestries involved. This simple model, which assumes that ancestry pairings can be explained by group size and ancestry complexity (itself a function of generation), explains most of the variation in frequency.

12. Because American Indian ancestry is so extensively intermixed with other old-stock ancestries, I will regard it too as an old-stock background throughout the book. This characterization, it should be underlined, is only applied to this ancestry among whites.

13. Occasional exceptions were made when respondents' responses seemed so confused or uncertain that it appeared as if they had given little thought to questions about ethnic background and presented no consistent image of themselves.

14. Logistic regression analysis is appropriate here because of the dichotomous nature of the dependent variable (identifying in ethnic terms). Note that in the table the coefficients of categorical independent variables

result from so-called effect coding, which requires that coefficients sum to zero. A good introduction to logistic regression is provided by Aldrich and Nelson (1984). I have followed their lead for significance tests (see Aldrich and Nelson, 1984: 55–61). As they recommend, the overall chi-square goodness-of-fit test is a joint test of significance for all of the coefficients except the intercept. The BMD program PLR was used to carry out the analyses.

Since the results of such an analysis, presented in the form of changes to the logged odds of the dependent variable, can be very difficult to interpret, I have also translated them into percentage changes. But, for those unfamiliar with the properties of log-linear analyses, a warning must be given: the magnitudes of the percentage changes depend on the choice of a reference point (for more information about calculating percentage changes, see Alba, 1987), and therefore these magnitudes must not be reified. (Note, for instance, that positive and negative effects of the same magnitude translate asymmetrically into percentage changes, as the dichotomous independent variables show.) The reference point throughout this book for percentage calculations is always the overall mean of the dependent variable.

15. The statistically minded reader will note that I do not limit the discussion to results significant at the conventional level of significance (.05), but also use those significant at the .10 level (two-tailed). In fact, my departure from convention is not very great since a two-tailed test at the .10 level is equivalent to a one-tailed test at the .05 level, and a one-tailed test is justified much of the time because the results are in a predictable direction. In other words, it is generally appropriate to view the significance level as .05. In any event, a good case can be made for the .10 level here. Given the exploratory nature of the study and the relatively small number of cases (reduced even further by exclusions in some subsequent analyses), it is important to avoid as much as possible the error of overlooking possible relationships (in statistician's language, this is type II error, failing to reject a false null hypothesis). This dictates a more generous level of type I error.

16. The generational variable is defined based on the most recent immigration on either side of the family (for example, a respondent whose paternal grandparents and maternal great-grandparents were immigrants would be defined as a member of the third generation, based on the more recent immigration on the paternal side). This definition presumes that the generation variable should measure the possibility of contact with immigrants (on either side) or family members raised in immigrant homes.

There are some respondents who do not know the recency of immigration on one or both sides of their family. In some cases, this still leaves no ambiguity about their generational placement (e.g., an American-born respondent with an immigrant parent must belong to the second generation by the preceding definition, no matter how distant the immigration on the other side of the family). In other cases, generation cannot be deduced, and is labeled "unknown."

17. Education was selected over other measures of social class, such as

occupation and income, for practical as well as theoretical reasons. Using occupation would have led to difficulties for people not in the labor force, such as young people still in school, elderly persons, and many women. This would have forced an undesirable choice between excluding such persons and thus artificially truncating the analysis or substituting another family member's occupation where available. The income variable was also missing for a substantial number of cases (for a different reason: because of refusals to answer the question); using it would also have produced many exclusions and weakened the analysis. Education is not without a difficulty as well: the historical rise in educational attainment implies that specific levels of educational achievement have somewhat different meanings for persons born at different times (since it was harder, for example, to attend college for someone born during the 1930s than for someone born in the 1960s). But this is mitigated by the use of birth cohort as a control.

18. The question about proximity was, "Aside from the people living with you, do you have any immediate family—such as parents, children, brothers or sisters, or in-laws—living in this area, that is, within about an hour's drive of here?"

19. The analysis is limited to respondents who previously identified themselves in ethnic terms (N = 310, slightly reduced here by missing data).

20. As Paul DiMaggio has pointed out to me, an alternative explanation might be that the effect of education on identity represents defensive reactions on the part of upwardly mobile ethnics attempting to establish themselves in new and somewhat threatening environments. But if so, one would expect statistical interactions with variables such as generation, since these effects should be most pronounced among the second and third generations, who come from less prestigious ethnic backgrounds. The interactions do not exist, indicating that the effect is associated with education in general.

21. I am indebted to Paul DiMaggio for suggesting this apt term to me.

22. This is the first table in which significance test results appear. For two-variable tables in the rest of the book, I will report the significance level of the standard chi-square test. For three-variable tables such as this, the significance levels are obtained by log-linear methodology (Knoke and Burke, 1980). The significance of each independent variable is tested in a model containing the other.

23. We asked, "There are many ways that we reveal our ethnic backgrounds to others. Names are obviously important, but sometimes people indicate their backgrounds by ethnic decals on cars, or by observing certain holidays. What are the chief ways someone else would know your ethnic background?"

CHAPTER THREE: Cultural Expressions of Ethnic Identity

1. This approach, which originates with Frederik Barth (1969), has much to recommend it, but risks slighting the importance of some cultural distinctiveness for an ethnic group (Cornell, 1988).

2. Directly indicated in chapter 1 is a massive decline in childhood exposure to mother tongues; and implied by the dramatic changes in intermarriage and mixed ancestry is the reduction of gross differences in culture, which are incompatible with widespread relations of social intimacy that cross ethnic lines and also with the socialization of children within ethnically mixed family settings. But neither trend speaks to the possibility of muted cultural patterns that are still capable of signaling ethnic group membership and contributing to feelings of ethnic group solidarity.

3. For instance, John Rockwell's (1984) book on Frank Sinatra identifies some of the ethnic antecedents of Sinatra's singing style, which has deeply influenced American popular music, and J. L. Dillard (1976) describes immigrant and ethnic influences on the American language.

4. There appears to be some misreporting involved here, and this figure is modified in subsequent discussion of the experience.

5. The ethnic-enclave model (Portes and Bach, 1985; cf. Sanders and Nee, 1987), which holds that some immigrant groups advance socioeconomically through ethnically based enterprises drawing on common ethnic bonds shared by owners and workers, is but the latest version of the ethnic assistance scenario. Other writers (e.g., Lieberson, 1980; Waldinger, 1986) have also called attention to the importance of ethnic labor-market niches, i.e., jobs that are basically controlled by members of specific ethnic groups.

6. Given the popularity of an "American" identification in the nonidentifying group, one may wonder whether the experiences reported by it are frequently nonethnic (for example, citing American foods as ethnic ones). But, in general, it appears that the experiences are in fact related to respondents' ethnic backgrounds, rather than their nonethnic identifications. I draw this conclusion from a detailed examination of the specifics respondents described for us in detailing the nature of each experience.

7. In chapter 2, I also employed a measure of the personal meaningfulness of an ethnic identity, namely, whether the respondent qualified or disavowed an identity. It has been dropped from this and subsequent chapters because it is so closely linked, conceptually and empirically, to the salience of identity that it contributes little to the analysis. The salience measure appears to be the more general one.

8. In probing for more details of respondents' ethnic-food experiences, we began, "Which foods or dishes from your ethnic background do you eat?" (an open-ended question) and "How often do you eat them?" (a closed-ended one). Below, I report other question wordings when I think that they might contribute to the reader's understanding.

9. No doubt, this is helped by the general acceptability of Italian food to American tastes. A New York Times article (August 10, 1988) proclaims the "Italianization of America," albeit mostly in food terms, and notes that there were more than 5,000 Italian restaurants in the U.S. in 1987, an increase of more than 1,000 from 1985.

10. These figures may overstate slightly the frequency of consumption

of Italian food, since a few Italian food consumers eat dishes associated with other parts of their backgrounds as well, and the frequencies of the different ethnic cuisines cannot be separated in the data.

11. The prominence of Italians among strong identifiers with undivided ancestry and also among ethnic-food consumers contributes, of course, to these patterns, but they do not depend solely on this group. The patterns appear also when the Italians are excluded, although the overall frequencies of ethnic-food use are lower among non-Italians.

12. Persons with mixed ancestry are included in the endogamously married category when their spouse's ancestry is the same as their own (see chapter 5, where intermarriage is discussed in detail). This may seem a peculiar classification, but it still guarantees that the spouse's culinary heritages are the same as the respondent's, which is the issue.

13. Our question was, "Overall, how would you say that the ethnic dishes prepared in your home compare to those you remember from your childhood?" Responses were open-ended and were coded into three summary evaluations: worse, same, or better. To avoid confounding the comparisons to the cooking of an older generation with the evaluations of respondents who still live with their parents, the percentages reported in the text are limited to respondents who reported that they or their spouses do the preparation of ethnic foods.

14. Perhaps this oddity stems from an ambiguity in the description of the experience in the list we presented to respondents. Since that description did not exclude English as a mother tongue, it may be that persons with ancestry from the British Isles were encouraged to check the experience. At least, this explanation is suggested by the fact that such persons, and the Irish in particular, seem especially numerous among those claiming the experience but indicating no knowledge of a non-English mother tongue. The explanation, however, does not account for the surprisingly low level of mother-tongue use among persons claiming the experience, since the detailed data make clear that many people who checked the experience have some knowledge of a mother tongue but make no use of it.

15. Unfortunately, data are lacking in general about the extent of non-English languages among immigrants from the British Isles and their descendants. But Irish, Scots, and Welsh must have been known and used to some extent. Writing of Irish immigrants to London around 1850, a period when many were also coming to the United States, Lynn Lees (1979: 189) notes that "their Irish was said [by contemporary observers] to be better than their English," although "it is doubtful that it was used much outside the homes of the first generation."

16. One might question the inclusion of respondents with any degree of ancestry from the British Isles in this percentage. But elimination of these respondents biases the results by excluding persons whose mixed ancestry represents one outcome of the assimilation process (see chap.1, n. 7).

17. For descriptive purposes, the percentages reported here include respondents whose ancestry is entirely from the British Isles. Eliminating

them strengthens the relationships between mother-tongue knowledge and identity type and salience.

18. Our question was, "Do you ever use [name of language] at all in daily life?" This question immediately followed one about the respondent's ability to speak a mother tongue, and it was clearly understood to mean speech or conversation in an ethnic language.

19. Our question was, "Do you ever use words or phrases from these languages when you are having a conversation in English?"

20. In her study of suburban Catholic ethnics, Mary Waters (1990) also finds a great deal of confusion about ethnic customs. Asked for example to describe the wedding and funeral customs of the groups they identify with, respondents were quite uncertain what was ethnic and what was specific to their families, and ended up describing putative ethnic traits that varied little from group to group.

21. There is admittedly room for argument on this point because of the linkage of religion with some ethnic traditions (see, e.g., Abramson, 1973). Thus, for example, Irish Catholic respondents have perhaps a legitimate claim that Catholic practices are ethnic practices for them because of the close association of Irish ethnicity and the American Catholic Church (Greeley, 1972). But having examined all of the descriptions of cultural practices, I am convinced that uncertainty over the appropriate definition of ethnic cultural practices is the more important reason for the frequent citing of purely religious observances in this context.

22. There is some evidence that the popularity of these festivals is waning. Because of small crowds, summertime German, Irish, and Italian festivals held at the Empire State Plaza, a centrally located site in Albany, were discontinued in the late 1980s. Organizers of the festivals were encouraged by state government, owner of the mall, to band together into a multiethnic festival, according to the *Albany Times-Union* (May 1, 1988).

23. Since the dependent variables, the various cultural indicators, are not scales, they were analyzed as a series of dichotomies; for example, the food indicators were analyzed as: eating ethnic foods at all (versus not eating them); eating them at home (versus not eating them at all or eating them only outside the home); eating them at least once a month (versus eating them less frequently or not at all); and eating them on special occasions (versus no such use). For such contrasts, logistic regression is the appropriate type of multivariate analysis.

Each equation contained the same set of basic variables, and additional variables could be included when they were significant. The basic set included ethnic identity status, the subjective importance of ethnic background, and major demographic and socioeconomic variables—to wit, generation, age, confidence in ancestry knowledge, education, and gender. These last variables, with the exception of gender, obviously reflect the transformation of ethnicity. The additional variables, appearing only in equations where they are significant, included living with parents, living near relatives, and growing up in a rural area, and a statistical interaction between identity status and subjective importance (whose function is discussed later in the text). All of the language equations include a term to take into account the low probability of mother-tongue knowledge and use among persons whose ancestry is solely from the British Isles.

Respondents who do not know their ancestry were omitted from the equations. Since their levels of ethnic experience are quite low, their inclusion as a separate category of identity status made its coefficients unstable in some cases. Hence, they were dropped consistently.

24. This percentage difference is calculated by the same method used in chapter 2 (for further details, see Alba, 1987).

25. Mary Waters (1987) points out, based on studies of ethnic identity in California and Philadelphia, that some of her young respondents indicated learning about ethnicity from reports that were prepared for school. Presumably, this reflects the introduction of ethnicity into school curricula during the 1960s and 1970s, following the abandonment of the melting pot view of American society.

26. These categories are the ones reported by respondents, even in the cases of respondents who did not identify ethnically and therefore may have been evaluating the American, or some other nonethnic, identity. Despite the error involved in retaining such original responses, there is no practical alternative. Some of the nonidentifying respondents did appear to answer the question on importance in terms of their ethnic background, while others did not; it is not possible to separate these two groups cleanly, and in any event we cannot know how the second group of respondents would have answered the question had they been thinking in terms of ethnic background. Alternatively, dropping many nonidentifiers from the analysis would defeat one of its main purposes—to investigate further the relationship between identity and experience. The most practical strategy for addressing this heterogeneity, given data limits, is to include an identity-importance interaction, which allows subjective importance to have a different slope among identifiers than among nonidentifiers. But this strategy is still not very effective: although an interaction was tested in every equation, it is only occasionally significant. The heterogeneity in the subjective importance variable undoubtedly means that the analyses yield a conservative estimate of its role. Moreover, since this variable emerges as the most consistently strong predictor throughout, it is reasonable to conclude that its true association with ethnic experience is very robust.

One other data problem was that for a small number of cases, values for the subjective importance are missing due to a flaw in the questionnaire design and were assigned for the analysis. This happened when respondents could give no answer *at all* to the basic identity question (saying, e.g., "I don't know" or "I am never asked that question"); in this situation, they were not asked the follow-up question about how important they felt their ethnic background to be. But dropping these nonidentifying respondents from the analysis seemed quite undesirable, because in general their characteristics are very nonethnic (shown by detailed analysis); therefore they were assigned to the "not important" category, a decision that seems reasonable based on their lack of interest in ethnicity and their overall similarity to the members of this category. The number of respondents affected by this decision is about twenty.

27. The interaction is created by multiplying a variable representing ethnic identity status (1 if the respondent identifies in ethnic terms, and -1 otherwise) by the subjective importance variable. Thus, for ethnically identifying respondents in the equation for eating ethnic foods (in table 3.10), the slope of subjective importance is actually .683 (i.e., .262 + .421). For nonidentifying respondents on the other hand, the slope is $-.159$ (i.e., .262 $-$ .421), which is surely not significantly different from zero.

28. The variance of a dichotomous variable is given by the formula $p(1 - p)$, and is larger as p, the proportionate frequency of the variable, is closer to .5.

29. There is an ambiguity here, for unfortunately the questionnaire did not ask for the language or languages in the case where a respondent reported only knowledge of words and phrases. Thus, the figure in the text possibly overstates knowledge of Italian, since some of those of mixed Italian ancestry may not know Italian words but those from some other ancestral language. But this error is not likely to affect the *relative* comparison among ancestry groups, in which Italian clearly stands out.

CHAPTER FOUR: Ethnicity's Shadow in Social Experience

1. As this book is being written, four white youths are on trial for beating three black men, and causing the death of one of them, in the Howard Beach section of Queens, New York. The only offense of the victims was to have gotten out of their disabled car at night in a largely white area.

2. This aspect of ethnicity is discussed at length in chapter 1. I note again that a tendency to interact with fellow group members is a feature of any social group, not just of an ethnic group (Merton, 1968).

3. This information emerged from our follow-up questions concerning the experience of curiosity about ethnicity. We said to respondents, "You mentioned feeling curious about the ethnic backgrounds of people you know. How often would you say you feel this—all the time, often, occasionally, or hardly ever?" We also inquired, "Do you ever ask people directly about their ethnic background?" following up this question with one about the frequency with which this happens.

4. We asked respondents who discussed their backgrounds, "Could you tell me more precisely what you talk about?" The question was open-ended, and interviewers copied down what was said to them.

5. We asked respondents with this experience, "What specific things about this person (or persons) made you especially feel this sense of shared background?" These respondents were also asked, "Of the people you now consider as your friends, with how many do you have this special sense of shared ethnic background?"

6. In each case, a global comparison between the identifying and non-identifying groups by z-test (for the percentage difference between two groups) shows significance levels below those reported in table 4.2. For instance, the z-value for the percentage feeling curious is 2.42 (p < .02), and that for feeling a special sense of relationship is 2.90 (p < .01).

7. Despite the insignificance of the relationships in table 4.3, a z-test shows that persons with the most intense identities are significantly different from everyone else (z = 3.13, p < .01).

8. In addition to the dependent variables in the table, I considered the variables: curious often or a lot (versus all others); asks about others' backgrounds; has three or more ethnic friends; and discusses own background sometimes or a lot. In general, the patterns for these other variables are quite similar to those reported in the tables and discussed in the text.

9. In the logistic regressions, the subjective importance variable includes the responses of nonidentifiers, some of whom were evaluating nonethnic identities (such as being "American" or "Catholic"). Even though their inclusion confounds the variable somewhat, it is not possible to "correct" the evaluations of nonidentifiers. The result is probably a conservative estimate of the effect of subjective importance (see chap. 3, n. 26).

10. This implication is evident in the justifications that undergirded the use of quotas to limit the number of Jewish students at Harvard during the 1920s (Steinberg, 1974). Jewish academic success was perceived in terms of damning character traits, which were then used as "tests" to limit the number of Jewish entrants.

11. We asked respondents who encountered stereotypes, "Do you think that some of those stereotypes are in fact true?" and "Do you think that some of them are true of you?"

12. We asked, "Do you ever find that other people expect you to behave according to the stereotypes?" and if the answer was positive, "How often does this happen—all the time, often, occasionally, or hardly ever?"

13. Our questions were worded: "How much discrimination is there today against people with your ethnic background? Would you say that there is a great deal, some, a little, or none?" and "Do you think that the discrimination against people with your ethnic background is less today than in the past? Would you say that it is much less, somewhat less, about the same, somewhat more, or much more?"

14. Regrettably, the time reference was not more specific. What constitutes the "past" undoubtedly differs among respondents—almost certainly, between older and younger respondents. But the uniformity of responses probably guarantees that the sense of a trend is captured, even if the time points involved are ambiguous.

15. Moreover, this high level may be a bit misleading. The category in question includes a small number of respondents who identify ethnically as Jews. They are classified as having mixed ancestry on the basis of the countries of origin of their ancestors, but probably most of them have unmixed ancestry when viewed in terms of the Jewish ethnic group (unfortunately,

the ancestry data cannot reveal this). Since Jews have higher levels of experience with prejudice and discrimination than other whites, their presence raises the overall levels in this category, even though most of the Jewish respondents could equally well be placed in a single-ancestry category. Without the Jewish respondents, the level of encounter with stereotypes falls to 33 percent among persons of mixed ancestry who identify with a single group—still higher than in the other categories of ethnic identity status.

16. The comparison between ethnic identifiers who feel strongly about their background and all other whites is statistically significant ($z = 2.54$, $p < .02$).

17. This statement may seem an inaccurate characterization for the personal experience with discrimination, but this experience is so rare that one has to proceed cautiously in drawing conclusions from relatively small shifts among the logit coefficients. These make clear that the principal contrast occurs between the fourth and other generations.

18. Although the Jewish group has been overlooked in the discussion up to this point—because the small number of Jews in our data make the characteristics of the group difficult to establish with any degree of statistical confidence—it cannot be neglected in the discussion of prejudice and discrimination because of its unique degree of experience with these. For purposes of reporting in the text, the Jewish group is defined on the basis of religious upbringing, not ancestry as such. In the Capital Region sample, virtually all who were raised as Jewish regard themselves as Jewish by religion, and most identify ethnically as Jews.

19. Jews of Polish ancestry are excluded from this percentage, since the discrimination they have suffered is covered under that of the Jewish group.

20. Specific issues were elicited in the following way in the interview: "You indicated that you have felt strongly about an issue because of your ethnic background. Please take a minute to think of the issue or issues you care about now or have cared about in the recent past because of your ethnic background. These may be international, national, or local issues. I'd like to know which two are most important to you. Please tell me what the most important issue is and how you feel about it. . . . Now tell me what the second most important issue is and how you feel about it." These were open-ended questions, and interviewers were instructed to write down what respondents said.

21. Despite the group's small presence in the data, the level of political concerns among Jews is significantly different from that in the rest of the sample ($z = 3.19$, $p < .01$).

CHAPTER FIVE: Ethnicity in Families

1. The strength of the common-school tradition can be exaggerated. It was not always the case that the children of European immigrants were

force-fed American language and culture, as hallowed legend would have it. Bilingual school systems, and even systems that were monolingual in a non-English language, were widespread in the nineteenth century and survived in some places well into the twentieth century. Their persistence is attested to by late-nineteenth-century legislation aimed at forcing some public school systems in the midwest to provide instruction in the English language. (In many of these systems, German was the language of instruction; see Fishman et al., 1966.)

2. Notwithstanding the criticism that often greets public figures who belong to elite private clubs that discriminate against blacks, Jews, and women, no one disputes the right of minority groups to form organizations that serve ethnic purposes. Such organizations, of which the B'nai Brith and the Sons of Italy are well-known examples, can be found throughout the United States.

3. Excluded here and elsewhere in the discussion of intermarriage is the small number of respondents who were unable to report about their own backgrounds.

4. On the still very distinctive geographies of different ancestry groups, see Lieberson and Waters (1987).

5. In general, these marriages have only recently come into being—roughly 60 percent existed for less than five years at the time of the survey. An apparent implication is that knowledge about a marital partner's ethnic background grows over time. But also implied is that, for some respondents, ethnicity is of so little consequence in choosing a spouse that they do not bother to find out about it.

6. Since the survey data are necessarily reported from the respondent's point of view, I have also opted to define marital type from this same vantage point. That is to say, a "complete overlap" means that a spouse's background includes all the elements in the respondent's; it *can* also include other elements not found in the respondent's background. In the strictest sense, therefore, the degree of endogamy, i.e., of identical ancestry in a marriage, is somewhat inflated by the figures reported in table 5.1 and discussed in the text. One "correction" of a sort has also been made. Since, for Jews, country of origin is generally not a meaningful indicator of ethnic background—religion is—I have placed marriages between individuals who were both born Jewish in the complete-overlap category, regardless of the degree of overlap in their nationality backgrounds. This results in a small increment to the total of endogamous marriages.

7. A fair number also do not identify themselves. When respondents do not identify *and* do not know the identities of their spouses' identities, they have been assigned to the latter category for reporting in the tables.

8. One should not expect it to be comparable. Even if individuals chose marital partners without any regard whatsoever for ethnic and religious origins, interreligious marriage would be less common than interethnic marriage. This fact is a function of the division of the population into a small number of religious groups (counting Protestant denomina-

tions as part of one group) and the numerical dominance of just two of them—Protestants and Catholics.

9. The importance of this phenomenon for intermarriage was originally identified in Robert Merton's ([1941] 1976) classic paper on the subject. Merton went so far as to assert that marriages where the perception of crossing a boundary is absent should not be viewed as intermarriages.

10. Specifically, our question was, "Would you say that you and your [husband/wife, as appropriate] are originally from the same or different ethnic backgrounds?" We then asked respondents to explain their answer.

11. We asked respondents, "Has having a [husband/wife] from [the same/a different] ethnic background made a difference in your marriage?" The interviewer's choice of wording between "the same" and "a different" ethnic background was made on the basis of the respondent's perception of his or her type of marriage. Respondents were also requested to explain their answer.

12. The question was, "Do you want your children to think of themselves as having a definite ethnic background?" If the respondent answered positively, he or she was then asked, "What ethnic background is that?" and "How important is this to you—is it very important, somewhat important, or of little importance?"

13. Children living at home are presumably seen as more open to the influence of their parents, which increases the relevance of the findings. They are, for the most part, young. There are only a few instances of adult children living with elderly respondents—more than 80 percent of the parents in the group under examination have at least one child under the age of twenty, and virtually all of the remainder have a child at home who is in his or her twenties.

14. In this respect, interethnic marriage presents a strong contrast to interreligious marriage, where agreement between parents on a religion for their children is very common (see Silberman, 1985: chap. 7, for some data on the decisions of parents in Jewish-Gentile pairings). The contrast is revealing, for it suggests a general lack of social importance attached to membership in an ethnic group and the absence of an institutional framework to maintain ethnicity. Despite the secularism of American society, there is still a normative expectation that individuals will have some religious training and affiliation, however loosely the latter may be observed. Hence, even parents who have married without much regard for religious differences take steps to ensure that their children receive some religious instruction; their decisions are assisted by social pressures from grandparents and other relatives and by the existence of institutions to provide this training. There are simply no equivalents for most interethnically married couples.

15. The difference with the endogamous group is statistically significant ($z = 2.11$, $p < .05$).

16. Two explanations seem plausible for the large effects in table 5.8. One is that parents' desires for their children's identities are determined

largely by their own identities, and thus factors linked to identity have very large effects. The other is the small number of cases involved because of the restriction of the analysis to parents with children at home. Because of this, only large effects can be detected. (These points apply also to table 5.11.)

17. For the purposes of this analysis, this variable has been treated as an optional independent variable, which can enter an equation when it is statistically significant but otherwise does not appear. Its appearance in table 5.8 does not change the significance levels of other variables (hence, it does not suppress the effects of such variables as generation). Because of the skewed distribution of the index and the possibility of nonlinear effects, it has been divided into a small number of discrete categories for use in the equation. Also, in order to prevent any confounding of dependent and independent variables, the one experience directly connected with socialization, namely, teaching children about their ethnic background, has been removed from the index.

18. The omission of one variable from the equation in table 5.8 should be noted, namely, age of children, which does not appear to affect parents' desires for their children's identities. Specifically, the age of the youngest child was tested in the model, and since it was not statistically significant, it was not retained in the final equation.

19. Were they a larger group in our sample, Jews might join the Italians here. Certainly, the evidence of other studies indicates Jewish concern with children's identities (Silberman, 1985). But the number of Jewish respondents in our survey who have children at home is so tiny that no meaningful conclusion can be drawn.

20. Judgments that children are too young to learn about their ethnic backgrounds emerged from responses to a question about whether children showed any interest in ethnicity. A significant number of parents with young children told us that their children were still too young. These parents are eliminated from the analysis in this section.

21. Because the small number of cases in the analysis raises the risk of failing to detect effects (in statistical language, the risk of type II error), I have given the benefit of the doubt to the effect of educational attainment. This variable seems especially likely to have fallen a victim to type II error, given the plausibility of its role and also the fact that some preliminary analyses showed it to be statistically significant.

22. As with education, one must be wary of accepting too readily the null hypothesis of no effect for ethnic identity status, given the small number of cases and the substantial number of variables in the equation reported in table 5.11. Even more to the point, when nonsignificant variables such as age and generation are dropped from the equation, identity status is statistically significant. Nevertheless, I have retained the standard set of demographic variables to make the reported analysis of teaching parallel analyses of other ethnic behaviors.

23. To keep the equation as simple as possible, parental desires for children's identity and endogamy were not included in the final equation,

presented in table 5.11. But these variables were included in preliminary analyses, as were a number of others, which also turned out not to be significant. Worthy of special mention is that, net of the variables in the final equation, the age of children has no relationship to whether or not they are taught by their parents about ethnicity.

24. The interviewer asked, "I'm interested in finding out how your children view their ethnic background. Do your children show any interest in the ethnic background they have from you?" If the respondent answered positively, this was followed by: "Are they very interested, somewhat interested, or interested only a little?"; "How do they show their interest?"; and "Do you care how interested they are?" If the respondent answered negatively, he or she was asked, "Does it matter to you that they don't?" These questions immediately preceded the questions about parents' desires for their children to identify. Hence, it cannot be the case that parents are answering them to maintain consistency with what they said about their desires for their children's identities.

CHAPTER SIX: Ethnic Social Structures

1. Plotnikov and Silverman (1978) provide a telling illustration of the use of ethnic expressions that are widely known within a group but not outside of it. The use in this case is to verify tacitly membership in the group. The story concerns two Jewish women, one named Mrs. Scolnick, who meet for the first time in the presence of a Gentile. Each woman is interested in establishing whether the other is Jewish, but without drawing attention to their ethnicity. This end is accomplished when Mrs. Scolnick is asked whether she is related to the "show biz personality," an oblique reference to Menashe Sculnik, a Yiddish comedian unlikely to be known to non-Jews. When Mrs. Scolnick readily replies that she is not, she acknowledges her recognition of the reference and hence her Jewish origins.

2. A handful of respondents refused to participate in this part of the survey.

3. Five seems a good number. In the General Social Survey data discussed by Peter Marsden (1987), for instance, only 6 percent of Americans named more than five people as part of their "core discussion networks."

4. Readers may wonder how this examination of friendship differs from the discussion of some of the experiences in chapter 4. There, the focus was on the respondent's sensitivity to ethnicity as an aspect of the social world. Thus, one of the experiences analyzed in that connection was "feeling a special sense of relationship to someone else" because of ethnic background, which depends not only on having a relationship to someone of the same background but also on recognizing a special quality in it. Here, by contrast, the focus is on the more or less objective characteristics of the respondent's social milieu, and the attempt is made to link these characteristics to the state of the respondent's identity.

5. Interestingly, kin were not as frequently named in our survey as

they were in the national survey discussed by Marsden (1987), presumably because of differences in the friendship question put to respondents. The key difference is that the General Social Survey asked for persons with whom a respondent "discusses important matters," while our survey asked only for the names of good friends. By focusing on the discussion of "important matters" (which are not further defined), the General Social Survey may limit the lists for some respondents to those persons to whom they are willing to reveal intimate details of their lives and hence may call forth a disproportionate number of relatives. A similar emphasis on kinship is evoked by questions that focus on exchanges of various sorts, such as borrowing money (Fischer, 1982: chapter 3). By highlighting instead a sense of closeness, or felt affinity, the question in our survey seems better attuned to our purpose—the discovery of relationships that may revolve around common outlooks and values rather than everyday necessities or extraordinary concerns.

6. Nominations of spouses as close friends are not counted, here or elsewhere in the chapter—not because spouses cannot also be good friends, but because the ethnic role of the marital relation has already been analyzed. In the few cases where respondents named their spouses among their close friends, this exclusion reduces the number of friends analyzed.

7. Since respondents of unknown background cannot have friends of overlapping ancestry, they are not considered here or anywhere else in the rest of the discussion of friendship. Such respondents were also eliminated from the consideration of ethnic overlap in marriage. In addition, the friendships of the small number of Jewish respondents are treated differently from the rest. Since Jewishness is the defining ethnic status for most of these respondents, religious overlap was substituted for ethnic overlap. A similar substitution was used in chapter 5 to define ethnic endogamy for the Jewish group.

8. While in principle it would be possible to calculate the proportion of friendships involving common ethnicity to be expected on the basis of chance, the practical hurdles are large. These involve the handling of mixed ancestry, which implies that ethnic categories are not mutually exclusive; the frequent simplification in the reporting of friends' ancestries, the basis for which remains unknown; and the large proportion of friends whose ancestry is not known to respondents. I do not believe that the minor contribution the calculation would make to the discussion is worth the effort required to overcome these difficulties.

9. This estimate draws only on respondents who report four or more friendships; and this restriction will be repeated throughout the chapter whenever characteristics of friendship circles, as opposed to individual friendships, are discussed. The restriction was imposed to avoid confounding the count of ethnic overlaps in friendship with the total number of friends named (obviously, the more friends who are named, the greater the chance that one or more of them have an ancestry overlap with a respondent). It still keeps about 80 percent (N = 355) of native-born whites in the analysis.

10. This calculation is straightforward, involving an application of the binomial distribution (Blalock, 1979). Assumed is that each friendship has the same probability of ancestry overlap—approximately .34, the overall proportion of friends whose backgrounds overlap respondents'.

11. Even though the overall relationship of subjective importance to having one or more friends of overlapping ancestry does not appear to be significant in table 6.4, the category of the strongly identified is significantly different from all others ($z = 2.63$, $p < .01$).

12. The index is based on the first two ancestries named for each friend and hence can go as high as ten in value.

13. Like other analyses of the friendship circle, the regression results in the table are based on respondents who named at least four friends. Two further steps were taken to negate any possible confounding influence of the total number of friends named. Since the analysis includes respondents who named only four friends, the maximum value for the dependent variable is set at four. Also, the number of friends named is included as a control variable to take into account the additional opportunity to name a friend of overlapping ancestry when five friends are named. These steps are repeated in similar analyses throughout the chapter.

14. A seeming anomaly in the effect of length of residence—namely, that nonkin friendships involving shared ethnicity are more common among the most recent arrivals than among persons who have lived in their community for one to five years—is probably due to the carry-over of friendships from a former place of residence. Since very recent arrivals have not yet had the opportunity to form many close friendships in their new communities, they still tend to name friends in their former communities.

15. This difference is not caused by the use of ordinary regression analysis here, as opposed to the logistic regression analysis of earlier chapters. When logistic regression is applied to a dependent variable contrasting respondents with any friends of overlapping ancestry to those with none, the lower effect of subjective importance remains. Nor is it a question of the demographic and other background variables explaining a stronger zero-order relationship, for this is barely stronger than the relationship in table 6.5.

16. Because of limited reporting of mixed ancestry for friends, this accounting does not distinguish between friends of mixed and single Irish ancestry.

17. Even though there are just a small number of Jewish respondents in our study, the data on their friendships are very much in line with those from national studies of American Jews; for example, Steven Cohen (1983: table 3.2) finds that about half of Jews say that all or most of their friends are Jews.

18. The logistic regression analysis has a somewhat different format from previous analyses of this type. The unit of analysis is the friendship relationship rather than the respondent. Thus, each friendship is treated as a separate unit and is analyzed in terms of such variables as its length of

existence, its manner of origin, and properties of the respondent's ethnic identity.

19. In the context of questions about respondents' top five friends, we asked, "Do you ever really talk about your ethnic background with any of them?"; if the answer was positive, we then asked, "Which ones?" Discussing one's ethnic background (within the preceding five years) was also one of the experiences analyzed in chapter 4. The data for the earlier analysis were based on the list of ethnic experiences; the data for the present one come from a separate part of the interview. Although there is not perfect consistency between the two measures (which can hardly be expected given differences in the framing of the questions), there is a reassuringly strong relationship. At one extreme, only 20 percent of respondents who do not talk about their backgrounds with any of their close friends checked the earlier experience of discussing their ethnic background (and most who did so said such discussions were infrequent). At the other, about three-quarters of those who talk about their backgrounds with four or more friends checked the experience (and most said the experience was more than infrequent).

20. When limited to a contrast between identifiers and nonidentifiers, the comparison is more statistically significant than the chi-square test result in table 6.7 indicates ($z = 2.68$, $p < .01$).

21. The index of ethnic experiences, first used in chapter 3, has to be modified because the experiences of social sensitivity (see chapter 4) are too closely related to the friendship variables, potentially confounding the analysis. Hence, these experiences were removed from the index, which varies from zero to twelve as a maximum for this analysis.

22. I have further confirmed this effect in some ways not reported in the text; for example, the number of friends of unknown ancestry affects the measured character of the friendship circle—thus it could be that this variable, which can be construed as a reflection of the respondent's identity rather than his or her friendship circle, is confounded in the effect of the number of nonkin friends of overlapping background. But controlling for it does not change the results of the analysis; nor are the results changed when the analysis is limited to respondents who know the backgrounds of all of their friends. The impact of friendships with nonkin coethnics holds firm under a variety of revisions.

23. To simplify the presentation in table 6.8, I have not separated out relatives from the "other friends" with whom ethnicity is discussed (since having relatives as friends generally does not affect ethnic experience). A further breakdown along these lines does not alter the result.

24. Admittedly, the distinction between avowedly ethnic organizations and organizations with ethnic memberships can be trickier to apply than to state in the abstract. It is not clear where organizations such as veterans' groups formed along ethnic lines should be placed, to take just one problematic example. In general, I have relied on respondents' own sense of whether an organization is ethnic in purpose or something else, although we did make some changes based on a close reading of the lists of organizational affiliations for our sample. As a rule, these changes went in the direc-

tion of classifying additional organizations as ethnic in purpose. Very few of the organizations on our respondents' lists challenged our sense of the boundary line; the problematic aspect of the definition turned out to present little empirical difficulty.

25. Thus, ethnic organizations have the ability to foster what Mark Granovetter (1973) has called "weak ties."

26. I am indebted to Claude Fischer for the list of organization types which was presented to respondents for the purpose of inventorying their memberships. The list is one he developed for use in a survey of Northern Californians (Fischer, 1982).

27. As noted, we combed through the lists of organizations respondents gave us, looking for ethnic organizations that might have been missed; for example, we searched for colonial-ancestry organizations (e.g., the DAR), on the grounds that these may not be thought of as ethnic by their members and hence may be misclassified from our point of view. In the end, our efforts did result in a few classification changes, most of which involved adding new entries to the roster of ethnic organizations.

28. It is necessary to control the overall number of organizational memberships in order to take into account the increased opportunity to name an ethnically homogeneous organization added by each membership. Without this variable in the regression equation, the adjusted R-square sinks to .025, demonstrating the low explanatory power of the identity and demographic variables by themselves.

CHAPTER SEVEN: The Changing Map of Ethnicity

1. For whites, the best recent statistical evidence on ethnic distinctiveness in residential patterns dates to the 1970 census; see Guest and Weed (1976). Limited results from the 1980 census are presented by Lieberson and Waters (1988).

2. The importance of an ethnic community's "institutional completeness" was first pointed out by Raymond Breton (1964).

3. The powerful role of competition with newer groups, who are often racially stigmatized, is borne out in Jonathan Rieder's (1985) account of the occasionally violent resistance to black in-migrants on the part of white ethnic residents of the Canarsie section of Brooklyn, New York.

4. Although hers is not a study of suburban ethnic neighborhoods, Mary Waters (1990) has examined the state of ethnicity in suburbia, as have John Roche (1982) and Salvatore LaGumina (1989).

5. In constructing this linkage, I will draw on the ethnic ancestry data collected in 1980 by the U.S. census. These data make it possible to characterize the ethnic composition of very small areas, so-called census block groups. Since the block group of each respondent was known at the time of the survey, it is only a small computer feat to merge ethnic information from the census with each respondent's survey data. More will be said shortly about the precise way in which the census data have been used.

6. Few areas are, of course, truly homogeneous. In his study of an

Italian-American neighborhood in Boston during the late 1950s, Herbert Gans (1962) found a diverse population, including Jews, Poles, and other groups. Thus, from the population point of view, ethnic neighborhoods are a matter of degree. The ethnic character of a neighborhood may be more identifiable from the nature of its small businesses and local organizations, although this is also a fallible indicator since this infrastructure can survive ethnic turnover. It is not knowable from census data, the only data source I have for determining the ethnic character of an area.

7. Given data about the numbers of group members who reside in different areas, the index of dissimilarity between any two groups, i and j, can be computed by the formula below, where p_{ik} and p_{jk} represent the proportions of groups i and j residing in area k:

$$\frac{1}{2} \sum_k |p_{ik} - p_{jk}|$$

8. The exposure index is given by the following formula, where p_{ik} is the proportion *of group i's members* who reside in area k and P_{jk} is the proportion *of area k's residents* who belong to group j:

$$\sum_k p_{ik}P_{jk}$$

Note that the index is asymmetric and the roles of i and j can be exchanged.

9. The term *block* is most easily applied in cities and least so in the countryside. Nevertheless, the Census Bureau does divide up the countryside into blocks on the basis of natural and manmade boundaries, such as streams and roads. Outside of cities, individual blocks can enclose large areas, but not necessarily a large population.

10. A few small block groups, containing fewer than thirty people each, are excluded from the analysis.

11. The data in table 7.1 are derived from block-group tabulations of the Census Bureau (taken from Summary Tape File 3); these tabulations present ancestry data with the foreign-born included, and it is not possible to separate them out.

12. In a formal sense, the index of dissimilarity controls for group size, and this is presumably one of its major strengths (but see Cortese et al., 1976). However, complications arise here because the ancestry data are derived from a sample and because the fine level of geographic data means that small ancestry groups are entirely absent from most block groups. These complications are best explained through an example. Consider the Greek single ancestry group, which has approximately 2,150 members in the four-county Capital Region. The average sampling rate used by the Census Bureau—roughly one in five households—implies that just slightly more than four hundred persons of single Greek ancestry, and even fewer households, are included in the sample from which the census ancestry figures are derived. Obviously, then, it is not possible for all block groups

(there are 748 of them) to contain at least one sampled person of single Greek ancestry, even if all in fact contain some Greeks. Further, the difference between block groups with and block groups without sampled Greeks is exacerbated by the weighting process used to inflate sample figures to approximate population ones, since this will blow up a tiny number of sampled Greek residents of a block group to a figure five or six times larger. These numerical considerations cannot explain the large value of the index of dissimilarity for blacks, however, since the black group is ten or more times as large as the smallest white ethnic categories.

13. There are some discrepancies between census ancestry data for the region and the ethnic composition data presented earlier, in chapter 1. Some old-stock groups—in particular, the English and Germans—appear smaller in census data than they do in ancestry data collected by our survey. As noted elsewhere, the explanation undoubtedly lies in deficiencies in the census data, especially the confounding of ancestry and identity and the truncation of ancestry, which particularly affect the old-stock groups.

14. In describing ethnic residential concentrations, I have made use of data far more detailed than the summary in table 7.2. These data describe the precise location, identifiable on U.S. census maps, of block groups with ethnic concentrations. For assistance in understanding the locational configurations in the detailed data, I am especially grateful to John J. McEneny, an extremely knowledgeable local historian, who readily shared with me his extensive knowledge of ethnic settlement patterns in the region. I owe to him many of the specifics in the discussion of the interrelationship between industrial development and ethnic concentration.

15. An interesting story lies behind the one suburban block group with a large black proportion. As is true also for many similar areas of white ethnic concentration, the area does not appear to represent a recently arisen suburban enclave of middle-class blacks. Located in Saratoga Springs, it is, according to John McEneny, a local historian, a long-standing concentration of blacks who are occupationally connected to the nearby race track.

16. In discussing the major white ancestry groups, for which the census provides mixed ancestry data, I deal only with the patterns of the composite ancestry categories, which combine persons of single and of mixed ancestry from the group. This seems to me the most sensible approach, since it is capable of recognizing concentrations that include some intermarried ethnics and their mixed-ancestry children. For other ancestry groups, however, I have no choice but to rely on the residence patterns of persons of single ancestry, since the census provides no residential information for mixed-ancestry group members. Partly for reasons of space and partly because I view these data as less accurate, I have not summarized them in table 7.2.

17. The urban-suburban-rural distinction is implemented with help from the Census Bureau's "urbanized area" concept. An urbanized area is defined as a major city (at least fifty thousand in population) and the "surrounding, closely settled, contiguous" suburbs. As a practical matter, the

latter are identified primarily on the basis of a population density criterion (at least one thousand persons per square mile). In the Capital Region, this concept appears to work well in distinguishing urban and suburban areas from rural ones. Accordingly, I have defined rural block groups as those outside of an urbanized area. To distinguish between urban and suburban block groups, however, I have taken into account one further aspect of the region's geography. In addition to its three major cities, the region includes several smaller, old industrial cities, such as Cohoes, a nineteenth-century manufacturing city. Although they do not rival the major cities in size, these once heavily industrial cities must be classified with them, because their patterns of ethnic settlement can be traced back to the period of mass immigration from Europe and resemble those found in larger cities like Albany. (Included here are the cities of Cohoes, Mechanicville, Rensselaer, and Watervliet, the town of Rotterdam, and the village of Green Island.) Any urbanized block group not in them or in a major city is classified as suburban.

18. There are also some rural and suburban block groups among the majority Irish areas, but their number is somewhat deceptive. These areas are mostly quite small, and hence they generally contain few Irish. All told, they account for just 12 percent of the Irish who reside in majority Irish areas, and just .2 percent of the entire ancestry group.

19. Some of the suburban areas of Irish concentration are not recent in origin, but date back to immigrant settlements. This is manifestly true of some Irish areas on the northern fringes of Albany, which were initially settled by immigrants coming to work in railroad and stock yards.

20. The foreign-stock definition of previous censuses obviously does not identify the whole of any group, and therefore the number of Italians counted in a given area in prior censuses cannot be compared directly to that in the 1980 census (which uses a broader, ancestry definition of ethnicity). Hence, I resort to viewing the number in a neighborhood as a proportion of the group as counted in a census year. Also, since the accuracy of the foreign-stock definition deteriorates as the temporal distance to a group's period of immigration increases, the intercensus comparison in the text is not sensible for older groups, such as the Irish or Germans. Another difference between the 1980 and previous censuses is that the prior censuses did not report data at the block-group level. Hence, the comparisons of the next few paragraphs are based on census tract data.

21. The correlation between the Italian-ancestry proportion of a block group and its proportion foreign born is .260 (p < .001). This, it should be noted, is an ecological correlation and does not constitute direct proof that the foreign-born residents of Italian areas are in fact Italian (there is no way to verify this at the block-group level of census data). But the presumption is strong, especially since Italians are, by a wide margin, the largest contingent among the Capital Region's foreign born.

22. An indirect indicator is the decline of the school-age population in the Schenectady Italian neighborhoods during the late 1980s, forcing the

school system to close and consolidate schools—a strong contrast to bur-
geoning school populations in the region's suburbs. I am grateful to Gordana Rabrenovic for pointing this connection out to me.

23. For evidence bearing on the use of the Russian category to represent Jews, see Rosenthal (1975) and Lieberson and Waters (1988: chap. 1).

24. Such individuals represent 56 percent of native-born whites. Since
I place somewhat greater credence in the standardized values derived from
composite groups, I must limit the analysis in this way, or run the risk of
muddying it with individuals whose neighborhoods are more imperfectly
characterized (because composite data are not available for some of the
components of their ancestries). Restricting the neighborhood analysis to
individuals in the six major ancestry groups has the added benefit of avoiding a problem that can occur with standardization, namely, that for small
ancestry groups, like the Greeks, large standardized values can be found for
areas with small absolute numbers of group members, merely because a
moderate concentration is much larger than the group mean.

The analyses I present are limited in the way the text describes, but I
have run many other analyses, including larger subsets of whites. All the
analyses are quite consistent with respect to the points subsequently made
in the text.

25. It would not be helpful here to select the standardized value corresponding with an individual's ethnic identity for at least two reasons. First,
only a minority of persons of mixed ancestry identify with a single group.
Many others identify in a mixed fashion or do not identify ethnically at all,
and the characterization of their neighborhoods would be left problematic.
Second, use of identity to define neighborhood would confound the crucial
examination of the relationship between the two.

26. Here, I save space by reporting only results based on standardized
neighborhood values derived from composite groups. The results would not
differ in any significant way if values derived from single-ancestry groups
were used instead.

27. The small-city category in the table includes the small, older industrial cities in the region; they are identified above. Also, in this table, I
have included all native-born whites, not just those in the major-ancestry
groups, since neighborhood identifications based on ancestry are not
involved.

28. This is significantly different from the suburban proportion in the
rest of the sample (z = 3.72, p < .001).

29. Negative standardized values, indicating group concentrations below the mean, are set to zero. The recognition of only positive standardized
values as meaningful is tantamount to positing that there is no difference
between living in an area that has an average proportion of residents from
an ethnic background and an area that has less than average—both are
nonethnic for a person with that ancestry.

30. As in chapter 6, the index has been modified for this analysis by
removal of the social experiences, because of the seemingly intrinsic rela-

tionship between these experiences and residence in areas of ethnic concentration.

31. That is, all of these variables are insignificant when they are present together. This indeterminacy results from the correlations among the variables and the small number of cases involved.

CHAPTER EIGHT: The Emergence of the European Americans

1. One should not forget that, only a short time ago, racial distinctions received official sanction in many parts of the United States. Until the Supreme Court's Brown decision of 1954, segregated school systems in many southern states were erected on the basis of race. Antimiscegenation laws in many states had an even longer life (until finally banned by the Supreme Court in 1967). Race was a basis of official distinction among citizens also during the World War II internment of Japanese Americans, and the federal and state governments continue to draw legally significant distinctions in terms of Indian tribal membership. But in none of these ways have distinctions been made among whites.

2. Charles Silberman (1985: chapter 5) points out the increasing role of choice as a fundamental condition of Jewish identity. He notes that, in the past, there were three reasons for Jews to remain Jews: "because they believed that was what God demanded of them; because they were born into an organic community with powerful sanctions and rewards; or because anti-Semites would not permit them to become anything else" (Silberman, 1985: 159). Each of these reasons has been abrogated for most Jews in the contemporary United States, making fidelity to a Jewish identity a matter of choice in a way that has rarely been true before. Silberman believes, probably correctly, that most Jews make the choice to continue to be Jewish. Below, I address why this choice may be different for Jews than for most other white ethnics.

3. It will be objected that some of these experiences are probably more common than respondents report, since the reports may be influenced by forgetfulness, etc. Even if true, it is consequential that the experiences most remembered are the ones with a generally benign character.

4. In Habits of the Heart (1985), Robert Bellah and his colleagues express the hope that Americans can overcome the centrifugal tendencies of their individualism by resurrecting and refurbishing collective memories and sentiments of which ethnicity represents a prime example. On the basis of my analysis, however, ethnicity is a poor candidate for this role, at least among whites, because it has adapted to and is conditioned by American individualism.

5. The one form of ethnic social structure I have not examined is that arising from ethnic concentrations in specific jobs, but I think it very unlikely that it could materially change the findings. Practical as well as theoretical reasons led to the omission. Given the size of my sample, declining occupational segregation among white ethnic groups would make it

difficult to identify a substantial enough set of jobs where specific ethnic groups are concentrated to give any empirical leverage to the analysis. Lieberson and Waters (1988: chap. 5), who find declining segregation and very low absolute levels of segregation across broad occupational categories, still are able to identify a few specific occupations for each group that display traces of once stronger ethnic patterns—for example, a disproportionate number of Norwegians among fishermen. But, in general, the occupations they cite account for such a small proportion of the work force that they would not be represented in more than tiny numbers in our survey. Moreover, since an analysis of occupational concentrations must be limited to the part of our survey sample in the work force, it would be problematic in execution.

But the strong evidence of decline in ethnic occupational concentrations implies that these cannot serve as anchors for ethnic identities on a large scale. Hence, the conclusion in the text seems sound.

6. Frances FitzGerald's (1979) examination of American history as taught by widely used school texts reveals a strong shift during the 1960s away from a nation "conceived as male and Anglo-Saxon" to one "filled with blacks, 'ethnics,' Indians, Asians, and women" (FitzGerald, 1979: 93). The new multicultural emphasis undoubtedly encouraged teachers to utilize family backgrounds as classroom material and students to relate their backgrounds to the multiethnic conception of the nation they were being taught.

7. Events among whites thus display some of the paradoxical features associated with what Yinger (1981) has described as assimilation combined with "dissimilation."

8. The suggestion was made in personal conversation.

9. Both campaigns featured politicians who made much of their ethnic origins, casting them as American archetypes. In 1984, however, Geraldine Ferraro's Italian ancestry became a focal point for attack, which involved among other things allegations that her parents and husband had ties to organized crime. Less was made of Michael Dukakis's Greek ancestry in 1988, but it is noteworthy that country-music celebrities campaigning for George Bush made fun of Dukakis's name as unpronounceable and, by implication, foreign (*New York Times*, October 16, 1988). To my knowledge, this behavior was never repudiated by Bush. The example of both campaigns suggests that the newer, European-American identity is not fully accepted in all regions of the country or among all old-stock Americans. One must be careful, however, not to overgeneralize from the peculiar conditions of presidential campaigns.

10. Reported in the *New York Times*, December 21, 1988.

11. Erickson also detected a "Third World" form of panethnicity, which allowed blacks and Hispanics to feel a sense of solidarity with one another.

Index